Oxford Studies in British Church Music

ANGLICAN CHANT AND CHANTING IN
ENGLAND, SCOTLAND, AND AMERICA

Anglican Chant and Chanting in England, Scotland, and America 1660 to 1820

RUTH M. WILSON

CLARENDON PRESS · OXFORD
1996

Oxford University Press, Great Clarendon Street, Oxford OX2 6DP

Oxford New York

Athens Auckland Bangkok Bombay Bogata
Buenos Aries Calcutta Cape Town Dar es Salaam
Delhi Florence Hong Kong Istanbul Karachi
Kuala Lumpur Madras Madrid Melbourne
Mexico City Nairobi Paris Singapore
Taipei Tokyo Toronto

and associated companies in
Berlin Ibadan

Oxford is a trade mark of Oxford University Press

Published in the United States
by Oxford University Press Inc., New York

British Library Cataloguing in Publication Data
Data available

Library of Congress Cataloging in Publication Data
Wilson, Ruth Mack.
Anglican chant and chanting in England, Scotland, and America,
1660–1820 / Ruth M. Wilson.
p. cm.
Includes bibliographical references and index.
1. Chants (Anglican)—History and criticism. 2. Church music—
—Church of England. 3. Church music—Anglican Communion.
I. Title
ML3166.W55 1996 782.32'23—dc20 96–17388
ISBN 0–19–816424–6

1 3 5 7 9 10 8 6 4 2

Typeset by Hope Services (Abingdon) Ltd.
Printed in Great Britain
on acid-free paper by
Biddles Ltd.,
Guildford & Kings Lynn

To
my 'in-house' editor
the other Dr Wilson

EDITOR'S FOREWORD

THE church music of Britain, like its church buildings and liturgical texts, is a national heritage that transcends religious controversy and the decline of faith. Unlike them—because of the ephemeral nature of music—it needs revival, interpretation, and advocacy if it is to be preserved and appreciated. Such processes must rest on a sound basis of fact and understanding. This series serves to encourage and present some of the best efforts of modern scholarship in the field.

The great Anglican cathedral tradition, with its roots in the Middle Ages, naturally takes the central place in this heritage. For centuries it has raised the music of worship to a high art, with its own style and history and its own series of composers, performers, and critics. It constitutes a school of musical art that is effortlessly distinctive, recognizably English, without being in the least nationalistic. Much though we may appreciate cathedral music as art, it also has a function in religious worship, and indeed in society. It shares this function with many other kinds of British church music—not all Anglican, not all English, not all achieving or even attempting high artistic value, but each playing a certain part in the life of a denomination and a community. The books in this series all, in their several ways, link developments in church music with the life of the individuals and societies that produced them.

Ruth M. Wilson's study of Anglican chant does, indeed, involve a great deal more than the cathedral tradition in which it had its roots. Originating in the practice of singing plainchant in faburden, Anglican chant gradually took on a distinct character, which was remarkably transformed during the eighteenth century into the form that is now familiar: the miniature, balanced melody of ten or twenty notes in a set rhythm, adapted, with more or less flexibility, to a prose text. Although this process certainly began in cathedrals and choral foundations, it was already, early in the eighteenth century, beginning to be imitated in English parish churches. Dr Wilson follows these developments, and traces them further into almost completely unknown territory, as she explores the beginnings of Anglican chanting in Scotland and the United States.

Anglican chant is a distinctively British practice, so much so that when comedians adapt it to the Highway Code, or to less innocuous texts, it is instantly recognizable. But it is no longer evolving. On the contrary, its standing is precarious in the profoundly altered conditions of worship today. It could be called an endangered species, carefully maintained and preserved in some churches. So this is the ideal moment to write its history. It is a story that has been largely ignored in the many books that have been written about English church music. Dr Wilson has broken new ground, and in doing so has uncovered some fascinating details that may surprise her readers.

NICHOLAS TEMPERLEY

Urbana, Illinois
October 1995

PREFACE

THIS study of chant and chanting in the Anglican tradition began with a search for the sources of liturgical music sung in the newly independent Protestant Episcopal Church in the United States of America. The initial research raised many questions about earlier practices in the old country. Liturgical chant had a long history in the Church of England, but little information had accumulated about English chant and chanting after the late sixteenth century. Establishing a history in more detail became the main task, because it was in the seventeenth century that the plainsong chanting inherited from the old Latin rite evolved into its present forms. The Protestant Episcopal Church in the United States was never left out of the equation, for the opportunity it presented to study Anglican liturgical music in a new and different setting has kept the focus on the transmission and synthesis of partly oral traditions. Moreover, a parallel investigation of the music of the Episcopal Church in Scotland yielded surprising results.

The body of music that makes up the chanting practice of the Anglican and related Episcopal Churches in Scotland, America, and other parts of the world is indeed diversified. In cathedrals and churches with trained choirs, several texts of the liturgy are harmonized in four vocal parts, with or without organ accompaniment. Others are recited in unison to traditional plainsong melodies. The largest group of chants, those for the psalms and canticles, has an idiosyncratic written form in conjunction with a performance practice that continues to evolve in oral tradition. It is this music which, since about the mid-nineteenth century, has been called the Anglican Chant.

It is not commonly appreciated that all these species of chant, whatever their individual styles, derive historically from the plainsong tones with four-part harmony in faburden style that were an integral part of the liturgical language of the Latin Sarum rite. At the Reformation, when the Mass and choir Offices were translated and consolidated into the one-volume English Book of Common Prayer, detailed musical directions, except for the psalmody and a few other texts, were no longer spelt out in the rubrics. In the reformed Church of England, therefore, the determinants of liturgical performance practice have always been the distinct customs of the various religious jurisdictions—cathedral and parish churches, royal chapels and royal peculiars, and collegiate churches and chapels.

In the evolution of Anglican chanting practices, the choral tradition belonged largely to cathedrals and churches where musical establishments were maintained. Historically, the separation of parish and cathedral musical customs is perceived as intrinsic to their nature, hence they are treated separately. Even so, since the intermingling of the formal elements of cathedral and parochial worship in the eighteenth century and the spread of the Anglican Communion in the nineteenth, the performance of the liturgy in all types of Anglican and Episcopal churches has come to be thought of as part of the same musical heritage.

Since English chant developed in partly written and partly oral tradition, the materials necessary to its study cover a wide and disparate range of manuscript and printed documents. The completion of this study owes a great deal, therefore, to the generosity and cooperation of archives and libraries in England, Scotland, and the United States. Permission to examine and quote from documents and manuscripts in their care was graciously granted by the Dean and Chapters of Norwich, St Paul's, Westminster, Chichester, Exeter, Lichfield, Wells, Canterbury, Bristol, Hereford, Durham, Gloucester, Peterborough, Ely, Worcester, and Winchester Cathedrals, and Lincoln and York Minsters; Deans and Canons of Windsor; Governing Bodies of Christ Church, Oxford and Peterhouse College, Cambridge; Master and Fellows of Pembroke College, Cambridge; Provost and Fellows of King's College, Cambridge; President and Fellows of St John's College, Oxford; Rectors of Wimborne Minster and Leeds Parish Church; Keeper of Manuscripts of the British Library Board; Keeper of Manuscripts of the Bodleian Library; Parry Library, Royal College of Music; Aberdeen City Library; Edinburgh City Library; Mitchell Library of Glasgow; City Libraries of Manchester, Birmingham, Leicester, and Norwich; Public Record Offices of London, Norfolk, Berkshire, Dorset, Kent, West Sussex, Gloucestershire, Devon, Suffolk, and Essex; Scottish Record Office in Edinburgh; Strathclyde Regional Archives in Glasgow; the Episcopal Theological College in Edinburgh and the Diocese of Edinburgh; the Diocese of Aberdeen and Orkney; St Andrew's Episcopal Church in Banff; St Andrew's Cathedral in Aberdeen; Aberdeen University Special Collections; National Library of Scotland; diocesan archives of the Protestant Episcopal Church in the United States of America in Boston, Hartford, and Philadelphia; City Libraries in New York, Philadelphia, and Boston; Newberry Library, Chicago; and the Huntington Library, San Marino, California.

Many official and unofficial persons have been especially helpful over the years I have spent in England and Scotland, and I am deeply indebted to them all. My initial research in England as a University of Illinois doctoral candidate was supported by a Fulbright–Hayes scholarship, and I thank the US–UK Educational Commission for their courteous and helpful oversight. I am beholden to many colleagues and friends for sharing ideas and information, especially H. Diack Johnstone, Peter Horton, Robert Ford, Ian Spink, Peter Dickinson, Walter Hillsman, Peter Marr, Alan Luff, Margaret Laurie, J. Joseph Wisdom, John Aplin, Percy Young, Brian Crosby, Margaret Cranmer, Tom Roast, Sarah Boyer, Bennet Zon, Ralph Valentine, and the late Mason Martens. Bruce Phillips and his expert staff at Oxford University Press have guided me through the many stages of the publication process with an extraordinarily high level of competence, and it is much appreciated. Above all, I wish to thank especially Professor Nicholas Temperley, without whose informed critical judgement and steady encouragement this study would never have seen the light of day.

RUTH M. WILSON

Evanston, Illinois

CONTENTS

List of Illustrations   xiv
List of Tables   xv
Hymn Tune Index Source Codes   xvi
Abbreviations   xvii

1. The Ecclesiastical Settlement and the 1662 Book of Common
   Prayer   1
2. The Restoration of Choral Service in Cathedrals and Collegiate
   Churches and Chapels   23
3. The Evolution of the Chant Tune   59
4. Chanting Service and Double Tune   103
5. Chanting and Choral Service c.1690–c.1820   125
6. Chants and Chanting in Parish Churches c.1710-1820   163
7. Music and Liturgy in the Episcopal Church of Scotland   192
8. Early Episcopal Music in America   217
9. Per Retro et Recte   259

Appendices
A. English Chant Tunes: Manuscript Sources 1635–1750   271
B. Parish Music Books with Chants 1718–1820   279
C. Scottish Music Books with Chants 1742–1820   283
D. Episcopal Liturgical Music Printed in America 1783–1820   286
E. Performance of Choral Service: Selected Documents 1668–1791   289
   1. Orders of Bishop Anthony Sparrow, visitation to Exeter   289
   2. Orders for the conduct of choral service in York Minster   289
   3. Granville Sharp's directions for chanting   292
   4. Funeral of Dr Boyce, 16 February 1779   293
   5. The organ in church, John Marsh, Eighteen Voluntaries, 1791 294
F. Autobiography and Journals of John Marsh: Selected Entries   298

Bibliography   307
Index   325

ILLUSTRATIONS

1. 'Tunes in foure parts to the Psalms of David', Add. MS 17784, fo. 177^{r-v} 62–3

2. King David, Add. MS 17784, fo. 178^r 64

3. St Paul's Psalter, MS A.1.8vo   66

4. Schematic diagram of psalm-tone and chant-tune melodies   71

5. 'Chappel Tunes', Bennet Organbook, Add. MS 39868, fo. 100^{r-v} 142–3

6. Responses used at Durham, St Paul's Music MS Chant Book I   153

7. Gloria in excelsis, William Smith, *The Churchman's Choral Companion to his Prayer Book* (New York, 1809), 32–3   236–7

TABLES

1.1.	The 1662 rubrics for Morning and Evening Prayer	14–15
1.2.	The 1662 rubrics for the Holy Communion	18–19
2.1.	1662 rubrics interpreted by Lowe, Playford, and Clifford	55–8
3.1.	The 'royal chapels repertory'	68
3.2.	Imperial, Canterbury, tone 1.4 tunes: MS sources	70
3.3.	Cathedral chant books in print: 1752–1820	87
4.1.	Chanting services: manuscript sources	106
4.2.	Chanting service in C minor: formal design	108
4.3.	Chanting service in D: formal design	111
5.1.	The Bennet organbook: 'Chappel Tunes'	141
5.2.	Litany by Thomas Wanless: manuscript sources	148
6.1.	Pre-1800 parish sources of Turner in A	172
7.1.	The Dallas/Bremner canon	214
8.1.	John Cole's 1805 service manual for Christ Church and St. Paul's	228
8.2.	Jacob Eckhard's organbook: service music	243
8.3.	William Smith, *The Churchman's Choral Companion to his Prayer Book* (1809): musical sources	256–8

HYMN TUNE INDEX SOURCE CODES

Codes beginning with an asterisk are Generic Codes, each representing a set of sources of the same type. For example, *SCT = Scottish Common Tunes; *TS = Tune Supplement; *UC = Untitled Collection.

Codes beginning with a number sign are Title Codes for anonymous sources; the letters that follow are the initial letters of a few principal words from the title of the source. For example, #VH = *Village Harmony*.

All others are Compiler Codes, beginning with the first four letters of the compiler's last name and the initial of his first name, and continuing with initial letters of a few principal words in the title. For example, PlayJI = John Playford, *An Introduction to the Skill of Music*.

A number or letter after a space at the end of the code indicates an edition of the source represented (letters for unnumbered editions), or in the case of *UC, one of a number of untitled collections. A number without a space before it is a volume or part number.

ABBREVIATIONS

Sources

BCP	Book of Common Prayer
Cuming, *HAL*	G. J. Cuming, *A History of the Anglican Liturgy* (London, 1982)
EECM	Early English Church Music
HM 54457	The Huntington Library, MS HM 54457, 37 vols., Autobiography and Journals of John Marsh, 1752–1828
HMPEC	*Historical Magazine of the Protestant Episcopal Church*
HTI	Nicholas Temperley (ed.), *The Hymn Tune Index* (Oxford, forthcoming)
JAMS	*Journal of the American Musicological Society*
JEH	*Journal of Ecclesiastical History*
JRMA	*Journal of the Royal Musical Association*
le Huray	Peter le Huray, *Music and the Reformation in England, 1549–1660* (Cambridge, 1978)
MD	*Musica Disciplina*
ML	*Music and Letters*
MR	*Music Review*
MT	*Musical Times*
New Grove	*The New Grove Dictionary of Music and Musicians* (1980) (library sigla in tables and figures are from *New Grove*)
PRMA	*Proceedings of the Royal Musical Association*
RRMR	Recent Researches in the Music of the Renaissance
SRO:RSEC	Edinburgh General Register House, Scottish Record Office, Records of the Scottish Episcopal Church
Temperley, *MEPC*	Nicholas Temperley, *The Music of the English Parish Church*, 2 vols. (Cambridge, 1979)

Texts

Ag	Agnus dei		Cr	Creed
AthCr	Athanasian Creed		Dm	Deus misereatur
Bc	Bonum est confiteri		Dx	Doxology
Ben	Benediction		Glp	Gloria patri
Bn	Benedictus		Glt	Gloria tibi
BnA	Benedic anima mea		Glx	Gloria in excelsis
Bte	Benedicite		Jd	Jubilate deo
Cd	Cantate domino		Ky	English Kyrie
CoR	Commandments responses		Mg	Magnificat

Nd	Nunc dimittis	Sn	Sanctus
Ps	Psalm	Td	Te deum
Sd	Surge domino	Ve	Venite
Se	Sentence		

Manuscripts and Music

A	Anthem end, double entry ptbk	org	organ
anth	anthem	pr	printing
arr	arranged	ptbk	partbook
B	bass	r	reverse
can	cantoris	S	Service end, dbl ptbk
ch	chant	Sc	Score
cho	chorus	sgl	single
cplbk	commonplacebook	T	tenor
Ct	countertenor	tr	transposed
dbl	double	Tr	treble
dec	decani	vv	voice, voices
M	medius	v., vv.	verse, verses
O	organbook		

Library Sigla

BE	Berkeley, University of California, Music Library
CA	Canterbury, Cathedral
CHc	Chichester, Cathedral
Cfm	Cambridge, Fitzwilliam Museum
Ckc	Cambridge, King's College, Rowe Music Library
Cpc	Cambridge, Pembroke College
Cu	Cambridge, University Library
DRc	Durham, Cathedral
EXc	Exeter, Cathedral
GL	Gloucester, Cathedral
H	Hereford, Cathedral
Lbl	London, British Library, Reference Division
Lcm	London, Royal College of Music
Ldc	London, Dulwich College
Lpro	London, Public Record Office
Lsp	London, St Paul's Cathedral
Lwa	London, Westminster Abbey
LF	Lichfield, Cathedral
LIc	Lincoln, Cathedral
NWr	Norwich, Norfolk and Norwich Public Record Office

NYp   New York, Public Library at Lincoln Center, Library and Museum of the
       Performing Arts
Ob   Oxford, Bodleian Library
Och   Oxford, Christ Church
Ojc   Oxford, St John's College
PHf   Philadelphia, Free Library of Philadelphia
W   Wells, Cathedral
WB   Wimborne, Minster
WO   Worcester, Cathedral
Y   York, Minster
Yi   York, Borthwick Institute of Historical Research

1

The Ecclesiastical Settlement and the
1662 Book of Common Prayer

> The Stuart age witnessed a search for a 'religious settlement' that lasted as
> long and was as difficult as the quest for a constitutional relationship
> between crown and parliament.[1]

THE reinstatement of the Church of England coincided with the return of the
king in 1660. This singular dramatic episode did not, however, bring with it
immediate consolidation of episcopal government and instantaneous restoration of traditional liturgical practice. Even so, the relatively rapid progress of
these events belies the century of tumultuous religious change which preceded the abolition of the monarchy and the state church in the early 1640s.
The sixteenth-century Reformation, Catholic reaction, and Elizabethan settlement were the prelude to a period of growth in the union of church and
state during the early Stuart years. Several archbishops of Canterbury were
active in this process, but it is William Laud whose name is inextricably linked
with the turbulent decade leading up to the Commonwealth.

The century opened quietly enough, without a change in religion, on the
accession of James I in March 1603. The Millenary Petition, a document in
which Puritan nonconformists outlined the points at issue between their theology and practice and that of the state church, was presented to the king barely
a month later.[2] The petition contained requests to shorten the long morning
service, to moderate church songs and music for 'better edification', and to
eliminate 'popish opinion'. This last was at the heart of objections to certain
'ceremonies', which included bowing at the name of Jesus, using cap and surplice, making the sign of the cross in baptism, and kneeling to receive communion.[3] James responded positively by calling the Hampton Court
Conference in January 1604, but the results provided few concessions to the
Puritan point of view. The main liturgical outcome of the conference was the

---

[1] Barry Coward, *The Stuart Age* (London, 1980), 418.
[2] Text in H. Gee and W. Hardy, *Documents Illustrative of English Church History* (London, 1896; repr. New
York, 1966), 508.
[3] Cuming, *HAL*, 104–5.

authorization of a new translation of the Bible. A new Book of Common Prayer enacted by royal decree in letters patent issued in February was followed the next month by a new series of Canons, which consolidated various Elizabethan directives. The Puritans brought out a new petition in 1605. In the next year, the influential anonymous *Survey of the Book of Common Prayer* appeared. Widely read, it compared the Canons of 1604 with the 1549 and 1552 prayer books and recommended the substitution of the Scottish *Book of Common Order*.[4]

The 'Laudian' church, however, was moving in the opposite direction with a greater emphasis on the externals of worship. Chapels and cathedrals adorned with magnificently carved woodwork and marble tile floors, and a liturgy performed by officiants in sumptuous vestments were earnestly promoted. Uniformity in worship and the silencing of dispute were also considered to be worthwhile goals. It is widely believed, erroneously, that Laud made substantial alterations in the prayer book, although 'as Archbishop [from 1633] he concentrated his attention, liturgically speaking, on placing the altar against the east wall of the chancel, fencing it with rails, making the communicants come to the altar to receive, and reading the Ante-Communion at the altar, not in the reading-pew'.[5] As visible and therefore potentially divisive as these 'high church' practices were, their effect in the long term came intrinsically from their theological underpinning, the doctrine of Arminianism.[6]

The writings of Arminius, a Dutch theologian, were intended to refute the Calvinist doctrine of the arbitrary predestination of divine grace and exclusion from the sacraments by strict moral control. The movement which became known as Arminianism stressed the availability of divine grace in the sacraments to those who confessed their sins. Infant baptism, confession, and the regular receiving of communion could bring one the grace denied to any but the elect in Calvinist theology. The idea of belief in God's universal grace and the free will of all men to obtain salvation was revolutionary for a society 'steeped in Calvinist theology as was England before the Civil War', and religion as a major issue in the Civil War crisis must be considered within the context of the rise to power of Arminianism in the 1620s.[7]

The open conflict which ushered in the political and military upheavals of the early 1640s came in the aftermath of an attempt to enact a prayer book along English lines for the church in Scotland. James had begun efforts in this direction with the restoration of a valid episcopacy to Scotland in 1610, and in

[4] Cuming, *HAL*, 104–5.   [5] Ibid. 107.
[6] Nicholas Tyacke, 'Puritanism, Arminianism and Counter-Revolution', in Conrad Russell (ed.), *The Origins of the English Civil War* (London, 1973), 119–43.
[7] Ibid. 119, 130.

1616 he obtained the sanction of the General Assembly at Aberdeen for compilation of a prayer book.[8] The English book was prescribed for use in the
chapel royal of Holyrood in 1617. The set of Five Articles adopted under great
pressure in the next year enforced kneeling at communion, private baptism
and communion, observance of four holy days corresponding to Christmas,
Good Friday, Easter, and Whit Sunday, and an episcopal blessing of children.
These proved universally unpopular and stimulated cries of popery, creating
an unfavourable climate for liturgical reform. An Ordinal was adopted in 1620,
but the move towards a prayer book was halted until the next reign.[9]

Charles I took up the matter with a fair measure of personal zeal and a
Scottish Prayer Book was finally introduced in the spring of 1637. There were
some concessions to Scottish practice, although other completely unacceptable features, such as the proclamation prefixed to the liturgy ordering its use
by royal prerogative alone, alienated much potential support. The calendar
was expanded rather than simplified and changes in the communion were
largely in the direction of the communion service of 1549, considered popish
by many Scots. The new prayer book was immediately resisted, little used, and
not enforced.[10]

In England, criticism of Laudian 'high church' practices and of the Book of
Common Prayer became more insistent, but religious discourse was increasingly overwhelmed by civil and political conflict. A committee of lay peers of
the House of Lords and clergymen attempted to negotiate various matters at
issue, but they had little success in finding some basis for compromise.
Nothing could be done to avoid the parliamentary declaration in January 1645
that the use of the Book of Common Prayer was illegal. Events moved swiftly
with the trial and execution of Archbishop Laud, followed by the execution
of the king, and the British experiment with republican government under the
Commonwealth was underway. The Church of England ostensibly ceased to
function and many high-ranking clergymen went into exile or took refuge in
the homes of Anglicans. Yet 'although Parliament abolished episcopacy, at no
time during this period did it disestablish the Church'.[11] Anglicans found ways
to worship using the Book of Common Prayer in private homes and clandes-
tine venues. Nonetheless, Protestant dissent multiplied and diversified
throughout Britain under Oliver Cromwell's firm belief in a national church
that would include everyone.[12]

---

[8] F. Procter and W. H. Frere, *A New History of the Book of Common Prayer* (London, 1955), 144–5.
[9] Ibid.
[10] Gordon Donaldson, 'Reformation to Covenant', in D. B. Forrester and D. M. Murray (eds.), *Studies in the History of Worship in Scotland* (Edinburgh, 1984), 48–9.
[11] M. C. Cross, 'The Church in England 1646–1660', in G. E. Aylmer (ed.), *The Interregnum: The Quest of Settlement, 1646–1660* (London, 1972), 99.   [12] Ibid. 99–113.

The interregnum years fell unevenly on different Church of England jurisdictions. In cathedrals and collegiate churches and chapels, where the liturgy
was customarily sung, services ceased entirely by about 1647 and a fair amount
of destruction of fabric and furnishings, especially in cathedrals, took place.[13]
Many cathedrals were turned into secular public buildings and served as sta-
bles or military quarters. In parish churches, however, worship went on as
before, with less dramatic change. The ordinances laid down between 1643
and 1649 to suppress the Book of Common Prayer and the old Christian festivals, especially Christmas, Easter, and Rogationtide, were largely ignored or
resisted.[14] There were prayer books in one-third of all parishes whose inven-
tories were surveyed by John Morrill, along with substantial evidence that regular administration of the sacraments, Communion in particular, was widely
practised.[15]

Musical practice in parish churches also remained substantially as it was
before the Commonwealth. Singing metrical psalms, the congregation led by
the parish clerk, had long been the custom, and the *Directory for the Public
Worship of God*, like the Scottish *Book of Common Order*, authorized metrical
psalm singing as the only proper formal church music. 'In parish churches, as
opposed to cathedrals, the Puritan ideal for music scored a decisive victory.
The resulting clear separation between cathedral and parochial music was not
seriously challenged until the eighteenth century.'[16] By the time of the
Commonwealth, the parish clerk was often the only musical official, for
organs and choirs had gradually disappeared with the cessation of endowments
for choral music after the Reformation.[17]

Historians of the civil wars of the mid-seventeenth century and the
Restoration era have substantially altered the old maxim that the Interregnum
was a great divide. The near extinction of the episcopal succession was possibly the greatest threat to the survival of the Church of England.[18] Nine bishops remained in 1660 and their average age was 74.[19] One of the urgent tasks
of the returned monarch was the appointment of new bishops to the episcopal bench and their ordination of as many clergymen as possible to fill the large
number of vacancies in parishes. The relative speed with which the episcopal
system was reinstituted and the collapse of the Puritan opposition, viewed
against the background of Cromwellian politics, is believed to be the outcome

---

[13] le Huray, 53–4.
[14] John Morrill, 'The Church in England, 1642–9', in id. (ed.), *Reactions to the English Civil War* (London, 1984), 90.
[15] Ibid. 91, 105–7.   [16] Temperley, *MEPC*, i. 75–6.   [17] Ibid.
[18] I. M. Green, *The Re-establishment of the Church of England, 1660–1663* (Oxford, 1978), 81–2.
[19] Ibid. 90.

of the alliance of high church clergyman and country squire.[20] Many Anglican clergymen, prominent and otherwise, were provided employment and haven during the Commonwealth in private houses and chapels, where they served as tutors and chaplains. They were able to reinforce there the traditional view of order founded on the rule of law and the rights of property.[21]

On the other hand, John Morrill makes the compelling argument that 'the strength of the Anglican reaction of 1660 lay not exclusively, or even principally, in the response of a gentry who craved the return of a hierarchical government and society, but in the popularity of traditional religious forms at all levels of society'.[22] A conservative settlement, in any event, was not a foregone conclusion, for Presbyterians were intimately involved in the negotiations to bring back the monarchy. The Convention Parliament, which recalled the king and sat until December 1660, was made up of representatives of both sides in the political and religious debate.

The first phase of the Restoration settlement was a political one which saw the union of church and king, that is, 'the trappings of monarchy were restored with the person'.[23] Leading gentry resumed power by reissue of commissions of the peace and in the universities, former chancellors were returned to their old posts. Settlements of property and the transfer of lands and livings purchased during the Commonwealth were undertaken. The speed and ease with which cathedral chapters were restored varied from place to place, but positions were being filled within weeks of the king's return and the 'varied tasks of cathedral and collegiate churches resumed'.[24] Traditional forms of worship came into use fairly quickly in the capital and in many places outside as well; for example, the Book of Common Prayer was probably used for a thanksgiving service in August 1660 for repossession of Winchester Cathedral.[25]

The accommodation of different sorts of Protestants in a national church seemed attainable in the early months of 1660.[26] The Declaration of Breda, issued on 4 April by Charles II before his return to England, held out some promise of negotiations in that direction.

And because the passion and uncharitableness of the times have produced several opinions in religion, by which men are engaged in parties and animosities against each

---

[20] R. A. Beddard, 'The Restoration Church', in J. R. Jones (ed.), *The Restored Monarchy 1660–1688* (London, 1979), 155–9; Green, *Re-establishment*, 180–201.

[21] Beddard, 'Restoration Church', 157; Robert S. Bosher, *The Making of the Restoration Settlement 1649–1662* (London, 1957).

[22] Morrill, 'Church in England', 91.   [23] R. Hutton, *The Restoration* (Oxford, 1985), 128.

[24] Green, *Re-establishment*, 61.   [25] Ibid. 73.

[26] Hutton, *Restoration*, 143; Bosher, *Restoration Settlement*, 144–9; Beddard, 'Restoration Church', 159; Green, *Re-establishment*, 1–2.

other (which, when they shall hereafter unite in a freedom of conversation, will be composed or better understood), we do declare a liberty to tender consciences, and that no man shall be disquieted or called into question for differences of opinion in matter of religion, which do not disturb the peace of the kingdom; and that we shall be ready to consent to such an Act of Parliament as, upon mature deliberation, shall be offered to us, for the full granting that indulgence.[27]

Upon his return, Charles implemented several policies designed to unite Presbyterians with the church. He appointed nonconformist chaplains, admitted their patrons to the Council and Household, and sponsored talks between their representatives and the episcopal divines.[28] The first of several meetings in London led to the Worcester House Declaration of 25 October, which promised, among other concessions, that representatives of different religious persuasions would be invited to meet and discuss 'such alterations as shall be thought necessary' in the Book of Common Prayer.[29]

The proposed conference became a reality the next year with the appointment of a commission composed of twelve clergymen representing each side, the nonconformists and the Church of England. They met in the Savoy from 15 April through 21 July 1661, but their deliberations produced few substantive changes in the liturgy. Moreover, the general election of 1661 returned a Commons in which the Anglican side was heavily represented. The Cavalier Parliament imposed the sacrament on its members, restored the bishops to the House of Lords, and introduced a Bill 'to provide for an effectual conformity to the liturgy of the Church', even though the Savoy Conference was in session at the time.[30] When the Cavalier Parliament met again in the autumn, 'it chose to regard the hastily summoned Convocation, elected under episcopal supervision, not the Savoy Conference, nominated by the King and including Presbyterians, as the authoritative voice of the Anglican clergy'.[31] This second phase of the Restoration settlement also saw the obliteration of the constitutional reforms of 1641 to 1654 and the public burning of the Solemn League and Covenant, which had been passed in 1643 in Scotland.[32] Not to be was the 'British church on the presbyterian-puritan model', for which the Covenant was the legal basis.[33]

The work of the Savoy Conference has an important place in the history of the English liturgy, despite its lack of success in accomplishing substantive reform in the national church. Objections to the prayer book were formally

---

[27] Gee and Hardy, *Documents*, 585.   [28] Beddard, 'Restoration Church', 160.

[29] E. Cardwell, *The History of Conferences and Other Proceedings connected with the Revision of the Book of Common Prayer* (Oxford, 1840), 297.   [30] Beddard, 'Restoration Church', 165.

[31] Ibid.   [32] Hutton, *Restoration*, 154.

[33] G. Donaldson, *Scotland—Church and Nation through Sixteen Centuries* (Edinburgh, 1972), 85.

presented with a list of general principles and proposals as 'The Exceptions against the Book of Common Prayer', and the response was given as 'The Answer of the Bishops to the Exceptions of the Ministers'. Taken together, these documents summarize the main issues between Anglicans and Puritans on the liturgy and its public observance. The commissioners were 'mostly chosen for their moderation'[34] and their warrant was appropriately cautious:

to take into your grave and serious considerations, the several directions, rules and forms of prayer, and things in the said Book of Common Prayer contained, and to advise and consult upon and about the same, and the several objections and exceptions which shall now be raised against the same. And if occasion be, to make such reasonable and necessary alterations, corrections, and amendments therein, as by and between you and the said archbishop, bishops, doctors, and persons hereby required and authorized, shall be agreed upon to be needful or expedient for the giving of satisfaction unto tender consciences, and the restoring and continuance of peace and unity, in the churches under our protection and government; but avoiding, as much as may be, all unnecessary alterations of the forms and Liturgy wherewith the people are already acquainted, and have so long received in the Church of England.[35]

The proposals for revision fall into three main categories: general principles, defects in wording, and objectionable usages.[36] Few deal with music specifically, although many are as a matter of course pertinent to the performance of the liturgy in its entirety. The revised prayer book under discussion was largely the work of John Cosin, Bishop of Durham, and Matthew Wren, Bishop of Ely. Both men had been in positions of leadership before the civil wars; both were deprived during the Commonwealth, Wren in the Tower and Cosin in exile. Cosin was a liturgical scholar of exceptional breadth, conversant with ancient liturgies as well as those of his own time. He had been involved with the printers in correcting the text of the Book of Common Prayer in the time of Charles I and was commissioned to compile a book of devotions for the ladies of the Court.[37] *A Collection of Private Devotions* was organized mainly by the ancient calendar of 'hours of praiers', with the Creed, Lord's Prayer, Ten Commandments and duties and sins thereof, 'Divers principles of Religion', Litany, and special prayers for feast and fast days.[38] It earned for Cosin the reputation of a Roman fellow traveller, even though he was a lifelong Church of England man, admittedly more amenable to dissenters after his exile during the Commonwealth than before it.[39] His love of ceremonial is well known because of the controversy surrounding his involvement in the

[34] Cuming, *HAL*, 117.
[35] Cardwell, *History of Conferences*, 300.
[36] Cuming, *HAL*, 117.
[37] Ibid. 107.
[38] J. Cosin, *A Collection of Private Devotions* (London, 1626).
[39] G. J. Cuming, *The Anglicanism of John Cosin* (Durham, 1975), 5, 14–15.

performance of the choral service in Durham Cathedral in the 1620s and his
introduction of choral service in Peterhouse College Chapel, Cambridge
around 1635.[40] Cosin's predecessor as Master of Peterhouse was his colleague
Matthew Wren, and it was during Wren's tenure that the chapel was consecrated on 17 March 1632 with half the ceremony in Latin, establishing clearly
a conservative and ritualistic direction.[41]

Early in his career, Matthew Wren had been chaplain to Lancelot
Andrewes, Bishop of Winchester, known for his attention to 'outward adorn-
ing' and elaborate ceremonial. Bishop Wren's major appointments were to the
sees of Norwich and Ely. His proposed amendments to the prayer book, the
'Advices', were written during his term in the Tower (1641-60).[42] Cosin
probably saw them soon after his return from exile in 1660 and produced his
own recommendations in a paper entitled 'Particulars to be considered,
explained, and corrected in the Book of Common Prayer'.[43] It may have been
in preparation for the Savoy review that Cosin and Wren combined their suggestions; these were entered in a prayer book dated 1619 and called the
Durham Book. 'Their object was to restore the characteristic elements of the
1549 Prayer Book without alienating a House of Commons which would
have been content to revive that of 1604. This task was then further complicated by the attempt to reconcile the Presbyterians to using the Prayer Book
at all.'[44]

The accomplishment of the Savoy Conference was slim in terms of substantive revision. The bishops conceded only seventeen points out of ninety-
six brought up by the Presbyterian side, mostly removing archaisms in
language, but approving one significant revision with the introduction of the
Authorized Version of the Bible.[45] A number of suggested changes in text or
ritual were relevant to items that were sometimes sung or intoned. For example, the grounds of objections to repetitions of the Lord's Prayer, the doxology after each psalm or canticle, and responses to the Commandments in the
Holy Communion rested on the view that these were inappropriate repetitions and interruptions in Scripture passages. The traditional alternatim musical practice in choral service would have been affected if the customary form
of verse and response in the litany and the alternate reading of psalms and
hymns were eliminated. The bishops countered these objections by saying that
the ministers 'directly practise the contrary in one of their principal parts of
worship, singing of psalms, where the people bear as great a part as the minis-

[40] le Huray, 47–50; J. Morehen, 'The Sources of English Cathedral Music c.1617–c.1644', Ph.D. diss.
(Cambridge University, 1969), 119–23.

[41] D. Mateer, review of EECM 13, in *ML* 68 (1987), 303.   [42] Cuming, *HAL*, 113.

[43] G. J. Cuming, *The Durham Book* (London, 1961), intro.; id., *HAL*, 113–16.

[44] Cuming, *Durham Book*, p. vi.   [45] Cuming, *HAL*, 118–19.

ter. If this way be done in Hopkins, why not in David's Psalms; if in metre, why not in prose; if in a psalm, why not in a litany?'[46]

The central musical request of the ministers was official recognition of metrical psalm singing as part of the liturgy. The only time that metrical psalms had been required to be sung in church was under the *Directory for the Public Worship of God*, although widespread use before that time encouraged the equally widespread notion that singing of metrical psalms in church was enjoined by law. The ministers stated in their twelfth general proposal that 'because singing of psalms is a considerable part of publick worship, we desire that the version set forth and allowed to be sung in churches may be amended; or that we may have leave to make use of a purer version'.[47] The bishops absolved themselves of pronouncing upon this important matter at all when they responded that 'Singing of Psalms in metre is no part of the Liturgy, and so no part of our commission'.[48]

The ministers also raised objections to the rubric 'in such places where they do sing, there shall the Lessons be sung, in a plain tune, and likewise the Epistle and Gospel'. Their aversion stems from the doctrine that only psalm and hymn texts are authorized by Scripture for singing in church. 'The Lessons, and the Epistles, and Gospels, being for the most part neither psalms nor hymns, we know no warrant why they should be sung in any place, and conceive that the distinct reading of them with an audible voice tends more to the edification of the church.'[49] The response of the bishops simply noted that 'the rubric directs only such singing as is after the manner of distinct reading, and we never heard of any inconvenience thereby, and therefore conceive this demand to be needless'.[50] Cosin summed up arguments for retention of the disputed rubric:

And this is the reason that in places where they sing, all our prayers are sung in a plain and audible tone. Reading hath not the force to affect and stir up the spirit, which a grave manner of singing has; and singing, if it be not tempered with that gravity which becomes the servants of God in the presence of His holy angels, is fuller of danger than of edification; therefore hath our Church most prudently appointed the lessons and prayers so to be sung as may make most for the dignity and glory of God's high and holy service, and be also a means to inflame men's affection to stir up their attentions, and to edify their understandings; which is answerable to St. Augustine's desire.[51]

Despite eloquent advocacy, the much disputed rubric was omitted in the review at Convocation.

---

[46] Cardwell, *History of Conferences*, 339.   [47] Ibid. 308.   [48] Ibid. 342.
[49] Ibid. 315.   [50] Ibid. 351–2.
[51] J. Cosin, *The Works of the Right Reverend Father in God John Cosin, Lord Bishop of Durham* (5 vols.; London, 1843–55), v. 58–9.

The Presbyterian request for less ceremonial in the matter of special observances went unheeded. Specifically, they wanted the elimination of holy days
not found in the 1549 and 1552 prayer books and the renaming of the remaining festivals without appointing special services for them. This would have
obviated a need for special music on these days, since their status would have
been lower than 'the Lord's-day' morning worship. A number of holy days
had been added in the 1604 prayer book. New services drawn up in 1661
included the anniversaries of the king's return on 29 May and the martyrdom
of Charles I on 30 January, and 'Forms of Prayer to be used at Sea'.[52]

There were clergymen who represented a middle position between conservative traditionalists and nonconforming Presbyterians regarding ceremonial
and music as well as church government. John Gauden, elevated to the see of
Exeter in 1660, was not in exile during the Interregnum and was one of several clergymen working on a form of modified episcopacy, which was
intended to function with the assistance of presbyters.[53] Gauden's views on
church music were likewise at the centre, between those who favoured a
return to the musical liturgy of the first Edwardian prayer book, such as Cosin,
and the nonconformists, who wanted music in church limited to metrical
psalm singing.

I know some (also) have been more at discord with the Liturgy, because they find in
cathedrals and other great churches the use of music, both vocal and organical, hath
been applied to some parts of it, which certainly is as lawful as any meter, psalmody,
hymnology, or singing to tunes; which was never questioned by learned and godly
men for lawful, in the worship of God public or private, especially that of praising and
giving of thanks. . . . The gift and use of music is so sweet, so angelical, so heavenly,
and divine, that it is a pity God should not have the glory and honour of it in his service, and the Church an holy comfortable use of it; that such an orient pearl may not
be used only in civil conventions, or abused in wanton carols and vain effusions, which
is to put a jewel in a swines snout;

  Tis true, (possibly) there may be some discreet regulations and emendations, even
in our Church Music; so as not to sing, either the Creeds, or Commandments, as not
the Lessons, or those parts of the Liturgy, which are most plain, doctrinal, and fundamental, (which ought to be fitted to the meanest auditors ears and understanding),
considering, that in the pauses or intervals of the lessons, and in the close of Divine
Service; the Psalms and Hymns, or holy and devout Anthems may be very aptly used;
not only as read or plainly sung, but as advanced with excellent music; so as may sometime suit with and regulate the common peoples tunes and singing; other while, it may
be elevated to those perfections of skill, which are worthy of the best choirs, and those
chief singers, or masters of symphony, which were and still are in the Church of

---

[52] Cuming, *HAL*, 126.   [53] Hutton, *Restoration*, 143.

England; it was only fit for those mens rudeness to abandon Church Music, who intended to fill all things with the alarums of war, and crys of confusion.[54]

The 'discreet regulations and emendations' which Gauden tentatively endorsed as reasonable were all possible within the framework of traditional practice. The legacy of the sixteenth-century reformers, who 'went upon the principle of expressing only the most essential things in the Rubric, and left many others to tradition',[55] allowed wide latitude for interpretation of directions for ritual and ceremonial actions, including chanting or singing. Deciding which texts were to be read in the ordinary speaking voice and which to be recited to a musical tone or sung in a composed setting was left in the hands of local authorities, who were more often clerical than musical. The customs of different religious jurisdictions—cathedrals, royal peculiars, collegiate churches and chapels, parish churches—had been the decisive determinants of liturgical performance practice since the Reformation, and the new prayer book did little to alter the traditional process.

Convocation met on 21 November 1661 to finish the revision of the prayer book, and 'official policy was to rush the book through with the minimum of debate'.[56] The new Book of Common Prayer was passed on 20 December 1661 and annexed to the Act of Uniformity; both received the Royal Assent of Charles II on 19 May 1662. The Act of Uniformity required every beneficed person to read prayers according to the new prayer book and to declare his consent to all things in it before the feast of St Bartholomew on 24 August. All who did not do so, as well as persons not in holy orders by episcopal ordination, unless so ordained priest or deacon before 24 August, were deprived of their benefices. In addition, every ecclesiastical person and every tutor or schoolmaster was required to promise conformity, to declare the illegality of taking arms against the king, and to make further declaration within twenty years that the Solemn League and Covenant was unlawful. It was now the turn of nonconforming clergymen to be ejected from their livings in substantial numbers, some to be replaced by old incumbents turned out during the Commonwealth, others not to be replaced for some time.[57]

None of the changes in the new Book of Common Prayer led to the kinds of reforms in liturgical practice that were earnestly desired by both sides in the protracted negotiations. Bishop Sanderson's preface indicates the modest accomplishment of the revision process.

[54] J. Gauden, *Considerations Touching the Liturgy of the Church of England* (London, 1661), 35–6.

[55] J. H. Blunt, *The Annotated Book of Common Prayer* (2 vols.; London, 1903), i, p. xxi.

[56] Cuming, *HAL*, 121.

[57] Green, *Re-establishment*, 177; Beddard, 'Restoration Church', 51; W. J. Sheils, *Restoration Exhibit Books and the Northern Clergy 1662–1664* (York, 1987), intro.

most of the alterations were made, either first, for the better direction of them that are to officiate in any part of the Divine Service; which is chiefly done in the Kalendars and Rubrics: or secondly, for the more proper expressing of some words or phrases of ancient usage, in terms more suitable to the language of the present times, and the clearer explanation of some other words and phrases, that were either of doubtful signification, or otherwise liable to misconstruction: or thirdly, for a more perfect rendering of such portions of holy Scripture, as are inserted into the Liturgy; which in the Epistles and Gospels especially, and in sundry other places, are now ordered to be read according to the last translation [King James].[58]

The largest part of the prayer book is taken up with the official texts of the liturgy, those for the unchanging or ordinary orders of worship and those for holy days and special state occasions. The full title is inclusive and general, specifying separately only the order for ordination and the prose psalter:

The Book of Common Prayer and Administration of the Sacraments—And other Rites and Ceremonies—of the Church According to the use of the Church of England Together with The Psalter or Psalms of David Pointed as they are to be sung or said in Churches And the Form or Manner of Making, ordaining, & consecrating of Bishops, Priests & Deacons.

The feasts and fasts of the liturgical year, the holy days, are governed by the Calendar and Tables of Rules, which specify the psalms and lessons proper to these days. Compared with the elaborate rubrics of the old pre-Reformation Sarum liturgy, which spelt out in great detail the music and ritual for festivals, the 1662 prayer book hardly touches upon these matters. Even so, custom continued to dictate the observance of holy days and singular occasions with special ceremony and traditional musical adornment.

The manner of reading the psalms and Scripture passages in the lessons are also part of the preliminary directions. The 'order how the Psalter is appointed to be read' governs the psalmody for daily and weekly use. The title wording 'pointed as they are to be sung or said' refers to the punctuation, a colon between the two phrases of the psalm verse and a full stop at the end of each verse. A note explains that 'the psalter followeth the division of the Hebrews, and the Translation of the great English Bible, set forth and used in the time of K. H. VIII and Edw. VI'.

The psalter shall be read through once every month, as it is there appointed, both for Morning and Evening prayer. But in February it shall be read onely to the twenty eighth or twenty ninth day of the month.

---

[58] *Facsimile of the Original Manuscript of the Book of Common Prayer Signed by Convocation December 20, 1661, and Attached to the Act of Uniformity 1661* (London, 1891); hereafter *Annexed Book.* Quotations below from the 1662 BCP are from this edition.

And, whereas January, March, May, July, August, October and December have one and thirty dayes a yeere; It is ordered that the same psalme shall be read the last day of the said monthes which were read the day before: So that the psalter may begin again the first day of the next month ensuing.

And, whereas the CXIX psalm is divided into xxii portions, and is overlong to be read at one time: It is so ordered, that at one time shall not be read above four or five of the said portions. And at the end of every psalm and of every part of the CXIX psalm shall be repeated this Hymn . . .

> Glory be to the Father, and to the Son: and to the holy Ghost. As it was in the beginning, is now, and ever shall be: world without end. Amen.

The Sunday morning worship was commonly called *Divine Service* and included the Order for Morning Prayer, the Litany, and the ante-Communion, or full Communion, when celebrated. Morning Prayer was prescribed for daily use and formed the main part of Sunday worship. The term *service* is used in both general and specific ways in conjunction with the liturgy and its music, with the precise meaning depending upon its context. For example, service can refer to Morning Prayer by itself, or to the several orders subsumed under Divine Service. *Service music* denotes all the music for a service or services, while a *musical service* is a setting of paired canticles from Morning or Evening Prayer, or a complete musical setting of all texts customarily performed with music.

Performance directions in the rubrics for each item in the liturgy can be reduced to one or a combination of three words, *read*, *say*, and *sing*. Their surrounding context, no matter how imprecise, is needed to fill out a picture of how the Morning Prayer service proceeded. For this reason, the rubrics in abbreviated form for each segment of the liturgy are set out in Table 1.1. The different canticle texts in the Evening Prayer service are noted, but the sequence of events is essentially the same as morning service. *Canticle* is used collectively for the texts said or sung after the reading of each Lesson, although in its strictest sense it pertains to texts from the Scriptures. Texts from the Psalms, Jubilate deo for instance, and the Te deum, technically a hymn since it is not a scriptural text, are still called canticles.

The Litany followed Morning Prayer by order of the rubric 'Here followeth the Litanie, or generall supplication, to be sung, or said after Morning Prayer, upon Sundaies, Wednesdaies, and Fridayes, and at other times when it shall be commanded by the Ordinarie.' The rubric restores the first Edwardian prayer book (1549) option of chanting, whereas in 1552 and later editions the rubric merely required the Litany 'to be used' at the same times. The form of the Litany is primarily verse and response and incorporates the texts of Agnus dei, Kyrie, and Doxology in its petitions and their answers. The Lord's Prayer is

TABLE 1.1. *The 1662 rubrics for Morning and Evening Prayer*

Liturgy	Text incipit	Rubric
Sentences	verses from the Bible	. . the Minister shall read with a loud voice, some one, or more of these sentences of the Scriptures that follow.
		And then he shall say . . .
Exhortation	Dearly beloved brethren	. . to be said of the whole congregation after the Minister, all kneeling
General Confession	Almighty and most merciful Father	. . to be pronounced by the Priest alone, standing, the people still kneeling. The people shall answer here, and at the end of all other prayers. Amen.
Absolution	Almighty God, the Father of our Lord	. . the Minister shall kneel and say . . . with an audible voice: the people also kneeling, and repeating it with him both here, and wheresoever else it is used in divine service.
Lord's Prayer	Our Father, which art in Heaven	Priest: Then likewise he shall say 'O Lord . . .' Answer: 'And our mouth . . .' Priest: 'O God, make speed to save us.' Answer: 'O Lord make haste to hear us.'
Preces and Responses	O Lord, open thou our lips	Here, all standing up, the Priest shall say 'Glory be . . .' Answer: 'As it was . . .' Priest: 'Praise ye the Lord.' Answer: 'The Lord's name be praised.'
Doxology	Glory be to thee	Then shall be said or sung this Psalm following: Except on Easter Day, upon which another Anthem is appointed: and on the nineteenth day of every month it is not to be read here, but in the ordinary course of the Psalms.
Invitatory Psalm	O Come let us sing unto the Lord	Then shall follow the Psalms in order as they be appointed. And at the end of every Psalm throughout the yeare, and likewise in the end of Benedicite, Benedictus, Magnificat, and Nunc dimitis shall be repeated 'Glory be. Answer: 'As it was . . .' read distinctly with an audible voice . . . out of the Old Testament as it is appointed in the Kalendar. Except there be proper Lessons assigned for that day. He that readeth standing and turning himself, as he may best be heard of all . . .
Psalms in Course	from the Psalter	. . said or sung in English . . . daily throughout the yeare.
First Lesson	from the Bible	Note that before every Lesson the Minister shall say, Here beginneth such a Chapter, or verse . . . And after every Lesson, Here endeth the first, or the second Lesson.
Te deum	We praise thee O God:	
Magnificat (Evening) or Benedicite	My soul doth magnify O All ye works of the Lord	
Cantate domino (Evening)	O sing unto the Lord	

Second Lesson	from the Bible	. . . read in like manner . . . out of the New Testament.
Benedictus	Blessed be the Lord God	said or sung . . . (except when that shall happen to be read in the chapter for the day, or for the Gospel on saint John Baptists Day
Nunc dimittis (Evening)	Lord now lettest thou	
or Jubilate deo	O be joyful in the Lord	
Deus misereatur (Evening)	God be merciful	
Apostle's Creed	I believe in God, the Father	. . . sung or said . . . by the Minister and the people standing: Except only such Dayes as the Creed of saint Athanasius is appointed to be read.
Athanasian Creed	Whosoever will be saved:	These praiers following, all devoutly kneeling, the Minister first pronouncing with a loud voice 'The Lord . . .' Answer: 'And with thy spirit.' Minister: 'Let us pray.' Minister: 'Lord have mercy upon us'; Answer: 'Christ have mercy . . .' 'Lord have . . .'
Lesser Litany	The Lord be with you	
Lord's Prayer	Our Father, which art in Heaven	Then the Minister Clerks and people shall say . . . with a loud voice.
Versicles and Responses	O Lord, show thy mercy	. . . the Priest standing up shall say . . . Answer: 'and grant us thy salvation.' Priest: 'O Lord save . . .' Answer: 'And mercifully heare us . . .' Priest: 'Endue thy ministers . . .' and so on
Collects	Almighty God, unto whom all hearts be open	Then shall follow three Collects. The first of the day, which shall be the same that is appointed at the Communion. The second for Peace. The third for grace to live well. And the two last . . . daily be said at Morning Prayer . . . all kneeling.
Anthem	variable	In Quires and places where they sing . . .
Prayers	for the King, Royal Family, Clergy and People, Prayer of St Chrysostom, Benediction	five Prayers . . . to be read here, Except when the Litany is read . . . then only the last two . . . to be read . . .

also said as part of the Litany, which ends with closing prayers and a benediction.

The third part of Divine Service is the Communion, or more often in the seventeenth and eighteenth centuries a portion of it called the ante-Communion. 'The direction for the "ante-communion service" is an attempt to revive the old custom, current in primitive times, of saying the introductory part of the Liturgy on solemn days when there was no celebration of the whole.'[59] In the 1552 prayer book the order was transferred to the holy days and in 1662, 'when it had long been evident that even a regular Sunday communion was a thing of the past', [60] the rubric refers to both:

Upon the Sundays and other Holidays (if there be no Communion) shall be said all that is appointed at the Communion, until the end of the general Prayer (for the whole state of Christ's Church militant here in earth) together with one or more of these Collects last before rehearsed, concluding with the Blessing.[61]

The rubrics for Communion in abbreviated form, with the ante-Communion portion marked, can be read in Table 1.2. The Sacrament was to be administered only when a convenient number of persons was present, according to the priest's discretion. Parishioners were supposed to take communion at least three times a year, including Easter, while 'in Cathedral and Collegiate Churches and Colleges, where there are many Priests and Deacons, they shall all receive the Communion with the Priest every Sunday at the least, except they have a reasonable cause to the contrary'.[62]

The custom of reading continuously Morning Prayer, the Litany, and ante-Communion as one interconnected service under the general heading Divine Service was said to be an innovation in 1709,[63] but the practice appears to have developed during the seventeenth century:

The old custom had been to have, on Sundays and holy days, prayers at six, and the Litany at nine, followed after a few minutes' interval by the Communion service. Even in Charles I's time they had often become joined, as a concession to the later hours that were gradually gaining ground. . . . But 'long after the Restoration' the distinction was maintained in some places, as in the Cathedrals of Canterbury and Worcester.[64]

The rubrics of the liturgy received their most drastic revision in the sixteenth century, when the old Sarum orders were rearranged, condensed, and

[59] Procter and Frere, *New History*, 498.　　　　[60] Ibid.
[61] *Annexed Book*, 249.　　　　[62] Ibid. 250.
[63] J. Johnson, *Clergyman's Vade Mecum*, i. 12, quoted in C. J. Abbey and J. H. Overton, *The English Church in the Eighteenth Century* (2 vols.; London, 1878), ii. 477.
[64] Abbey and Overton, ibid. ii. 477.

adapted to the new English liturgy. Directions previously spelt out for many texts were either omitted along with the texts, or abbreviated for those items that were retained. Of the two Edwardian Prayer Books of 1549 and 1552, the first was 'a moderate, though extensive, adaptation of the Sarum service-books, the second a decided step towards the doctrinal standpoint of the continental reformers'.[65] The most severe pruning of the Communion liturgy occurred from 1549 to 1552; in the first, rubrics mentioned clerks singing with the Introit, Kyrie, Gloria in excelsis, Creed, Offertory sentences, Sanctus, Proper preface, Agnus dei, and post-Communion, but only the Gloria in excelsis was to be said or sung in the second.[66] There was no change in the rubrics mentioning music in Morning and Evening Prayer: Venite exultemus and the proper psalms in Morning Prayer, and the Athanasian Creed for major feasts and saints' days were directed to be said or sung. The Book of Common Prayer restored in 1660 was essentially the Elizabethan prayer book, revised minimally and reissued in 1604 in the reign of James I.

The interpretation of the rubrics of the liturgy in terms of how each text was to be delivered and what ritual would accompany it, in the absence of detailed instructions, depended on received custom and on the participants. The terms *read*, *say*, and *sing* are used singly or in tandem for almost all texts and none excludes a musical tone. The plainest form of recitation on a single tone is not confined to the least significant items in the liturgy, but may be used for all liturgical texts. Conversely, 'the direction to be "said or sung" is not so much an order to sing those portions of the service which the direction precedes, as a license to read them in the ordinary tone of voice, provided there is no choir'.[67] 'Read', broadly meaning recitation from a book, is the usual term referring to an entire order of service in the act books of cathedral Dean and Chapters, irrespective of specific methods of delivery for particular texts. This general meaning conveys the sense of the old Latin rite's *cantare officium*, which admitted 'the double translation of "to sing" or "to say" the Office'.[68] As Roger North put the matter,

The Liturgy allows some passages to be *said or sung*, one would consider the difference. It seems not to be so much as is commonly understood; for in that sense *Singing* is not according to melody and harmony, but in a distinct and sonorous voice without any modulation at all, as the use is in our great churches in rehearsing the Pater Noster and Credo; and in that respect only, *singing* differs from common speech.[69]

[65] Cuming, *Durham Book*, p. xi.　　[66] Cf. Sarum and reformed use in le Huray, 20–1, 27.
[67] W. Dyce, *The Order of Daily Service, the Litany, and Order of the Administration of the Holy Communion, with Plain-Tune* (London, 1843), preface.
[68] S. J. P. Van Dijk, 'Medieval Terminology and Methods of Psalm Singing', *MD* 6 (1952), 8.
[69] John Wilson (ed.), *Roger North on Music* (London, 1959), 269.

TABLE 1.2. *The 1662 rubrics for the Holy Communion*

Liturgy	Text Incipit	Rubric
Lord's Prayer	Our Father, which art	And the Priest standing at the north side of the Table shall say the Lord's Prayer with the Collect . . . people kneeling.
Collect for Purity		
Commandments	God spake these words, Lord have mercy upon us	Then shall the Priest, turning to the people rehearse distinctly all the ten Commandments; And the People still kneeling, shall after every Commandment ask God for mercy . . .
Collects	for the King	. . . the Priest standing as before, and saying.
Epistle	from the Bible	. . . the Priest shall read the Epistle, saying, [follows the Collect of the day, directions for announcing chapter, etc.]
Gospel	from the Bible	Then shall be read the Gospell (the people all standing up) saying, The holy Gospel is written in . . . And the Gospel ended, shall be sung or said the Creed following, the People still standing as before.
Nicene Creed	I believe in one God	
Announcements		
Sermon or Homily		
Sentences	selections given	Then shall the Priest return to the Lords Table and begin the Offertory saying one or more of these . . .
Offertory		
Prayers	Let us pray for the whole state of Christ's Church Militant here in earth. [Ante-Communion ends after the above prayer, with the addition of the final collects and blessing.]	And when there is a Communion, the Priest shall then place upon the Table so much bread and wine as he shall think sufficient. After which done the Priest shall say.
Exhortation	several texts given	At the tyme of . . . Communion, the Communicants being conveniently placed for the receiving of the Holy Sacrament, the Priest shall say . . .
Prayer	Ye that do earnestly repent	Then shall the Priest say . . .

Confession	Almighty God, Father of our Lord Jesus Christ	. . . in the name of all those that are minded to receive . . . Minister and all the people kneeling humbly upon their knees and saying . . .
Absolution	Almighty God, our heavenly Father	Then shall the Priest (or the Bishop being present) stand up, and turning himself to the people, pronounce . . .
Comfortable Words	Hear what comfortable words	Then shall the Priest say.
Preface	Lift up your hearts.	. . . the Priest shall proceed saying 'Lift up . . .' Answer: 'We lift them up unto the Lord.' Priest. 'Let us give thanks unto . . .' Answer. 'It is meet and right so to do.' Then shall the Priest turn to the Lord's Table and say. 'It is very meet . . .'
Proper Prefaces	texts for specific feasts	
Sanctus	Therefore with Angels . . . Holy, holy, holy	After each of which Prefaces shall immediately be sung or said,
Prayer of Humble Access	We do not presume to come to this thy table	Then shall the Priest kneeling down at the Lord's Table, say . . .
Consecration	Almighty God, our Father	. . . he shall say the Prayer . . .
Communion	Take, eat	. . . Priest shall say . . .
Lord's Prayer	Our father, who art	Then shall the Priest say the Lord's Prayer, the People repeating after him every petition.
Thanksgiving	O Lord and Heavenly Father	. . . said as followeth
Gloria in Excelsis	Glory be to God on high	Then shall be said or sung.
Blessing	The peace of God	Then the Priest (or Bishop, if he be present) shall let them depart with . . .
Collects		to be said after the Offertory, when there is no Communion

'Say', the single directive term most often used in the rubrics, has several traditional ecclesiastical meanings, including recitation on a speaking tone, a musical monotone, or chanting with inflections in unison, or in harmony as in the preces and versicles and their responses. The opening sentences, exhortations, confessions, prayers, lessons, and collects in Morning and Evening Prayer, and most of the texts in the Communion liturgy, were customarily said 'in a monotone, slightly varied by occasional modulations'.[70] Liturgical and practical considerations governed cadential inflections:

at the close of each Prayer or Collect a certain modulation, inflection or change of voice, such as is accustomed, is both necessary and becoming: becoming, because being placed upon that constant close 'thro' Jesus Christ our Lord,' or the like it is a proper testimony, that we rejoice in God our Saviour; necessary, because it serves as a public sign or warning to the Choir to join in the approaching Amen. For the same reason it is also necessary in Chaunting the Versicles and Responses, distributed throughout the Liturgy. This modulation of the voice of the Priest has the same use, and is of the same necessity, in our Cathedral worship, as the cadence or other variation of it is, when he only says or reads the Service in our Parochial Churches.[71]

When 'say' is used in conjunction with 'sing', the usual meaning is chanting in unison or harmony, or singing a composed setting, unaccompanied or with organ. Venite and the proper psalms, creeds, canticles, the Litany, and the Sanctus, Creed, and Gloria in excelsis in Communion are all ordered to be said or sung. 'Sing' is used by itself only for the anthem in Morning and Evening Prayer, traditionally a composed setting of an appropriate text.

The position of the text in the liturgy and the person or persons to whom it is addressed, in other words the context of the liturgical action, is perhaps the most important factor in the choice of a method of recitation. A variety of conventions determined the proper approach to particular texts and those specially for the officiant were sometimes spelt out in printed guides, such as Thomas Seymour's *Advice to the Readers of the Common Prayer*. Seymour gave practical suggestions for the appropriate gestures, choice of vocal delivery, and progress of the service. The reader was advised to conduct the worship, for instance, with 'such postures as the Church hath ordered, as standing or kneeling in such parts of Worship as is proper to each, but also with such natural actions, as lifting up the Eyes or Hands, &c. which the Church hath not ordered; because they are so obvious to the reason of all Mankind . . .'.

He ought also to give to each part of the Service the proper accent or measure of Voice belonging to the same: For it is not seemly that all should be read in one Tone;

---

[70] John Jebb, *The Choral Service of the United Church of England and Ireland* (London, 1843), 156.
[71] Thomas Bisse, *A Rationale on Cathedral Worship or Choir-Service* (London, 1721), 32–3.

but those parts that are for *Instruction*, wherein he speaks to the people, should have one manner of reading; the *Prayers*, wherein he alone speaks for them, another, and those *Psalms* and *Prayers* wherein they speak with him by turns, another. He that hath no understanding of this, nor doth observe it as it ought to be, can never read well.[72]

Another guide was more precise in listing the Sentences, Exhortation, and Absolution under the first category of texts directed to the people, and the Confession and Lord's Prayer, among others, in the second group of texts spoken to God. In the third category were the psalms and prayers spoken 'by turns', to 'be read with the voice *kept up*, as the Suffrages are required to be and the Minister's part, thro' the whole Benedictus and Litany'.[73] Although the subtle nuances that were considered appropriate are not always clear, the voice 'kept up' can reasonably be equated, for most purposes, with the 'elevated voice', which was similarly associated with the opening sentences, Lord's Prayer, and lesser Litany in Morning Prayer. These items were to be 'read with a loud voice, or a clear and audible one: the word, loud, not signifying there, that it should be in any way strain'd, or kept up beyond its strength, but that it should be raised and adapted to . . . an extended Elevation, above the ordinary course of Reading'.[74]

From all accounts, the 'elevated voice' almost always meant a higher pitch, depending on the particular position of the text in the liturgy, and could also require a louder dynamic level in certain cases. Additionally, the term elevation is found in conjunction with the pronunciation of a particular word within the sentence structure, 'the elevation and depression of the voice in proper places and periods; I call them proper, not only with regard to the art of music, but even to the sense of the words'.[75] This kind of elevation was related to well-defined concepts of language, grammar, and proper expression, which were the subject of much study later in the eighteenth century. For example, the steady kind of monotone, 'the continuation of the voice on one single tone, as in cathedral service', was considered proper, but 'a uniformity in raising and falling the voice where the tune . . . is alike in every sentence', was not.[76]

The elevated voice required in liturgical recitation was more than a monotone on a different pitch level, however, for a subtle approach to phrasing seemed to be expected. But this did not mean licence to vary the tone beyond the bounds of accepted convention, which is the basis from which Anselm

---

[72] Thomas Seymour, *Advice to the Readers of the Common-Prayer* (London, 1682), 9.

[73] *The Rubrick of the Church of England, Examin'd and Considered* (London, 1737), 19.　　[74] Ibid.

[75] J. Gardiner, *Advice to the Clergy of the Diocese of Lincoln, in order to his Primary Visitation* (2nd edn.; London, 1697), 12.

[76] Anselm Bayly, *A Practical Treatise on Singing and Playing with Just Expression and Real Elegance* (London, 1771), 20.

Bayly argued his condemnation of too much variation in tone: 'some begin every sentence with the same tone elevated, and sink alike: others rise from a depressed tone to an octave, and then fall again to the same tone one while on a sudden, another while leisurely, either of these ways is speaking as some men live and argue, in a circle'.[77] Discussion of the use of the elevated voice in the recitation of the preces and responses and in other parts of the liturgy will continue in due course, but first we turn our attention to the liturgy as it was conducted in the seventeenth century.

Restoration sources concerned with the manner of performing Divine Service were the direct consequence of the special circumstances which caused routine procedures, normally taught by example, to be written down and published. They make it possible to draw an outline of the performance of choral service. Coordinating the rubrics of the Book of Common Prayer with the instructions and music in these publications will go a long way towards explaining the nature of the revival of tradition in the early 1660s. Their retrospective contents open a small window on liturgical practice in the earlier seventeenth century, before the cataclysm of the Commonwealth descended upon the choral establishments of the Church of England.

[77] Anselm Bayly, *A Practical Treatise on Singing and Playing with Just Expression and Real Elegance* (London, 1771), 20.

2

The Restoration of Choral Service in Cathedral and Collegiate Churches and Chapels

Gentlemen.

It is too well known what hath bin practised in Cathedrall Churches (in order to the publique worship of God, for many years past) instead of Harmony and Order. And therefore it may be rationally supposed, that the Persons and things relating to both, are not easily rallyed, after so fatall a Route. But Since the mercy of God hath restored a Power, and by it put life into the Law, to promote and settle it as it was. It hath been judged convenient, to revive the generall practise of the ordinary performance of Cathedrall service for the use of them, who shall be called to it, and are desirous to doe it with devotion and alacritie. To this end a Person is willingly imployed, who hath seen, understood, and bore a part in the same from his Childhood: And therein thinks himselfe happy to be now a Meane Instrument to doe God, and the Church service, in such a time when there are so many Cathedralls to be furnisht, and so few Persons knowing enough (in this particular) to performe the solemnity requisite in them.[1]

THE organs were back in service in Westminster Abbey and the Chapel Royal in 1660.[2] Common Prayer was restored in Oxford University's college chapels by about June 1660, and Anthony Wood reported that on 11 November 'the canons and students of Christ Church began to wear surplices and the organs plaid . . . Great flocking'.[3] Edward Lowe, restored to his post as organist of Christ Church in 1661, promptly published a complete manual with directions and music in response to the urgent need he and certain clergymen perceived for authoritative information on the performance of

---

[1] Edward Lowe, *A Short Direction for the Performance of Cathedrall Service* (Oxford, 1661), preface.

[2] Samuel Pepys, *The Diary of Samuel Pepys,* ed. Robert Latham and William Matthews (11 vols.; Berkeley, 1970), i. 176, 283.

[3] Anthony Wood, *The Life and Times of Anthony Wood*, ed. Andrew Clark (5 vols.; Oxford, 1891–1900), i. 319, 347.

the choral service. The dispersal of singing men and organists during the Commonwealth, often to non-musical pursuits, had left in short supply singers trained in recitation and chanting who remembered the plainsong melodies of the liturgy. The traditional methods of transmission whereby singers learned their craft from fellow musicians had been seriously compromised by the fifteen-year hiatus. At only one other time since the Reformation were the chants for ordinary service published, and then in direct response to the translation of the liturgy into English. The liturgical relevancy of John Merbecke's *Book of Common Praier, Noted* was short-lived, however, for its use was curtailed almost immediately by the far-reaching revisions of 1552. Its musical relevancy was another matter, for Lowe used it as a source for many of his melodies.

Some of the music in Lowe's manual, and in the two other Restoration publications of James Clifford and John Playford, is adapted from earlier composers, including Merbecke, and some can be traced back to forms of liturgical chant that were inherited from the old Latin rite at the Reformation. Plainsong melodies, for instance, can be identified with their Sarum antecedents and harmonized plainsong tunes show some of the features of improvised performance. The forms of liturgical chant inherited from the sixteenth and early seventeenth centuries were inevitably altered through changing liturgical demands, but evolution is part of the process in oral traditions. The suppression of choral service for fifteen years did not sound the death knell for the ancient choral tradition, but its resuscitation did present a challenge to clergymen and musicians alike.[4] The first steps were taken with the resumption of cathedral and collegiate routine and the refurbishment of choral establishments.

The appointment of officials and the restoration of cathedral life began promptly and proceeded steadily after the return of the king. Partly due to the survival of an above average number of old prebendaries, Winchester may have been among the first to restore the statutory number and form of services.[5] Dean John Cosin was at Peterborough within weeks of returning from exile and in July 'took possession of the cathedral, and, "to the great satisfaction of the whole city," revived daily choir services. On 1 August he held his first chapter meeting, at which livings were filled, leases granted, and orders made for resuming the collegiate life of the foundation.'[6] In Exeter Cathedral, chapter meetings began again in August 1660 and the number of residentiaries

---

[4] As an example of the problems of rebuilding where there was extensive destruction see Nicholas Thistlethwaite, 'Music and Worship 1660–1980', in Dorothy Owen (ed.), *A History of Lincoln Minster* (Cambridge, 1994), 77–9.

[5] Green, *Re-establishment*, 74.   [6] Beddard, 'Restoration Church', 163.

reached the statutory nine by September; 'within the next few months the canons set out to recover and restore to its pristine use cathedral and chapter property, to reinstitute the traditional corporate and choral worship and to lease out again the chapter estates.'[7] The College of Vicars Choral was reinstated within a few months and early in 1661 John Loosemore was paid 'for perfecting the Organs newly erected in the Cathedral'.[8]

In Norwich Cathedral, five of eight lay clerks resumed in 1660 the posts they had vacated during the Commonwealth, and the purchase of '4 surplices for singing boys' indicates that choristers joined them a year later. A small organ was used in the cathedral services until a new one was erected in 1664.[9] Under the leadership of Dean Robert Creighton of Wells Cathedral, the organ was repaired, choir stipends raised, new books ordered, and in 1664 a new organ, commissioned in 1662, was in place.[10] Similar entries in Dean and Chapter Act books and account ledgers from other institutions show that many followed the same path in returning musicians to their posts and replacing music and instruments.[11]

The publication of Edward Lowe's *Short Direction* was of immense value in making available to anyone the basic directions and music for the performance of a choral liturgy. As the subtitle stated, it was 'published for the information of such Persons, as are Ignorant of it, And shall be call'd to officiate in Cathedrall, or Collegiate Churches, where it hath formerly been in use'. Lowe's long career qualified him to assume the role of a reliable authority. He was trained in the Salisbury Cathedral choir and took the post of organist in Christ Church, Oxford in 1630. Deprived of his post under the Commonwealth, he was returned in 1661 and in the same year was appointed Professor of Music and organist in the Chapel Royal.

A Short Direction includes 'the Ordinary and Extraordinary parts, both for the Priest, and the whole choir', in liturgical order. The Extraordinary parts were for the special days in the church calendar, traditionally observed with different ceremonial and music than the daily service. Polyphony replaced plain recitation in responses and doxologies, and canticles were sung to composed settings rather than chanted to four-part tunes. In the old pre-Reformation Sarum use, the ceremonial for special occasions had been spelt

---

[7] Anne Whiteman, 'The Re-Establishment of the Church of England, 1660–1663', *Transactions of the Royal Historical Society*, 5th ser. (London, 1955), 113.

[8] Exeter Cathedral, Dean and Chapter 3787, Extraordinary Solutions (1635–46, 1660–66), 2 April 1661.

[9] Norwich Public Record Office, Norwich Cathedral DCN/R 229 A/3, Act Books; DCN/Q 231 A/1, Audit Books.

[10] L. S. Colchester, *Wells Cathedral: A History* (Shepton Mallet, Somerset, 1982), 162.

[11] For other examples see Christopher Dearnley, *English Church Music 1650–1750* (New York, 1970), ch. 1, pp. 65–81; ch. 7, pp. 116–34.

out in minute detail in terms of ritual and music, but these rubrics had been discontinued in the sixteenth century. As John Cosin pointed out, the Book of Common Prayer 'does not everywhere enjoin and prescribe every little order, what should be said or done', but takes 'it for granted that people are acquainted with such common things always used already'.[12] The rubrics contain few references to holy days and special occasions, but they do appoint psalms proper to the feasts of Christmas, Easter, Whitsun, and Ascension, and the fasts of Ash Wednesday and Good Friday. The Athanasian Creed is prescribed for fourteen festival and saints' days.

The Ordinary service music is organized in liturgical order for recitation of prayers and responses in the three main parts of Divine Service: Morning Prayer, Litany, and Communion. In the 1661 edition there are two psalm-tone melodies for the daily psalms, a plainsong and a four-part litany, and three psalm tones harmonized in four parts for canticles and psalmody on festivals and fasts. The unison litany is based on the melody of Cranmer's printed edition of 1544 and the harmonized version was adapted from Tallis.[13] A larger selection of psalm-tone melodies, seven for the days of the week, four 'single tunes formerly in use for the Psalms', and two more for Ps. 136 and the Athanasian Creed, were added in Lowe's second edition of 1664.[14]

These same unison and harmonized melodies were published in the same year by another cathedral musician, James Clifford, minor canon of St Paul's Cathedral. He, too, spanned the Commonwealth, having been a chorister of Magdalen College from 1632 to 1642. 'Brief Directions for the understanding of that part of the Divine Service performed with the Organ in S. Paul's Cathedrall on Sundayes and Holy-dayes' was first published in 1663 with rubrics only. In the 1664 edition, Clifford added the music and complete texts for the canticles and Nicene Creed. He intended, according to his preface, to 'inform and direct all other Choirs (that are remote) with the exact and uniform performance both at his majesty's Chapel Royal, and at (the mother of all cathedrals) St. Paul's in London'. The shortened rubrics begin after the psalms in 'the first service in the Morning', at the same point in Evening Prayer, and after the Commandments in 'the second, or Communion Service'. The complete texts of the canticles and Nicene Creed are printed as parts of the liturgy that were to be accompanied on the organ. Clifford also implied that the psalmody and the Athanasian Creed were accompanied:

---

[12] John Cosin, 'Notes on the Book of Common Prayer', *Works* (Oxford, 1855), v. 5.

[13] [Thomas Cranmer], *An Exhortation unto Prayer. A Letanie with Suffrages* (London, 1544); facs., ed. J. E. Hunt, *Cranmer's First Litany, 1544 and Merbecke's Book of Common Prayer Noted, 1550* (London, 1939).

[14] Edward Lowe, *A Review of a Short Direction for the Performance of Cathedrall Service* (Oxford, 1664).

I have here inserted all the *Tunes* now in use with us in all parts of the Service (viz.) the *Venite, Te Deum, Benedicite, Benedictus, Jubilate, Magnificat, Cantate Domino, Nunc dimittis*, and *Deus misereatur*, (when more solemn composures are not used) and also in the Psalms for the day of the Moneth, and for the *Quicunque vult* upon its proper days: which I hope will in some measure encourage the studious, inform the ignorant, and abate the mallice of the foul Detractor, when he shall see that we make use of nothing in Gods worship that we are either affraid or ashamed to publish.[15]

The revival of plainsong was critical to continuity in liturgical and musical tradition, thus the source of the plainsong melodies is a matter of considerable interest. The close concordances between most of Lowe's and Clifford's single and harmonized tunes is either an extraordinary coincidence of good memories, or attributable to another mutual source. Both men published this music in second editions in the same year, and a source may be inferred by the dedication in both volumes to the Revd Walter Jones, canon of St Paul's and sub-Dean of Westminster Abbey and the Chapel Royal. Clifford states that 'since my knowledge at Oxford (improved further at London) of your Eminency this way, [I] cannot so far disoblige the world as not to believe you have the supreme Mastery in religious Musick'. Lowe no doubt also knew Jones in Oxford and acknowledged that 'obedience to the Commands of some Reverend Persons brought this trifle first into the world'.

All the Versicles, Responsals, and single tunes of the Reading Psalms [prose psalms] (as many as we retain of them) are exactly the same that were in use in the time of K. Edward the sixth: This I can aver from the perusal I had of an ancient copy (sent me by the Reverend Dr. Jones) printed in the year 1550.[16]

In his second edition Lowe introduced the plainsong melodies for Ps. 136 and the Athanasian Creed with the remark 'the two tunes following were anciently used at Salisbury', so these melodies were presumably remembered from Lowe's early years there. As for the others, the Oxford associations of both Lowe and Clifford raise the possibility of the preparation by someone of a manuscript set of liturgical melodies. The scribe may have been Walter Jones, who could have supplied such a manuscript of tunes and the copy of Merbecke in the interest of assisting the restoration of choral service.[17] Oxford was, after all, the seat of Anglican orthodoxy for most of the seventeenth century.

---

[15] James Clifford, 'Brief Directions', *The Divine Services and Anthems usually sung in His Majesties Chappel, and in all Cathedrals and Collegiate Choires in England and Ireland* (2nd edn.; London, 1664), preface. The last is a jibe at Puritans for criticizing choral service on grounds of secrecy and exclusiveness.

[16] Lowe, *Review of Short Direction*, preface.

[17] Walter Jones (1605–72) was educated at Christ Church, Oxford and came to London in 1660 as canon of Westminster Abbey and St Paul's Cathedral. The sub-Dean of the Chapel Royal in the Restoration era was an important music copyist, and Dr Jones was paid £73 between May 1662 and December 1669 for 'pricking Services and Anthems'; Pipe Office Accounts, quoted in David Baldwin, *The Chapel Royal* (London, 1990), 193.

The third Restoration publication, 'The Order of Performing the Divine Service in Cathedrals and Collegiate Chappels', was a virtual reprint of Lowe's *Short Direction*, with minor changes in notation and some rearrangement of voice-parts. John Playford added this version as a supplement to the seventh edition of his *Introduction to the Skill of Music* (1674). It had a wide influence, especially in parish circles, and was still included in the nineteenth edition of 1730. Several musicians and singing masters in the eighteenth century copied its rubrics and its music. Playford was a vicar choral of St Paul's Cathedral and for many years clerk of Temple Church, a royal peculiar, and his empathy with cathedral worship helps to explain the presence of a manual for choral service in a popular book intended primarily for the domestic market. There were also six chant tunes in four parts 'sung in His Majesties Chapel with the organ to the Psalms, Te Deum, &c. composed by Mr. John Blow and Mr. William Turner', printed only in the 1674 edition. These chant tunes were part of the royal chapels repertory sent out from the capital to outlying cathedrals, described in the next chapter.

The interpretation of the Book of Common Prayer rubrics and their key directive words in all three publications are grounded in pre-Commonwealth liturgical practices. They demonstrate the continuity of musical tradition and repertory in the conduct of Divine Service and the manner of performing the chanted parts of the liturgy. Some minor changes in the first years of the Restoration are noticeable from Lowe's first to second editions, for example, those in some responses and the doxology, due to features of the new 1662 Book of Common Prayer. Since Playford's order of service came out ten years after Lowe and Clifford it might be expected to indicate new practices, but the rubrics are essentially Lowe's. Different wording and fuller explanations of some items, however, may have been intended to interest London and provincial churches with choirs in chanting portions of their services. As Table 2.1 shows (see end of chapter), musical performance is determined by the particular text and its historical context, and not spelt out in detailed rubrics in the prayer book. Of the twelve items in Morning and Evening Prayer that were customarily performed musically, for example, eight are ruled by *said* and only four by *said or sung*. In the ante-Communion portion of the liturgy, the rubric for four items with music is *said*, and for one other is *said or sung*.

Some music in the performance of the liturgy is prescribed by customary use only. Clifford's directions specify a second anthem after the sermon in Morning and Evening Prayer, and organ voluntaries after the psalms in Morning and Evening Prayer and at the conclusion of the Litany. Custom alone dictated the singing of the response to the announcement of the Gospel, 'Glory be to thee, O Lord', in the Communion Service. Although Bishop

Cosin succeeded in having the rubric for the congregation to stand while the Gospel is read reinserted in 1662, his attempt to restore the Gospel acclamation failed. Even so, its continued performance is directed by both Lowe and Clifford, and many four-part settings were still being composed in the early nineteenth century. 'This usage borrowed from the ancient Liturgies our Reformers continued in ours', wrote the Chancellor of Hereford, 'and tho' afterwards discontinued in the Rubric, yet custom still continues the use of it in most Cathedral and in many Parochial Churches: and the voice of Custom is in many cases the voice of Law'.[18]

The music specified in Table 2.1 for the different parts of the liturgy is almost entirely retrospective and has its antecedents in earlier forms. These will be explored in due course, but first let us look at the shape of the liturgy described by Lowe, Playford, and Clifford as it moved through its prescribed ritual and action. The choral part of Morning and Evening Prayer began with the officiant and the choir reciting the Lord's Prayer on one tone. The preces were sung by the officiant a tone lower, the choir answering on the same tone. There was a practical reason for changing pitch levels in the recitation of these items, according to commentators such as Thomas Bisse and Roger North. Bisse mentioned a signal to the choir to be ready to answer in the preces and responses, and North wrote: 'we have also a rationale of changing the tone, for by that the remoter people [outside the choir in the nave] might know what the prayers are, and also, by the cadence tone at the end, when the prayer is done; so also for the suffrages'.[19]

The Venite exultemus and the psalms for the day were sung 'for sides', that is, sung alternately by sections of the choir facing each other from opposite sides of the aisle. From the Reformation, the Venite exultemus was treated as a separate canticle and set in polyphony, usually as part of a full morning service. Formerly, the Venite had its own set of Invitatory tones and was preceded and followed by a responsorial chant, whose mode and melodic ending matched the Venite chant in the same way that antiphons matched their particular psalm tone.[20] Sometime after the mid-sixteenth century, the practice of chanting the Venite as its own invitatory to the daily psalms became the favoured procedure.[21] For the psalms proper to the day that follow Venite, Playford's rubrics require one lay clerk to sing the opening phrase or half verse

---

[18] Thomas Bisse, *The Beauty of Holiness in the Common-Prayer* (London, 1721 edn.), 141.

[19] Wilson, *North on Music*, 269; Bisse, *Rationale on . . . Choir-Service*, 32–3.

[20] John Aplin, 'Anglican Versions of Two Sarum Invitatory Tones', *MR* 42 (1981), 182.

[21] Sarah Boyer reports that Venite is 'found in about 60% of services written by composers who died before 1600, in about 40% of services whose composers died between 1600 and 1650 and in about 10% of services written by composers who died in the following half-century', 'The Manchester Altus Partbook MS 340 Cr 71', *ML* 72 (1991), 211.

of the psalm, the rest of the choir joining in the second half verse and continuing the alternatim performance. Accounts from Norwich Cathedral confirm the observance of this practice there through at least 1687, with payments to one of the singing men for beginning the psalms.[22]

Which parts of the service were routinely accompanied on the organ is not always clear, and practice no doubt varied from place to place. In the immediate Restoration period, some evidence shows that the role of the organ began with the canticle after the first lesson, except on festivals when the responses were sung in harmony. A direction to the organist of Westminster Abbey supports Lowe and Clifford on this point:

It was ordered that the back door of the organ loft be shut up and that the organist come into the choir at the beginning of Prayers in his surplice and betake himself to his stall till towards the end of the Psalms (except on festival days when the Answers are to be performed with the organ), then to go up the stairs leading from the choir to the organ and perform his duty.[23]

Lowe's 1664 preface directed that 'all the Tunes for 4 Parts, whether in Black or White notes (excepting the buriall song) may easily be ordered to be plaid on the Organ to the Quire, if there be any one that can prick out the upper, and lower parts, one over against another, and hath but so much ability only, as to play a Psalme from Notes'. Clifford indicated that the organ accompanied the Venite and the daily psalms, but whether this included the plain tunes is a moot point. Playford simply leaves the accompaniment optional, saying that the canticles and psalms could be sung 'to the Organ, or sometime without it'. According to Clifford, an organ voluntary followed the psalms in St Paul's Cathedral and the Chapel Royal, a custom that apparently went back at least as far as the early seventeenth century.[24]

After the first Lesson was read, the Te deum or the alternate canticle, Benedicite, was chanted in harmony or sung to a setting. The officiant recited the opening phrase and the choir joined on the second. The same directions apply to the Benedictus and its alternate, Jubilate deo, sung after the second Lesson. The sense of Lowe's rubric is that chanting the canticles to plainsong tunes in four-part harmony was a temporary expedient: 'when Quiremen are well skild in song & can perform the varietys composed for this service, then either of these tunes may serve for the Psalmes on festival days.' It also implies that the four-part tunes were well known in their other context, the psalmody in special services. Clifford's list of composers indicates again the preference for singing the canticles to composed settings.

[22] Norwich Public Record Office, Norwich Cathedral DCN/Q 231 A/1–3.
[23] Westminster Abbey, Muniment Room and Library, Chapter Act Book 3, fo. 30ʳ, 18 Dec. 1660.
[24] le Huray, 115.

The Apostle's Creed, or the Athanasian Creed on major feasts, was recited on one tone by officiant and choir. The suffrages and their responses followed in the same manner as the earlier preces and their responses, officiant beginning and choir answering. Then the whole choir recited the Lord's Prayer on one tone. The shorter Versicles and responses followed in the same manner as above. The Collects were recited by the officiant and answered by the choir with Amen on a single tone. Clifford was alone in mentioning the anthem, the only item which was ruled by the single key word, *sung*, but it can be assumed that Lowe left it out as being self-explanatory. The Anthem was followed by the closing prayers and benediction. A second anthem after the sermon was sung at St Paul's Cathedral, according to Clifford.

Divine Service continued with the Litany on Sunday, Wednesday, and Friday, and at other specially appointed times. According to custom, two persons recited the verses, kneeling at a special desk in the centre of the choir. The form of the Litany was mainly verse and answer sung 'in an Ordinary way', that is, chanted to the unison melody of Cranmer's 1544 English litany. For feast or fast days, the Tallis harmonization of Cranmer's plainsong melody was arranged by Lowe in four parts. Few composers set the litany responses after the Restoration, influenced perhaps by the almost universal adoption of the Tallis setting in cathedrals and collegiate churches and chapels.

The Second Service, or Communion, was celebrated more often in cathedral churches than in parishes, where a monthly or quarterly communion was usual. Few Communion texts were sung in polyphony. Clifford's Second Service includes the Responses to the Commandments, Gloria tibi, Nicene Creed, and the direction for a 'last Anthem' after the sermon. Lowe's instructions begin with the rubric for the opening Lord's Prayer, recitation by the priest 'in one grave tone, the deeper (if strong and audible) the better' indicating a lower pitch than the 'solemn and grave tone' required for the Creed in Morning and Evening Prayer. A Collect preceded the Commandments, which were chanted on a higher tone, the choir responding with 'Lord have mercy . . .' on the same tone when the organ was not playing. Conventions such as the higher pitch for chanting the Commandments were still observed in the next century (see Ely service, Ex. 5.1 below).

The Collects before the Epistle were also recited, the choir intoning the Amen after each reading. The Gospel was named when the Epistle reading ended and the customary response, Glory be to thee, O Lord, was sung in harmony by the choir. The Nicene Creed was directed to be sung, either on a solemn tone or in a composed setting. Lowe's Service ends with the priest reading the general prayer which, with one or more collects and the final blessing, closes the morning service when there is no Communion. The only

other music he mentioned is the choir Amen sung on one tone after each collect. The Second Service was first reprinted by Playford in the 1683 edition of
the *Introduction*.

The Divine Service on feast and fast days generally followed the same order
as Morning and Evening Prayer, Litany, and Holy Communion or ante-
Communion. For some special liturgies, a separate order is printed in the Book
of Common Prayer, for example, Baptism, Burial of the Dead, and
Matrimony. Some specific occasions, for example, the commemoration of
Gunpowder Treason on the fifth of November, begin with the rubric: 'The
Service shall be the same with the usual Office for Holy Days in all things;
Except where it is hereafter otherwise appointed.' Propers for certain texts follow. Musical performance included polyphony in place of recitation in choral
responses, canticles, and the litany. Proper psalms might be chanted in harmony or sung in a composed setting. Amens to the collects were also sung in
four parts and Playford indicates that the Athanasian Creed was sometimes
chanted in four parts. Organ music could also be added with voluntaries at
appropriate points in the service. In the Communion, the responses to the
Commandments could be sung in harmony.

Clifford and Playford printed all their service music in the standard white
mensural notation of the seventeenth century, but Lowe adopted the older
style of black notation used by Merbecke for all the music recited on one tone,
and for the four-part psalm tunes which required flexibility in the recitations.
He changed the note-values; Merbecke's oblong semibreve became a breve
and Merbecke's diamond pycke a semibreve. The recitation of the plainsong
tunes was intended to be flexible and the relationship between long and short
interpreted in terms of text rather than metrical pattern. In Lowe's words, 'the
Ordinary Responses are done in notes that are intended to signify no exact
measure, only the square black notes (or breves) are put, where the syllables
are to be sung slower than the other'. Clifford's directions are essentially the
same, though slightly more precise: 'the Minim and Semibrief are only put
where the syllables are to be sung slower and more emphatically than the rest.'
These directions follow precedents for interpreting notated recitations in
terms of flexible speech rhythm, that is, in the way a speaker would naturally
pronounce his language in a liturgical context.[25]

The single melodies for chanting the psalms in all three Restoration publications speak with the 'voice of Custom', for they trace their descent back to
pre-Reformation Latin plainsong. There were eight general classes in the
Sarum tonal system, each with its own formulae for specific groups of texts—

---

[25] Mary Berry (Mother Thomas More) discusses this issue in the Latin liturgy in 'The Performance of
Plainsong in the Later Middle Ages and the Sixteenth Century', *PRMA* 92 (1965–6), 121–34.

introit, gospel and canticle, and psalms. The melodies and their endings were written out in the Sarum Tonal, which 'arose as a systematic classification of the antiphons of Divine Service and of the tones and endings which are to be used with them'.[26] This system was abandoned in the mid-sixteenth-century reform and ceased to have any official liturgical function, but the familiar plainsong melodies had far from outlived their usefulness. John Aplin has described many items to show the continuity they provided in composition for the new English rite, as evidenced in part by the service music preserved in the Wanley and Lumley partbooks, and printed in Daye's *Certaine Notes*.[27] A unique item in the Wanley books provides an especially appropriate example. One Venite has a mode 4 Invitatory tone in the top voice, the only piece in the Wanley repertory for which the plainsong does not have to be supplied (the tenor book is missing).[28] Aplin discusses this Venite and one other to reinforce his point that while the use of chants may seem at the outset to be archaic in conception, 'clearly there were advantages in continuing to draw on proven structural methods, the causes being musical, not doctrinal'.[29] The same can be said for the continued use of Sarum psalm-tone melodies for chanting the daily psalms. But it must also be said that while antiphons, responses, invitatories, and 'suche like thynges' were eliminated from the reformed liturgy, the Venite was still ordered by rubric to be said or sung. It came to be treated as an invitatory to the proper psalms and the same rubric was customarily applied to both. Thus there was liturgical authority and a compelling musical reason for chanting the Venite and proper psalms to the familiar melodies.

There is little written or musical evidence about the nature of chanting practices in the century between the Reformation and the Restoration, although there is some reference to chanting the psalms. An Elizabethan clergyman mentions the psalms being sung 'by note' in cathedrals and collegiate churches, and a document of 1581 concerning the conduct of services in the parish church of Ludlow specifies that 'the psalms as well before the chapters [lessons] as after [meaning the canticles] shall be sung in plainsong in the choir'.[30] An oblique reference to chanting the psalms in plainsong emerges from the Lincoln Minster records during William Byrd's tenure (1563–72), particularly towards the end of the 1560s, when the influence of the Puritan Archdeacon John Aylmer had an adverse effect on the choral service. Roger Bowers notes that 'there was overt friction between Byrd and the chapter; the

[26] W. H. Frere, *The Use of Sarum* (2 vols.; Cambridge, 1901), ii., p. xxxiii.

[27] John Aplin, 'The Survival of Plainsong in Anglican Music: Some Early English Te-Deum Settings', *JAMS* 32 (1979), 247–75; ' "The Fourth Kind of Faburden": The Identity of an English Four-Part Style', *ML* 61 (1980), 243–65.

[28] Aplin, 'Anglican Versions . . . Invitatory Tones', 183.

[29] Ibid. 182.   [30] le Huray, 157–8.

latter disapproved of his practice of leaving the singing of the (plainsong) psalms to the men, and instructed that the boys should participate also.'[31]

The strongest evidence of the persistence of Sarum melodies in the psalmody comes from two sets of psalm tunes in which the four-part texture is ruled by tenor psalm-tone melodies. In 1597 Thomas Morley published his 'Eight Tunes' not as 'the true and essential forms of the eight tunes or usual Modes', but as examples of 'the forms of giving the tunes to their psalms in the churches which the churchmen (falsely) believe to be the *modi* or tunes, but if we consider them rightly they be all of some imperfect Mode, none of them filling the true compass of any Mode'.[32] These are written out as part of a discussion of composing in the modes, so there is no text underlay or other direction concerning their performance. There is more information in the other set of tunes, a small repertory copied out for Peterhouse College chapel in Cambridge around 1635, at the time that John Cosin reintroduced choral service there.[33] The tunes, on psalm tones 1, 2, 3, 7, and 8, are carefully laid out to match the first verse of Venite exultemus. Only three parts survive, but the bass can be reconstructed satisfactorily to supply the fourth part. The Peterhouse tunes are the only extant written psalm chant formulae representing what is now presumed to have been the common practice in cathedrals and collegiate chapels and churches.

Psalm-tone tenors have been identified by Nicholas Temperley in two metrical psalm collections published in the mid-sixteenth century. Ps. 146 in Francis Seager's *Certayne Psalms select out of the Psalms of David* (1553) is set in four parts with a tone 6 tenor. Tone 7 is the tenor part of Robert Crowley's sample tune for Ps. 1 in the first metrical translation of the complete psalter, *Psalter of David* (1549). The four-part tune harmonized in faburden style was intended to show how any metrical psalm text could be fitted to the same or similar tunes. 'The obvious inference is that these metrical psalms were to be sung in exactly the way the Latin prose psalms had been sung under the old rite. Even though only one psalm tone is printed . . . church choirs would have had little difficulty in applying the familiar faburden technique to the metrical psalms using any of the other traditional tones.'[34] It has even been suggested

[31] Roger Bowers, 'Music and Worship to 1640', in Owen, *Lincoln Minster*, 67. Direct assaults on music can be seen in the orders limiting the role of the organ to giving the pitch for the choir chanting of the canticles and even the anthem, which Byrd was ordered to sing with the choir. See Bishop Sparrow's visitation orders for Exeter Cathedral a century later in App. E.

[32] Thomas Morley, *A Plain and Easy Introduction to Practical Music* (London, 1597); ed. R. A. Harman (London, 1952), 206. Morley was choirmaster at Norwich Cathedral 1583–7 and organist of St Paul's Cathedral in London 1589–92.

[33] Morehen, 'Sources of English Cathedral Music', 119–23. Five psalm melodies are copied with a treble part in Music MS 479 and a countertenor part in Music MS 486.

[34] Temperley, *MEPC*, i. 25.

that the prayer book rubric directing the psalter to be read as appointed (the complete psalter through once every month) was 'probably purposely phrased so as to allow both prose and metrical forms, sung either in unison or in simple polyphony'.[35]

The psalm-tone melodies published by Lowe, Clifford, and Playford for the daily psalms offer their own strong evidence of the survival of the Sarum melodies. All eight tones are represented, in some cases by more than one melody. For the two tunes in his 1661 edition, Lowe assigned tone 1 to days of the week and tone 8 to Sundays and Holy days. In the 1664 revision, each day of the week has its own tune, called 'the Common Tunes' by Clifford. Playford's tunes are assigned in the same manner as Lowe's but to different days, possibly according to the use of St Paul's or Temple Church.[36]

Some changes in the form of Sarum melodies could be expected during their long use, especially after antiphons were no longer sung and they were not governed by a prescribed liturgical order and detailed rubrics. Intonations appear in only two of Morley's tunes and in none of the seventeenth-century psalm tunes, though the custom of intoning the first phrase of certain hymn (canticle) and psalm settings was still followed. The number of different endings used with each psalm tone narrowed to two for tones 5, 7, and 8 and one for the rest, as the psalm tones evolved into self-contained pieces adaptable to any of the 150 psalm texts in the monthly rotation. Even so, points of arrival and departure were still emphasized in the processes of memorization and transmission, and cadences remained the focal point of melodic progression. The peregrine tone, for instance, lost its second-phrase recitation on G in Restoration tunes, but the termination, even with some pitches omitted, retains enough of its distinctive ending to preserve its identity (Ex. 2.1). Lowe noted that the peregrine tone was 'anciently used at Salisbury' for Ps. 136, and the final cadence pattern would have been reinforced by the repetition of its second text phrase in every verse.

In all three Restoration sources, several tones are represented by more than one melody. For example, Lowe has two melodies on tone 1; the second, added in 1664, is transposed a fourth higher with a B♭. Otherwise, it and melodies in Peterhouse, Clifford, and Playford copy the Sarum tone with its fourth ending. Morley gives a different ending for tone 1, also for tone 3, but Restoration sources follow Peterhouse in their choice of ending. For tones 2 through 6, Restoration sources have a single melody, transposed in most cases

[35] Paul Doe, *Tallis* (2nd edn.; Oxford, 1976), 56.

[36] Perry Marshall is of the opinion that the assignment of days indicates that different tones were used from cathedral to cathedral, and concordances between Lowe and Playford show that a single tone for chanting daily psalms was a uniform practice throughout 17th-c. England; 'Plainsong in English: an Historical and Analytical Survey', SMD. diss. (Union Theological Seminary, 1964), 125.

Ex. 2.1. The peregrine tone (Lbl Arundel 130) and its use in Ps. 136 (Lowe)

In   e - xi - tu Is-rael de E-gyp-to ...

O give thanks un-to the Lord for he is gra- ci-ous: and his mer-cy en-dur-eth for-ev-er.

except 6, the same as Sarum in all sources except Lowe, where the transposition is a fifth higher. Lowe and Clifford use alternate clefs to indicate the
optional choice of transposition for bass or tenor. Changes in melodic contour
are often due to omitted inflections, such as the last pitch in the mediant in
tones 2, 4, and 5, and shortened terminations. In Ex. 2.2, the melody shown
below the Sarum psalm tone has been selected to represent transposition or
melodic change in cadences. (In the examples tone and ending are indicated
as, for example, 1.4.)

Ex. 2.2. Sarum psalm tones (Lbl Arundel 130) and their form in: (*a*) Lowe 'Munday'
tune; (*b*) Peterhouse no. 5; (*c*) Peterhouse no. 3; (*d*) Lowe 'Wensday' tune; (*e*) Clifford
no. 8; (*f*) Clifford no. 10

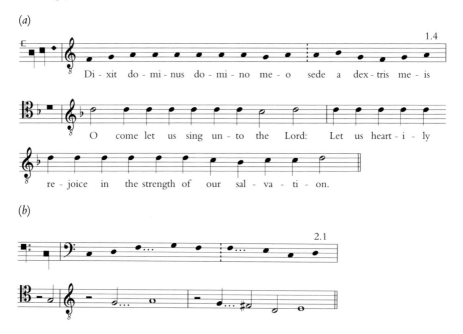

(*a*)

1.4

Di - xit do - mi - nus do - mi - no me - o   sede a   dex - tris me - is

O   come let us sing un - to the Lord: Let us heart - i - ly

re - joice in   the strength of   our   sal - va - ti - on.

(*b*)

2.1

There are two melodies for tone 7 in Lowe, Playford, and Clifford, one with the Sarum first ending unchanged and one with it shortened by two pitches, as it appears in Peterhouse. Tunes with the short final cadence in Restoration sources accommodate the first verse of the Athanasian Creed (Ex. 2.3). The earlier Peterhouse tune is laid out for the first verse of Venite. Half the tone 7 tunes are transposed a fifth down.

The largest and most varied number of melodies are those belonging to tone 8. Lowe and Clifford printed four tunes each on tone 8 for different days of

Ex. 2.3. Sarum psalm tone 7.1 (Lbl Arundel 130) and the Athanasian Creed (Lowe)

the week. Some tunes use a short gospel-canticle form in the first phrase, and a majority of tunes have dropped the last pitch in the mediant. Merbecke used a tone 8.1 melody with shortened mediant for Venite, and it and the Morley, Peterhouse, and Lowe 1661 tunes all show different combinations of tone and ending (Ex. 2.4). Each of Clifford's four tone 8 melodies has a different configuration of first and second phrases (Ex. 2.5).

All the four-part tunes in Restoration publications are harmonizations of psalm tones and all have titles, most likely in imitation of the way in which metrical psalm tunes were named after towns and villages, or specific churches. Hence Canterbury Tune and Christ Church Tune came from Canterbury Cathedral and Christ Church Cathedral, Oxford, and two others in the Peterhouse partbooks, Lincoln and Ely Tunes, came from their respective cathedrals. Two chants are associated with individual composers, Adrian

Ex. 2.4. Sarum psalm tone 8 (Lbl Arundel 130) and its use in: (*a*) Merbecke; (*b*) Morley's Eighth Tune; (*c*) Peterhouse no. 1; (*d*) Lowe 1661

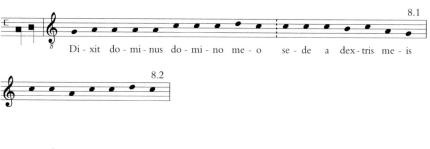

Ex. 2.5. Clifford's tone 8 cadences: (*a*) short 8.1, tune no. 2; (*b*) 8.2, tune no. 5; (*c*) 8.1, omitted inflection, tune no. 4; (*d*) 8.1, tune no. 9

Batten and William Child. All these chants named for persons or places are simply institutional formulae for chanting the daily prose psalms, which in normal times would not need identifying titles, since they were not written down. The number of places that claimed their own tune on psalm tone 1.4 reinforces the notion that many choral establishments still used the traditional psalm melodies.

If the composer attributions in Lowe and Clifford are to be accepted at face value, and there are valid reasons for doing so, it can be said with a measure of certainty that psalms were chanted to four-part chant tunes by the early seventeenth century. Adrian Batten's death in 1637 and the Peterhouse tunes copied around 1635 date the practice back to the 1630s. Peter le Huray first speculated that this was the case in *Music and the Reformation in England*. Thomas Morley's written and musical evidence from the late sixteenth century should also be accepted for what he described as current liturgical practice, even though his 'eight tunes' were designed to illustrate a theoretical point.

The Canterbury Tune is the least complex of the harmonized prose psalm tunes, but this kind of straightforward recitation was often considered most suitable for the most serious theological statements. The middle voices recite on one pitch with a single inflection, at the mediant in the tenor and the termination in the countertenor. The top voice and the bass have a single inflection in each cadence. The tenor might belong to psalm tone 4 or 8, both with upward inflections in the first phrase. The Peterhouse copy (Ex. 2.6) is identical with Lowe (for Te deum) and Clifford (for Venite).[37] Playford has copied Lowe's tune for boys' voices, in which the second countertenor is put up an octave, creating sixths between the three upper voices.

The harmonization of the Merbecke tone 8 melody called 'for Boyes' and Christ Church Tune on tone 1.4 are the other four-part tunes in Lowe's 1661 edition, and both are for Te deum (and psalmody on festivals). In the tune for

---

[37] Cambridge University Library, Peterhouse MS 487, copied by Henry Loosemore (1627–70), organist of King's College, in a gathering of liturgical pieces between the Tallis Litany and a Pater de coelis. The Peterhouse MSS and copyists are analysed by John Morehen in 'Sources of Cathedral Music'.

Ex. 2.6. Sarum psalm tone 4.6 (Lbl Arundel 130) and the four-part Canterbury Tune (Cu Peterhouse MS 487)

boys' voices, the psalm tone is in the bass (Ex. 2.7). The four parts must have been conceived in linear sequence, for the F in the termination has been raised, but the mediant is left with F naturals against a B♮ in the top voice, unless the B♭ were expected to be added by faburden rule.

The prominence of the interval of the sixth in many of these early harmonized chants is a legacy of the old improvised faburden technique. Morley's seventh tune and the Peterhouse tune on tone 7, for example, reveal similar chord structure and parallel sixths—between treble and tenor in Morley (Ex. 2.8(*a*)), and between countertenor and treble in Peterhouse (Ex. 2.8(*b*)). The

Ex. 2.7. Lowe's 'tune for Boyes' (1661)

Ex. 2.8. Harmonizations of tone 7: (a) Morley's Seventh Tune; (b) Peterhouse no. 4

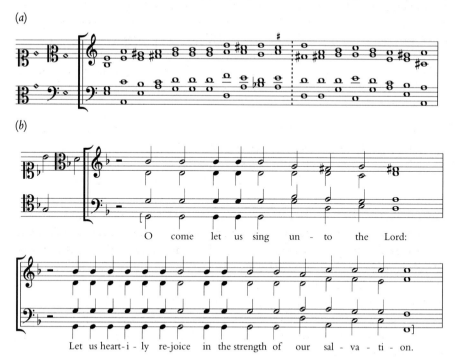

(a)

(b)

O come let us sing un - to the Lord:

Let us heart-i - ly re-joice in the strength of our sal - va - ti - on.

rules of faburden governed the older practice of 'singing upon a plainsong', which Morley pointed out 'hath been in times past in England (as every man knoweth) and is at this day in other places the greatest part of the usual music which in any churches is sung'.[38] The essentially oral practice of faburden was most useful in parts of the ritual that lent themselves to formulaic improvisation, for example, in processions where singers had to keep together while moving, and in psalmody, where verses were chanted alternately from each side of the divided choir.

Faburden originated early in the fifteenth century as improvisation in three parts, described by John Wylde of Waltham Holy Cross as 'the least process of Sights, natural and most in use' in one of two English tracts dealing with the subject.[39] The term 'faburden' is a composite of burden, a bass part, and the solmization syllable *fa* and is derived from technical characteristics of singing faburden:[40]

[38] Morley, *Plain and Easy Introduction*, 206.

[39] British Library, Lansdowne MS 763, fo. 116r–v, transliterated by Brian Trowell in 'Faburden and Fauxbourdon', *MD* 13 (1959), 47–8.

[40] Brian Trowell, 'Faburden–New Sources, New Evidence: A Preliminary Survey' in E. Olleson (ed.), *Modern Musical Scholarship* (London, 1980), 30.

The faburden proper, or lowest voice, is derived by singing fifths and thirds beneath the plainsong, which is the Mean, or middle voice. In order to be able to visualize these intervals from his book of chant, and within the four lines of the plainsong staff, the faburdener is told to imagine the notes a fifth higher than he sings them: that is to say, as unisons with and thirds above the plainsong. (This device of transposition or 'Sight' is borrowed from English discant.) The result is that the faburdener can never sing a B natural, but always sings B flats, as the imagined note for a B will always be the F-fa a fifth above.[41]

The treble voice doubled the plainsong at the upper fourth, the parallel movement of the voices producing a progression of first inversion chords. The intervals were often adjusted at beginnings and cadences, or on important words of the text, where the Mean and lowest voice frequently sang octaves or fifths.

Because the rules were taught by practitioners and handed down in oral tradition, few written examples are known, though 'faburden was no doubt used extensively for antiphonal psalm-singing'.[42] A single exception is the three-voice faburden for Ps. 134 which serves as an illustration of older technique in British Library Add. MS 4911, the other of the two English treatises that describe faburden. The plainsong from the third-mode psalm tone is transposed down a fourth in the middle voice. The outer voices maintain the interval of the sixth, and the middle voice proceeds in thirds and fourths from the upper and lower voices.

Some of the features of faburden harmonization were common to improvised psalmodic recitation in other parts of Christendom, for instance, a plainsong tone in one voice, homophonic texture, and binary verse form. Morley refers to this common practice in discussing singing on a plainsong; a 'ground' sung a sixth under true pitch but 'pricked a third above the plainsong', with an octave or unison at the close: 'this kind of singing was called in Italy "Falso bordone", and in England a "Fa burden" '.[43] Falsobordone, or false bass technique, is believed to have developed in Italy and Spain in the late fifteenth century from adding formal cadence formulae to Gregorian psalm tones.[44] The falsobordone produced mainly root-position chords highlighting the psalm tone in the highest voice, and all four parts were written out. In the sixteenth century, the plainsong foundation of the falsobordone gradually disappeared and more elaborate and varied pieces in the style were written, especially for the vesper psalms.[45] In Germany, several composers published

[41] Ibid. [42] Ibid. 68. [43] Morley, *Plain and Easy Introduction*, 207.
[44] Murray Bradshaw, 'The History of the Falsobordone from its Origins to 1750', Ph.D. diss. (University of Chicago, 1969), 291–5.
[45] In New Grove vi. 376 Bradshaw makes the statement: 'at the time when the practice of falsobordone writing was declining on the Continent, however, it received fresh impetus in England where it came to

polyphonic pieces in the falsobordone style for psalms to vernacular texts in Martin Luther's translation.[46]

In England, the improvised faburden replaced the plainsong itself as cantus firmus in four-part composition, and most of the large repertory of faburdens that survive in written form are of this type.[47] The practice of improvised faburden continued alongside the development of composition on faburden, both methods being governed by liturgical considerations.[48] The difference in approach to the performance of the psalms in daily service and on festival days accounts for the antecedents of all the four-part tunes in Restoration sources. The origins of Canterbury Tune and the Lowe tune for boys lie in the improvised method of singing on plainsong. The various four-part chants on tone 1 and tone 8 come from compositions on psalm tones that were part of a large repertory of special psalm settings.[49]

The psalms proper to major feasts in the liturgical calendar, or those appointed for state occasions and special commemorations, were often written out in measured polyphony. The Lumley and Wanley partbooks contain early examples of through-composed psalms on psalm-tone tenors in which the music is essentially the same for each verse. Ps. 47 in the Wanley partbooks, for example, composed on tone 5, third ending, repeats the same harmonization scheme, but the rhythm is adjusted to the text in successive verses (Ex. 2.9).[50] There are four psalms on

be known as Anglican Chant'. I take issue with this conclusion and with the similar analysis made of English chant by Ronald Makeley in 'Recitation Practices in Early Anglican Church Music, 1544–1676', Ph.D. diss. (University of California at Santa Barbara, 1975), 143–53. English church musicians had similar, but not identical, methods of improvising harmony to a plainsong, as Morley pointed out, and the English chant tune developed quite naturally from faburden technique. Applying the term falsobordone to faburden-derived chanting formulae is misleading in any case and begs the question of the long period of evolution of English chanting practice. Morley put it just right in 1597 when he wrote that improvising in harmony for chanting the psalms was called one thing in Italy and another in England. The Anglican Chant is a legacy of its own earlier traditions and there is no evidence to support a conclusion that falsobordone was reinvented in England after it had died out on the Continent.

[46] Friedrich Blume, *Protestant Church Music* (London, 1975), 73–8, 117. The Jena choirbook 34 (1510–20) contains 111 psalms based on plainsong, and was probably the model for Georg Rhau's vespers publications. See Bradshaw, 'History of the Falsobordone', 93.

[47] Trowell, 'Faburden–New Sources', Checklist of Surviving Faburdens (excluding Magnificat), appendices I, II, III; John Aplin, 'A Group of English Magnificats "Upon the Faburden" ', *Soundings*, 7 (June 1978), 90. Sources for these pieces are the Wanley, Lumley, and Barnard partbooks and John Day's *Certaine Notes*, published as *Mornyng and Evenyng Praier and Communion . . .* (1565).

[48] F. Harrison, 'Faburden in Practice', *MD* 16 (1962), 11.

[49] These psalms have been called 'festal psalms' since Edward Fellowes wrote about them more than fifty years ago in *English Cathedral Music* (1941), although the stylistically varied repertory, from elaborate pieces in imitative textures to homophonic settings on a plainsong tenor, is more accurately served by 'festival psalms'. This term takes its wording from Durham MSS E 4-11, 'Preces and psalmes proper for the Festival Dayes hereunder named', quoted in Kenneth Jennings, 'English Festal Psalms of the Sixteenth and Seventeenth Centuries', DMA. diss. (University of Illinois, 1966), 9.

[50] Bodleian Library, MSS Mus. Sch. E. 420–22, fos. 52^r, 52^v, 51^v; reconstructed on the psalm tone identified by Aplin in 'Fourth Kind of Faburden', 265; See also James Wrightson, *The 'Wanley' Manuscripts: A Critical Commentary* (New York, 1989), 172–3.

Ex. 2.9. Ps. 47, vv. 1 and 5 from the Wanley partbooks (Ob MSS Mus. Sch. e. 420–2)

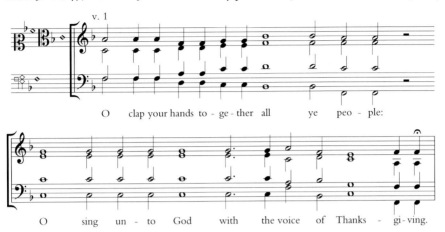

psalm-tone tenors in the Lumley partbooks and though only two parts survive, they are sufficient to indicate similar construction.[51]

The earliest festival psalms were written on psalm-tone tenors in a mainly homophonic texture, but the repertory gradually diversified to include elaborate verse settings without any psalm-tone basis.[52] Many were intended to be sung with particular sets of preces and responses. The earliest sequence of festival psalms was composed by Thomas Tallis, four sections of Ps. 119 appointed for evensong on the 24th of the month, two propers for Christmas Day, and four more sections of Ps. 119 for the 26th evening. They form a Christmas cycle of ten psalms, but only the second, third, and fourth sections of Ps. 119, on tone 1.4, and part of Ps. 110 for Christmas Day (verses 1–4), on

[51] Judith Blezzard, *The Tudor Church Music of the Lumley Books* (RRMR 65; Madison, 1985). There are twenty-nine pieces in mainly syllabic style, some on plainsong tenors and some with chant-like features, all composed according to Reformation principles of text setting. The music is reconstructed in four parts.

[52] Settings of Ps. 89 by John Amner, Ps. 47 by William Byrd, Ps. 21 by Richard Farrant, Ps. 119 by Thomas Morley, and Ps. 119 and Ps. 110 by Thomas Tallis are composed on a plainsong; see table of festival psalms in Jennings, 'English Festal Psalms', 67.

tone 5.1, survive in enough parts to be completed.[53] Ps. 119 is written for five voices, and although the musical formula repeats for successive verses, it is imaginative in its handling of the text. These psalms, like the Litany, writes Paul Doe, 'have the great merit that the texture is seldom merely chordal: each voice has a sense of purpose, and a rhythmic and melodic cogency of its own'.[54] The process of adapting the rhythm for each succeeding verse while repeating the plainsong formula, without the variable inflections of the Latin text, Doe points out, 'is clearly an important antecedent of Anglican chanting, which developed in the seventeenth century'.[55]

Tallis's Ps. 119 was the source and the model for a number of simpler four-part harmonizations of psalm tone 1.4. Lowe's Christ Church Tune and Clifford's 'Mr. Adrian Batten's Tune' are harmonized with most of the same chords as the third part of Ps. 119, 'O do well unto thy Servant'. The tenor is the untransposed psalm tone with mediant and final cadences on F. The fourth chord from the end is variously handled in all of the short formulae, Peterhouse included (Ex. 2.10). The tone 1.4 formula, called 'Mr. Thomas Tallis's Tune', is assigned to the psalmody and canticles in a 'Litany-service' arranged from

Ex. 2.10. Harmonizations of psalm tone 1.4: (*a*) Lowe, Christ Church Tune, 1661, 1664 cadence; (*b*) Clifford, Christ Church Tune; (*c*) Clifford, Mr. Adrian Batten's Tune; (*d*) Tallis, Ps. 119, Pt. 3, v. 17

(*a*)

We praise thee O   God: we know-ledge thee to   be   the   Lord.

[53] Aplin, 'Fourth Kind', 251–3, 265. Tallis's Ps. 119 is transcribed in EECM 13.
[54] Doe, *Tallis*, 56.   [55] Ibid.

(*b*)

O come...   Our   sal - va - ti - on.

(*c*)

O come...   our   sal - va - ti - on.

(*d*)

O do well...

Tallis by Henry Aldrich.[56] In the first volume of Boyce's *Cathedral Music*, the tone 1.4 chant appears as an integral part of Tallis's Dorian Service, which cemented Tallis's association with the chant for some time to come.

Another festival psalm, Richard Farrant's setting of Ps. 21 on tone 8, was adapted to a short formula, probably by William Child. James Clifford called it Imperial Tune, but Edward Lowe's title is 'D. Childs of Windsor'.[57] Farrant's psalms survive only in partbooks at Pembroke College, Cambridge where Pss. 21, 146, and 147 were appointed for Founder's Day. The same psalms, however, were assigned for Obiit Sunday at St George's Chapel, Windsor, where Farrant was Master of Choristers from about 1564 to 1580, and Child was organist from 1632 to 1697. The Farrant psalms were quite likely in the choir library before the destruction of music manuscripts during the Commonwealth. Child simply transcribed Farrant's harmonic structure

[56] Christ Church, Music MS 48, 170, Aldrich autograph; Westminster Abbey, Music MS Set 3, MS Organ 20, copied by John Church, Master of Choristers 1704–40 in his post-1720 hand.

[57] Pembroke College, Music MSS 1–6: 6.1, fo. 47ᵛ; 6.2, fo. 46ʳ; 6.3, fo. 49ʳ; 6.4, fo. 51ʳ; 6.5, fo. 49ʳ; 6.6, fo. 50ʳ. Kenneth Jennings identified Ps. 21 as the source of Imperial Tune in 'English Festal Psalms', 82.

Ex. 2.11. The Imperial Tune and its Source: (*a*) Lowe and Clifford; (*b*) Farrant Ps. 21, vv. 1 and 3 (Cpc MS 6: 1–6)

(*a*)

(*b*)

intact in a short formula, without the rhythmic variations of the original psalm verses (Ex. 2.11). The Te deum text was paired with a tone 8 melody many times in cathedral and parish sources, which suggests that Lowe's rubric, 'used for Psalmes (like the Canterbury Tune) on solemne daies, or Te Deum, at other times',[58] was widely followed. The Imperial Tune melody became in turn the tenor of another chanting formula called the Lincoln Tune.[59]

John Barnard, minor canon of St Paul's Cathedral, did as much as any musician to preserve the English cathedral tradition with the publication of *The First Book of Selected Church Musick*, the only printed anthology of liturgical music between 1565 and 1660.[60] It was the source used by many cathedral musicians, Edward Lowe among them, to arrange the service music of Tallis and Byrd for their own choirs. In his polyphonic responses and Litany, Lowe altered mostly the inner parts to reduce the texture from five to the four voices which had become standard for service music by the middle of the seventeenth century. His initial procedure was to move the tenor, wholly or in part, up to the treble and shift the upper parts down. This straightforward process usually produced a more homophonic texture. His version of the second response, 'O Lord make haste to help us', in Byrd's Second Preces and Responses, for example, highlights the contrast between Byrd's handling of inner voices and Lowe's chordal simplification (Ex. 2.12).[61]

In the doxology there is a little more shuffling of inner voices at the cadences. Lowe has placed Byrd's tenor up an octave in the countertenor at 'to the Holy Ghost' and shifted the first countertenor down to tenor. 'As it was in the beginning' is set to the same music as the opening of the doxology, note-values adjusted to the text. At 'without end' Lowe skips to Byrd's cadence, moving the tenor up an octave again, and proceeds with notes incorporated from Byrd's two countertenor parts. Lowe's concluding phrase, 'Praise ye the Lord', imitates Byrd in its first statement, omitting the first countertenor, but in the final statement, the lower four voices are reordered and the tenor melisma moved to the bass (Ex. 2.13).

To accommodate text revisions in the 1662 Book of Common Prayer, Lowe replaced the four-part doxology in his second edition. The priest recites

---

[58] Lowe (1664), 5.

[59] Cambridge University Library, Peterhouse MSS 485–90; Wells Cathedral, BCP with manuscript chant tunes.

[60] Robert Ford has suggested that the Barnard collection, though printed by Edward Griffin in 1641, was probably not published until after the Restoration (Playford, 1660); 'Some Notes on John Barnard and his *The First Book of Selected Church Musick*' (unpublished manuscript, 1979). For Barnard's place in the establishment of England's ancient music canon see William Weber, *The Rise of Musical Classics in Eighteenth-Century England* (Oxford, 1992), 25–8.

[61] Craig Monson has written about Byrd's debt to Tallis in these responses in 'The Preces, Psalms and Litanies of Byrd and Tallis: Another "Virtuous Contention in Love" ', *MR* 40 (1979), 257–71.

Ex. 2.12. Response from Preces and Responses: (*a*) Byrd; (*b*) adapted by Lowe

(*a*)

(*b*)

'Glory be . . . to the Holy Ghost' and 'Praise ye the Lord' on G and is answered in harmony. 'The Lord's Name be Praised' is actually a four-part recitation, sounding like a C to G plagal cadence. The short doxology which follows the Gospel acclamation in the Second Service likewise moves directly from recitation to final chord, D to A. The plain response replaces the more tuneful one from 1661, in which the tenor carries the chant-like melody.

For the suffrages and four-part responses that follow the Creed, and the versicles and responses recited after the Lord's Prayer, Lowe has used Tallis's First Preces and Responses and altered them mostly in the inner parts. Following his usual procedure, Tallis's second countertenor is omitted in some responses and in others, both countertenor parts contribute notes to one new part. A monotone replaces Tallis's plainsong inflection in the verse.

The Tallis Litany receives similar treatment in Lowe's four-part version for Extraordinary use. In the first four long responses, each repeating the priest's supplication, the plainsong is kept in the treble voice (Ex. 2.14). In the next several responses, the tenor is taken from the first response as it appears in Barnard. Pitches from the original first and second countertenor parts are selected to keep the range within a few notes either side of middle C. (In the examples, brackets enclose the second contratenor parts Lowe selected.) In the first response in Ex. 2.15 Lowe takes the countertenor down an octave so it

Ex. 2.13. The Doxology from Preces and Responses: (*a*) Byrd; (*b*) adapted by Lowe

(*a*)

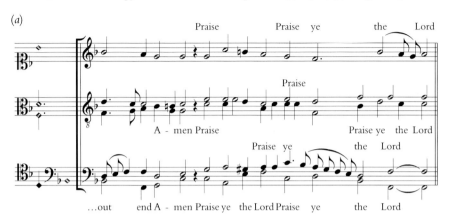

(*b*)

crosses the tenor, leaving an octave between treble and countertenor. This open spacing is characteristic of Lowe's plainsong harmonizations and may be his response to the acoustical properties of the buildings he worked in, or perhaps his own preference for adding variety to the texture. He used it in the response 'We beseech thee to hear us', where Tallis's second countertenor is moved up an octave, creating a wide space between it and the tenor. In the remainder of the Tallis Litany, Lowe reduced the five voice-parts to four in the same fashion, altering the inner parts and selecting countertenor pitches from the original first and second countertenor parts.

Polyphonic hymn settings for the Ordination service and for funerals complete Lowe's service music offerings. He explained that he published 'both the formes of Veni Creator, as they are set downe in the New Office of the Ordination of Priests, both set to 4 parts, the Notes of the latter transcribed

Ex. 2.14. Opening responses in the Litany: (*a*) Tallis; (*b*) adapted by Lowe

(*a*)

(*b*)

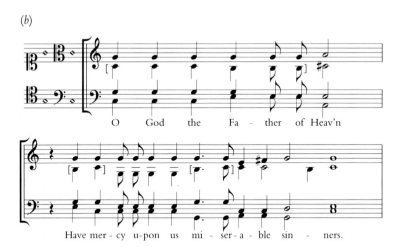

Ex. 2.15. Shorter responses in the Litany: (*a*) Tallis; (*b*) adapted by Lowe

(*a*)

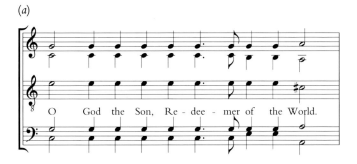

O God the Son, Re-dee-mer of the World.

We be-seech thee to hear us, good Lord.

(*b*)

O God the Son, Re-dee-mer of the World.

We be-seech thee to hear us, good Lord.

out of Ravenscrofts 4 part Psalmes, only the Plainsong, put in the upper part, instead of the Tenor'.

All the music for the liturgy in the Restoration publications was a legacy from the pre-Commonwealth years. Chanting practice, too, was firmly rooted in pre-Commonwealth procedures and underwent few changes until the next century. The psalms were sung to plainsong melodies at least up to 1700, and according to some observers well beyond. A note in the margin next to the 'Order how the Psalter is appointed to be read' in one Book of Common Prayer, for example, reads: 'Heretofore (as now in Cathedral & Collegiate Churches and some Colleges) 'twas customary to sing the Psalms in Plano Cantu.'[62]

Benjamin Payne refers to chanting practice in his recommendation that parish clerks imitate John Playford's way of reading the psalm 'distinctly and chantingly', or 'tunably, i.e., in a singing tone, and after the manner of chanting'. He added: 'a slight pause after the first four syllables will appear musical, much after the manner of plainsong used in cathedrals, or the chanting of the psalms'.[63] A dictionary entry on psalmody from 1739 also suggests that chanting the psalms to plain tunes had not died out: 'the plain song was only a gentle inflexion, or turn, of the voice, not much different from reading, like the Chant in our Cathedrals'.[64]

Though the music Lowe, Clifford, and Playford made available to church musicians in the Restoration era was not new, and the primary emphasis was on restoring older traditions, new forms began to evolve as a natural part of the process of revival. The plain tunes, chant tunes, responses, and litany were treated as common property and arranged by church musicians for their own needs. This is abundantly evident in the service music copied in cathedral and collegiate music manuscripts. The most enduring of the new forms of music for psalms and canticles are the main focus of the next two chapters.

[62] Exeter Cathedral, *Book of Common Prayer* (London, 1692). This volume is interleaved and extensively annotated and once belonged to Jeremiah Milles, Dean of Exeter from 1762 to 1784, among others.
[63] Benjamin Payne, *The Parish-Clerk's Guide* (London, 1709), 29–31, quoted in Temperley, *MEPC*, i. 97–105. Dudley Ryder, a Nonconformist of dissenting stock and later Attorney General and Chief Justice in the Court of King's Bench, naturally disapproved of chanting; his comment after service at St Paul's Cathedral, 14 June 1715, at least documents the practice: 'It is a very unhappy thing though that they make so ill a use of singing in the cathedral by using it even in their prayers and recitations of the Psalms that are no better at all than the Italian recitativo's'; Dudley Ryder, *The Diary of Dudley Ryder 1715–1716*, ed. William Matthews (London, 1939), 34–5.
[64] Thomas Broughton, *Bibliotheca Historico-Sacra* (2 vols.; London, 1737–9), ii. 295. Broughton was vicar of St Mary Redcliffe, Bristol.

TABLE 2.1. *1662 rubrics interpreted by Lowe, Playford, and Clifford*

Liturgy	Rubric	Lowe^a	Playford	Clifford
Morning Prayer				
Sentence	*read* with loud voice		*read* by the Priest in one continued and solemn tone	
Exhortation	*say*			
Confession	*said*			
Absolution	pronounce			
Lord's Prayer & Doxology	*say* with audible voice	The beginning of all is the close of the Doxologye of the Lord's Prayer . . . only to shew that whatever Tone ended that Prayer, the Priest is to begin O Lord open &c. a note lower and so on [tone given; 1664: Priest incipit on G]	the Priest and the whole Choir repeat the Lord's prayer: Thus [tone given]	
Preces & Responses Doxology	*say*	[inflected monotone for Priest; monotone responses] Extraordinary Responsals^b upon Festivals to Four Parts [Priest incipit G, Praise ye the Lord]	[above directions]	
Venite	*said or sung*	Then Venite Exultemus, and the Psalmes for the day to either of the following Tunes to be *sung* for sides [1661–2 tunes; 1664: 13 tunes]	begun by one of the Choir, then *sung* by Sides [7 tunes], observing to make the like break or Close in the middle of ev'ry Verse, according as it is shorter or longer	The Common Tunes [13 tunes]
Psalms	*sung or said*	[above directions] either of these tunes may serve for the Psalms on festival days. [3 4-part tunes] Those . . . may easily be ordered to be played on the Organ to the Choir . . .	These several Tunes of 4 parts are proper for Choirs to *Sing* the Psalms, Te Deum. Benedictus or Jubilate to the Organ, or sometime without it.	[3 4-part tunes]
			After the Psalms, a short Voluntary is performed on the Organ	After the psalms a Voluntary upon the Organ alone

Liturgy	Rubric	Lowe[a]	Playford	Clifford
First Lesson / Te Deum	*read* / *said or sung*	The Psalms ended follows the First Lesson; that done. Te Deum Laudamus &c. eitherset in variety as M. Tallis Birds &c. or else to one of these tunes next but one in foure parts . . . And so on, making the same break in the midst of each staff, though some of them are shorter [direction above for Organ; 1664: 4 tunes]	is *sung*, the Priest beginning alone, Then the whole Choir answer, . . . Composed usually in 4 parts for sides, by several Authors; Somtimes it is *sung* to one of these following Tunes of 4 parts with the Organ or without it. [8 4-part tunes]	After the first lesson is *sung* with organ; [3 4-part tunes]
or Benedicite				
Second Lesson	*read* / *said or sung*	as above		After the second lesson, [is *sung* with organ]
Benedictus or Jubilate deo		to one of these Tunes as before [directions above]	*Sung by the Choir, as* . . . variously composed, or else, to one of the following Tunes of 4 parts. [8 tunes above]	
Apostle's Creed or Athanasian Creed	*sung or said*	Then follows the Apostle's Creed, *sung* in one grave tone by the whole Choir [1664: tone 7 tune]	*sung* by the whole Choir in one continued solemn and grave Tone	[tone 7 tune]
			sung in the same Tune by sides; and sometimes it is *sung* to the Organ to one of . . . Tunes of 4 Parts. [tone 7 tune]	
Suffrages & Responses	*pronounce*	[inflected monotone for Priest and Choir; for Festivals 4 parts for responses only]	the Priest *sings* [Choir follows inflected monotone for both verse and answer]	
Lord's Prayer	*say with loud voice*	In one tone by the Whole Choir	The whole Choir in one Tone	
Versicles & Responses	*say*	[directions for suffrages]	[inflected monotone for Priest and Choir]	
Collects	*said*	Then follows the three Collects, which the Quite answers Amen. [Rubric in Second Service pertains;] The Amen	after every collect the Choir answers [monotone]	

Item	Action	Description		Rubric
Anthem	sung	is to be *sung* by the Choir at the end of each prayer in parts, . . . [4 parts for festivals]		After the third Collect O Lord our heavenly Father, is *sung* the first Anthem
Prayers	read			
Litany				
General Supplication & Answers	sung or said	And then (upon Lettany dayes) the Lettany sung (in an Ordinary way) by two of the Choir, the Responsalls follow as here. Answer the same by the whole Quite.	*sung* by two of the Choir in the middle of the Church, near the Bible-desk. The whole Choir answering in the same Tune. [inflected monotone]	After that the Litany O God the Father of Heaven
Lord's Prayer	say	either in the Last single Tone, or 4 notes lower		
Verse/Answer	say	[inflected monotone]	[inflected monotone]	
Prayers	say	[text incipit]	[text incipit]	
Doxology	say	[inflected monotone; 1664: monotone]	[inflected monotone]	
Verse/Answer	say	[inflected monotone]		
Prayers	say	[1664: Choir Amen on monotone, text incipit before Amen]	Choir Amen [monotone]	After the Blessing, . . . A Voluntary alone upon the Organ.
Communion				
Lord's Prayer	say	The Second Service is begun by the Priest who *reads* the Lords Prayer in one grave tone, the deeper (if strong and audible) the better:	[direction same]	
Collect	say	the Collect before the Commandements, and the Commandements in a higher tone, the whole Choir (if no singing to an Organ)		
Commandements	rehearse,		[direction same]	After every commandement the Prayer, Lord have mercy upon us, and &c.
Responses	ask			

Liturgy	Rubric	Lowe[a]	Playford	Clifford
		answering Lord have mercy . . . after each Commandement in the same tone.		
Collects	*saying*	Then the Priest *reads* the Prayers before the Epistle, the	[direction the same]	
Epistle	*said*	Quire answering Amen		
Gospel	*read*	When the Epistle is done and the Gospel named. The Choir *sings*, Glory be to thee O Lord, as is here set down. [1661: 4-part response; 1664:] in either of the two formes here set downe; which will serve to the Key of any Service, as the Organist shall apply it. [above response and shorter one]	[direction the same; short 4-part response from Lowe 1664]	After the Epistle, this heavenly ejaculation, Glory be . . .
		When the Gospel is ended, the		
Nicene Creed	*sung or said*	Priest (or whole Choir) *say* (or *sing*) the Nicene Creed		After the holy Gospel, the Nicene Creed; [with organ]
Sentences	*saying*			
Sermon				After the Sermon, the
Offertory				last Anthem. [with organ]
Prayers		The Priest *reads* the Prayer for Christ's Church Militant &c. and so goes on to the end of the Morning Service.		
Collects	*said*			
Blessing	*say*	The Amen . . . in a single tone.		

[a] Lowe's 1661 and 1664 editions are the same except where noted. Column entries are direct quotes; editorial remarks are in brackets.
[b] Extraordinary Service is separate in Lowe in the same liturgical order.

3

The Evolution of the Chant Tune

Set forms of prayer and praise have ever been characteristics of the Church, and she has always manifested a predilection for those melodies which are called Chants. Admitting a more extensive theme of praise than either Anthems or Metre Psalms, Chants have, in every age of the Church, been considered as eminently subservient to spiritual edification and comfort.[1]

CHANTING the prose psalms or canticles in harmony is a unique and distinguishing feature of the English liturgy. It has its own highly specialized genre of chant with an official name, Anglican Chant, a distinctive written form, and conventions which theoretically govern its performance. Over the long period of its development, from the fifteenth century to the present, English chant has evolved from a wholly improvised practice to one which is partially improvised from written music. Since the harmonized form of commonly used liturgical melodies began to be written down in the 1660s, church musicians have composed melodies and harmonized them especially for this purpose. In the old Sarum liturgy written chants were not needed, since familiarity with the canon of liturgical melodies and extempore methods of harmonizing them were required of all singers. Even in the simplified English liturgy of the Reformation, the old melodies continued to be used in a similar fashion. The routine practice of writing chant tunes out, except in the special circumstances already noted, coincided with new composition by individual composers after 1660.

From early on, chant tunes had two features that remained constant: a homophonic texture, and four-part harmony for the treble, countertenor, tenor, and bass voices of the normal English cathedral choir in the post-Restoration period. They were also governed by the formal structure of the prose liturgical text, the binary form of a psalmodic verse, in which the first phrase ends at the mediant and the second phrase closes with the terminal cadence. The internal musical features of chant tunes remained flexible, in keeping with the new practice of musicians creating and claiming these pieces

---

[1] William Smith, *The Churchman's Choral Companion to his Prayer Book* (New York, 1809), preface.

as their own, and with the traditional practice of adapting the musical unit to texts of varying lengths in performance.

When this music began to accrue its special notated form several centuries ago, the piece now called an Anglican Chant was known simply as a chant tune, or psalm tune. *Psalm tune* has now come to be associated almost exclusively with tunes for metrical texts,[2] but *chant tune* has always meant a musical formula intended for a prose liturgical text. The name Anglican Chant was coined much later, in the early nineteenth century, primarily for the purpose of distinguishing this harmonized form of English chant from the plainsong of the pre-Reformation Latin rite, which was receiving a great deal of attention from clergymen and musicians in the years preceding the Oxford Movement. The genesis of *chant tune* can be found in *tone*, used in earlier centuries to designate a melody intended for liturgical recitation, for instance, a psalm tone. After the Reformation, *tone* became transliterated into *tune*, as in Thomas Morley's 'Eight Tunes'. Typical headings for sets of chant tunes from the Restoration to about 1730 include 'tunes for the psalms', 'Wells tunes a 4 voc.', 'chappel tunes', 'proper tunes', 'psalms tunes', and 'chanting tunes'. The most precise name in terms of liturgical performance practice is 'chanting psalm tunes' in Ely Cathedral Music MS 4. By the middle of the eighteenth century, *chant tune* had largely given way to *chant* or *chaunt*.

The evolution of the English chant tune is an integral part of the history of the cathedral choral tradition. The evidence needed to trace its development from the Restoration to the late eighteenth century is contained in cathedral and collegiate church and chapel music manuscripts. The humble chant tune was not the kind of music that was carefully preserved, but a sufficient sample of chant-tune repertories remains to show what kinds of formulae were composed and something of the methods of their transmission. The earliest repertory to be circulated country-wide was sent out from the capital to choirs in outlying regions in the 1670s and was intended as an authoritative source and a model for composition, an encouragement to the restoration of the traditional choral liturgy and its ritual. The composers identified with chant tunes in the model set were all associated with the Chapel Royal, and it is very likely that these chant tunes belonged to the common repertory of functional music sung in the royal chapels in London and Windsor. Six of the generic model tunes were printed by John Playford in his 'Order of Performing the Divine Service' with the note 'these six Tunes are sung in His Majesties Chappel with

---

[2] Psalm tune is used for a large and well-known body of psalm and hymn tunes. Nicholas Temperley, *The Hymn Tune Index* (Oxford, forthcoming) defines a tune as 'a piece of music intended for strophic repetition with a sacred metrical text'. This also applies to chant tune, substituting prose for metrical.

the Organ to the Psalms, Te Deum, &c. Composed by Mr. John Blow and Mr. William Turner, Gentlemen of His Majesties Chappel'.[3]

Sections of overlapping segments of the original repertory are found in numerous manuscripts from widespread locations in Britain. The most complete segment survives in a Restoration bass partbook, British Library Add. MS 17784, which is linked to the Knights of the Garter and St George's Chapel, Windsor by its elegantly decorated ornamental capitals and coats of arms, and its repertory of services and anthems by William Child. St George's is a royal peculiar rather than a royal chapel, but its traditionally close ties to the royal chapels in Windsor and London are well documented.[4] Twenty-one chant tunes in four parts are copied on the first two pages in the service end of Add. MS 17784. The chant tunes are headed by a drawing of viol and lute, crossed in front of a music manuscript displaying 'Cantate domino' and 'Non nobis', with the ornate caption 'Tunes in foure parts to the Psalms of David' (Fig. 1). King David himself with instrument in hand is elaborately drawn in brown ink on the opposing page (Fig. 2).

The bass parts of the same twenty-one chant tunes in the same order were copied in Durham Cathedral Music MS C 28, and the tenor part to twenty in Music MS C 12. These are probably the items for which cathedral accounts record payment 'to Mr. Husbands for pricking 20 Tunes for the Psalms – 5., June 13, 1674'.[5] If Mr Husbands may be presumed to be Charles, Gentleman of the Chapel Royal (d. 1678), he may well have brought the chant tunes from London himself.[6] Durham Music MS C 28, the bass partbook, contains a total of twenty-five tunes, which may well have been the number in the original set, but there is a lack of concordances for the additional four tunes in other manuscripts. The Wimborne Minster repertory has several chant tunes not in Add. MS 17784, by William Turner, Michael Wise, and Thomas Heywood, all Chapel Royal composers, and these may also have been selected from the original set.

A third significant segment of the 'royal chapels repertory' is preserved in a psalter which came into St Paul's Dean and Chapter Library in 1988. The small

[3] John Playford, 'The Order of Performing the Divine Service in Cathedrals and Collegiate Chappels', *Introduction to the Skill of Music*, 4.

[4] Coats of arms of men knighted between 1661 and 1673, identified by the Hon. Mrs Grace Holmes, include James, Duke of York, and Henry Compton, Bishop of London. Edward III founded the 'Royal Free Chapel of Our Lady, St George and St Edward the Confessor within the Castle of Windsor' in 1348. Its status as a 'royal peculiar' comes from a 1351 order by Pope Clement VI conferring exemption from ordinary ecclesiastical jurisdiction. See Neville Wridgway, *The Choristers of St. George's Chapel* (Windsor, 1980), ch. 1.

[5] Durham Cathedral, Add. MS 110, Minutes of the Dean and Chapter relating to the Services of the Church, Treasury Book 1674, fo. 10[v].

[6] Brian Crosby, *A Catalogue of Durham Cathedral Music Manuscripts* (Oxford, 1986), 244.

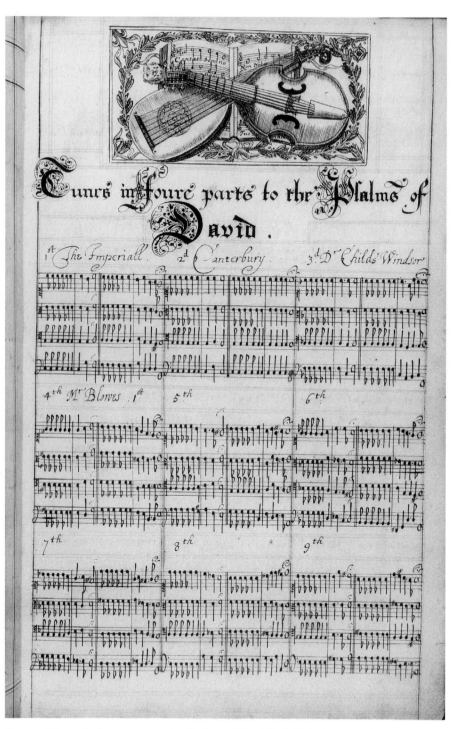

FIG. I. 'Tunes in foure parts to the Psalms of David', Add. MS 17784, fo. 177 ʳ⁻ᵛ. By permission of the British Library.

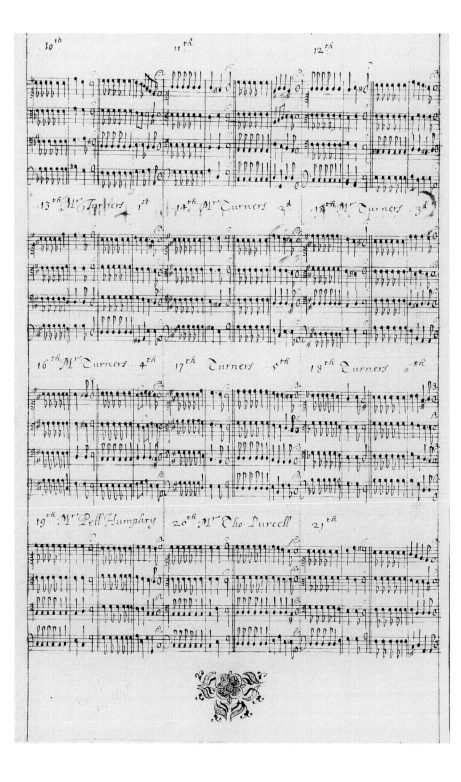

FIG. 2. King David, Add. MS 17784, fo. 178ʳ. By permission of the British Library.

volume, Music MS A.1.8vo, is made up of the printed psalter and additional music pages, on which are copied the bass parts to services, the whole inscribed with the title 'Twenty Morning & Evening Services of the best now performed in the Cathedrall Church of Pauls London'. The bass parts of twelve of the twenty-one tunes from Add. MS 17784 are copied out on the blank page opposite the first printed page of the psalter, beginning with nos. 1–4 (Fig. 3). The order of the remaining eight (Add. MS 17784 nos. 7, 6, 10, 13–15, 19, 11) is varied to suit the individual musician or cathedral official for whom it was intended. The chant tunes are written in the notational style of Restoration tunes and appear to have been copied in the 1670s, when the royal chapels repertory was circulated. On the other hand, chant tunes continued to be written in the same notation through the early eighteenth century, so a copying date in the 1690s, when St Paul's choir reopened, must be considered.

The great London fire of 1666 effectively curtailed the performance of choral service in St Paul's for thirty years, though occasional special services were held in a part of the building during the intervening years.[7] Music officials continued to be paid according to their appointments, but since the choral establishment of St Paul's was not officially functioning, they were allowed to hold positions elsewhere.[8] This complicates the question of where the St Paul's psalter was used, if it was assembled in the 1670s, as well as the relationship of the tunes to the service section, which matches the repertory in St Paul's partbooks copied in the 1690s. Music MS A.1.8vo contains the bass parts of services by Child, Gibbons, Bryne, Tucker, Dr (1677) Blow, Purcell, Humfrey, and Dr (1669) Rogers. The picture is further clouded by the number of successive scribes who copied the services and entered the titles in the index at the same time. One of these appears to be Stephen Bing (d. 1681), in which case the earlier date for the chant tunes would be the better choice.[9] The psalm tunes copied by Bing in York Music M 1/5–8s, the Gostling partbooks, are in the order of the St Paul's tunes, although he selected only eight (nos. 3, 4, 7, 10, 13, 15, 17, 19).

Besides the title, 'Twenty Morning and Evening Services', another inscription, 'For Mr. Short', is written on the inside cover in the same or very similar hand. Benjamin Short, resident of St Andrew Holborn and organist of St Sepulchre (1712–60), is one possible candidate.[10] He was born about 1674

[7] I wish to thank Sarah Boyer for sharing her research on the music of St Paul's Cathedral in the late 17th c.

[8] Watkins Shaw, *The Succession of Organists* (Oxford, 1991), 173–4.

[9] Sarah Boyer and Jonathan Wainwright, 'From Barnard to Purcell: The Copying Activities of Stephen Bing (1610–1681)', *Early Music*, 23 (1995), 620–48. See also Robert Ford, 'Minor Canons at Canterbury Cathedral: The Gostlings and their Colleagues', Ph.D. diss. (University of California at Berkeley, 1984). Ford remains sceptical about Bing's connection with the St Paul's partbooks (private correspondence, Nov. 1994).

[10] Donovan Dawe, *Organists of the City of London, 1666–1850* (Padstow, Cornwall, 1983), 142.

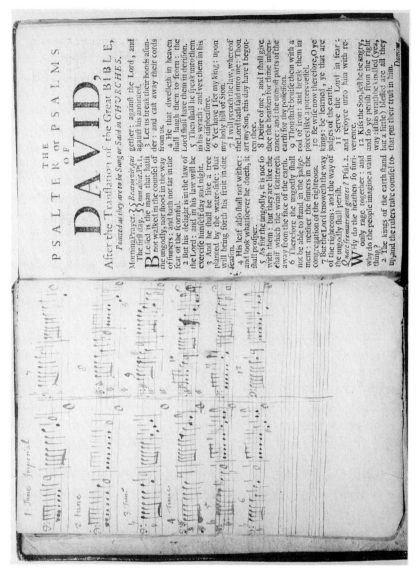

Fig. 3. St Paul's Psalter, MS A.1.8vo. By permission of the Dean and Chapter of St Paul's Cathedral.

and could have deputized for a lay clerk or minor canon in St Paul's after choral service resumed, even though the name Short does not appear in the official records. The original owner of the psalter was probably someone else, since the bass parts to the chant tunes and some of the early canticle settings may well have been copied during or before the 1670s. The hand of the chant tunes bears some resemblance to the informal writing of John Gostling, bass singer, music copyist, and minor canon of Canterbury and St Paul's, but the hurried appearance of the notation rules out a firm identification.[11] The style is in some respects like William Turner's autograph in Christ Church Music MS 49, although Turner did not place his descending or ascending stems on the left side of the note-head in the manner of the scribe of the St Paul's tunes.

Additional details of the provenance and persons associated with MS A.1.8vo may eventually emerge, but they do not need to be known to define the importance of this type of individual service manual. It can be said with a degree of certainty that the St Paul's psalter was prepared for a cathedral official to use in time of services, even though neither he nor the scribe can be named conclusively. The practical convenience of a small volume containing an individual voice-part for the regularly used service music in an immediately accessible form is obvious. There must have been many such small, portable volumes compiled for the personal convenience of cathedral musicians and other officials. Unfortunately, this type of manuscript music did not often survive the vagaries of time and daily use.

Copies of the royal chapels model repertory found their way to a fair number of cathedrals and collegiate churches and chapels around England. There are recognizable portions of the Add. MS 17784 set in organbooks and partbooks from Canterbury, Chichester, Durham, Hereford, Worcester, Ely, St Paul's, and Norwich cathedrals, York Minster, Wimborne Minster (a collegiate church in the seventeenth century), St John's College and Christ Church, Oxford, and King's College, Cambridge. Several sets of chant tunes are made up entirely of pieces from the model repertory and these include, besides those in the St Paul's psalter and the St George's, Durham, and Gostling partbooks, six numbered tunes copied on the last pages of Christ Church Music MSS 1220, 1223, and 1224 (Add. MS 17784, nos. 12, 17, 20, 21, 4, 5) and a set of seven in Ely Music MS 28, a tenor partbook (Add. MS 17784, nos. 14, 19, 18, 10, 4, 5, 11). The style of notation in royal chapels repertory tunes is nearly identical in seventeenth-century manuscripts, including York Music M 1/5–8s, St John's College Music MS 315, Christ Church Music MSS 1220–24, Durham Music MSS C 12, C 26, C 28, Worcester Music MSS A 3.2–5, and Bodleian Library Mus. Sch. B.7.

---

[11] See pl. V in Watkins Shaw, *The Bing–Gostling Part-Books at York Minster* (Croydon, 1986).

Of the chant tunes in Add. MS 17784 for which composers are named, six belong to William Turner, and one each to John Blow, Pelham Humfrey, William Child, and Thomas Purcell. Turner, a Gentleman of the Chapel Royal from 1669, was also a chorister prior to his service as lay clerk of Lincoln Cathedral (1667–9). John Blow was a Chapel Royal chorister in the 1660s also, and organist of Westminster Abbey (1668–79 and 1695). He was a Gentleman of the Chapel Royal from 1674, when he succeeded Pelham Humfrey as Master of the Choristers. William Child's Chapel Royal appointment as musician to his Majesty dates from the 1660s, and his post as organist of St George's Chapel, Windsor spanned the Commonwealth. Thomas Purcell, uncle of the famous Henry Purcell, was a tenor singer and composer, a Gentleman of the Chapel Royal from at least 1661, and a Musician-in-ordinary in the King's Private Musick from 1672.

Composers are not named for nine chant tunes in Add. MS 17784, but other manuscripts identify them as various members of the Purcell family (see Table 3.1). Ascriptions are written in manuscripts from the 1670s for tunes 7, 8, 10,

TABLE 3.1. *The 'royal chapels repertory'*

Chant Tune	Composer	Sources with attributions
1. Imperial Tune	—	see Table 3.2
2. Canterbury Tune	—	see Table 3.2
3. Psalm Tone 1.4	—	see Table 3.2
4. Tune in E m	John Blow	Lbl, Add. MS 17784; almost all MSS with attributions; Playford 1674
5. Tune in A m	[Thomas Purcell]	CHc, MS Kelway 4; Cu, EDC Music Ms/28; Lsp, MS 10
6. Tune in G m	[Thomas Purcell]	CHc, MS Kelway 4; Lsp, MS 10
7. Tune in G m	[Thomas Purcell]	Lsp, MS 10; Lbl, Add. MSS 9073 and 37027; Y, M 1/5–8s
8. Tune in D m	[Thomas Purcell]	Lsp, MS 10; WO, MS A 3.5
9. Tune in A	Thomas Purcell	Lsp, MS 10
10. Tune in D m	[Edward Purcell]	WB, Music P10; Y, M 1/5–8s; Lbl, Add. MS 9073; Cu, EDC Ms/28; Lsp, MS 10
11. Tune in G	[Purcell]	CHc, MS Kelway 4 (Thomas); Cu, EDC Ms/28 (Edward); Lsp, MS 10 (Henry); Lbl, Add. MS 37027 (Henry)
12. Tune in A m	[Henry Purcell]	CHc, MS Kelway 4; WB, Music P10; Lsp, MS 10; Lbl, Add. MS 9073
13. Tune in A	William Turner	Lbl, Add. MS 17784; CHc, MS Kelway 4; WB, Music P10; Och, MS 49; Lsp, MS 10; Y, M 1/5–8s; Playford 1674
14. Tune in A	William Turner	Lbl, Add. MS 17784; Lsp, MS 10; Playford 1674
15. Tune in D	William Turner	Lbl, Add. MS 17784; Och, MS 49; Y, M 1/5; Playford 1674
16. Tune in A	William Turner	Lbl, Add. MS 17784; CHc, MS Kelway 4; Lsp, MS 10; Playford 1674
17. Tune in B m	William Turner	Lbl, Add. MS 17784; Lsp, MS 10; Y, M 1/5–8s
18. Tune in G m	William Turner	Lbl, Add. MS 17784; Y, M 11s; Lsp, MS 10; Playford 1674
19. Tune in C	Pelham Humfrey	Lbl, Add. MS 17784; CHc, MS Kelway 4; Y, M 1/5–8s; almost all MSS with attributions
20. Tune in A m	Thomas Purcell	Lbl, Add. MS 17784
21. Tune in D m	[Purcell]	CHc, MS Kelway 4 (Mr. Purcell)

and 12, while individual associations for tunes 5, 6, 9, 11, and 12 come from early eighteenth-century manuscripts. Tunes ascribed to Henry Purcell could have been contributed by father or son. Henry, Sr. was a singer, Gentleman of the Chapel Royal, and Master of the Choristers of Westminster Abbey. His son and Pelham Humfrey after him were both Chapel Royal choristers under Henry Cooke. It is well known that choristers were encouraged to compose, and writing chant tunes would qualify as a useful introductory exercise in composition.[12] The intriguing Purcell attribution is to Edward, nearly always credited with Add. MS 17784 no. 10. The only Edward known to be a musician was the younger Henry's son, but he was not born until 1689 and is thus not the Edward in question; Stephen Bing's attribution in the Gostling part-books pre-dates his death in 1681. There are two other Edwards, the younger Henry's brother, who was a soldier, and a cousin about whom next to nothing is known.[13] Either Edward could have begun his education as a chorister, considering the family's strong connections with the Chapel Royal and Westminster Abbey, and efforts to recruit choirboys undertaken in the immediate Restoration period.

Music manuscripts that contain chant tunes from the royal chapels model repertory almost always count among them at least one of the first three, the psalm-tone pieces. When only one of the three is selected it is usually Imperial or Canterbury, while Imperial most often carries its tune name (Table 3.2; a tune so named is marked by the large X). When all three psalm-tone pieces are present, they are always in the same order as they appear in Add. MS 17784. These are the same tunes printed by Edward Lowe and James Clifford in 1664, and John Playford in 1674, except for minor alterations and different attributions. Imperial Tune is so named in Clifford and Playford, while Edward Lowe calls it 'D. Child's of Windsor'. The tone 1.4 tunes carry several different names, which simply indicate their presence in institutional repertories. In the St George's, Windsor repertory, the treble melody in Imperial Tune is exchanged with the psalm tone 8 tenor, and the tone 1.4 tune, credited here to Child, is arranged in Lowe fashion with the countertenor put up to the treble. Also, Lowe's open spacing between inner voices is followed in the Canterbury Tune.

The mainly homogeneous musical style of the royal chapels repertory can be seen in the half dozen most frequently copied items. These are chant tunes attributed to Blow (Fig. 1, no. 4), Humfrey (19), Turner (14), and Thomas (7),

[12] British Library, MS Harley 7338, Thomas Tudway's 'Collection of the most celebrated Services and Anthems', vol. ii (1716), preface.
[13] Franklin B. Zimmerman, *Henry Purcell, 1659–1695: His Life and Times* (2nd edn.; Philadelphia, 1983), ch. 1 and app. I, II.

Table 3.2. *Imperial, Canterbury, tone 1.4 tunes: MS sources*

MS		Canterbury	Imperial	Tone 1.4	Royal chapel tunes
Cu	EDC/Music Ms/4		X[a] (Td)		
	EDC/Music Ms/9		X		
	EDC/Music Ms/27		X		6 of 17
	EDC/Music Ms/32		X		8 of 27
	Peterhouse MS 486		x		
	Peterhouse MS 487	x (Ve)	x		
CA	Barnard Ct Can		X		
	Music MS 11		X (Child)		
CHc	MS Kelway 4	X	X		14 of 24
DRc	Music MS C 12	x	x	x	20 of 20
	Music MS C 28	x	x	x	25 of 25
H	Music MS 30. A. 30	X (Ath Cr)	x	x	8 of 12
Lbl	Add. MS 17784	X	X	X (Child)	21 of 21
	Add. MS 37027	X (Ath Cr)		X (Child)	10 of 13
	Add. MS 39868	x (Td)			5 of 16
Lsp	Music MS A.1.8vo	x	X	x	12 of 12
	Music MS Organbk 10	X	X	X (Child)	17
Lwa	Music MS Set No. 1			X (Tallis)	
Ob	MS Mus. Sch. c. 42	x (Td)			2 of 2
Och	Music MS 46	x			
	Music MS 48	X	X	x	
	Music MS 88	x			
	Music MS 437		X		
Ojc	MS 315	x (Ve)			5 of 8
WO	Music MS A 3.3	X (Ve)	X (Ve)		7 of 7
	Music MS A 3.4	X (Ve)	X (Ve)		7 of 7
	Music MS A 3.5	X (Ve)	X (Ve)		7 of 7
Y	Music MS M 1/5–8s		x (Ve)	X (Child)	8 of 8
	Music MS M 164/J1s	X	X		
	Music MS M 164/J3s	X	X		
	Music MS M 11	X	X		

[a] A large X means that the tune is named.

Edward Purcell (10), and Henry Purcell (12). The treble melodies move mostly by step, with a few leaps of a fourth or fifth. The tenor in some tunes, for instance nos. 7 and 12, ends on the tonic and acts as a countermelody to the treble. Almost all the mediant cadences in these tunes close on the dominant or relative major, except for the mediant on tonic in Turner (14). The final cadences are usually dominant-to-tonic progressions and, in typical late seventeenth-century fashion, end in an incomplete chord. The third is usually omitted, although Turner leaves out the fifth in the manner of Thomas Morley's eight psalm-tone tunes. One or two first-inversion chords can be found in these early chant tunes, most often in the first mediant cadence.

The melodic phraseology in the newly composed chant tunes is intimately related to their harmonization. The reciting tone in most is on a different pitch in the second phrase than in the first, as treble melodies move forward with harmonies that arrive at a mediant on the dominant or in the relative key, and work their way back to a final authentic cadence. Psalm-tone melodies, on the other hand, except for those on the irregular peregrine tone, move away from and return to the recitation pitch in the first phrase, and begin the second on the same note, leaving it altogether for the ending formula (see Fig. 4). The contrasting closed melodic shape of the royal chapel tunes foreshadows the type of melodies found in most later chants.

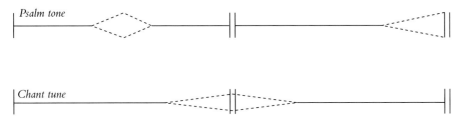

FIG. 4. Schematic diagram of psalm-tone and chant-tune melodies

The first individual composer who exercised more than an ordinary interest in the functional chant tune was William Turner. The pungent idiosyncratic elements of his tunes and the large number he composed give him a special status in the early history of the English chant tune. His predilection for exploring the relationship of relative major and minor keys and his use of the melodic interval of a fourth are characteristic of the six pieces in the royal chapels model repertory. In his autograph set of tunes in Christ Church Music MS 49, the largest (sixteen single tunes and one double tune) from this early period that has come to light, certain features seem to represent a compromise between older psalm-tone harmonizations with melodies of limited range and stepwise progression in slow harmonic rhythm, and the new chant tunes displaying more distinctive vertical sonorities. The fourth tune in Turner's autograph set, for instance, sounds in phrase one like two successive V–I cadences, the first in B flat and the second in C. The second phrase commences with recitation on an A minor chord, followed immediately by a modern-sounding IV–I–V–I cadence in F major (Ex. 3.1). In Turner's sixth chant tune in this set, a diminished chord in inversion is used in the mediant cadence and again in the second phrase recitation.

Some of Turner's terminations often feature clashing simultaneous dissonances and parallel seconds, while in others an anticipated tonic in the final chord is placed against a leading-note in another voice, as in nos. 6 and 12 from his autograph set (Ex. 3.2(a)). In the close of no. 10 an open seventh resolves in a complete final chord while in no. 14 a similar anticipation in the upper

Ex. 3.1. Fourth psalm chant in Turner's set (Och Music MS 49)

O   come   let   us   sing   un - to   the   Lord:

let us heart - i - ly re - joice in the strength of our sal - va - ti - on.

voices against the root of the dominant is followed by an incomplete chord
(Ex. 3.2(*b*)). Terminations in other contemporary chant tunes, by way of contrast, reveal a fairly consistent pattern of penultimate quaver anticipations, but
where dissonances are not omitted in incomplete final chords or masked in an
acceptable manner, as in Turner's A major chant tune (see Fig. 1, no. 14), they
are handled by staggered attacks in different voices (Ex. 3.3).

   In its dual role as generic body of authoritative material and model for chant
composition, the royal chapels repertory was an unqualified success. Later sets
of chant tunes compiled for particular institutions almost always contain a
number of the original tunes, plus pieces composed by organists and clergymen, two consistently represented groups. The content and breadth of these
repertories and something of their behaviour can be seen in the annotated catalogue of English manuscript sources in Appendix A. Most of these manuscripts are cathedral and collegiate chapel partbooks and organbooks, but there
are also several small volumes like the St Paul's psalter. An anthem wordbook
that belonged to an official of Chichester Cathedral, for example, contains an

Ex. 3.2. Cadences in Turner chant tunes (Och Music MS 49): (*a*) nos. 6 and 12; (*b*) nos. 10 and 14

(*a*)

(*b*)

interesting set of about twenty chant-tune bass parts notated in two forms, fourteen of them from the royal chapels repertory.[14]

Repertories of new and old chant tunes made their rounds in the manner of the royal chapels repertory, and index entries in music manuscripts sometimes record specific exchanges, for instance, this one from York Minster: '12 Psalm Tunes from Canterbury in a Sheet of paper'.[15] A group of six chant tunes from

[14] Robert Bridges, 'English Chanting', *Musical Antiquary*, 2 (1911), 136, examined this volume in one of the canons' stalls.

[15] The marginal note was written in Music MS M 11s by William Knight, vicar choral from 1718 and Succentor 1722–39 (York Minster S 3/4e). The tunes were probably brought to York by Edward Finch, composer and Canon of both cathedrals, who resided in the close at York.

Ex. 3.3. Cadences in seventeenth-century chant tunes: (*a*) Turner (Och Music MS 49); (*b*) E. Purcell (Fig. 1, no. 10); (*c*) T. Purcell (Fig. 1, no. 20); (*d*) Blow, psalm tune from A re service (Lbl Add. MS 31559)

St Paul's Organbook 10 indicate their source with the heading 'Windsor Chants'. There are seventeen of the model royal chapels tunes in this large collection of Thomas Sharp, Archdeacon of Northumberland and prebend of Durham Cathedral. Thomas was the son of John Sharp, Archbishop of York, and the family ties to both institutions are the main reason the majority of these chant tunes were compiled from repertories in use at York Minster and Durham Cathedral. The organbook was bequeathed to St Paul's by Thomas Sharp's son, Granville, in whose hand are many late eighteenth-century additions and annotations.

The smaller repertories of chant tunes were made up from the same categories as the larger ones, that is, royal chapels tunes, tunes by the local organist, and a contribution or two by a resident clergyman. Typical are the tunes copied on the back pages of a 1681 Book of Common Prayer from Wells Cathedral, 'Mr Jackson's Tunes'. These include a chant tune from the royal chapels repertory, two psalm-tone-like tunes, four composed by the local organist, and one attributed to a clerical member of the cathedral.[16] The first four are Jackson's (organist 1674–88); next the 'Ely Tune in B' and 'Lincoln Tune in C', probably brought by Jackson from Ely, where he was choirmaster (1669–70), or nearby Norwich, where he was organist (1670-2);[17] the seventh tune by Joshua Lasher, priest vicar of Wells;[18] and lastly, John Blow's E minor tune (see Fig. 1, no. 4). The first verse of Venite exultemus is underlaid to the first Wells chant tune in the customary way, with a crotchet or quaver per syllable.

A typical collegiate chapel chant repertory is the set of 'Proper Tunes' copied by Dean Henry Aldrich for Christ Church, Oxford. Seventeen of twenty-eight pieces are either royal chapels repertory tunes or have psalm-tone tenors. Aldrich borrowed the Canterbury Tune, Imperial Tune, and the melodies for three other psalm-tone harmonizations from Lowe, *A Review of Some Short Directions* (1664). Lowe's Tuesday tune on tone 3.4 becomes the tenor in one piece and the tone 1.4 melody, transposed up a fifth, is the countertenor in another (Ex. 3.4). The melodies in the new chant tunes by local composers, a Mr Smith, B. Isaack, Richard Goodson, and Francis Withye, are mostly of narrow range with some parallel sixths between voices, and are harmonized with dominant–tonic chords. The three chant tunes by Aldrich are harmonized with mediants on secondary dominants and second recitations in relative keys, except one tonic first-inversion chord in the A major chant tune. Aldrich gave the D minor chant tune from the royal chapels repertory attributed to Edward Purcell (Fig. 1, no. 10) a change of mode and harmony and counted it among his own, as 'Dr. A's second'.

Institutional chant repertories sometimes have idiosyncratic features and a large repertory of about fifty psalm chants from York Minster provides some curious examples. Among the new pieces contributed by local musicians are a number of unusual chants in five and six voice-parts. These are by Thomas Wanless (organist 1691–1712), Valentine Nalson (subchanter 1707–22),

---

[16] Noted in Roger Bowers, L. S. Colchester, and Anthony Crossland (eds.), *The Organs and Organists of Wells Cathedral* (7th rev. edn.; Wells, 1979), 20. The same chant-tune repertory is copied in a Wells organbook now in the Royal College of Music Library; see App. A.

[17] Norwich Public Record Office, Norwich Cathedral, DCN/Q 231/A, 2; Bodleian Library, Tanner MS 113, fo. 127.

[18] Wells Cathedral Library, Michael Windeatt, 'A Handlist of Vicars Choral—Wells AD 1592–1935'.

Ex. 3.4. Aldrich's use of psalm tones (Och Music MS 48): (*a*) T, tone 3.4; (*b*) Ct, tone 1.4

(*a*)

(*b*)

Charles Murgetroyd (organist 1712–21), and Edward Finch (prebend of York and Canterbury). Finch also added voice-parts to chant tunes written by colleagues, according to a note written by William Knight (subchanter 1722–39) in York Music MS 11s. The multi-voice chants seem to have been part of an experiment in sound effects, stimulated perhaps by the great open spaces of the Minster's large choir. There seems to be no other logical explanation for some of these elaborate constructions and they cause one to wonder if they could have been chanted in time of service. Nalson and Finch often blurred the binary psalm division with mediant appoggiaturas and Finch created thick textures with treble parts in thirds or parallel sixths, quite different from seventeenth-century chant tunes with open spacing and incomplete final chords. To one of Aldrich's popular tunes, Finch added two additional voice-parts, transposed it up a half-step, and spiced up the cadences with a seventh in the penultimate mediant chord and terminal anticipations (Ex. 3.5).

Borrowing material from chant tunes in general use became more frequent as more repertories circulated and organists made up chant-tune sets for their own choirs. Their functional nature had, from the beginning, made chant tunes susceptible to rearrangment and recomposition, processes in which a certain amount of predictable alteration in melody, harmony, and voicing crept in. Small melodic changes are fairly routine, such as filling in the intervals and adding or omitting inflections at cadences. In John Reading's 1720s organ score of John Blow's psalm tune for the A re service, compared with an

Ex. 3.5. Chant tune recomposed: (*a*) Aldrich (Och Music MS 48); (*b*) 'Mr Finch upon Dr. Aldrich' (Y Music M 11s)

(*a*)

(*b*)

earlier score in Ex. 3.6, an extra mediant inflection has been added.[19] His exchange of treble and tenor reciting notes in the first phrase of a Turner tune in D is another common device, in this case retransmitted in a manuscript compiled by John Church at about the same time.[20]

One of the known casualties among the many chant repertories that do not survive would have provided a comprehensive overview of psalm chants in early eighteenth-century institutional repertories. Humphrey Wanley asked Thomas Tudway to prepare a collection of tunes at about the time the latter was beginning work on his six-volume edition of English church music. This book of tunes might be extant if it had been solicited officially for the Harleian library and thus preserved in the British Library, but the correspondence between Wanley and Tudway suggests that Wanley's request was a personal one:[21]

---

[19] Dulwich College, MS 92B, 39–41, 'Choice Collection of Vollentarys and Fugues for the Organ with the Chanting Tunes, as they are Performed in the Cathedrall Churches', autograph of John Reading, organist of Dulwich College.

[20] British Library Add. MS 37027, fo. 50. Church, one of the important music copyists of his time, was Master of the Choristers of Westminster Abbey, 1704–40, and a Gentleman of the Chapel Royal from 1697. See Margaret Laurie, 'The Chapel Royal Part-Books', in Oliver Neighbour (ed.), *Music and Bibliography* (London, 1980), 28–50.

[21] Humphrey Wanley's diary is missing for the years August 1715 through January 1720, precisely when the collection of chapel tunes was prepared and sent. See Wrightson, *'Wanley' Manuscripts*, 32.

Ex. 3.6. Psalm tune adapted: (*a*) Blow (Cfm Mus MS 116); (*b*) Reading (Ldc MS 92B)

(*a*)

O come lett us etc.   Lett us hartyly etc.

(*b*)

56   ♭5   6   56 6   7
                                              4   ♯

17 October 1715, Tudway to Wanley
. . . I have made a Collection of most of the Chappell Tunes, us'd at the King's
Chappell, St. Paul's, Westminster, Windsor, here, [Cambridge] & at Oxford, & in the
Cathedralls over England; I have allso added the responses to the Suffrages in 4 parts
sung to the Organ Anciently on the great festivals, by Bird.
. . . I will send your book of Tunes etc. by the first opportunity.

5 November 1715 [received], Tudway to Wanley
I have finish'd the Little Collection of Chappell Tunes, which you desir'd, . . .

14 November 1715, Tudway to Wanley
I received your kind, and obliging letter, and am glad what I have sent you proves any
ways acceptable; . . .

10 December 1715, Wanley to Tudway
. . . Among the Notes you sent in your last, I observe the Tune of Mr Lamb, in a key
different from that you wrote in the Book you gave me. As to this [notated bass part
of tone 1.4 tune] I would gladly have the other parts in score, that I may insert the
same into the said Book.

20 December 1715, Wanley to Tudway
. . . I heartily thank you for your inclosed paper of Church-Tunes.[22]

The chant tune Wanley wrote out is the bass to 'Dr Childs Windsor' as it
appears in the St George's, Windsor repertory, which raises a host of intrigu-

[22] British Library, Add. MS 70481; MS Harley 3782, fo. 161ʳ. This correspondence is quoted by
Wrightson in *'Wanley' Manuscripts*, 267–72. William Weber quotes Tudway's letter of 17 Oct. in *Rise of
Musical Classics*, 41. The present musicological use of the term 'psalm tune', has presumably led him to guess
that the chapel tunes were metrical psalms rather than prose chant tunes.

ing questions. Was this tune among the 'notes you sent in your last' and why was Tudway sending bass parts only? Did Wanley have this bass part from another source, perhaps an individual set of chant tunes like the St Paul's psalter? Was the 'paper of Church-Tunes' an additional set which included the four parts for the tone 1.4 tune? Whatever the answers to these questions may be, the transmission of Tudway's chant-tune collection stopped with Humphrey Wanley and unless it comes to light some day, further details about its contents are lost.

The proliferation of institutional chant-tune repertories paralleled the development of a commonly accepted method of notation. The facsimiles and musical examples shown thus far have different written forms from choir to choir, but a few features, such as bipartite structure, short notes for recitation, and long notes in cadences, were mainly the same. Rhythm and the placement of barlines more often varied. In the York tunes, a barline marks off the last chord in each phrase, and another separates the second recitation from the final cadence. The earliest Restoration chant tunes had at most one barline marking the binary division and one note per syllable for the first verse of Venite (Ex. 3.7). A few others began to be written with a first phrase matching the corresponding first verse of Venite, and a second phrase that was not related to the text (Ex. 3.8).

Gradually over time, writing out chant tunes with one note per syllable for the full first verse of text, or with one schematic phrase and one phrase with a note per syllable, became obsolete. Already in a few Restoration chant tunes,

Ex. 3.7. Notations for Venite first verse: (*a*) Lowe; (*b*) WB MS P10; (*c*) W BCP; (*d*) Och Music MS 49; (*e*) WO Music MS A.3.2

Ex. 3.8. Notations with schematic second phrase: (*a*) Lbl Add. MS 17784; (*b*) Ojc MS 315; (*c*) Och Music MSS 1220–4; (*d*) CA Music MS 8; (*e*) Y Music MS M 1/5–8s)

elements of the future seven-bar chant are present. In chant tunes with bar-lines, the eventual shape of a two-bar mediant and three-bar termination can sometimes be seen, for example, in a chant tune from Gloucester Cathedral with three- and five-note patterns in cadences (Ex. 3.9).[23] Black note-heads represent the variable number of text syllables in the recitations, a device used by Edward Lowe and Henry Aldrich which reappears periodically in later chant notations, for example, a set of chants copied by John Travers in the 1730s in Hereford Cathedral Music MS R.14.iii (see App. A). An older chant notation still used in the Restoration period indicates where to sing an accented syllable, or the first syllables of a three-syllable word, by placing two dots over the penultimate note of the chant.[24]

Chant tunes shortened proportionally occupy another intermediate stage in the development of a standard notation. An early example is Robert Watton's long version of 'Tune in f fa ut' on fo. 29ʳ of Christ Church Music MS 437 (Ex. 3.10(*a*)), recopied in a short version on fo. 50ᵛ (Ex. 3.10(*b*)). It has five measures of semibreve value in the proportion of two to three, while the short version is written in three bars of semibreve value at one to two. Both short and long tunes preserve the relationship of the shorter first phrase of the first verse of Venite to its longer second phrase.

Many short verses occur in the course of the one hundred and fifty psalms, and these were the motivation for John Church's method of shortening the chant; 'if the verse is short and of but few syllables, it may be play'd as you see

---

[23] Gloucester Cathedral Organbook 1. Charles Wren was organist of Gloucester Cathedral, 1674–8.
[24] Christ Church Music MS 437, fo. 2ᵛ.

Ex. 3.9. Restoration chant tune by Charles Wren (GL MS 110)

the Base of the same Tune underwritten. In the same manner you may shorten all the other Tunes'.[25] These condensed bass parts take two forms; five bars of semibreve value (Ex. 3.11(*a*)), and four bars of the same value, the second bar divided by a double line at the mediant (Ex. 3.11(*b*)). Thirteen of the twenty-four chant-tune bass parts in the anthem wordbook, Chichester Cathedral

Ex. 3.10. Watton's chant tune (Och Music MS 437) (*a*) long form, fo. 29; (*b*) short form, fo. 50ᵛ

(*a*)

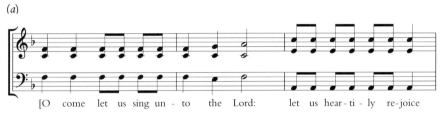

(*b*)

[25] British Library Add. MS 37027, fo. 50ʳ. Edward Skilton, Military Knight of St George's Chapel, amateur composer, and owner of the manuscript, added three upper parts to the Church shortened bass for each chant tune.

Ex. 3.11. Church's notations (Lbl Add. MS 37027): (a) tune shortened to five bars;
(b) tune shortened to four bars

(a)

O come let us sing etc.   let us hear-ti-ly re-joice etc.

our sal - va - ti-on

(b)

O   come let us sing etc.   let us heart-i - ly re-joice   etc.

our sal - va - ti-on

Music MS Kelway 4, were recopied in short form, but the reduction is not proportional in terms of note-values or rhythm. Whether the short forms were related to particular psalmodic verses is not indicated in the manuscript.

Experiments with written forms led to the final consolidation of a generally accepted shorthand notation for psalm and canticle chants, although of equal influence in the process was the practical requirement of adapting the prose text to its music at sight. For both organist and singer, chanting the variable number of recitation syllables and arriving at the cadences together was always a balancing act. Even 'where the most deliberate chanting is, the pronuncia-tion is at best a huddle unintelligible', observed Roger North, 'all run on non passibus equis, it is a wonder that where the organ is used, it is so well per-formed as it is; and where it is not used, who expects better than the music of Babel?'[26] John Marsh described how he 'had got on a verse too forward for want of being able distinctly to hear the Boys' in morning service at Salisbury, so in the afternoon, he writes, I 'got young Waterlane, one of the boys, to come into the Organ Loft and chant out of the book with me, in which he had like to have led me into another mistake, as he got wrong himself, so that instead of his being of Service to me, I was forc'd to correct him'.[27]

In psalm chants, a variable number of syllables were chanted to a fixed num-ber of small notes, whose relation to the length of the verse at hand might be wholly arbitrary. The potential for confusion in this system was eliminated by the logical and practical replacement of the variable number of small notes with a single reciting note of larger value. The only difficulty with the new single note for the recitation portion of the chant was its encouragement to performers to rush through the recitation, but that is another story. An early example of the beginning semibreve can be seen in Henry Aldrich's proper tunes (see Exx. 3.4 and 3.5). Here the semibreve serves as a gathering note, since it is not repeated in the second phrase. Aldrich has placed a barline to separate the phrases, each having the value of four semibreves. If the crotchets were eliminated in the first and consolidated in the second, the chant would look exactly like a modern Anglican Chant seven bars long:

The shorthand chant notation using large note-values in seven bars is con-sistently presented for the first time in a large repertory of chant tunes from Norwich Cathedral. The early portion of the repertory was copied by James

[26] Wilson, *North on Music*, 269.   [27] HM 54457, v. 114.

Cooper (organist from 1689 to 1721), whose unique device, a semibreve combined with a direct, represents the flexible recitation of variable length. His transitional notations include short tunes of five or six bars combining various rhythmic schemes and others seven bars long, some with semibreves and minims in the bass and different patterns in smaller notes in the treble (samples are given in Ex. 3.12). Later additions to the repertory are in the hand of Cooper's

Ex. 3.12. Transitional notations in Norwich Cathedral repertory (Ckc Music MS 9): (*a*) Purcell; (*b*) Cooper; (*c*) Wildbore; (*d*) Cotton

(*a*)

(*b*)

(*c*)

(*d*)

successor, Humphrey Cotton, organist to 1749. Although most of these are written in large note-values in seven bars, Cotton still uses the direct in combination with a semibreve for the recitation portion of the chant.

The origin of the chant of seven bars, which has become the universal written form of English chant for prose recitation, has been the subject of some speculation. Paul Doe and Peter le Huray both recognized the influence of proper psalm settings for special services, and Kenneth Jennings traced the Imperial Tune to Farrant's Psalm 21, noted in the previous chapter. Edmund Fellowes thought that the Anglican Chant owed its origin partly to festival psalm settings, 'but perhaps more directly to the harmonization of the eight Gregorian tones', for example, Thomas Morley's eight tunes. He also suggested that 'certain old melodies very closely foreshadowed the Anglican chant', such as Ravenscroft's Psalm 124.[28] Christopher Dearnley was of the opinion that the seven-bar notation crystallized from a residue of plainsong melodies, for instance, the 'characteristic rhythmic pattern' of psalm tone 1, fourth ending.[29] Little attention has been paid to the intimate relationship of text and music in extempore psalm chanting, yet it is text rhythm which established the standard notation of the Anglican Chant.

The reader will have observed that in the musical examples of psalm chants quoted thus far, the text assigned is the invitatory psalm, Venite exultemus, Ps. 95, prescribed by rubric to be said or sung in Morning Prayer daily or weekly, preceding the psalms appointed for the particular day. If the complete text is not underlaid, the notes of the chant are often laid out for the opening verse of Venite, as in the Peterhouse psalm chants, or the incipit 'O Come' is given. The proportional temporal relationships of the seven-bar Anglican Chant and its internal divisions were determined by this text. The unbalanced phrase lengths of the first verse—nine syllables to sixteen syllables—are reproduced in the chant's three bars in the first phrase and four bars in the second. The internal pattern of note-values in the cadences, with a rhythmic articulation on the penultimate syllable, mirrors the last three and five syllables, respectively, of the first and second phrases of the first verse of the Venite: '. . . to the Lord: . . . our sal-va-ti-on'. In chant tunes with a text incipit or text underlaid, except for some intended for canticles, it is the first verse of Venite exultemus that rules the pattern of notes and of bars when barlines are present. In printed chant collections from the second half of the eighteenth century, a sample verse showing syllable placement, where one is written in, is always the first verse of Venite. The historical evidence is incontrovertible. The final shape of seven bars, a three-bar phrase and a four-bar phrase, is

---

[28] Fellowes, *English Cathedral Music* (2nd rev. edn., London, 1945), 19–20.
[29] Dearnley, *English Church Music*, 105.

clearly the temporal representation of the unbalanced phrases of the first verse of Venite exultemus, which from the mid-sixteenth century was the primary text association of psalm chants.

The adoption of the seven-bar chant was accelerated by the publication of printed service music in the second half of the eighteenth century. Especially influential in terms of content and notation was the modest repertory of single and double chants in William Boyce's *Cathedral Music*.[30] Only chants by older Chapel Royal musicians were selected, in keeping with the antiquarian purpose of preserving sacred music from the past, and an older style of notation is also imitated in the longs, breves, and semibreves of the chants. A sample first verse of the Venite exultemus to show syllable placement is underlaid to the first chant in the customary fashion (Ex. 3.13). In the Arnold republication of Boyce at the turn of the century, a new chant repertory is notated in half the Boyce note-values, with barlines only at the mediant and before the terminal cadence.

Ex. 3.13. Example for psalm chanting in Boyce's *Cathedral Music*, i

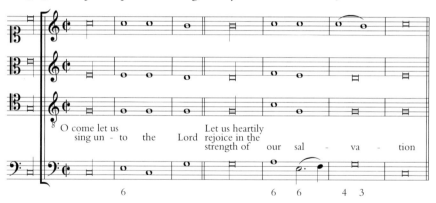

After Boyce, cathedral music publications began to combine services, anthems, and psalm chants in the same editions. Parish music collections had done so throughout the century, and it was in a 1788 parish collection that one of the earliest comprehensive sets of chants appeared.[31] A growing number of separate chant books were published for cathedral use from the first in 1752, many of them by individual composers. Chant books that appeared before 1820 are listed in Table 3.3 with a note about their contents. A few of these

---

[30] Vol. i (1760) contains thirteen single chants and a double chant by John Robinson; vol. ii (1768) has two more singles and three doubles by Morley, Dupuis, and Cooke.

[31] Ralph Harrison, *Sacred Harmony* (London, 1788), contains over seventy chants, mostly from cathedral repertories.

TABLE 3.3. *Cathedral chant books in print: 1752–1820*

Composer or editor	Title and imprint	Notes
John Alcock	*Divine Harmony*, Birmingham, For the Author and M. Broome, 1752	50 sgl, 5 dbl, own compositions except Athanasian Creed
[Granville Sharp], ed.	*Fifty Double and Single Chants*, London, C. and S. Thompson, [*c.*1770]	38 sgl, 12 dbl, collected from Durham, York, London, Windsor
Thomas Vandernan, ed.	*Divine Harmony*, London, Engrav'd and Publ'd by the Author, 1770	160 sgl, 48 dbl, mainly Chapel Royal composers
Thomas S. Dupuis	*Sixteen Single and Double Chants*, London, [*c.*1775]	no copy known
John Jones	*Sixty Chants*, London, For the Author, 1785	30 sgl, dbl, own compositions; first changeable chant
Thomas S. Dupuis	*Twenty four Double and Single Chants*, London, Preston & Son, [*c.*1795]	12 sgl, dbl, own compositions
—	*Sixty Chants, Single and Double*, London, 1795	chants by St Paul's musicians
Joseph Kemp	*Twenty Double Chants*, London, For the Author, [*c.*1800]	20 dbl, own compositions
John Stafford Smith	*Twelve Chants*, London, For the Author, 1803	7 sgl, 5 dbl, own compositions
John Marsh	*Twenty four New Chants*, London, For the Author, [1804]	8 sgl,16 dbl,1 Bte, own compositions
John Beckwith, ed.	*The First Verse of Every Psalm of David, With an Ancient or Modern Chant in Score, Adapted as much as possible to the Sentiment of each Psalm*, London, For the Author, 1808	Chant for each psalm in monthly course, first verse underlaid
John Marsh, ed.	*The Cathedral Chant Book*, London, Clementi & Co., [1808]	*c.*200 (sgl,dbl); for each psalm in monthly course
John Clarke-Whitfeld, ed.	*A Selection of Single and Double Chants*, London, Birchall & Co., [*c.*1810]	2 vols., dbls, sgls 17th–19th centuries

require more extended discussion in conjunction with the development of printed form and performance practice.

The first printed chant book contained a selection of single chants composed by John Alcock for Lichfield Cathedral, where he was the organist. His rather florid melodies and decorative ornaments were accompanied by an imaginative harmonic style. The sixth chant in E major, for example, closes at the mediant on a first inversion of the subdominant, followed by a second phrase recitation on a first inversion of the dominant. The voice leading in the terminal cadence is reminiscent of William Turner's earlier chant tunes, with an anticipation of the tonic, different rhythmic figures in each voice, and a final chord without its fifth. In Ex. 3.14(*a*), the chant is transcribed as Alcock printed it, in four voice-parts with figured bass for the organist. Alcock wrote his chants in phrases of two and three bars, using his own system of slurring

Ex. 3.14. Chant tunes by Alcock: (*a*) no. 6 in E; (*b*) no. 1, sample text underlay

(*a*)

56   6   9   6   8 7
                                    4 3

(*b*)

O come etc.-to the   Lord: Let us etc. our   sal - va - tion.

6   56   6   8 7

groups of notes in the cadences. In chant no. 1 he has underlaid the usual first verse of Venite, also showing the changed articulation of the last word, 'sal-va-tion', in the slurred notes of the penultimate measure (Ex. 3.14(*b*)).[32]

   The second separate chant collection is one of the most interesting, not only because it was the first printed compilation of chants from several cathedral manuscript repertories, but also because its editor is one of the most fascinating characters of the late eighteenth century. The Sharp family concerts on Sunday evenings and the brothers' large library of manuscript and printed

[32] See Peter Marr's facsimile edition of *Divine Harmony* (London, 1980) and Marr, 'An 18th-Century Collection of Anglican Chants', *Soundings*, 8 (1979–80), 71–80. The florid writing and harmonic boldness of Alcock's chants, as well as their decorative nature, lead one to wonder whether they were actually performed at Lichfield, given Alcock's outspoken criticisms of the state of the Lichfield choir and the regular absenteeism of singers. See, for example, the preface to *A Morning and Evening Service* (1753), dedicated to Dean Addenbrooke.

music are the better known musical activities of Granville Sharp, but he was also engaged in a lively exchange of music and ideas about performance practice in the liturgy with church musicians, clergymen, and others in his wide circle of friends. *Fifty Double and Single Chants*, Granville Sharp's 'Thompson collection', contained 'the most Favorite as Perform'd at St. Paul's, Westminster and most of the Cathedrals in England'. Sharp added fifteen new pieces to thirty-five from the manuscript set compiled by his father, Thomas, Archdeacon of Northumberland.[33] The printed collection contains a double chant by Thomas Sharp, the first printing of Luke Flintoft's double chant (see Ch. 4), an early Battishill double chant, and a 'curious' item, 'The Convent Chant, given by Pope Gregory the 1st to the Cathedral Church of Lyons and therefore . . . commonly call'd the Gregorian Chant'. The melody of this single chant in G minor bears an uncanny resemblance to Playford's Tuesday tune, but there are few other plainsong-like features except the minor sonority. Interest in Gregorian chant among Anglicans is supposed to have been an Oxford Movement phenomenon, but Sharp was not alone among his contemporaries in investigating other chant traditions than his own.

Sharp's concern with chants and chanting and his views on the reform of church music were those of the Evangelical wing of the Church of England.[34] Its members were in favour of congregational chanting of responses and prose psalms as part of their programme for a larger congregational role in a liturgy made more accessible, both textually and musically, to the ordinary lay person. Sharp's thoughts on the psalms and psalm chants were also influenced by his academic pursuits in the study of civil and religious law, and languages besides his own, especially Greek, Hebrew, and Latin. 'Chants are Tunes adapted to the Prose Psalms', he wrote, 'whereby any Psalm may be distinctly sung by a Congregation, without being tortured into *Metre*: the true sense & spirit of the Psalms are thereby retained, as nearly as they can be rendered in a literal translation from the original Hebrew.'[35]

Sharp's musical abilities and interests were wide-ranging and his personal papers are full of notations of various kinds of chants and other musical enquiries, including his father's plans for a 'traverse' harp, which Granville

---

[33] St Paul's Cathedral Music MS Organbook 10. Since the Sharp music library contained six copies of the 'Thompson collection', the psalms were probably chanted to some of its music during the family Sunday evenings of sacred music.

[34] Sharp was an associate of the Clapham sect, whose collective interests included timely social issues such as the abolition of slavery, temperance, and educational reform. Many of its members were Evangelicals. See also Temperley, *MEPC*, i. 207–23.

[35] MS annotations in *Fifty Double and Single Chants*, British Library shelf mark E. 487, transcribed in App. E. This copy was owned in the last century by antiquarian Edward Rimbault, who supplied the notes to be printed in the *Parish Choir*, 1 (July 1846), no. 6, 44.

built.[36] Sharp sang the service regularly with the choir of St Paul's Cathedral towards the end of the century and was reported to have engaged daily in chanting psalms:[37]

It was no uncommon practice with him, when his mind was religiously impressed, to take an appropriate psalm of David, to chant it in Hebrew, and to accompany his own voice with the harp. The writer of this article has seen him so employed; and it has often struck him, that if any one wished to know what David was, he might form some appropriate conception of him by taking a view of Mr. Sharp singing his Hebrew on these occasions.[38]

Sharp's activities on behalf of chanting and choral service also involved him in the preparation of several compilations, duplicated in manuscript, of responses, litanies, sanctuses, and chants, many of these published in the Thompson collection.[39] His musical hand is marked by the use of an idiosyncratic sideways sharp, always present in the G♯ he liked to use in place of his written signature. His avid interest in stylized and ornamental calligraphy produced bookplates for the Sharp library and the decorated manuscripts of liturgical music. The original copy of these items was no doubt Sharp's own, but the number of copyists he hired to reproduce them has created a graphological problem in the identification of Sharp manuscripts.[40] The content of these manuscripts of liturgical music, taken together with Sharp's publications of chants and a singing manual, are a significant statement of personal advocacy for the preservation and encouragement of cathedral choral tradition at a time when it was threatened by internal and external pressures.

The reasons which Alcock gave for publishing *Divine Harmony* are largely related to pressures of performance and raise some interesting questions about the nature of extempore chanting:

As I have always taken Notice how much the Contra-Tenor and Tenor Parts are neglected in chanting of the Psalms, &c. the Persons who perform those Parts being

---

[36] Gloucestershire Record Office, Lloyd-Baker Collection D 3549, Box 56, 54. Sharp's musical commonplace book contains mostly sacred music.

[37] Prince Hoare, *Memoirs of Granville Sharp, Esq.* (London, 1820), 454. Hoare's app. VI, xii–vi, has a letter of William Shield (1748–1829), Master of the King's Musick, recommending Sharp's *Short Introduction to Vocal Musick* (1767; 2nd edn. 1777).

[38] *The Philanthropist*, 12 (Oct. 1813), copy in Lloyd-Baker Collection D 3549, Box 15a.

[39] The music in Sharp's MS collections includes litanies by Wanless and Soaper (composed at Sharp's request to go with the Durham responses), responses by Ebdon, double and single chants, preces and responses 'used at Durham', and Sanctus settings. See below, Fig. 6.

[40] A substantial number of Sharp MSS have found their way to libraries in Britain and are easily identified by Granville's bookplates, by his niece Catherine's (administratrix of his estate) inscription, or by their ornamental calligraphy: Ckc Rowe Music MSS 331–3, 416, 420; Cu Ely Cathedral EDC/Music MS 23; DRc Music MSS M174, M89; Lcm Music MSS 813, 1065; Lsp Music MSS Organbook 8, 10, Chant Books I–V; Lwa Music MS 7; Ob Tenbury MSS 805, 812–26, 827–40, 857–76. See also below, Table 5.2 and App. A.

oblig'd to sing any thing that comes into their Heads, for want of a true copy of the Chants, is the Reason why I have ventur'd to publish these that I made for the Use of this Cathedral, by which means, the Contra-Tenor and Tenor Parts may not only be better sung than they usually are, but also, in case of those Voices being missing, any other Person in the Choir will now have an Opportunity of singing either of those Parts in order to compleat the Harmony.

In order to show the Necessity for the Members of Cathedrals having their proper Parts, I have inserted one exactly in the Manner I've heard most of them sung, which is in Eighths or Fifths to the other Parts, and so as they end with a Third, Fifth, or Eighth, it is thought to be all mighty well.[41]

Alcock seems to be commenting on chanting in general, not just at Lichfield, and suggesting that singers were expected to memorize their parts and chant the psalms from the text only. Benjamin Cooke said as much in his directions for chanting in a service composed for the military garrison at Gibraltar; 'the performer is required to sing the tune by heart and having the words only of the Psalm before him to break or subdivide the black notes'.[42] That is clearly what John Marsh had in mind when he printed a chant book for organ and outer voices and separate companion books for alto and tenor:

By having general chant-books of a convenient size dispersed through every choir, the Tenors and Counter-tenors, instead of chanting extempore, may always have the proper parts at hand, which will much improve the effect; it being scarcely possible that different extemporary singers, however each may separately harmonize with the Treble and Bass, should combine in any real system of Harmony. I instance only in the middle parts, because the Treble and Bass Singers are so much assisted by the Organ, as to render printed parts for them the less necessary.[43]

Musical and written sources all confirm that chanting in harmony was expected, but a century earlier, at the turn of the seventeenth to the eighteenth century, this was not the case. The recitation was sung in unison, according to reliable observers, and this practice may have had something to do with singers

[41] John Alcock, *Divine Harmony* (Birmingham, 1752). Alcock also published a number of parish music books, and besides his post at Lichfield Cathedral, he was organist at Sutton Coldfield 1761–86 and Tamworth 1766–90.

[42] Royal College of Music, Cooke Collection MS 819, 'Choral Service for the Garrison in Gibralter', 1787.

[43] John Marsh, *The Cathedral Chant Book* (London, [1808]), preface. The collection is erroneously dated 1804 and 1810 in many libraries, but Marsh tells of receiving the proofs 8 Mar. 1808, HM 54457, xxvi. 167.

not having music in front of them for the psalm chants. They would, in this case, need only to know their cadence notes to sing in harmony. This system apparently worked well, for as Roger North noted, 'when performed decently, the organ presiding, the music, tho' it chant most upon the key note, yet in virtue of the cadences which are artificial, the harmony is exceedingly good'.[44]

The Revd Arthur Bedford described the same style of chanted psalmody, but within a framework of ancient temple practice, predicated upon his assumption that the two were identical. In his view, the practice was 'conformable, not only to that of the Primitive Christians, but also to the Practice of the Church in all preceding ages', and his treatise on the subject aimed 'to Vindicate the Practice of our Cathedrals from the Prejudices which some have taken against the Manner of their Singing, and their Chanting Tunes':[45]

In the Cathedral Service, the greatest part thereof is sung in short notes, in unison to each other, and are pricked with quavers in our chanting tunes: and this we call the chanting part of our singing . . . in all this chanting space of our Reading Psalms, they have observed no manner of order, or uniformity in the accents; which they would certainly have done, had they designed in those places any other method in their singing.[46]

The recitation was flexible in length; in other words, the number of notes needed was determined by the text verse rather than the notation.

The cadences were another matter, for they were sung to longer notes in slower rhythm, and in harmony:

In our Cathedral Service, the voices alter (before they come to a colon or a period) from an unison, in order to make two closes, where these two marks are placed [: and .]; and accordingly the notes are longer, and usually marked with crotchets, and the last note of all with a minim, or semibreve. The middle close at the colon is usually made in some other place of the Gamut, differing both from the full close of all, and also from the chanting part, (the Base usually closing in the fifth above the key) and the full close of the period ends in the key itself in which the music is set . . . That the musical notes near these accents, as well as vowels, might be something longer than in other places; and consequently, the method of singing, to which these two accents seem to direct us, is observed in all the chanting tunes in our Cathedrals.[47]

The written form of a psalm chant pictured in Bedford's treatise reappears in James Bentham's description of chanting in Ely Cathedral, but there is no mention of a unison recitation:

[44] Wilson, *North on Music*, 269.

[45] Arthur Bedford, *The Temple Musick: or, An Essay concerning the Method of Singing the Psalms of David, in the Temple* (London, 1706), preface. Bedford was vicar of Temple Church, Bristol 1693–1715 and Newton St Low, Somerset 1715–45. For his importance in the development of an ancient music canon, see Weber, *Rise of Musical Classics*, 47–56.

[46] Bedford, *Temple Musick*, 162.   [47] Ibid.

Now let us observe how Chants are set to music, let us take a view of them in score, for that is the only way of judging of any piece of music; the following things are observable in them: that they are generally set in counterpoint; that they have a middle close, & a full close; & move by quavers, crotchets & minims; the first syllable in the verse a crotchet, the next syllables (till you come to the *antepenultima* of the middle close, or the division of the verse) quavers, the *antepenultima* & *penultima* crotchets, & the Ultima of that division a minim; (to take breath in, if the verse is long) thus far for the half close: then (beginning at the division of the verse) a crotchet, then quavers, till the last syllable but four, when they move by crotchets again, & the *antepenultima* a prick'd crotchet; (for a grace or little shake before the close) the *penultima* a quaver, & the *ultima* a minim. This is the general proportion as to time, in a well-composed Chant, & is strictly kept to by all other organists, as far as I have been able to observe: so that a Chant is as regular as to time, as the Services and Anthems are.[48]

At first reading, Bentham's regularity of time might be interpreted as strict metre, but closer examination reveals a different meaning. The complaint he made about the current organist at Ely playing short and long verses 'in the same time' makes this plain. What Bentham has explained is a performance convention by which quavers in the recitation portion of the chant were added or subtracted, according to the number of syllables in the text verse. In other words, 'their time or measure was govern'd by the measure and quantity of their words & syllables'.[49]

The number of syllables assigned to the cadences was determined by a rough rule of thumb known as the *rule of 3 & 5*, a corollary of shorthand chant notation in which the cadence patterns are those of the first verse of the Venite exultemus, three syllables in the mediant and five in the final cadence. John Beckwith printed the most concise statement of this commonly accepted rule with his 1808 psalm chants:

The perfect chant has four tones contained in three alla breve bars to the mediatio or breathing-place or double bar. The first of these tones is the reciting note, which serves all verses, long or short, to the third word or syllable before the middle of such

[48] Cambridge University Library, Add. MS 2961, James Bentham to Mr Gunning, 5 Apr. 1745, 20–1. Henry Gunning was minor canon and precentor (d. 25 Nov. 1764); Bentham was minor canon and historian of Ely Cathedral. See the complete text in R. M. Wilson, 'Anglican Chant and Chanting in England and America, 1660–1811', Ph.D. diss. (University of Illinois, 1988), app. F. Bentham's lengthy letter addresses many matters concerning performance, including balance of choral forces, the organ, service playing, and conduct, and discusses the neglect of the 'Antiphonal way of Singing in the Chants and Services'.

[49] British Library, MS Harley 7342, fo. 3ᵛ, introduction to vol. vi of Tudway's Collection of English Church Music.

verse. It has six more tones in four bars from the mediatio to the end; the first of these is also the reciting note, which like the other is kept until the fifth word or syllable from the conclusion.[50]

The *rule of 3 & 5* is strictly followed in a rare late seventeenth-century manuscript copy of chant-tune voice-parts written out for a complete canticle text.[51] The verses selected from a bass part for Venite to Turner in A and the bass and treble parts for Te deum to Canterbury Tune show the misplaced word accents that result if the rule is applied indiscriminately (Ex. 3.15). An alert organist might be able to lessen the adverse effect on word rhythm by lengthening appropriate notes, especially not rushing the quavers of the recitation, and this may well have been done. However, the limited written evidence that does exist points to a more general habit of applying the rule too rigidly.

Recommendations for adjusting the *rule of 3 & 5* can be found in a number of manuscripts and publications, and give an indication that organists and choirmasters did pay some attention to correct word accent in prose chanting. Benjamin Cooke favoured singing one syllable to two slurred notes or two syllables to one note where the text demanded it:

The white notes are to be sung in measured time like other music, but the black are to be subdivided into shorter notes more or fewer according to the number of syllables in the period. These black notes formerly called the strain notes [Merbecke's

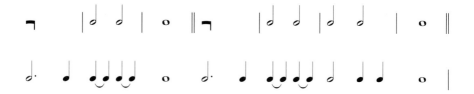

strene note] are therefore without any specific measure but may in some verses be twice or thrice longer than in others. . . . The performer is required to break or subdivide the black notes of each period into so many distinct and equal notes as may agree with the syllables always pronouncing the three last syllables of the first period to the three white notes, and of the second period the four (or sometime five) last syllables to the five white notes. . . . in the second period of the chant there are five white notes, but these will usually admit only the last four syllables of the verse, for the penultima and antepenultima note will generally be best apply'd both to one and the same syllable, namely the last but one in the verse.[52]

[50] John Beckwith, *The First Verse of Every Psalm of David* (London, 1808), 6. According to Beckwith, it was during his student days at Oxford (*c*.1775–7) that he heard the 'laws for chanting' from William Hayes.

[51] Bodleian Library MS Mus. Sch. c. 42, fos. 17–19. A cover to the chant tunes 'Papers for the 3 Songes on Saturday, 8th July 1676' does not appear to belong to the gathering.

[52] Royal College of Music, MS 819, Benjamin Cooke Gibralter Service.

Ex. 3.15. Vocal parts with full text (Ob MS Mus. Sch. c. 42): (*a*) Ve, vv. 1 and 9, B; (*b*) Td, vv. 11 and 15, Tr and B

Ex. 3.15

(*a*)

(*b*)

Granville Sharp suggested aligning the last three or four syllables of the first phrase of a verse with the second, third, and fourth chant notes, and the last four to six syllables with the last five notes. He wrote out a sample text verse for the first chant in his copy of *Fifty Double and Single Chants*, matching the last six syllables of the first verse of the Venite with the final five notes: − strength − of − our − sal − vation.[53]

The practical problems of coordinating music and text in prose chanting were addressed on several levels in a document 'for the regulation & improvement of the singing & chanting in this Choir', posted in the vestry of York Minster and copied out by Granville Sharp:

First that in Chanting of the Psalms, for the avoiding that confusion which arises from some Persons going before others, Every Member of this Choir do endeavour to Speak or Chant the same Syllables at the same time, by which means the Words themselves will not only be heard more distinctly, than they can be in Parish Churches where they are read alternately by the Minister and People, but likewise it will highly contribute to the Harmony, or rather indeed necessary for it, for all Psalm tunes being Counterpoint, unless this method be observ'd the Harmony will be much lessen'd, if not too often spoil'd, & therefore we do order that the Choir do meet together frequently to practice this way of Chanting till they are perfect in it, & agree among themselves which of them shall set the time for each side whom the rest are to listen & attend to, so as that they may the more easily & effectually keep together.[54]

The confusion caused by 'some persons going before others' was behind Anselm Bayly's concern that in the responses and chants, the choirmaster should 'teach the boys to speak exactly together, equally loud and distinct, not, as they generally do, in confusion and half words, hurrying with the utmost speed to the end of a sentence, then stopping at the last word with a tone like parish-boys'.[55] Charles Burney's reference to chanting practice in his music history expressed the same concern for balance between recitation and cadence; 'some of the words are uttered with too much rapidity, while others at the mediatio, or half-close, and termination, are protracted to an unreasonable length'.[56]

There is general agreement that the role of the organist was crucial in ruling the psalmody. 'Where the organ is not used which keeps the choir upright', observed North, 'the chanting is scandalous, such a confused din as

[53] Sharp MS annotations in *Fifty . . . Chants*, British Library shelf mark E. 487; see App. E.
[54] Gloucestershire Record Office, Lloyd-Baker Collection, MS D 3549, Box 33b, Bundle H, transcribed in App. E. Sharp's title is 'Copy of a Paper hung up in the vestry at York Minster', most likely dating from about 1762, when William Mason became precentor.
[55] Bayly, *Practical Treatise*, 38.
[56] Charles Burney, *A General History of Music*, ed. Frank Mercer (2 vols.; London, 1935; repr. New York, 1957), ii. 125.

no one living not pre-instructed could guess what they were doing.'[57] Bentham commented that 'Chanting, where it is perform'd with regularity & decency (as it is in most other Cathedrals & Choirs) is one of the finest & noblest parts of the Service', but he faulted the organist for causing disarray in the chanting at Ely:

> . . . the number of syllables in the verse is frequently disregarded & a short & a long verse play'd in the same time, or at least not in due proportion to the length of the verses; some part of the verse so hurried over, that it is impossible to utter the word distinctly; as other times a syllable is lengthened out by a long shake, so long that one might easily count ten or twelve in the time; then a short one where there should be a long one, & long where it should be short.[58]

Some of the problems of accomplishing uniform chanting stemmed from the current style of accompanying psalm chants. Preludes introduced them and interludes were improvised between verses, in similar fashion to organ givings out and accompaniments for metrical psalms. Melodic lines were often liberally decorated with graces, and trills were almost always played in final cadences. Running figures and trills can be seen in a rare notated example of a psalm chant prelude to Canterbury Tune from the late seventeenth century (Ex 3.16).[59] Even more elaborate accompaniments were common in the eighteenth century (see below, Fig. 5). Bentham complained that the chant accompaniments of Ely's organist, Thomas Kempton, 'are so disguis'd by Variations and running divisions from the one end of them to the other, that the master who composed any one of them would be puzzled to distinguish his own'.[60]

A plainer style of chant accompaniment and the adoption of a clear way of indicating main divisions in the chant to the singers was urged by Bentham and others:

> For the more distinctly playing a Chant, I think, it would be right to observe this rule, that, when the Chant begins in the Key, (as it generally does) the Organ should end in the lower octave, where it can be done, as it may always when the Key is in G, A, or B: This may perhaps at first sight seem an indifferent matter; (it may indeed with respect to the voices) but it is proper to be observ'd by the Organ; because the Chords being often the same in the beginning & end of the Chant, the Singers are apt without this distinction, to begin upon the last Syllable of the foregoing verse; but let this distinction be made, & let the last Syllable have its due length, & the Choir will know exactly when to begin the following verse. (The end of the Chant, or close of it, will be made more distinct, by taking the hand off, & making a fresh beat.)[61]

---

[57] Wilson, *North on Music*, 269.   [58] Bentham to Gunning (see n. 48), 21–2.

[59] Christ Church Music MS 46, fos. 11ᵛ–12ʳ. The Canterbury prelude follows Benjamin Rogers Service in D and three chant-tune accompaniments for canticles (see Ex. 3.15).

[60] Bentham to Gunning, 19.   [61] Ibid. 24–5.

Ex. 3.16. Prelude to Canterbury Tune (Och Music MS 46)

Anselm Bayly agreed that 'in the chaunts it would add greatly to solemnity and distinctness, were they played neat and plain, with the hands just taken off at the middle and end of each verse, and not held on with the chords, and hurried in the confused manner of the common practice'.[62]

One of the commonest complaints about chant accompaniments was their loudness, in terms of volume and registration. The voices were often overpowered by the organist, according to most commentators, both lay persons and musicians. The choice of stops was a technical matter addressed by several musicians. Bentham suggested that the Cornet, Furniture, and 'other loud shrill pipes' were generally unsuitable to accompanying voices, and recommended the use of those that had some mellowness to the sound, for instance, those 'made of wood of several sorts, & some of the metal ones, particularly the Trumpet for a full Chorus'. Similar suggestions were among those made by John Marsh in the preface to *Eighteen Voluntaries*, where he described in great detail the stops of the organ and the combinations which should accompany the various parts of the service (a summary is given in App. E). The general practice of deputizing the routine service playing to the organist's apprentice or a visitor, described throughout Marsh's journals (see App. F), must have prejudiced the prospect of good chanting in extempore situations.

The initial steps towards devising a generally adaptable system for indicating which text syllables should be sung to the notes of the cadences were taken around the turn of the century. Marsh proposed that prose texts could be uniformly marked in some way, adding that he had known such a method to have been adopted already in some choirs (i.e. before 1804):

---

[62] Anselm Bayly, *A Collection of Anthems used in His Majesty's Chapel Royal* (London, 1769), p. xi.

So far indeed is it from being a matter of course, for singers exactly to coincide in applying the proper syllables to the final cadence, even in the plainest chant, that in some choirs I have known the first of such syllables to be marked by a stroke underneath, which mark seems to me to be as necessary (to those at least who are not in the daily habit of attending cathedral service) as the colon dividing the two parts of the verse, and might therefore as well be printed.[63]

As an example, Marsh set out the beginning of the Venite with the concluding syllables 'applied just as they happen to stand' and again, in 'more properly chanted' fashion, with italicized cadential text syllables. The proper scansion is shown as follows:

1. Let us heartily rejoice in the *strength of our sal-vation.*
2. Let us come before his presence *with thanks-giving.*

The clear presentation and practicality of italicizing cadential syllables was apparent to others, and Marsh's method was widely imitated in later chant publications.

There was another important new direction in psalm chanting in the eighteenth century, the choice of a psalm chant to reflect the meaning of a particular text. It may be recalled that Restoration publications of Lowe, Clifford, and Playford printed unharmonized plain tunes for the daily psalms with the text of the invitatory psalm, Venite exultemus, to indicate that the same tunes would serve for any of the daily psalms appointed in the monthly round. By the mid-eighteenth century, matching psalm texts to appropriate music was more prevalent. Bentham noted 'a variety of Chants composed & adapted to the several subjects of the Psalms; those design'd for the Penitential Psalms, are grave & solemn; others grand and majestick, for Praises & Thanksgivings; others are adapted to the Narrative Style, which is frequently met with among the Psalms', and states that 'in other Choirs this propriety of the Chants is constantly regarded'. Also, one chant might supplant another when the sentiment changed during the course of a long psalm; 'it is usual in other choirs to change the tune as often as the subject requires it; and it would be absurd not to do it then'.[64] William Mason, Precentor of York Minster, recalled changing the chant for a succeeding psalm in a different mood during his student days (1742-7):

I remember, when I was a scholar in St. John's College, Cambridge, it was the constant practice with the organist, and I suppose a long established custom, after the

---

[63] John Marsh, *Twenty four New Chants* (London, [1804]), p. iv. This book is erroneously dated 1810 in most libraries and in New Grove. Marsh himself dates it 1804 in the preface to The Cathedral Chant Book and in HM 54457, xxvii. 11. Marsh's prefatory 'dissertation upon the nature of the plain chant' is transcribed in Wilson, 'Anglican Chant and Chanting', app. H.

[64] Bentham to Gunning, 26.

136th Psalm, O give Thanks, &c., had been chaunted in a major key, to change the chant into a plaintive one in a minor for the succeeding Psalm, By the Waters of Babylon. I know not whether this is still done, but I thought, at the time, it had a good effect.[65]

This practice may not have been as widespread in the second half of the century, for Anselm Bayly also expressed the thought that 'some regard too might be had to the general subject of the psalms for the day, using plaintive chants with mournful psalms, and cheerful with Thanksgiving'.[66] In the set of chants he sent to Benjamin Cooke, organist of Westminster Abbey, in the 1760s, Granville Sharp marked each chant according to the mood of the text to be paired with it.[67]

John Jones, organist of St Paul's Cathedral, published a system for classifying chants which he printed in a large collection of double and single chants of his own composition. The three categories are the same as Bentham's:

The Psalms of David being either Rejoicing, Penitential, or Historical, those chants which best suit such sentiments are mark'd with an R, P, or H; but where the psalms change from Rejoicing to Penitential, in the same Morning or Evening Service, Numbers XXX, of both single and double chants are particularly adapted.[68]

In chant number XXX, the same music is printed twice in succession, first in the major key and then in its tonic minor. The juxtaposition of chants in different keys to accommodate changes in mood could be simplified in this way by changing the mode of the same chant. This type of chant came to be known as a 'changeable chant'.

William Mason was among the first, if not the first cathedral musician, to suggest a fixed marriage of text and chant formula:

as the Psalms, in their present order, vary materially among themselves in this point, so that a penitential one is often immediately followed by another of a different cast, I would go farther, and wish that a Cathedral Psalter was composed by some judicious person, in which every Psalm should have a peculiar chaunt affixed to it; and that these chaunts, succeeding one another in the allotted portions of the Rubric for the day, should pass from major to minor keys, and vice versa, according to the established rules of modulation. For this purpose no new chaunts need be invented, but only a good selection made from the great variety now in use. The metrical Psalms, we

[65] William Mason, 'A Critical and Historical Essay on Cathedral Music', in *A Copious Collection of Those Portions of the Psalms of David, Bible, and Liturgy, which have been set to Music, and Sung as Anthems in the Cathedrals and Collegiate Churches of England* (York, 1782), p. li.

[66] Bayly, *Collection of Anthems*, p. xii.

[67] Royal College of Music, Cooke Collection MS 813.

[68] John Jones, *Sixty Chants, Single and Double* (London, 1785), preface.

know, have long had their peculiar melodies, and I know no reason why those in prose have not as good a right to their peculiar chaunts.[69]

John Marsh began implementing these ideas in *The Cathedral Chant Book* by printing a choice of single and double chants for each day's psalms in Morning and Evening Prayer. Marsh also added two more classifications to Jones's R (Rejoicing) and P (Penitential): O for Ordinary and Ch for Changeable:

By their being arranged in different classes, according to the character of the psalms for each morning and evening of the month, it will no longer be left, as is too frequently the case at present, to the Organist's apprentice to play the first chant that occurs to him, or to select any one, merely because the air is pleasing, without regard to the peculiar nature of the psalms to be chanted.[70]

Printing a chant to match the first verse of each psalm was the innovative aspect of John Beckwith's chant publication of the same year. The first decade of the new century thus saw the first systematic experiments in joining psalm text and tune.

The cathedral chant collections listed in Table 3.3 give an idea of the extent and nature of the psalm-chant repertories printed by the early nineteenth century. Manuscript chant repertories were by no means obsolete, although their content was substantially influenced by the growing quantity of printed chants. Organists and choirmasters continued to compile their own manuscript sets of psalm chants for their own choirs on into the late nineteenth century.[71] Some of the old traditional psalm chants were still sung, including pieces from the royal chapels model repertory, but both the experienced church composer and the amateur musician could negotiate the straightforward compositional requirements of the binary chant tune, and composing chants became the order of the day.

The standard seven-bar chant of three- and four-bar phrases, with its corollary performance convention, evolved as a convenience to performers. In its strict form, *the rule of 3 & 5* was not satisfactory in terms of musical accent and text accent, and indeed, it was probably intended only as a general rule. In any case, the ideal performance remained the same, to recite 'the verse as well as the close in distinct counterpoint time, with respect to long and short syllables, and then come off in the cadences all exactly together'.[72] Uniform chanting was not automatically achieved, however, and wide discrepancies between

---

[69] Mason, 'Essay on Cathedral Music' (1782), p. li.   [70] Marsh, *Cathedral Chant Book*, preface.
[71] Here are a few representative examples: King's College, Rowe Music Library, Music MS 127, set of 25 double and single chants used at Westminster Abbey to 1828; Bristol Cathedral, Music MS 8, tenor, 'Approved Chants as sung in Bristol'; Exeter Cathedral, MUS/2/11 and MUS/2/13, collection of fifty chants; York Minster, Music MS M 77, chants by Matthew and John Camidge for York Minster choir.
[72] Wilson, *North on Music*, 269.

institutions produced satisfactory chanting in some places and unacceptable performances in others. Nevertheless, the usefulness of the written chant formula had been securely established. The practicality and versatility of chant tunes for singing prose texts, in which a varying number of syllables in each verse was a constant factor, ensured them a permanent place in the body of acceptable music for the English liturgy.

4

Chanting Service and Double Tune

> The object of saving time could have been more readily attained, and a
> far better effect produced, by reserving certain portions of the work to be
> sung in harmony; and chanting, either in unison or harmony, the rest.
> Such a course would have been . . . more in accordance with the primi-
> tive model; and would also afford great opportunity for the development
> of modern genius. For Short Services, this idea may not be without value
> to future composers for the Church, should any such arise.[1]

THE task of the church-music composer to provide suitable and acceptable
liturgical music for the 'daily round' has often required new approaches and
special techniques, whether the primary object was to respond to a historical
imperative, to satisfy some theological or aesthetic prescription, or simply to
save time. The chanting service and the double tune represent two quite different approaches to musical performance in the liturgy, and both had their
antecedents in earlier forms of service music. Some of these developed in the
sixteenth century, in the wake of the far-reaching liturgical reforms of the
Reformation. The new English liturgy offered fewer opportunities to composers of music for the church than the pre-Reformation Latin rite and less
elaborate music gradually replaced the large forms of Ordinary of the Mass,
votive antiphon, and Magnificat. Even so, some of the old compositional
processes, especially those involving plainsong, continued to supply methods
and general techniques.

One structural principle in music for the old Latin liturgy which lost little
of its prominence in the new English service was the practice of alternatim
singing, an important idea behind the late seventeenth-century chanting service and the double tune. Alternatim performance was realized in a number
of ways. Certain texts were traditionally set by verse in contrasting musical
textures. In Sarum settings of the Magnificat, for example, every other verse
was sung in polyphony composed on the faburden of the plainsong.[2]
Alternate sections of some liturgical items were traditionally performed by

---

[1] S. S. Wesley, *A Morning and Evening Cathedral Service* (London, 1845), p. iii. I wish to thank Peter
Horton for this reference.

[2] See Harrison, 'Faburden in Practice'.

distinctly different forces. These procedures were combined in responsorial chants and hymns where soloists alternated with the choir singing plainsong or polyphony, or the organ substituted for the soloist. Alternatim practice took other forms than the opposition of plainsong and polyphony; the one that concerns the chanting service most directly is chanting the psalms antiphonally.

English practice was to chant the psalms prescribed for the day, or psalms proper to special days, by verse from alternate sides of the choir aisle. In the century before the Restoration, many polyphonic psalm settings were written to be performed in this manner. These psalms were often set in chordal note-against-note style, for example, Tallis's Christmas psalms written on a psalm-tone cantus firmus.[3] Many others were composed following the example of William Byrd in his early festival psalm, Teach me O Lord (Ps. 119:33–8), where solo verses alternate with choral sections.[4] The same types of composition found their uses in service writing, the setting of hymn and canticle texts.

'The unified Service cycle rapidly began to take shape even before 1552, as soon as an English rite was presented to composers in 1549. In the works of this period one may discern real attempts to construct workable schemes of unity as a response to fundamental changes in the relationship between polyphony and liturgy.'[5] These procedures included beginning and ending motifs and sequential writing to create interconnecting segments, for example, Thomas Tallis's handling of successive verses in the Dorian Service.[6] The Dorian Service is the paradigm for the idea and form of the short service; there is little or no text repetition and note-against-note homophony dominates the texture. The basic musical structure for each text verse is repeated and the musical rhythm is adjusted to that of the text.

Canticles for Morning and Evening Prayer are customarily arranged in pairs, Te deum with Benedictus or, more often, Jubilate deo, and Magnificat with Nunc dimittis, or the alternate evening texts together, Cantate domino with Deus misereatur. The fundamental musical organization for a set of canticles is a unified harmonic scheme, but composers used other structural devices as well. The chanting service is a hybrid form, a pair of canticle settings in which ideas from both the verse and short styles of service are combined with the additional element of chanting. The mixture of performance styles results from certain verses being chanted to a formulaic tune and others sung in a set metre. For short texts, verses for one or more solo voices are preceded and followed

   [3] EECM 13, ed. L. Ellinwood, rev. Paul Doe (1974).
   [4] Byrd, *The English Services I*, ed. Craig Monson (*The Byrd Edition*, 10a; London, 1980), 43.
   [5] John Aplin, 'Cyclic Techniques in the Earliest Anglican Services', *JAMS* 35 (1982), 409–35 at 410.
   [6] Ibid. 428–33; EECM 13.

by verses sung to a chant tune. For longer texts, verses set for solo voices alternate with verses to the four-part chant tune according to a pattern devised by the composer.

A chanting service could be sung by three or four singers and thus provided a means of performing a verse service of some complexity to good effect with small forces. This may have been the motivation for its composition, or it could have been inspired by an approach from a different direction, a wish to create more musical contrast in canticles chanted entirely to a four-part tune. There were a number of cathedral choirs in the late seventeenth century who followed Edward Lowe's note in *Short Direction* to chant the canticles until enough trained singing men were available to sing composed services. The scarcity of singers prompted Thomas Mace's observation that 'in most Quires there is but allotted one man to a part; and by reason of which it is impossible to have that Service constantly performed, although but in a very ordinary manner (thinly, yea very thinly).'[7]

The reasons for this state of affairs were mainly economic and part of the legacy of earlier institutional change:

in all Cathedrals where choirs were first founded, I dare say, then, their stipends were a maintenance; But Deans & Chapters, since the Reformation, tying their clerks down to the same allowance, now, when money is not a 5th part in value, to what it was then, have brought a general neglect of the Service, & a very mean, & lame way of performing it, for want of encouragement; I can't forbear to say, it was an oversight at the Reformation, to constitute a daily Service, for chanting and singing of hymns, &c., & not provide a sufficient maintenance for those, upon whom the performance of that duty lay; whereas before the Reformation, their clerks were provided for, in their way, in the colleges, & cloisters, &c., in which they were establish'd, & had their meal, drink, lodgings, &c. provided; they were by that means at leisure to practice & prepare, what was necessary for divine Service in public, & were not encumber'd with families to provide for; this insufficient provision, I take to be, the source of the decay of Cathedral Service with us; and what makes this, yet more evident, is, that where there is encouragement, or a maintenance, as at the Royal Chapel, St. Paul's, Westminster Abbey &c. they abound in good voices, and the Service is perform'd, with such decency and solemnity, that God is truly worship'd, as of old, in the beauty of holiness.[8]

At the end of the seventeenth century a different set of circumstances prevailed than in 1660 and, while the restoration of the choral service was no longer the most pressing need, the practical problems of adequate resources

---

[7] Thomas Mace, *Musick's Monument* (London, 1676), 23.

[8] British Library, MS Harley 7342, fo. 11ᵛ. Extensive documentation of Reformation period changes in cathedral foundations and finances can be found in Stanford Lehmberg, *The Reformation of Cathedrals* (Princeton, 1988).

and well-trained personnel were still formidable and led to the situation Tudway describes. Efficiency may well have been the main motivation for the chanting service.

Chanting services survive in manuscripts from Ely and nearby cathedrals in Norwich, Peterborough, Lincoln, and in the west country at Bristol and Exeter. Institutional and personal connections account for the spread of the chanting service, and some of these can be traced in the extant manuscript sources catalogued in Table 4.1. A number of other projected relationships

TABLE 4.1. *Chanting services: manuscript sources*

Composer	Text/Key	Sources	Notes
James Hawkins, Organist, Ely, 1682–1729	Mg, Nd in C min	Cu EDC/Music MSS/3:146 [A]	Org Sc
		EDC/Music MSS/7:392	Sc, autograph
		EDC/Music MSS/9:29v	Org Sc; tr B min
		EDC/Music MSS/15:24	Sc
		EDC/Music MSS/19:(2)25	Vocal Sc
		EDC/Music MSS/25:56	B
		EDC/Music MSS/33:9	T, B
		Ob Tenbury MS 1504:23	Sc
		Lbl Add. MS 31445, fo. 106	Sc, autograph
		EXc MS Mus/2/12:89	B; tr
		Norwich Cath. Music MS 1, fo. 1 S	Tr
		Music MS 2, fo. 5ᵛ S	Ct
		Music MS 3, fo. 4 S	Ct
		Ckc Music MS 9	Org Sc
		Peterborough Cath. Music MS Small Folio No. 7:143S	B
James Hawkins	Cd, Dm in D	Cu EDC/Music MSS/9:10 [A]	Sc
		EDC/Music MSS/18:49	Sc
		Norwich Cath. Music MS 2, fo. 22ᵛ S	Ct
		Llc Music MS 48:5 [S]	B; ed. Norris
		Peterborough Cath. Music MS Small Folio No. 7:77 [S]	B; ed. Norris
William Norris, Master of Choristers, Lincoln, 1690–1702	Td, Bn in G min	Cu EDC/Music MSS/3:183 [S]	Org Sc
		EDC/Music MSS/25:42	B
		EDC/Music MSS/26:54 [S]	T
		Peterborough Cath. Music MS Small Folio No. 7:172[S]	B
Thomas Kempton, Organist, Ely, 1729–62	Mg, Nd in B♭	Cu EDC/Music MSS/9:58	Sc
		EDC/Music MSS/25:70	
		EDC/Music MSS/26:150 [S]	T
		EDC/Music MSS/30:92 [S]	Ct
		EDC/Music MSS/13:376	Sc; tr C
		EDC/Music MSS/24:63	Sc; tr C
		Ob Tenbury MS 1504:30	Sc
Richard Langdon, Organist, Exeter, 1753–77 Ely, 1777–8 Bristol, 1778–82 Armagh, 1782–94	Td, Jd Cd, Dm in A	Bristol Cath. Music MS Tom V:31	Sc
		EXc MS Mus/2/10:29	Ct

have been explored elsewhere.[9] Some chanting services have not survived, for example, an 'Evening Service in Chant' by Thomas Deane, listed in a 'Catalogue of Musick Books in the Choir at Chichester Cathedral October 3, 1767'.[10] It would be interesting to know whether this service was of the chanting-service variety, or written in the manner of later nineteenth-century services composed on a plainsong. If the latter, it would be an early example of service writing quite different from the typical four-square eighteenth-century short service of Charles King or James Nares.

Another lost chanting service was composed by Robert Creighton, Precentor of Wells Cathedral. The Te deum was seen by Samuel S. Wesley in the last century and he referred to it in his discussion of the chanting service above, noting that the chanting service concept 'had often occurred to the writer, before he was made aware that some such idea had been acted upon by the late Precentor Creighton, of Wells: . . . who had composed a Te Deum of this nature, but which, it will be regretted, from its mutilated condition is not likely to become of any future use'.[11]

James Hawkins, organist of Ely Cathedral, is presumed to have invented the chanting service. His C minor evening canticles and D major setting of the alternate evening texts are copied in manuscripts belonging to most of the institutions where chanting services were probably performed in the late seventeenth and early eighteenth centuries. Hawkins worked out a symmetrical formal design for each text, verse by verse, with various performing forces and musical textures. For the Magnificat in the C minor service outlined in Table 4.2, verses in triple time for countertenor, tenor, and bass alternate with verses sung in four parts to the homophonic chant tune. The shorter text of the companion Nunc dimittis is set in three solo verses, framed by the opening verse and the closing doxology to the chant tune.

Hawkins's chant tune for the C minor service is composed in late seventeenth-century style, the upper voices proceeding in sixths and the termination sounding like a royal chapels tune, with double anticipation of the dominant and tonic rhythmically ordered to avoid dissonances. In the third verse of the canticle, the common-time chant gives way to the first solo verse in triple metre and the musical contrast is immediately enhanced with successive imitative entries from the countertenor, tenor, and bass (Ex. 4.1).

The harmonic plan designed by Hawkins for the C minor service is organized on the alternatim principle. The chant-tune chorus, with a mediant

---

[9] See Wilson, 'Anglican Chant and Chanting', 127.
[10] West Sussex County and Diocesan Record Office, Cap. I/21/7, 80. Deane was organist of Warwick and Coventry.
[11] Wesley, *Morning and Evening Service*, p. iii.

TABLE 4.2. *Chanting service in C minor: formal design*

Verse and text incipit	Setting	Voices
MAGNIFICAT		
1. My soul doth magnify	Chant tune C	Tr, Ct, T, B
2. For he hath regarded	Chant tune C	Tr, Ct, T, B
3. For behold, from henceforth:	Verse 3/2	Ct, T, B
4. For he that is mighty	Chant tune C	Tr, Ct, T, B
5. And his mercy is on them	Verse 3/2	Ct, T, B
6. He hath shewed strength	Chant tune C	Tr, Ct, T, B
7. He hath put down	Verse 3/2	Ct, T, B
8. He hath filled the hungry	Chant tune C	Tr, Ct, T, B
9. He remembering his mercy	Verse 3/2	Ct, T, B
Glory be to the Father	Chant tune C	Tr, Ct, T, B
As it was in the beginning	Chant tune C	Tr, Ct, T, B
NUNC DIMITTIS		
1. Lord, now lettest thou	Chant tune C	Tr, Ct, T, B
2. For mine eyes have seen:	Verse 3/2	Ct, T, B
3. Which thou hast prepared	Verse 3/2	Ct, T, B
4. To be a light to lighten	Verse 3/2	Ct, T, B
Glory be to the Father	Chant tune C	Tr, Ct, T, B
As it was in the beginning	Chant tune C	Tr, Ct, T, B

Ex. 4.1. Hawkins in C minor (Cu EDC/Music MS 7): (*a*) chant tune; (*b*) 'Vers a 3 voc' (v. 3)

(*a*)

(b)

cadence in the relative major and a terminal cadence on the tonic, alternates with verses closing in the key of the dominant. In each solo verse, as in verse three, voices enter in imitation. The even quavers and dotted crotchet and quaver figures of the chant tune are carried over to moderately florid vocal lines in these verses, while in the fifth and seventh verses (Ex. 4.2) two voices in thirds move against the other one. The ninth verse extends to thirty-five bars and ends with a coda in which the final eleven bars are repeated. The

Ex. 4.2. Hawkins in C minor (Cu EDC/Music MS 7), v. 7

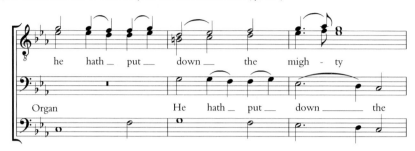

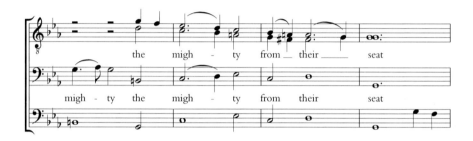

three solo verses in the Nunc dimittis incorporate a fresh theme of smaller figures from the Magnificat.

The overall symmetrical formal design of Hawkins's D major setting of the alternate canticles in Evening Prayer is laid out in a similar pattern to the C minor service (Table 4.3). There is more imitative writing in this service, and the contrast between the angular chant tune and the florid melodic lines in solo verses, especially in the Cantate domino, is also more striking (Ex. 4.3). The centre sections of Cantate domino are the two duet verses, 'Praise the Lord' for countertenor and bass and 'With trumpets also' for treble and tenor. The opening two verses and the doxology are sung to the choral chant tune, and intervening verses are set for four voices in triple metre (3 and 10) and in common time (4 and 9).

A four-voice verse is the centrepiece of the Deus misereatur, framed by solos for countertenor and tenor. Hawkins again employs successive imitative entries and there is more text repetition in the coloratura solo verses, especially in response to the text at 'Praise the Lord upon the harp' and 'Let the floods clap their hands' in Cantate domino, and 'O let the nations rejoice' in Deus misereatur. The choral chant tune is sung only for the opening verse and for the doxology in the Deus misereatur, but two of the four-part verses, both to the text 'Let all the people praise thee', repeat the same note–against–note statement of the text. This more elaborate setting of the alternate evening canticles may have been intended for a special occasion, a holy day in the church calendar or a state visit.

Hawkins's D major chanting service was copied in partbooks from Lincoln and Peterborough, but it appears there under the name of William Norris, Lincoln's Master of the Choristers, who is presumably the composer of its new chant tune. The only other alteration from the Hawkins original is a sixteen-bar coda to the chant tune in the fifth verse of Cantate domino. The first verse of Cantate domino to the chant tune is written out below a staff on which a direct replaces a musical note as a non-durational pitch sign, one direct for each syllable, implying that the text was chanted in even rhythms.

Norris composed his own chanting service in G minor for Morning Prayer in which the harmonic structure and vocal scoring imitate the Hawkins model. The solo verses are scored for treble, countertenor, and bass in Ely copies of the service, but in Peterborough there is an alternate version with the countertenor part written for a bass. In Norris's formal design for the long Te deum text, two choral chant-tune verses alternate with two, and occasionally three, solo verses, mostly in triple metre. Verse 16, 'when thou tookest upon thee to deliver man', receives the most florid treatment. The chant tune

TABLE 4.3. *Chanting service in D: formal design*

Verse	Setting	Voices
CANTATE DOMINO		
1. O Sing unto the Lord	Chant tune C	Tr, Ct, T, B
2. With his own right hand	Chant tune C	Tr, Ct, T, B
3. The Lord declared	Verse 3/2	Tr, Ct, T, B
4. He hath remembered	Verse C	Tr, Ct, T, B
5. Show yourselves joyful	Chant tune C	Tr, Ct, T, B
6. Praise the Lord	Verse C	Ct, B
7. With trumpets also	Verse 3/2	Tr, T
8. Let the sea make a noise	Chant tune C	Tr, Ct, T, B
9. Let the floods clap	Verse C	Tr, Ct, T, B
10. With righteousness shall	Verse 3/2	Tr, Ct, T, B
Glory be to the Father	Chant tune C	Tr, Ct, T, B
As it was in the beginning	Chant tune C	Tr, Ct, T, B
DEUS MISEREATUR		
1. God be merciful unto us	Chant tune C	Tr, Ct, T, B
2. That thy way may be known	Verse C	Tr, Ct, T, B
3. Let the people praise thee	Verse 3/2	Tr, Ct, T, B
4. O let the nations rejoice	Verse 3/2	Ct
5. Let the people praise thee	Verse 3/2	Tr, Ct, T, B
6. Then shall the earth	Verse C	T
7. God shall bless us	Verse 3/2	Tr, Ct, T, B
Glory be to the Father	Chant tune C	Tr, Ct, T, B
As it was in the beginning	Chant tune C	Tr, Ct, T, B

Ex. 4.3. Hawkins in D (Cu EDC/Music MS 9): (*a*) chant tune; (*b*) 'Vers a 4 voc'

(*a*)

O   sing   un - to   the   Lord   [a new song:]
With his own right hand etc.

(*b*)

and a few bars of verse three illustrate the composer's dependence on his
model (Ex. 4.4).

Thomas Kempton's essay in the chanting service genre adds nothing new to
the basic design; rather, its mainly chordal texture simplifies the Hawkins
approach. Musical variety and contrast are provided through rhythmic figures
rather than imitative part-writing. The original key may have been C major,
although autograph copies in Ely manuscripts and a later copy from Exeter are
in B flat. The transposed version was perhaps intended to accommodate the
pitch of the organ in Ely Cathedral, reported as 'three quarters of a note higher
than the pitch of the organs are now'.[12] Like Hawkins's C minor chant tune,
Kempton's chant in B flat appears on its own in Ely Music MSS 27 and 32 and
thereafter in many chant repertories. The psalms for the day and the canticles
were sung to these chant tunes in an 'ordinarily chanted' service, and although
the chanting services themselves are no longer performed, the choruses have

Ex. 4.4. Norris in G minor (Cu EDC/Music MS 3): (*a*) chant tune; (*b*) v. 3

(*a*)

We praise thee O God: We ack-now-ledge thee to be the Lord.

(*b*)

To thee all ___ an - gels cry ___ a - loud the heav'ns and all

the Pow'rs there - in

---

[12] Dickson, *A Catalogue of Ancient Services and Anthems. . . Ely*, quoted in Maurice A. Ratcliff, 'Ely', *New Grove*, vi. 150.

taken on a life of their own as Anglican chants. A smoothed-out version of Hawkins's chant tune was printed anonymously in the second volume of Boyce's *Cathedral Music* (1768), but beginning with its next printing in Thomas Vandernan's *Divine Harmony* (1770), the C minor chant is commonly attributed to William Croft.

Richard Langdon used a new device for the chant verses in his Morning and Evening chanting service in A major. The opening and closing verses, and two intervening sections in the longer texts, are set to a double chant (Ex. 4.5). One of these, in the Te deum, serves as a shortening device and accommodates the tenth through thirteenth verses. The Te deum, except for two very brief text repetitions, is composed in note-against-note short service style. Two verse sections, one for the decani and one for the cantoris side, are

Ex. 4.5. Double chant tune from Langdon in A (Bristol Cath. Music MS Tom V)

enlivened with brief imitative points, but the texture remains full throughout. There is less harmonic variety than might be expected for a long text, mainly excursions into D major, E major, and the relative and tonic minor keys.

The companion alternate morning canticle Jubilate deo has a bit more variety in texture, with a 3/2 decani verse marked 'lively' and introduced in imitative counterpoint (Ex. 4.6). It is followed by a slower fourth verse for the cantoris side in D major. The evening canticles for the alternate texts are handled similarly, with a little more adventuresome approach to the text in the decani and cantoris sections.

Ex. 4.6. Decani verse from Jd in Langdon in A (Bristol Cath. Music MS Tom V)

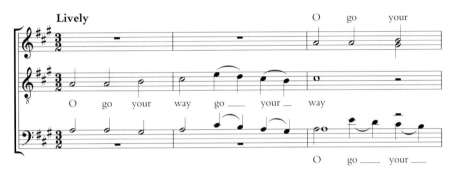

The chanting service was but one of a number of ways of performing the liturgy with a few singers. Chanting the entire service was another, a temporary expedient in Edward Lowe's time, but still a viable choice on into the nineteenth century. It lost none of its appeal as a solution to deficiencies of personnel, shortage of practice time, and other practical demands made upon musicians and resources. One of these was the pressure of the busy organist's multiple activities necessary to afford him a reasonable living. John Alcock commented that at Hereford Cathedral 'and at Gloucester, as well as at some others where I have been, they always chant the Service without the Organ, every Wednesday and Friday, which gives the Organists an opportunity of attending their scholars out of town'.[13] The service was often entirely chanted at St George's Chapel, Windsor in the last quarter of the eighteenth century.[14]

The first double tunes may have been designed to add more musical contrast in a service with psalms and canticles chanted, or in a long text chanted to a single tune. Festival psalms composed on contrasting musical formulae also provided models for the double chant tune. John Amner, for instance, set the long Christmas evening prayer text, Ps. 89, to four different formulae in varying sequences.[15] In Thomas Morley's setting of four sections of Ps. 119, for the fourth Sunday in Lent or Evening Prayer on the 26th of the month, one musical formula is sung by the decani side of the choir and answered by a different formula on the cantoris side in three of the four sections. The first two parts especially, for verses 145–52, 'I call with my whole heart', and 153–60, 'O consider mine adversity', are homophonic and chant-like in texture.[16]

Several entertaining stories circulated in the last century about the origins of the double chant. One of the most persistent featured a confused eighteenth-century organist's apprentice, who inadvertently slipped into a different chant in the course of playing a long psalm and created a pleasing effect that 'caught on'. The composition of a double chant in four phrases was far less haphazard than that, however, for its intentional beginning as a separate species of liturgical chant can be documented in the late seventeenth century. Two 'duble tunes' were composed before 1700, one by the prominent William Turner and one attributed to the less well-known Bartholomew Isaack. The Venite exultemus is the assigned text for both tunes, linking them to the proper psalms for each day. The use of a formula that accommodated two verses reduced by half the number of times the same music was sung, since the second side answered the first with a different melody.

The Isaack double tune is part of the repertory of chant tunes copied in Oxford Restoration manuscripts: Christ Church Music MS 437; the corresponding organbook St John's College MS 315; and Christ Church partbooks Music MSS 1220, 1223, and 1224. Isaack was a chorister in the Chapel Royal in the 1670s and organist of St Saviour, Southwark (now Southwark

---

[13] John Piper [John Alcock], *The Life of Miss Fanny Brown* (Birmingham, 1760), 219.

[14] St George's Chapel, Windsor, The Aerary, Attendance Books V.B.3 (1762–83) and V.B.4 (1783–1825). Services and anthems for daily Morning and Evening Prayer are listed with the attendance roster.

[15] Jennings, 'English Festal Psalms', 61, 138.

[16] *Thomas Morley I*, ed. John Morehen (EECM 38; London, 1991), Ps. 119:145–52, 76 and 119:153–60, 81.

Cathedral) from 1705 to his death in 1709.[17] His whereabouts from 1676, when his voice broke and he was discharged from the Chapel Royal, to about 1686 when he may have been in Dublin, are at present unknown. Perhaps he was in Oxford after he left the Chapel Royal. The double tune, ascribed only to B. Isaack, is the fifth in the sets of chant tunes in both Christ Church Music MS 437 and St John's Music MS 15. There was another B. Isaack in Oxford, Barnabas, possibly a brother, appointed *organarius* of St John's on 14 July 1682.[18] Later copies of the double tune from around the last decade of the century and from Oxford are ascribed to Bartholomew, and as he was probably then back in England, that may settle the question of authorship. One of the later copies is in the hand of Simon Child, organist of New College, and another appears in Bodleian Library MS Mus. Sch. D. 217.

The Isaack double chant tune in F follows a straightforward harmonic plan of tonic and dominant sonorities, with a typical dissonance for added spice in the anticipation of the final chord. The treble melody is built around the interval of the fourth, and the direct leap in the first and last phrases is balanced with an approach through an intermediate step in the centre two phrases. The chant on fo. 4ᵛ of Christ Church Music MS 437 is written in organ score on a six-line staff, at choir pitch (Ex. 4.7). An unexplained transposition a fifth higher is copied on fo. 50ᵛ.[19]

Ex. 4.7. Isaack's double tune (Och Music MS 437, fo. 4ᵛ)

O come ...

[17] Biographical information on the Isaack family from Peter Holman, 'Bartholomew Isaack and "Mr Isaack" of Eton', *MT* 128 (1987), 381–5. [18] Ibid.

[19] See J. Bunker Clark, *Transposition in Seventeenth-Century English Organ Accompaniments and the Transposing Organ* (Detroit, 1974), 59.

The autograph score of William Turner's double chant tune in Christ Church Music MS 49 eliminates any doubt of authorship. Turner uses contrasting keys in the way that is familiar from his single chant tunes in the model royal chapels repertory, beginning and ending in A major with intermediate cadences on E, F sharp minor, and G minor. The voice-leading is conservative, with the treble and countertenor separated by parallel sixths in the first two recitations, likewise the three upper voices in the third and fourth phrase recitations. The melody follows the contour of psalm tone 5, third ending, with certain intervals adjusted to fit the keys of A major and F sharp minor. An extra downward inflection is added at the mediant in the first phrase. In phrases three and four, the mediant cadence takes a different pattern, but Turner returns to the psalm tone 5 cadence a minor third higher in the fourth phrase (Ex. 4.8).

The distinctive shape of the psalm tone 5.3 cadence can be found in a fair number of other composed chant tunes, usually with the first descending

Ex. 4.8. Psalm tone 5.3 (Lbl Arundel 130) and Turner's double tune (Och Music MS 49)

interval a major rather than minor third. The Imperial Tune melody is also commonly used and in Turner's double chant it appears in the tenor of the second part, where it has the half-step downward inflection at the mediant accrued in many later versions of the melody. While its presence here may be entirely coincidental, a conscious use of well-known material in functional music of this type cannot be dismissed out of hand.

The 'Duble Chant Tunes' copied by Simon Child in an early eighteenth-century organbook include one of his own, Isaack's, and a set of five composed by Henry Hall. Stylistically, these belong to the late seventeenth century and were probably the work of Henry Hall, senior, organist of Exeter (1674–88) and Hereford (1688–1707), although the authorship of Henry Hall, junior, organist of Hereford in succession to his father (1707–14), is also possible. The melodic figures and phrase patterns are similar to Isaack's and an ascending fourth is prominent in at least one of four phrases in each chant tune. A descending fifth, with or without intervening fourth, is present in all but the first tune. Hall's melodic design for each piece is unified by connections between phrases, and in ten cases out of fifteen, the final pitch in the treble of each phrase is the same as that of the following recitation.

Every melodic phrase connection in Hall's double chant in E flat, which was taken over into many other chant repertories, is on the same pitch. The sequential pattern of phrases in the bass line is another device Hall used consistently. Chants four and five contain the rubric 'always end with the first part' to accommodate verses of text beyond division into two, such as the eleventh and final verse in Venite exultemus. A three-part ABA form results if these directions are followed. In the fifth chant tune in E minor, for example, the third phrase ends in V of V and the fourth closes on the dominant chord, B major, the sharp third making it a final cadence for the verses sung to the entire chant. The reciting tone, which proceeds by leap over the first two barlines between phrases, remains on the same pitch for the next two connections, the second being the final cadence and the first-phrase recitation tone. If the last verse of text is sung to part A, the terminal cadence is appropriately in E minor (Ex. 4.9).

A number of early double tunes similar to Hall's in melodic and harmonic features were composed by the Norwich Cathedral organist James Cooper. These were written for the same reasons, to create musical variety and to extend the customary alternatim psalm-chant performance beyond the limitations of chanting every text verse to the same music. The double tune allowed every other verse to be chanted to different music, and Cooper's direction assigning the first part to the decani side and the second to the cantoris side of the choir maintained the traditional performance of alternating verses 'by sides'.

Ex. 4.9. Hall's ABA double tune in E minor (BE Music MS 173)

Two other early eighteenth-century double chant tunes that have been called the first require special mention. William Morley is presumed to have composed a double chant which was published anonymously in the second edition of Boyce's *Cathedral Music*. Thomas Vandernan reprinted it in 1770 with credit to Morley, a Gentleman of the Chapel Royal from 1715 to his death in 1721. Accepting Vandernan's authorship places this double chant tune much earlier in the repertory than it appeared in print. The other double chant thought to be the first was composed by Luke Flintoft, using the melody of a Long Metre psalm tune for Ps. 125 printed first in Richard Allison's *Psalmes of David in Metre* (1599).[20] Flintoft's immediate source appears to have been John Playford's well-known *Whole Book of Psalms in Three Parts* (1677), where Playford recast the tune in Common Metre and called it Salisbury.[21] Flintoft borrowed the beginnings of the first and third phrases and most of the second and fourth phrases of the metrical tune melody (Ex. 4.10).

The same process of borrowing melodic segments without destroying the identity of the original tune also converted chants into metre. One of these, 'Sterling', was arranged by Ralph Harrison from the parish alternatim canticle setting incorporating William Turner's chant tune in A, the Chetham Te deum, by adjusting the chant to the rhythm of a long metre tune (see below, Ex. 6.10). Another of Harrison's conversions, the short metre tune 'Westminster', is constructed in the same manner from a popular cathedral

[20] Flintoft was priest vicar-choral of Lincoln Minster (1707–14), Gentleman of the Chapel Royal (1715–27), and minor canon of Westminster Abbey from 1719.

[21] Playford previously printed the tune for Ps. 121 in *Psalms & Hymns in Solemn Musick* (London, 1671). A copy of *Fifty Double and Single Chants*, British Library shelf mark F. 1120. a, in which the Flintoft double chant was first printed, contains a lengthy exchange between Henry Parr, A. H. Mann, John Bumpus, and William Cowan about the history of the Flintoft tune. It was William Cowan who traced the melody back to Allison. See also 'Clerical Chant Composers', *MT* 48 (May 1907), 312–13.

Ex. 4.10. Double tune adapted by Flintoft (Lsp Orgbk 10) (a) from Salisbury Tune (b)

(a)

(b)

double chant printed anonymously in the second volume of Boyce's *Cathedral Music*, but attributed to Mr Davis by Thomas Vandernan in *Divine Harmony* (Ex. 4.11).

The composition of double chants increased in quantity and sophistication in the second half of the eighteenth century, and the proportion of double to single chants in printed collections rose steadily (see above, Table 3.3). John Marsh called the double chant 'the first innovation upon the original plain Chant':

This Chant comprising therefore four cadences instead of two, all of which may be in different keys, a much greater variety of modulation may be obtained. On this account, I cannot but look upon it as a great improvement upon the single Chant, especially when the portion of psalms happens to be long; as it not only prevents the constant recurrence of the final cadence, but obviates the monotonous effect of a few notes, repeated for sometimes fifty or sixty times together, by reducing the repetition one half.[22]

Not all church musicians approved of double chants, especially those with too much harmonic movement. 'If the modulation and harmony be perplexed with flats and sharps, or unexpected intervals', wrote Anselm Bayly, 'the ear is offended like the hand or foot amidst thorns or briars; which way so ever you move is liable to be hurt: hence ariseth a strong objection against all double chants.'[23] Marsh himself expressed disapproval of chants that are 'of too

---

[22] Marsh, *Twenty four New Chants*, p. ii.   [23] Bayly, *Practical Treatise*, 74–5.

Ex. 4.11. Westminster Tune adapted by Harrison (*a*) from a chant by Davis (*b*)

(*a*)

(*b*)

extensive compass, . . . abound in chromatic passages, and also all those that are too much loaded with appoggiaturas and divisions. . .'.[24] The grounds for an argument against double chants later on in the nineteenth century rested on a common perception that single chants better represented the true practice of the primitive church.

A number of methods for composing double chants came into general use, described by Marsh in his preface to *Twenty four New Chants*. The basic principle, he wrote, is a 'degree of relation or connexion with each other so that when the first half is chanted on one side of the choir, the second from the opposite side may form a natural, or corresponding sequel to it'.[25] The early double chant tunes accomplished this purpose through harmonic and melodic relationships, while many later ones tended towards structural contrivances. According to a dedication to Weldon Champness, sub-Dean and succentor of St Paul's and Precentor of Westminster Abbey, Marsh brought out his own publication of chants 'to guard against all unnecessary and inexpedient innovations upon the simplicity and purity, as well of the plain Chant as of Cathedral Music in general'.[26]

Marsh especially recommended composing double chants with connections between phrases, by repeating melodic phrases in different voices or keys, and inverting or reversing them. As an example, he offered his arrangement of Canterbury Tune to the Athanasian Creed, 'the bass of the whole of such

---

[24] Marsh, *Twenty four New Chants*, p. iv.   [25] Ibid. p. ii.   [26] Ibid.

second division consisting of exactly the same notes as the treble of the first division, so that between the two, a constant conversation, as it were, is kept up throughout the Creed.'[27] The prime example of a chant melody inverted and reversed is William Crotch's chant *per recte et retro* (Ex. 4.12(*b*)), to which Marsh gave conditional approval for its clever construction.

Ex. 4.12. Late eighteenth-century chants compared: (*a*) Battishill (Lsp Music MS T Dec 1, p. 264); (*b*) Crotch

New types of chants described by Marsh in not so favourable terms were the octave chant, and one he called an intermediate between a double and single chant, both having the first and third phrases the same. The octave chant, in which the first and third phrases are sung in unison to a descending or ascending arpeggiated octave, was published first by John Jones, organist of St Paul's Cathedral. The classic example is Jones's chant in D major, sung for a special service in commemoration of King George's recovery in 1789. This is the much written about occasion when Haydn was present and heard the

[27] Ibid. p. iii.

psalm chanting, and went away impressed with the grandeur of such simple music.[28] Although Marsh thought most octave chants suffered from lightness, and were 'partaking more of the nature of a jolly song, than of a style suited to the church', he conceded that Jones's chant was sufficiently solemn. He described another type of octave chant he called a 'semi-octave chant', in which only the first phrase is sung in octaves. These, he said, 'exactly coincide with the manner of chanting the *first verse* at St. Paul's, and some other choirs'.[29]

The only redeeming feature of the intermediate chant, one with the first and third phrases the same, was decreasing the number of times the final close was heard, quipped Marsh. Despite this general censure, he conceded that Jonathan Battishill's well-known double chant in E was well written, and printed it transposed to D major. A copy in organ score in St Paul's Music MS Tenor 1 is claimed to be the original in Battishill's hand. Whether this is true has never been conclusively established, but the copy is, in any case, an interesting example of ornamentation in chant tunes of the late eighteenth century. Most of the skips between melody notes in the second and fourth phrases are filled in with appoggiaturas (see Ex. 4.12(a)). In contrast to the contrived effect of Crotch's inverted and reversed melody, the Battishill double chant is a good example of the type of chants with tuneful melodies that became repertory standards.

By the early nineteenth century, double chants had become a well-established genre with a number of formal conventions governing their composition. Also, double chants were constructed from single ones by joining two, or by integrating a new chant with an old one. The chanting service, on the other hand, achieved only a regional and temporary popularity. The Hawkins model, chant-tune verses arranged symmetrically with verses set for one or a few voices, had the virtue of being new. Even though it satisfied the needs of economy of means and musical variety, the chanting service concept was eclipsed by the double tune for the same reasons that single chant tunes took over much of the work of the daily service. Single and double chants could be readily adapted to any prose text and provided enough musical variation within an easily comprehended framework to meet the demands of the ordinary performance of the liturgy. Most importantly, they could be negotiated by amateur singers as well as accomplished and highly trained performers. Double and single chants would, in time, meet the crucial test of adaptability to congregational participation in various denominational settings, at the same time maintaining their established place in the cathedral service.

[28] Gerald Gifford, 'John Jones', *New Grove*, ix. 701. See Temperley, *MEPC*, Ex. 49, ii. 128, for the Jones octave chant written out in full for Jubilate deo by Benjamin Jacob in *National Psalmody* (1817).

[29] Marsh, *Twenty four New Chants*, p. vi.

5

Chanting and Choral Service
c.1690–c.1820

If there be any of our own communion (as we hope there are not many) who, taking Church-Music for a relic of popery, would have it altogether silenc'd, they may assure themselves, that the letting it drop would by little and little make room for weightier alterations. And therefore, tho' they look upon it as a disagreeable piece of antiquity, 'twere safer to let this ruin stand, than by rashly blowing it up endanger the cathedral to which it joins.[1]

NOT all churchmen concerned about the state of the national church in the early eighteenth century predicted such dire consequences as these from compromises and abrogations proposed in the traditional performance of cathedral choral service. Chanting the prose texts of Morning and Evening Prayer, Litany, and Communion, nevertheless, was at the centre of the liturgical ritual which had defined choral worship for centuries. The extraordinary character of cathedrals and collegiate churches and chapels seemed to depend as much on whether or not they chanted the prayers as on their special status at the top of the hierarchy of institutional bodies within the Church of England. Chanting the prose psalms in harmony 'by sides' was not viewed in exactly the same way, for in places where orders were given to cease chanting prayers, the psalmody was exempted. Even though it was not destined to remain for long the exclusive property of choral establishments, the strength and centrality of psalm chanting within the choral service tradition is evident in its history, which has already been accorded its own chapter. The other texts that were recited on one tone or chanted with traditional inflections were another matter, and at least in the eighteenth century they were still chanted almost exclusively in institutions with choral establishments. There was serious concern that if this practice were to cease entirely or be diluted beyond recognition, special musical characteristics of cathedral service would no longer set it apart from public worship in other churches.

[1] W. Dingley, *Cathedral Service Decent and Useful. A Sermon Preach'd before the University of Oxford . . . on Cecilia's Day* (Oxford, 1713), 18–19.

All churches, from large to small and town to country, were governed by the same liturgy, the Book of Common Prayer, whose rubrics dealt with few of these matters of music and ceremonial in sufficient detail to ensure their continuation. Tradition and established custom rather than legislation or written rule determined the musical practice of different jurisdictions within the Church of England, and precedent could just as well be circumvented as upheld. Some clergymen, like Thomas Bisse, Chancellor of Hereford, urged parishes to imitate their mothers, the cathedrals, and some parishes did so by adopting certain of the chanting traditions of cathedral choirs. Other clergymen and laymen supported orders of Dean and Chapters to speak rather than chant the prayers, responses, litanies, and creeds, and by so doing moved closer to the customary parochial practice. It is not altogether surprising, then, that general principles governing the performance of service music in Church of England cathedrals and churches are difficult to systematize. The choices could be just as confusing to clergymen and members of musical staff as to outside observers:

It is said of the Venite Exultemus, the Hymns for Easter-day, Gloria in Excelsis, the whole Psalter, and Gloria Patri; that they shall be said or sung. But it is not said whether this shall be done by the Priest or the People; or if by both, whether jointly, or alternatim. Custom therefore is our only authority for those various ways, in which we perform these parts of the Office in Choirs and Parish Churches.[2]

Musicians had little difficulty defining the difference between the performance of the liturgy in 'choirs' and parish churches. Thomas Tudway isolated the main issue as one of musical consonance:

When St. Gregory the great, compos'd, for the making more regularly the responses, what we call now, the Chanting of the Service, in the Church of England; as we may see it set down in notes, in the Missals &c., that is, that all the responses made to the suffrages, or at the end of ev'ry pray'r &c., should be in a musical uniformity of sound, or tone, and not at random, as those made by Congregations in Parochial Churches, where, no order is observ'd, of uniformity, or agreement of sound, but only, a disagreeable murmuring noise is heard, by a confus'd mixture of tones; tis true indeed, that this art of making musical, & regular responses, cannot be had, but where Choirs are established, & therefore this is not said, to upbraid as indecent, Parochial Service, but to show the disparity of these two ways.[3]

Many other perceived distinctions had little to do with music and liturgy and much to do with episcopal administration, economics, and social hierarchy, but all had their impact on public worship. A generally held concept of the

[2] Thomas Sharp, *The Rubrick in the Book of Common Prayer* (London, 1753), 77.
[3] British Library MS Harley 7342, fo. 9ᵛ.

proper separation between cathedral and parish would still be abroad at the end of the eighteenth century, but the clear boundaries between cathedral music and parish music that were commonly accepted in the Restoration era had become less marked as the eighteenth century gave way to the nineteenth.

An appreciation of the forces that had created an adverse environment for the welfare of choral establishments in the early eighteenth century must begin with some understanding of events surrounding the Glorious Revolution and its aftermath. The accession of William III and Mary II in 1689 ushered in a period circumscribed by the Toleration Act of the same year, in which Protestant dissenters were exempted from legal penalties. Though they were still excluded from civil and military office by the test of acceptability based upon membership in the established church, the Test Act of 1673, they had more licence to preach, to write about, and to practise their own style of public worship. The emphasis between nonconformist and Church of England member was on differences rather than similarities, and 'introduced into the life of society a lasting division: a division between privileged conformist and unprivileged nonconformist, between "Church" and "Chapel" '.[4] This division was exacerbated by the Test Act, which effectively kept nonconformists and Roman Catholics out of civil and military office for 150 years; it was not repealed until 1828–9.[5]

Some attempts were made to broaden the base of the state church to include dissenters in the Restoration decades, but none succeeded. The temper of the times was not conducive to compromise: 'in the latter years of Charles II and throughout the short reign of James II even toleration was suspected, not indeed without reason, of bringing with it an equal toleration of popery'.[6] The same assessment could be made of the climate in James II's reign as was made of the immediate pre-Civil War period, when 'English Protestants had been told for years that Catholicism was politically seditious, morally evil, and doctrinally damnable. It was indelibly associated with foreign attempts to invade England, with domestic plots to assassinate its monarchs.'[7] It is not surprising that opposition at many levels of society to the king and his efforts to extend the influence of Roman Catholicism eventually brought his exile.

Fear of Roman Catholic domination fed deep-seated and long-lasting prejudice in England against anything reminiscent of Catholic doctrine or practice, including its traditional liturgical music. This was still true in the early nineteenth century:

[4] Beddard, 'The Restoration Church', 166.
[5] G. M. Trevelyan, *The English Revolution 1688–89* (Oxford, 1938, 1965), 15.
[6] Procter and Frere, *New History . . . Common Prayer*, 207.
[7] Robin Clifton, 'Fear of Popery' in Russell, *Origins of English Civil War*, 156.

But the same prejudice, which has operated to the rejection and continued exclusion of the Organ from an entire division of the National Church, has been connected with Chaunting also. That it is employed by Roman Catholics, is sufficient in some quarters to stamp it with the mark of the beast; and even in the Church of England, on occasion of its re-introduction after a suspension, the writer once heard this sentiment solemnly uttered, 'Ah! we shall have *Mass* next:' Such is the power of the association of ideas.[8]

If the Athanasian Creed was recited less and less in the eighteenth century, it was surely due to the implications of the text, of which the first verse stated outright, 'Whosoever shall be saved: before all things it is necessary that he hold the Catholick faith.' 'In his *Free and Candid Disquisitions* (1749) John Jones urged the authorities in church and state to purge the Liturgy of its anomalies, excise the ferocious dogmatism of the Athanasian Creed and remove some relics of popish ritual.'[9]

Prejudice against Roman Catholicism received periodic dramatic reinforcement throughout the eighteenth century, especially in the Jacobite disturbances of 1715 and 1745. The three main categories of Catholic discourse in the eighteenth century, according to Colin Haydon, were political distrust, theological disagreement, and popular fear.[10] The latter was stimulated by the commemoration of the Gunpowder Plot every fifth of November in a special order of service in the Book of Common Prayer. Popular demonstrations associated with the occasion and the sermons preached in the service were especially effective in keeping alive fear of a Roman Catholic threat to the English way of life.[11] Although the service became less important in the second half of the century and severe restrictions against Catholics began to ease at the end of the century, 'no Popery' continued as a rallying cry for 'all sorts and conditions of men' on many issues affecting religious and non-religious life.

After the departure of James II, an effort to revise the Anglican liturgy was undertaken by a Commission of ten bishops and twenty other clergymen called in September 1689. They prepared a series of 598 articles, which included textual changes in the Prayers, Collects, and Canticles and procedural changes to accommodate the views of dissenters, but the proposals for revision were never taken up by Convocation. Comprehension of dissenters within the Church of England was defeated largely by inaction.[12] The administrative

---

[8] Minimus [Edward Hodges], 'Church Music' No. X, *The Bristol Mirror*, 12 May 1821.

[9] John Walsh and Stephen Taylor, 'Introduction: The Church and Anglicanism in the "Long" Eighteenth Century', in John Walsh, Colin Haydon, and Stephen Taylor (eds.), *The Church of England c.1689–c.1833* (Cambridge, 1993), 38. Even today there is a common confusion among 'ordinary folk' about the catholicity, small c, of the Protestant Episcopal Church.

[10] Colin Haydon, *Anti-Catholicism in Eighteenth-Century England, c.1714–80* (Manchester, 1993), 3.

[11] Ibid.; see 30–5, chs. 3 and 4, and 175–6.   [12] Procter and Frere, *New History*, 207–21.

system of the restored church also remained the same until the nineteenth century, 'but much of the spirit of conviction which still animated it when it was revived, and made tolerable its shortcomings, was gradually to disappear. In ecclesiastical administration as well as in theology, it was rather the change in mental climate in the last years of the seventeenth century than the cataclysm in the middle of it' which separated the early seventeenth-century from the early nineteenth-century church.[13]

The removal of nonjurors from the main body of the Church of England after 1690 had a profound effect on the church, especially in eighteenth-century Scotland. The official end of episcopacy and the re-establishment of Presbyterianism as the state church placed Episcopalians in the position of outsiders. The nonjurors administered to their congregations without legal status, attempting to gather their forces to the Stuart cause, while both old and new congregations willing to pray for the reigning monarch were allowed to worship, after 1712, according to the English Book of Common Prayer. These two strands of episcopalianism would again become one at the beginning of the nineteenth century, when the 'qualified chapels' agreed to be governed under the administration of the Scottish Bishops, forming the Episcopal Church in Scotland.

Among the 300–400 nonjurors who could not take the oaths of allegiance to William and Mary were those most inclined to liturgical scholarship and liturgical practice. Even though they were separated from the main body of the state church, their influence continued through their writings and in certain areas of activity, such as Magdalen College, Oxford and Manchester Collegiate Church.[14] Much has been written about the mainstream position in the English church being increasingly occupied by men who were centrist in their thinking and opposed to radical change on either end of the religious spectrum. Latitudinarianism, which gives the Georgian age its defining character for many religious historians, was as much a concept of 'moderation; the practice of Christian charitableness and tolerance' as it was a 'school of liberal religious thought with a set of well-defined tenets'.[15] Norman Sykes's opinion is well known, that 'the eminently practical character of this presentation of religion was well suited to the temper of the age which, in reaction from the furies of theological strife of the seventeenth century and the extremes of Independency and Popery, desired to expend its energies in the profitable task of advancing the national wealth by the pursuit of trade and commerce and in the enjoyment of domestic peace.'[16]

---

[13] Whiteman, 'Re-Establishment', 131.
[14] Walsh and Taylor, 'Church and Anglicanism', 32–3.   [15] Ibid. 36.
[16] Norman Sykes, *Church and State in England in the XVIIIth Century* (Cambridge, 1934, repr. 1962), 283.

But as John Walsh and Stephen Taylor point out, 'there was divergence as well as consensus in Latitudinarian religion'.[17] Different groups representing significant shades of thought had always existed in the Church of England and this was most definitely the case in the eighteenth century. The liberal, Evangelical, and 'High Church' schools 'existed as identifiable tendencies in the Georgian Church'.[18] It may yet be possible to correlate the resurgence of 'High Church' influence at the end of the century with the restoration of choral service in some cathedrals where it had been given up. Evangelical aims for church music are more easily documented in terms of practice. There are encouraging signs of a reassessment in the commonly held perception that in the 'secular age' the Church of England was in a century-long stupor, that it was a time when the distractions of an increasingly urban and industrial society and the debates of scientific inquiry and reasonable discourse relegated religion to the position of an unessential ingredient of social dynamics. The Canterbury Convocation did not meet regularly from 17 May 1717 onward, supposedly symbolizing the irrelevance of the church. This general overview does little justice to the Church of England; 'though one might never guess it from modern historical writing, there was still a Protestant world in the eighteenth century to which the Church of England belonged, to which it was acknowledged to belong and to which it regarded itself as belonging'.[19] Anglican thought was neither eclipsed by science and technology nor by the challenges of dissenters, although it is true that the state church was increasingly in competition with other religious bodies for allegiance from the well-to-do and the wider population. The growth of Methodism and the 'chapel' movement, in particular, contributed to a diversification of religious thought and practice which culminated in the next century with denominationalism on a grand scale.

All these currents and cross-currents circumscribed the daily and weekly routine of public worship, but none more so than the economic factors which adversely affected the maintenance of cathedral fabrics. Funds for cathedral musical establishments did not profit from the growth in real income in other sectors of society and salaries for musical personnel, for example, did not improve. Lay clerks were paid 'identically the same as at the Reformation: without the least regard to their being at that time a competent maintenance, or the difference between the value of money at that and the present time, which is very considerable', wrote William Hayes at mid-century.[20] Salaries of

---

[17] Walsh and Taylor, 'Church and Anglicanism', 37.   [18] Ibid. 45.

[19] W. R. Ward, 'The Eighteenth-Century Church: A European View', in Walsh, Haydon, and Taylor, *Church of England*, 285. Ward goes on to discuss the astonishing amount of English religious and theological literature reaching European readers in the 18th c.

[20] William Hayes, *Remarks on Mr. Avison's Essay on Musical Expression* (London, 1753), 96.

£8, £10, and £12 yearly were so far out of line with the cost of living that very few singing men could support themselves and their families on one source of income. Pluralities became commonplace, and since one person could not be in two or more places at once, choirs were certain to be short-staffed. Under these conditions, any absence due to sickness or accident, or obligations away from the cathedral, compromised musical performance. From his study of the church and cultural patronage in the cathedral city of Bristol, Jonathan Barry has concluded that 'in music at least, the Church had to accept a partnership with other forms of support, because the resources were lacking to offer complete support to talented musicians. The consequent pluralism and dependence on lay financial support, and hence approval, were not unique to the Church's cultural position, of course, but reflected its general urban condition.'[21]

The wide gap between salaries in provincial cathedrals and those paid in the capital only complicated matters (as Thomas Tudway had pointed out earlier):

There are several singing Gentlemen, that belong to his Majesty's Chapel-Royal, St. Paul's, and Westminster Abbey, whose yearly income is about 150 pounds and others, who sing at the same King's-Chapel, Westminster Abbey, Windsor Chapel, and Eton College, that have not less than 120 pounds per annum, perquisites included, for their attendance at those places of worship. But, on the contrary, I'm extremely sorry to find, that at the cathedrals of Bristol, Rochester, Carlisle, St. Asaph, and some others, that the salaries are not more than ten pounds a year; to which (as a later writer observes) must be attributed the lay-stalls being filled with mechanics; and in consequence of that, the miserable performances which we generally hear in country cathedrals.[22]

Cathedral choirs were also affected by the diversion of funds intended for music to other purposes.[23] And Hayes pointed out another serious problem directly influencing the adequate performance of choral service: the musical incompetence and indifference of many cathedral officials, including non-musical deans and precentors who had the official oversight of the musical establishment. Many of these officials were non-resident and little concerned with the weekly and daily observance of the liturgical calendar, with notable exceptions like William Mason of York Minster. John Marsh has left a telling summary description of the 'state of the Chapter' of Chichester in the late 1780s (see App. F).

[21] Jonathan Barry, 'Cultural Patronage and the Anglican Crisis: Bristol c.1689–1775', in Walsh, Haydon, and Taylor, *Church of England*, 207.

[22] Piper [John Alcock], *Fanny Brown*, p. xxxiii. The 'later writer' was William Hayes, *Remarks*, 98.

[23] Nicholas Temperley, 'Music in Church', in H. D. Johnstone and R. Fiske (eds.), *Blackwell History of Music in Britain: The Eighteenth Century* (Oxford, 1990), 358–9.

Tudway worried about misunderstandings of the role of the traditional choral liturgy 'when Cathedral Service lies under so many & great discouragements & disregards; nay ev'n when, (so little is Church Music understood), it is much to be feared, the use of it may soon going to be laid aside.'[24] Prejudice against the choral service was partly caused by cathedrals themselves, Tudway suggested, when they tried to imitate the elaborate music heard in the Chapel Royal with inadequate resources, resulting in poor performance and justly deserved condemnation.[25] The debate was more often joined on the question of sung creeds, prayers, and responses, an ongoing issue for nonconformists or 'Sectarians, who suppose singing to be a light exercise, and unfit for churches'.[26] The oft-debated theological question about music in church had not lost any of its controversiality: is music appropriate for any, all, or only some of the prose texts in the English liturgy?

Clerical arguments for and against choral service, pronounced in sermons and treatises, revolved around perceived requirements of public worship such as order and uniformity, decorum and taste, and, above all, comprehension. 'All true Christian Worship, whatever the externals of it are', reminded the Dean of St Paul's, 'is the Worship of the Mind and Spirit'.[27] Nonconformists often cited passages in Paul's letters, for instance, Col. 3:16 exhorting the faithful to sing to one another in psalms, hymns, and spiritual songs, to support their contention that only metrical psalms were authorized by Scripture to be sung in church. The same text served equally well to argue for the necessity of singing the liturgy:

> Though they are not an Apostolical Institution of a Choir, nor do prescribe the particular Forms of Cathedral Worship, yet they justify it all, as far as it is fitted to the true ends of devotion; for the Apostles knew after what manner they sung in the Jewish Church; and had this been so unfit, as is pretended for Christian worship, they would not have exhorted Christians to sing, without giving them a caution against Jewish [antiphonal] singing.[28]

In similar fashion, Paul's letter to the Corinthians I 14:15 served both sides of the argument on what texts should be sung, nonconformists maintaining that the words in any chants and composed service music were equally unintelligible to the people, while a canon of Worcester Cathedral preached that the traditional choral liturgy was better understood than when spoken:

---

[24] British Library MS Harley 7342, fo. 2[r].   [25] British Library MS Harley 7338, fo. 3[r].

[26] Wilson, *North on Music*, 269–70.

[27] William Sherlock, *A Sermon Preach'd at St. Paul's Cathedral, November 22, 1699, Being the Anniversary Meeting of the Lovers of Musick* (London, 1699), 4.

[28] Ibid. 14–15.

I presume men sing, especially in the Church, with the same design that they speak, i.e., to be understood. And therefore clearness and perspicuity will always be an excellency in singing, as in speaking: for the want of which no accomplishment can atone. Unless, according to St. Paul, I sing with understanding, i.e. so as to be understood; and give an articulate distinction to the sound; there can be no such thing as edification; if any kind of devotion is raised, 'tis that which hath ignorance for its' mother; and a sort of Popery is brought even into music.[29]

The aesthetic expectations of persons on opposite sides of the church music question met on the desirability of uniformity and order, although they recommended different means of obtaining it. The need for order and regularity is not by any means the exclusive property of religious bodies, but could safely be called a universal norm within all formal organizations operating for whatever purpose in human society. In orderly worship, for instance, 'may be expected an harmony of all the parts of divine worship: that agreeable uniformity, which carries a spirit of devotion through the whole Office, and several branches of the Service, the Lessons, Prayers, and Thanksgivings: whereby your warm and rapturous strains are not immediately succeeded by the dangerous symptom of a cold fit'.[30]

To choral service advocates, chanting in plainsong created the desired uniformity in public worship in liturgical and musical terms. The widely influential Thomas Bisse put forth a concise and useful summary of this position when he preached that 'this evenness or uniform tenour of pronunciation used in our Cathedral Service was introduced and continued for these three reasons':

1. By necessity. For the great extent and amplitude of our Cathedral Churches . . . obliges the voice of him that officiates therein, to put forth its strength. For the extent of the voice must bear a proportion to that of the house, so as to be heard throughout the congregation: which would be impracticable, were the Reader allowed to alter it by variable cadences. For to let down the voice would be to lose it thro' the vastness of the Sanctuary. Whereas in Chaunting the voice is (as I observed) enabled to be much stronger, as well as melodious.

2. Commended by uniformity. For the Choirs, as the voice of the Priest keeps one uniform tenour, so the voices of the congregation, of young and old, tho' of a different pitch or elevation, are obliged at the public answers of Amen, and other Responsals, to conform to it, so as to keep the same tenour or tone, or to be unisons to it . . .

3. Thereby to prevent the imperfections of pronouncing in the Reader, as well as to cover the disagreements of voice in the Congregation . . . For which cause the fore-cited Public appointed even the Lessons, Epistles and Gospels to be sung in a plain

---

[29] George Lavington, *The Influence of Church-Music* (London, 1725), 14–15. The occasion was the annual Three Choirs meeting on 8 Sept. 1725.

[30] Ibid. 23.

tune, as the Prayers were, that is, to be read in one even pronunciation: . . . But at the last revival of our Liturgy at the Restoration, at which many useful rubrics were added, this remarkable rubric was struck out and cancelled, for reasons unknown, and therefore not to be judged.[31]

In Bisse's view, maintenance of the choir service '1. as an emblem of the delight; 2. of the cheerfulness of our Christian Profession; 3. as giving to Divine worship a greater dignity; and 4. a greater efficacy and power to edification' fully justifies 'this ancient usage of singing, as termed in the rubric, but in common appellation, Chaunting, the Public Service'.[32]

The presence of serious challenges to the continuation of the choral service should not be taken as a sign that the traditional musical performance of the liturgy was everywhere compromised. Neither was the trend towards the elimination of chanted prayers inexorable, for some institutions changed their policies a number of times. Unfortunately, a balanced picture of the state of choral service for the whole country is as yet unavailable, since much of the basic information about cathedral musical life which would contribute to that assessment has not been collated.[33] But there is a good deal of evidence relating to choral service that can be examined in other sources, for instance in the writings of musicians and knowledgeable observers. Unfortunately, controversy engenders more attention than the smooth process of ordinary routine, so there is more evidence of the issues involved in places where choral service was given up than where it proceeded in customary fashion.

Chanting the prayers, creeds, and responses apparently continued in the traditional way in places where choral service was performed. A visitor in 1729 observed that 'in the royal chapels, the cathedrals, and collegiate churches the services are chanted in a tone resembling that used by the Roman Catholics in their services'.[34] 'A distinct and sonorous voice without any modulation at all, as the use is in our great churches in rehearsing the Pater Noster and Credo', was the way Roger North described liturgical recitation.[35] Directions and notated music from Ely Cathedral for chanting the liturgy in the three parts of Divine Service show in more detail how recitation and response proceeded, beginning with the opening sentences in Morning Prayer:[36]

[31] Thomas Bisse, *Rationale . . . Choir-Service*, 33–7.   [32] Ibid. 28.

[33] Although studies of organs, organists, choristers, and a few catalogues of music MSS provide essential information, there are no separate comprehensive musical histories of cathedrals, except the now out-of-date Norwich Cathedral monograph. There are important chapters on music in histories of York and Lincoln Minsters and in a new history of Norwich Cathedral (in press).

[34] Cesar de Saussure, *A Foreign View of England in the Reigns of George I and II*, ed. and trans. Madame Van Muyden (London, 1902), 318–19, 29 Apr. 1729.

[35] Wilson, *North on Music*, 269.

[36] Cambridge University Library, Ely Cathedral EDC MS 10/12. Ian Spink has published a complete transcription in *Restoration Cathedral Music 1660–1714* (Oxford, 1995), app. A.

Begin the Sentences or exhortations in a reading tone which being ended, Elevate your voice to a Moderate pitch & begin the confession, in as even a voice as you can keeping your voice stedfast in the same tone, after this manner

[confession recited on A]

Then proceed to the absolution with the same Elevated voice, which being done, begin the Lord's prayer in the same tone, which the Choire will take from you & finish.

[reciting tone A is again given for the preces and responses]

At the end of the Apostles Creed, which is allways Chanted by the choir, Elevate your voice at first, or to such a pitch as you can best keep your voice to, without varying, & proceed after this manner

[reciting tone on A for lesser litany]

At the end of the next Lord's Prayer, chanted by the choir, is the rubric 'at the end of the Lord's Prayer you are at Liberty to take a new pitch, & proceed after this manner.' The suffrages follow, recited with the traditional plainsong inflections, but the recitation tone in the music remains on A (Ex. 5.1).

Ex. 5.1. Chanting morning service, Ely Cathedral, 1702–8 (Cu EDC/MS 10/12)

A shorter version of 'chanting the pray'rs', written out by Thomas Watkins, begins with preces recited on D, a fifth lower to accommodate a bass voice—perhaps his own?[37] The recitation tone for the prayers following the suffrages is on G, one tone lower than above; otherwise the order and method of performance is essentially the same (Ex. 5.2).

Ex. 5.2. Watkins's 'chanting the pray'rs', Ely Cathedral (Cu EDC/Music MS 33)

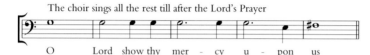

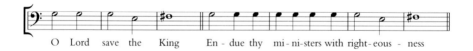

---

[37] Cambridge University Library, Ely Cathedral EDC/Music MS 33. The small folio is dated 1719 inside the cover and inscribed 'Tho. Watkins book'.

The earlier Ely directions mention a reading tone, normally a monotone, and the elevated voice, which is shown to be at a higher pitch, although, depending on the position of the specific text in the liturgy and whether the text was sung by officiant or choir, the elevated voice might also be at a louder dynamic. The orders for the officiant in reciting the Lord's Prayer and Creed at York Minster indicate a higher pitch and louder dynamic for the officiant and a softer voice for the choir:

The Minister who officiates shall here be always the Leader of the Choir, and therefore that he do Elevate his voice, and endeavour to be louder than the rest of the Choir, and for this reason that they do not only attend to him, and endeavour to keep his time exactly as to the pronunciation of each syllable, but also that they do this in a lower voice, that the Minister may be heard more distinctly without too much straining himself.[38]

Word accent and rhythm were not automatically excluded from the type of voice required for recitation on one tone. The 'decencies of pronouncing', wrote Thomas Bisse, dictated 'due emphasis upon words, varying the voice with the signification of each, . . . to observe the length, order and form of sentences in a period, and to distinguish and terminate them by proper rests and cadences'.[39] Anselm Bayly wrote a great deal about the proper voice required in parts of the service, suggesting that 'to avoid monotony let the speaker now and then vary the key in the beginning of sentences, with the pitch sometimes higher according to the length of the sentence, and sometimes lower'; further, 'in whatever key you begin, a kind of melody natural and suitable to it should be preserved throughout in rising and falling'.[40] Bayly's concern for comprehension and the expressiveness of the text at the same time prompted another remark: 'let those who chaunt the prayers, sing them less, and be more deliberate, more emphatic, more devout'.[41]

As a demonstration of his opinion that cadences should be 'deeper in proportion to the finishing of the thought, or point of discourse', Bayly offered his pointing for recitation of the Lord's Prayer. 'After a semicolon, or colon properly placed, the voice may sometimes be a little elevated, as it were half a tone, but should never be depressed much below the tone in the preceeding words.'

Our father, [count 1 for comma] which art in heaven, hallowed be thy name; [count 2 for semicolon]
thy kingdom come;

[38] Gloucestershire Record Office, Lloyd-Baker Collection D 3549, Box 33b, Bundle H, transcribed in App. E.
[39] Bisse, *Rationale . . . Choir-Service*, 37.   [40] Anselm Bayly, *Practical Treatise*, 21–5.
[41] Id., *Collection of Anthems*, pp. x–xi.

thy will be done in earth, as it is in heaven: [count 3 for colon]
give us this day our daily bread, and forgive us our trespasses as we forgive them that
    trespass against us;
and lead us not into temptation, but deliver us from evil:
for thine is the kingdom, and the power, and the glory forever and ever: Amen. [count
    4 for full stop][42]

Bayly's comment that the Lord's Prayer 'will always move, if pronounced with
solemnity, and with propriety' may stem from a generally perceived fault in
reciting too slowly. John Alcock observed that the time taken up in reading
the Lord's Prayer was one minute when chanted at the slowest rate, and double that time when 'drawled out', as he had sometimes heard it.[43]

The parts of Morning Prayer that were customarily recited in harmony
included responses on festivals, although Tudway indicated that 'those few
places or churches who still make any use of responses on great days always use
Mr Byrd's'. He added: 'they are still used I believe on those occasions at
Windsor but whether anywhere else I am not sure'.[44] The psalms in daily and
weekly Morning and Evening Prayer continued to be chanted in harmony
from alternate sides of the choir, in places where the full choral service continued and in those where it did not. The development of the psalm chant and
the conventions for its performance described earlier indicate that the Venite
and psalms were chanted as a unit.

A few composers wrote a chant for Venite as an integral part of a complete
service. John Blow's four short services, each with their own chant for the
psalmody in the same key, are possibly the best-known examples.[45] In these
tunes, the melodies move around the key note within a range of a few tones,
and the cadences are similar to those in the royal chapels repertory (see above,
Exx. 3.3 and 3.6). Thomas Tudway composed psalm chants for Morning
Prayer and Evening Prayer as part of a service composed for the projected con-
secration of Lord Harley's Chapel at Wimpole in 1721.[46] Two of John
Alcock's services from Lichfield Cathedral include their own psalm chant in
the same key, and one is similar in melodic design to the canticle which follows it.[47] Another eighteenth-century service, Charles Wesley's service in E
flat, has its own chant preceding the Te deum.[48]

---

[42] Bayly, *Practical Treatise*, 19–20; punctuation marks p. 10.

[43] John Alcock, *The Pious Soul's Heavenly Exercise* (Lichfield, 1756), preface, quoted in Peter Marr, 'The
Life and Works of John Alcock (1715–1806)', Ph.D. thesis (University of Reading, 1978), 92.

[44] British Library, Add. MS 70481, Tudway to Wanley, 5 Nov. and 14 Nov. 1715.

[45] Fitzwilliam Museum Music MS 116 contains the organ score for the tune with the A re service; all
four tunes are copied in four parts by John Christopher Smith in British Library Add. MS 31559.

[46] British Library Add. MS. 36268, autograph score. A note states that the chapel at Wimpole was never
consecrated.

[47] Lichfield Cathedral Library, Music MS 1, 48.   [48] Bristol Cathedral Music MS 3, 264.

The way in which the canticles in Morning and Evening Prayer were sung depended on the same variety of factors that influenced the rest of the service music. Edward Lowe had recommended chanting canticles to chant tunes as a temporary solution for the lack of trained personnel in the 1660s, a solution that was just as convenient in the next century. The practice also became a matter of choice in some churches and chapels. Benjamin Rogers was reportedly dismissed in 1686 from his post as organist of Magdalen College, Oxford because of 'complaints from the choir that he would not play services "as they were willing and able to sing, but out of a thwarting humour would play nothing but Canterbury tune!" '[49] John Alcock noted in 1752 that 'at several Choirs it often happens, either for want of proper Voices, or a sufficient Number of Persons well skill'd in Musick, or from the too frequent absence of the members thereof, that they commonly chant the Te Deum, Jubilate, and the other Hymns.'[50] He noted another reason, too, that at Hereford and Gloucester cathedrals 'as well as some others where I have been, they always chant the Service without the Organ, every Wednesday and Friday, which gives the Organists an opportunity of attending their scholars out of town.'[51]

The service was often entirely chanted at St George's Chapel, Windsor in the second half of the century, although a positive correlation with low choir attendance is not immediately apparent in the records.[52] John Marsh criticized the frequent use of Pelham Humfrey's 'Grand Chant' for the canticles at Winchester, pointing to its customary use for psalms on festivals:

It is remarkable that this Chant which at St Paul's, Westminster Abbey, and many other Cathedrals, is always used on high festivals, [for the psalms] is at Winchester, instead of the grand Chant, called '*Common Tune*,' and so far from being selected at festivals, it is seldom used but when the choir happens to be particularly weak in voices, when instead of a service, *Common Tune* is frequently put up for the Te Deum, Magnificat, &c. – It is therefore not uncommon at Winchester, to hear a person express his disappointment at there being *only* common tune at the Cathedral, instead of a service.[53]

Through-composed paired canticle settings may have been reserved for festivals in some cathedrals and collegiate chapels and the more straightforward chant tune used in daily services. An idea of how such a service proceeded can be gained from a unique manuscript chant-tune service from the early

[49] Shaw, *Succession of Organists*, 382. See above, Ex. 3.15.

[50] Alcock, *Divine Harmony* (1752), preface.   [51] Piper [Alcock], *Fanny Brown*, 219.

[52] Windsor, St George's Chapel, The Aerary, Attendance Books V.B.3 (1762–83) and V.B.4 (1783–1825). Services and anthems for Morning and Evening Prayer each day are listed with the daily roster.

[53] Marsh, *New Chants*, p. ii.

eighteenth century. The music is notated in organ score, with captions and rubrics in red lettering in the style of the rubrics in the old Sarum manuals (Fig. 5). The set of 'Chappel Tunes' set out in liturgical order occupies the first two pages of John Bennet's organbook, inscribed 25 March 1724 and given to Thomas Bennet on 8 August 1728.[54] What is known at present about these Bennets places them securely in Cambridge, but whether this John Bennet is the John Bennett listed by Venn as Mus. Bac. in 1725 is unclear, for no college affiliation is given. A Mr Bennett is listed in the Mundum Books of King's College as lay clerk beginning in 1726, but without a Christian name recorded, he cannot, of course, be confirmed as Thomas.[55]

The title, 'Chappel Tunes', is reminiscent of the collection of chant tunes Thomas Tudway compiled for Humfrey Wanley and might even have been a source for the Bennet tunes. They include Tudway's Wimpole psalm tunes and a tune by Mr Wendy Fuller, who succeeded his father, Robert, as organist of King's College in 1728.[56] A tune of Thomas Bennet's is also there, and he is the most likely candidate for copyist of the set.[57] Thomas may have belonged to the same family as James Bennet, identified by A. H. Mann as organist of St Michael's Church and 'in the choir' of Trinity, King's, and St John's.[58]

The Bennet organbook contains a first complete set of morning and evening chant tunes, a second set with the alternate canticles, and a choice of additional music, listed with a few directions in Table 5.1. For the alternate evening, a voluntary follows the psalms and precedes the first lesson. The Canterbury Tune is paired exclusively with Te deum, a preference seen throughout the century for plain recitation of important theological statements. In another chant repertory, John Church noted with the Canterbury Tune, 'this Tune is never us'd with the Psalms; but always with St. Athanasius's Creed'.[59] The Bennet chant tunes make up a typical institutional repertory: a few well-travelled pieces from the seventeenth-century royal chapels model repertory, Thomas Tudway's tunes for the psalms in his 1721 service for the Wimpole Chapel, a tune from Windsor by Benjamin Lamb, and a few anony-

---

[54] British Library Add. MS 39868, fo. 100^r–v.   [55] King's College, Mundum Book vol. 45, 1726.

[56] King's College, Rowe Music Library, MS File compiled by Margaret Cranmer, Librarian, and Andrew Parker.

[57] British Library Add. MS 39868, fo. 66, contains a Magnificat by 'the late Dr. Tudway' (d. 1726) copied by the scribe of the chant tunes.

[58] King's College, Rowe Music Library, MS Notebooks of A. H. Mann. Mann gives James's death as 1763.

[59] John Alcock in *Divine Harmony* (1752) and Thomas Vandernan in his *Divine Harmony* (1770) also assigned the Canterbury Tune to the Athanasian Creed. Te deum was still sung to Canterbury Tune in the early 19th c. Cf. Highmore Skeats's autograph, St George's Chapel, Windsor Music MS 89, 'Te Deum Chant'.

TABLE 5.1. *The Bennet organbook: 'Chappel Tunes'*

Morning Prayer	Evening Prayer
First set	
Ve: Wendy Fuller, B♭	
Tune for the day of the Month	Tune for the day of the Month
Ps: John Blow, G minor	Ps: Purcell, G minor
Tune after the First Lesson	Tune after the first Lesson
Td: Canterbury Tune; 'This tune is to be play'd only to the Te Deum.'	Mg: Humfrey, D
Tune after the second Lesson	Tune after the second Lesson
Jd: B. Lamb, G	Nd: Tudway, D minor; 2nd tune, 'At the Glory Patri play this last part'
Alternate set	
Tune for any day of the month	Tune for any day of the month
Ps: Tudway F	Chant G
	First the Voluntary and after the first Lesson this
After the first Lesson	tune
Td: Canterbury Tune	Cd: Turner A
After the second Lesson	After the second Lesson
Bn: Chant E	Dm: Gilbird D
or this	or this
Chant G	Bennet C minor

mous tunes. The remaining chant tunes are by other local musicians and include, besides Tudway and Fuller, a Mr Gilbird (not listed as a clerk of King's, but possibly a chorister), and Thomas Bennet himself.

The Bennet organbook chant tunes are amply ornamented with shakes and graces of several kinds, even in the tunes for solemn texts, Magnificat to Humfrey's 'Grand Chant' and Te deum to Canterbury Tune. The shorthand signs, explained in 'Rules for Graces' prefixed to the third (1699) edition of Henry Purcell's *Choice Collection of Lessons for the Harpsichord or Spinnet*, were used in English keyboard music of the late seventeenth and first quarter of the eighteenth century.[60] Few organ accompaniments for chant tunes survive for they were mainly improvised, but those that do have some ornamentation, almost always at cadences. Certain of these appoggiaturas and trills are merely decorative, but trills used in interludes, such as those in an organ score for Magnificat from Christ Church, and the cadential trills in the Bennet tune for the daily psalms, could also have been a form of musical signal to the singers to prepare for the end of the phrase. In Ex. 5.3, the short double slash is the

---

[60] H. Diack Johnstone, 'Ornamentation in the Keyboard Music of Henry Purcell and his Contemporaries', in M. Burden (ed.), *Performing the Music of Henry Purcell* (Oxford, 1995). I wish to thank Dr Johnstone for allowing me to read the article before publication.

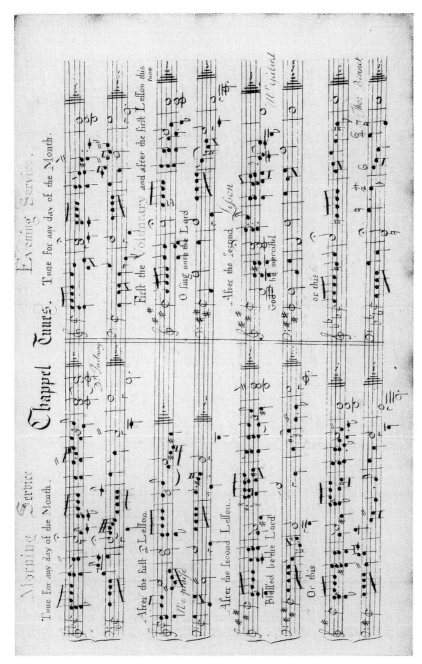

FIG. 5. 'Chappel Tunes', Bennet Organbook, Add. MS 39868, fo. 100r–v. By permission of the British Library.

Ex. 5.3. Organ accompaniments: (*a*) Mg (Och Music MS 46); (*b*) Ps. 1 (Lbl Add. MS 39868)

(*a*)

sign for a trill or shake; the backfall in the treble third bar of the Bennet tune is written out.

It is not commonly appreciated that chants were routinely ornamented, because almost all early chant tunes in use after 1820 have been melodically and harmonically smoothed out, and modern Anglican Chants have few passing tones and even fewer graces. Furthermore, Anglican Chant standard notation seems to have inspired the statement that while the crotchet became the main time unit for much music in the seventeenth century, the minim remained the beat in music for popular consumption, such as metrical psalms and hymns, 'indeed it still survives as the normal beat in hymn tunes and Anglican chants.'[61] In the late seventeenth century, however, harmonized

[61] 'Notation', *New Grove* xiii. 380–1.

chants for prose texts were almost always notated in alla breve time, with quavers in recitations and crotchets in cadences, a minim for the final held chord.
This was still the case in the mid-eighteenth century, even though some musicians had begun to write semibreves for recitations and minims in cadences,
the final sometimes a semibreve, depending on the text. The time signature,
nevertheless, remained alla breve into the nineteenth century.

The second part of Divine Service was the Litany, prescribed by rubric to
follow Morning Prayer on Sunday, Wednesday, and Friday. The performance
conventions surrounding the Litany stem from its special penitential character,
its verse and answer structure, and its use in special services on separate occasions. Also, the Litany was recited from a special place, a desk in the centre of
the church, or choir. Two minor canons were ordered to chant the Litany by
Bishop Compton at his visitation to St Paul's Cathedral in 1696.[62] In other
cathedrals, two lay clerks or one lay clerk and one minor canon led the recitation. Ely changed its procedures in 1708, when the Dean and Chapter ordered
that instead of two lay clerks, 'for the more decent and pious performance of
that solemn office in the public Liturgy called the Litany it is agreed and
order'd by the Dean and Chapter that one of the Minor Canons do always
chant or sing that whole service at the desk on Litany days.'[63] In the Ely directions with notated music, the officiant is told, 'who ever goes out with you to
the Litany, let him pitch the beginning about E la mi, or F fa ut, for fear of
leading you, out of the compas of your voice'.

Though the presence of a litany desk in eighteenth-century churches was
thought to be rare earlier this century, 'such were in use in most cathedral
churches, such as Canterbury, Durham, and Lincoln, besides St. Paul's; and in
parish churches, too.'[64] A new litany desk was ordered for Westminster Abbey
in 1711.[65] Payments for mending 'Litany Books' are recorded in St George's
Chapel Audit Books in 1763 and 1765 and 'a cushion for the Litany Desk' was
purchased in 1783.[66] An inventory the same year from the parish church in
Bledlow records 'a Wainscot Litany Desk with Silk Covering a Stool and
Cushion and Litany Book in Quarto.'[67]

In earlier times the litany was not read immediately after Morning Prayer,

---

[62] Guildhall Library, St Paul's Cathedral MS 25663/1, 1. A transcription of the Compton visitation
orders is printed in W. Sparrow Simpson, *Registrum Statutorum et Consuetudinum Ecclesiae Cathedralis Sancti
Pauli Londinensis* (London, 1873), 281–6.

[63] Cambridge University Library, Ely Cathedral EDC 2/1/2, 276, 25 Nov. 1708.

[64] J. Wickham Legg, *English Church Life from the Restoration to the Tractarian Movement* (London, 1914),
149.

[65] Westminster Abbey Muniment Room, Dean and Chapter Acts, Book 5, fo. 165ᵛ.

[66] Windsor, St George's Chapel, The Aerary, Audit Books XII.B.6, 28 Jan. 1763; XII.B.7, 11 Dec. 1765;
XII.B.11 (1782–7).

[67] Legg, *English Church Life*, 161.

but a few hours later, followed shortly thereafter by the Communion or ante-Communion.[68] This practice survived in a few cathedrals, Worcester and Canterbury among them, in the late 1730s.[69] In the Oxford colleges, a number of different customs prevailed:

At Merton College their great bell rings out every Friday morning between ten and eleven of the clock for half an hour; after which they have the Litany by itself, upon account of their Founder's being drowned (as they say) about that time, and upon that day of the week, in the River Medway, as he was going to Rochester, there being no bridge there.

At Christ-Church they have a little bell that rings upon Wednesdays and Fridays as soon as the Te Deum is over, to give notice to those that had been at early Prayers, to come and join with them in the Litany.

And so was it not long ago at Maudlin College; but now those who had been at early Prayers come very properly at the very beginning of the Choir Service.

It begins the Service with the organ at St. Mary's every term. It is performed every Saturday morning there too, for the determining Bachelors during the whole Lent.

It is used every year in the same place too upon Scholastica the Virgin, Sister to St. Benedict . . .[70]

The Litany was chanted in plainsong for most ordinary services or to the Tallis setting when sung in harmony. The majority of the many editions in cathedral music manuscripts are in four parts, plainsong in the tenor, and preserve Tallis's note-against-note texture.[71] There is an occasional elaboration on the basic formula, for example, Tudway's arrangement with plainsong in the treble and additional moving passages in the inner parts (British Library Harley MS 7337, fo. 22ʳ).

In a separate 'Litany-service' for Christ Church, Henry Aldrich arranged together Tallis's Preces and Responses for Morning Prayer, the psalm chant on tone 1.4 intended for both psalms and canticles, and Tallis's Litany scored for two countertenors, tenor, and bass. Aldrich added his own setting of the second suffrages in the litany, which were not set by Tallis, beginning at 'O Lord deal not with us after our sins; Neither reward us after our iniquities'. John Church's copy of the Aldrich service for Westminster Abbey prescribes its use on the following festivals: Christmas Eve, Day, and three days following; Easter Eve, Day, and two days following; Whitsun Eve, Day, and two days

[68] Abbey and Overton, *English Church . . . Eighteenth Century*, ii. 477.
[69] *Rubrick of the Church of England*, 74.   [70] Ibid. 74–5.
[71] John Jebb collated several versions of the Tallis Litany in *The Choral Responses and Litanies of the United Church of England and Ireland*, i (London, 1847): arrangements of Aldrich (in four and five parts) and Tudway; a copy from Magdalen College, Oxford; Boyce's copy from *Cathedral Music*, i (1760).

following; and Election Sunday and three succeeding days.[72] As an alternative choice, Aldrich set the second countertenor part in the preces, versicles, and responses up an octave for boys' voices. In the litany, a five-voice alternate version has the tenor marked to be put up for the boys, and a new alternate tenor is appended for the men. Aldrich's second suffrages are included in the Latin edition of the Tallis Litany published by William Crotch.[73]

Few composers after Tallis set the Litany, perhaps because the old plainsong melody was simply too familiar and too much a part of tradition to be superseded.[74] The only new composition that was much used beyond its place of origin, a setting by the organist of York Minster Thomas Wanless (1691–1712), was still sung in the Minster in the early nineteenth century.[75] The catalogue of manuscript sources in Table 5.2 lists copies from Norwich, Durham, Ely, Lichfield, St Paul's, and Westminster Abbey. Surviving sources are in D minor for a tenor reader, or C minor for a bass. The priest's opening recitation moves directly to the dominant at the mediant. The second phrase closes with a semitone upward inflection, minor third descent, a move up a tone to the fifth, and down to the tonic final. The response is similarly shaped and traditionally chordal with sixths between the upper voices (Ex. 5.4). The shorter responses beginning at verse five are merely extended dominant–tonic cadences, but the harmony is varied in the short petitions containing the Agnus dei and Kyrie texts, the first section ending with a cadence in the major key at 'Grant us thy peace'. The priest sings 'O Christ hear us' on C–Bb–Eb with a hopeful subdominant–dominant–tonic response in B flat major; 'Lord have mercy upon us' is on Bb to Ab, the response in G minor (Ex. 5.5). The remaining two Kyrie petitions move from F recitation to Eb chord response, and D recitation and response returning to C minor. Wanless has managed overall to retain some of the modal feeling and understated eloquence of Tallis's treatment of the text.

In terms of transmission, the alterations and additions to the Wanless Litany in manuscripts from several choirs place it in the same category as the Tallis Litany. James Cooper's copy for Norwich Cathedral and those in short score in Durham Music MS A.7 are closest to the date of composition, and there are

---

[72] Westminster Abbey Muniment Room, Music MS Organbook 20.

[73] William Crotch, *Tallis's Litany. Adapted to the Latin Words with additions by Dr. Aldrich* (London, 1803; 2nd edn. 1807). Tallis adaptations enjoyed a new lease of life in the 19th c., for instance, 'Tallis's Grand Chant', a setting of selected phrases from the litany in four parts plus trumpets, horns, and tympani obbligati, the voices doubled by woodwinds and strings, in William Gardner's *Sacred Melodies* (London, 1815), ii. 211.

[74] Tudway states that the Tallis Litany responses were always sung in churches 'who still make any use of responses on great days'; British Library Add. MS 70481, Tudway to Wanley, 14 Nov. 1715.

[75] A bass part in York Music MS 164/H 1s is dated 14 Aug. 1812 by the organist, Matthew Camidge. In E minor, this bass part supports Jebb's assertion that a score copy in E minor was among the York manuscripts he saw after the organ loft fire in 1829. Jebb printed three other versions: one from an unidentified Durham MS and two of Granville Sharp's copies with alternate responses.

TABLE 5.2. *Litany by Thomas Wanless: manuscript sources*

MS (provenance)		Key	Format	Notes
Ckc	Music MS 10:63 (Norwich)	C	2 Tr, 2 Ct, 2 T, 2 B	hand of James Cooper; Reader's part, MS 17: 'If a Bass Chaunts tis to be play'd in C flat, if a Tenor in D sol re'.
	11:69s			
	12:1			
	13:23s			
	14:62			
	15:69			
	16:60a			
	17:59–60a			
	Music MS 416:151	C	Sc	copied for G. Sharp
Cu	EDC/Music MS/8:229–30 (Ely)	D	Sc	Thomas Watkins MS, 'The York Litany': 2 Tr, M, B
	EDC/Music MS/32ᵛ:11	D	Sc	James Bentham MS, 2 Tr, Ct, B
DRc	MS Mus. A. 7:129–30 (Durham)	D	O, 2 edns. in short Sc	Tenor reader, p. 129, note: 'If two Basses go to the litany desk play in Cfaut'; Bass reader, p. 130 in C, Tr and T ex-changed
	MS Mus. A. 8:66	D	O, short Sc	hand of Cuthbert Brass, 1740s
	MS Mus. A. 29:66	D	Sc	
	MS Mus. B. 17ᵛ:26	D	Ct	
	MS Mus. B. 28:296–7	D	B	
	MS Mus. B. 35:10	D	B	
	MS Mus. B. 36ᵛ:41	D	B	
	MS Mus. C. 8:548–9	D	Ct	
	MS Mus. C. 21ᵛ:101–2	D	T	
	MS Mus. C. 29:112–13, v:8	D	B	
	MS Mus. C. 35:96–7	D	T	
Lwa	Music MS 813: fos. 104–9 (Westminster)	D	Sc	sent to Benjamin Cooke by G. Sharp; Sharp annotations in score
Lsp	Music MS Chant Bk I:8–19 (St Paul's)	C	Sc & Priest's part	alternate responses; G. Sharp's personal copy
	Music MS Chant Bk II:91–102	C		Copied for G. Sharp
	Music MS Chant Bk III:69–80	C		Sharp copy
	Music MS Chant Bk IV:105–16	C		Sharp copy
	Music MS Chant Bk V:69–80	C		Sharp copy
LF	MS Mus. 65:44–6 (Lichfield)	D	O, Sc	Prelude added ?John Alcock
Y	Music MS M 8s:388 (York)	D	Sc	William Knight's MS, litany in late 18th-c. hand
	Music MS M 164/H 1s:142	E	B	Matthew Camidge autograph, unison second suffrages

already voice-parts arranged differently and small variations in rhythm and melody. The C minor version in Durham MS A.7, for example, exchanges treble and tenor parts in a closed chord voicing. In later copies from York and Lichfield, the first phrase in the opening recitation has been brought closer to the Tallis plainsong, though the mediant is on the fifth instead of Tallis's

Ex. 5.4. Wanless Litany, opening petition and response (Ckc Music MSS 10–17)

fourth. The absence of the Wanless Litany in Rowe Music MS 9, the organ-book to the Norwich partbooks, probably indicates it was sung unaccompan-ied.

The Wanless Litany accrued a set of alternate responses, an organ prelude, and a set of second suffrages. The Sharp alternate responses for the short Kyrie petitions were intended for days when the litany was sung in the 'common way', that is, recited in unison. They are written in four parts with the priest's verse on C and the final cadences of responses in C minor. The prelude for Lichfield Cathedral, perhaps added by John Alcock, is written in the style of those composed for metrical or prose psalm tunes, in this case crotchet figures over a pedal bass. The second suffrages were added by Matthew Camidge for the York Minster choir with text underlaid in both verses and responses. A few of these will show how word accents were handled, and the use of dotted rhythms and grace notes at certain cadences (Ex. 5.6).

The least amount of music required by rubric in any part of Divine Service was in Communion, called in the eighteenth century the Second Service, pre-scribed by the Book of Common Prayer to follow the Litany. The full Communion was supposed to be celebrated every Sunday in cathedrals, but in

Ex. 5.5. Wanless Litany, shorter responses (Ckc Music MSS 10–17)

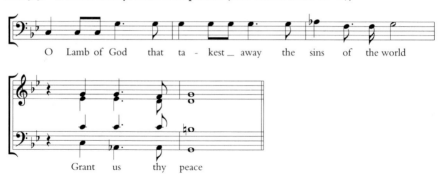

Ex. 5.6. Second suffrages by Camidge (Y Music MS M 164/H 1)

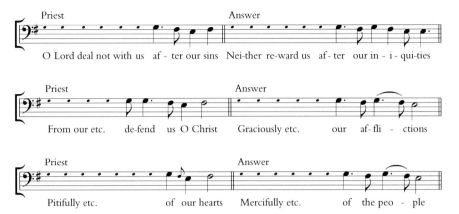

parishes a monthly or quarterly observance was more usual, depending on the region of the country.[76] In addition, the Sacrament was celebrated on Easter and other major feast days. Different customs prevailed in some places; for example, it was reported that 'at Winchester College, one of the Fellows reads the Communion Service by itself, upon all Holidays, at Eleven of the Clock, before their Sermons.[77]

The rubrics in the Communion liturgy require the Creed, Sanctus, and Gloria in excelsis to be sung or said, and each text was governed by different liturgical requirements. The Creed was part of the ante-Communion and therefore a regular part of weekly services (see above, Table 1.2). It was traditionally recited when not sung in a composed service setting. Roger North deplored the occasions when the Creed was not chanted, saying that 'requiring it to be *sung* doth not imply melodiously, but distinctly and with a sonorous voice all in the same tone; but our usage in the Second Service is otherwise.'[78] Puritan theology, of course, would militate against delivery of the creeds in any but the spoken voice, and this argument carried substantial weight in terms of the expected goal of comprehension. The prayers preceding the Creed were also chanted, according to the Ely Cathedral service: 'The 2d Service begins the Lords Pray'r with a pretty Elevated voice, but not so high but that you may raise your voice higher at the Pronouncing of the Commandments, & so, keep to that Pitch up to the Epistle & Gospell, which being ended Give the Pitch to the Choir, for the Nicene Creed; &c.'[79] Raising

[76] F. C. Mather, 'Georgian Churchmanship Reconsidered: Some Variations in Anglican Public Worship 1714–1830', *JEH* 36/2 (1985), 269–75.

[77] *Rubrick of the Church of England*, 74.　　　　　　　　　[78] Wilson, *North on Music*, 270.

[79] Cambridge University Library, Ely Cathedral EDC 10/12.

the pitch for recitation of the Commandments was a legacy from the seventeenth century (see Edward Lowe's rubric, above, Table 2.1).

Two items from the ante-Communion portion of the liturgy, the Responses to the Commandments and the Gospel acclamation, continued to be chanted or sung in harmony by custom rather than rubric. There are many simple syllabic settings of the latter, 'Glory be to thee, O Lord', patterned after those of Lowe and Playford. Similarly in parish churches, the custom of saying a thanks for the Gospel reading or singing a Hallelujah is reported to have continued in its place at the end of the reading.[80] A monotone recitation and response for the Commandments was indicated in Granville Sharp's rubric for the Durham responses: 'It is earnestly recommended that no Chant or intonation should be used by the Priest but merely a monotone in the proper Key of the Service in the same manner as they read the Commandments when the Responses are Chanted in the Communion Service' (see Fig. 6).[81] The Responses to the Commandments can be found in many complete musical services that contained all or most of the liturgical items of Morning and Evening Prayer and Communion usually set to music.[82] Of the many separate Commandment responses, William Mason's miniature verse setting was the most popular in the late eighteenth century.

The Responses to the Commandments and certain doxologies were still improvised in the early part of the century, and Roger North described the method of chanting them as 'plainsong practice':

There are certain grave airs to be found, or composed for the purpose, and some used in the cathedral services very proper, as the versicle between the Commandments, which may be sounded in this manner: [see below Ex. 6.2(*b*)]

I might instance further in the Gloria Patri and other of the ecclesiastical hymns, which are short and plain, and are readily to be acquired, . . . as a pattern I have shadowed a consort part to the hymn above, . . . This is set for a lower part, but the same methods serve for the superiors, the notes being disposed accordingly.[83]

The celebration of the full Communion service is indicated in places where the Sanctus and Gloria in excelsis were sung, since they come after the point

[80] Legg, *English Church Life*, 181.

[81] St Paul's Cathedral, Music MS Chant Book I, 20. The Preces and 'Responses used at Durham' were only one of the liturgical items Sharp assembled in his manuscript collections. They included the Wanless Litany and another by John Soaper, lay clerk of St Paul's (composed at Sharp's request), responses by Thomas Ebdon, organist of Durham, double and single chants, and ten Sanctus settings. Sharp sent these various collections, many with his annotations, to organists at Ely and Westminster Abbey, among others.

[82] Norwich composers continued the practice into the 18th c. Complete services by William Pleasants, John Connould, and James Cooper all contain settings of the 'Kyrie'; R. M. Wilson, 'Music and Musicians at Norwich Cathedral', Brian Runnet Music Library, Norwich Cathedral.

[83] Wilson, *North on Music*, 237–8.

Fig. 6. Responses used at Durham, Music MS Chant Book I. By permission of the Dean and Chapter of St Paul's Cathedral

in the liturgy where ante-Communion ends. For example, Bishop Compton's visitation orders for St Paul's Cathedral in 1696 requested that the choir sing the Trisagion and the Gloria in excelsis,[84] probably associated with the reopening of the choir in 1697. In the Chapel Royal 'the Organ and Voices assisted at Holy, Holy, &c., and at Gloria in excelsis', according to the Bishop of Carlisle.[85] References to the Communion elsewhere are few. The Sanctus and Gloria in excelsis were set in only one complete service written in the eighteenth century, and it was for Durham Cathedral, where some Communion ceremonial was still retained.[86]

The Sanctus accrued its own conventions and came to be sung as an introit to the Second Service rather than in its liturgical position. An annotation next to a Sanctus in Durham Music MS C 10, 'Sanctus to the Alter', points to a seventeenth-century origin for this practice. By the early eighteenth century, 'in choirs this Service [ante-Communion] is performed at the Communion Table after the playing of a Voluntary, or the singing of the Trisagion, i.e., the Holy, Holy, Holy, Lord God of Hosts.'[87] William Mason said he was imitating the Chapel Royal in instituting the Sanctus as an introit at York in the 1760s, where 'instead of two unmeaning voluntarys a fine Sanctus of Dr. Boyce's [is] performed going & coming from the communion table'.[88] John Hawkins also approved: 'particularly St. Paul's and Canterbury, and at Westminster, the practice has been, and still is, instead of a voluntary, to sing the Sanctus to solemn music in the interval between morning prayer, concluding with the Benediction, and the second or communion service, which is certainly a change for the better.'[89]

In choirs that carried on choral service, prayers, verses and responses, creeds, and psalms continued to be chanted in the customary way in the three parts of the morning service. In the places where chanting the prayers was given up, the choir part of Morning Prayer began with the Venite and proper psalms for the day, for the psalmody was usually not included in restrictions imposed on chanting other texts in the liturgy. The canticles were also chanted in harmony to a composed tune or sung in a setting. Even though these texts were still sung, most of the liturgy was read 'with a distinct & audible voice', an unmistakable and marked change in traditional procedure. Whether 'singing or say-

---

[84] Guildhall Library, St Paul's Cathedral MS 25/663/1, 5. See Simpson, *Registrum Statutorum*, 285.

[85] William Nicolson, *Diary of Bishop Nicolson of Carlisle*, 4 Nov. 1705, quoted in Fellowes, *English Cathedral Music*, 32.

[86] Thomas Ebdon's service for Durham Cathedral published in *Sacred Music, Composed for the Use of the Choir of Durham* (2 vols.; London, 1790).

[87] *Rubrick of the Church of England*, 84.

[88] L. Whibley and E. Pearce (eds.), *The Correspondence of Richard Hurd and William Mason* (Cambridge, 1932), 120–1, Mason to Hurd, 25 Jan. 1796.

[89] John Hawkins, *A General History of the Science and Practice of Music* (London, 1776; repr. 1853), ii. 690.

ing' won out influenced the perception of decorum, uniformity, legitimacy, and vitality in the English cathedral tradition. Since recitation and response in plain tune and chanting the prose psalms were the features of choral worship which distinguished its practitioners and institutions from parishes and non-conforming congregations, it was a matter of grave concern that some choirs were abandoning the ancient tradition:

with what more than ordinary concern must it be observ'd, that in the churches of Worcester and Lincoln, the Choir Manner should be degraded into the Parochial, and instead of its being gloriously perform'd by persons that have been bred up at the Universities, and have, as it were, appropriated themselves to chanting, . . .[90]

In addition to Worcester and Lincoln, Ely Cathedral had taken the decision to give up chanting parts of the liturgy by the third decade of the century. The Chapel Royal itself, the arbiter of taste in the choral tradition, had already (1721) adopted its 'Rules for the Decent & Orderly Performance of Divine Service', which specified that 'the Common Prayer shall be read throughout, with a distinct & audible voice'.[91] This order apparently did not pertain to special occasions, for M. Saussure reported a few years later that 'the service is entirely musical, some of the laymen having superb voices; they are aided by a dozen or so of chorister-boys and by some very excellent musicians, the whole forming a delightful symphony, and what is not sung is intoned by the clergy'.[92]

Chanting in the service was replaced by spoken texts in certain cathedrals and churches during penitential seasons, particularly Lent, which provoked Richard Banner to preach:

I can see no grounds for the practice peculiar to some churches of this nation, who have wholly laid aside the laudable custom of chanting the Divine Service, or of others who excluded this so useful and necessary help to devotion in the time of Lent, and other penitential seasons of the year.

As our Church has given no direction, for this practice, so we ought to consider that the Soul has more need of assistance in its dejected than in its exalted state, and consequently ought not to be denied those helps, which, as the great Mr. Hooker has observed, are as seasonable in grief as in joy. And accordingly our Church has thought music not improper to accompany the most solemn and grave part of our devotions, the Litany being appointed to be sung, as well as the Hymns, and other of the most seraphic parts of her Service.[93]

[90] *Rubrick of the Church of England*, 17. Choral service was resumed at Worcester after the new bishop, Richard Hurd, took office in 1781.

[91] London Public Record Office, MS PRO 28, 1 (1592–1736), fo. 9ʳ, 1721.

[92] Saussure, *Foreign View of England*, 42–3, 17 Sept. 1725.

[93] Richard Banner, *The Use and Antiquity of Musick in the Service of God* (Oxford, 1737), 21–2. Richard Hooker, author of *The Laws of Ecclesiastical Polity* (London, 1597), was widely quoted on the aesthetics of

Saying and not chanting the Litany was sometimes condoned on the grounds that two lay clerks should not lead the recitation. Thomas Bisse's argument against such a suggestion was based on a parallel case of the solemn Confession in Communion, the old rubric directing it to be 'said either by one of the Communicants in the name of the rest, or else by the Minister himself', a rule applied to the Creed and the petitions of the Litany. This was adequate precedent for either minor canons or lay clerks or one of each 'singing the Litany, and that with the organ'.[94]

The ordinary ways in which cathedral and parish churches interacted in the conduct of the musical part of services contributed little by little to the build-up of interconnections. There was regular movement of musicians between them as cathedral organists normally supplemented their income with posts in nearby parishes and singing men functioned as parish clerks in the same churches. Ely's directive for special circumstances refers also to regular practice:

Whereas during the silence of the organ it is necessary that some one of the Lay-clerks should set a Psalm, not only on Sunday at Sermon, but also at morning and evening prayers in Trinity Parish, as has hitherto been done, and that office does not belong to the Clerk of Trinity Parish in particular, while the choir attend prayers there: We do enjoin every of such Lay-clerks to officiate as Clerk by weeks, the senior by admission next week and the rest in course . . .[95]

Ely Cathedral was one of the institutions where chanting was given up and the service music limited to psalms, canticles, and the anthem in Morning and Evening Prayer. The Dean and Chapter initiated the first fundamental move in 1730 when they ordered 'that the whole Morning & Evening Service be read for the future with a distinct & audible voice except the Psalms & Hymns & Anthems which are to be sung as usual.'[96] It had become customary for the congregation to sing a metrical psalm when they gathered in the nave to hear the sermon after Morning Prayer and a cathedral musician usually acted as precentor. This role is confirmed by the Dean and Chapter order in 1745, 'that every singing man in his turn give out the Psalm at sermon or procure one of his brethren to do it for him beginning next Sunday.'[97] In 1749 the Chapter ordered 'that a gallery be built for the singing men, choristers and as many of

church music, for example, 'an admirable faculty which is in music, to express and represent to the mind more inwardly than any other sensible thing, the rising and falling, the turns and varieties of all the passions whereunto the Soul is subject', quoted in Ralph Battell, *The Lawfulness and Expediency of Church-Musick, Asserted* (London, 1694), 16. Battell was sub-Dean of the Chapel Royal, preaching at the anniversary meeting of 'gentlemen lovers of musick'.

[94] Bisse, *Rationale . . . Choir-Service*, 42–4.
[95] Cambridge University Library, Ely Cathedral EDC 2/1/4, 210, 14 June 1758.
[96] Ibid. 9, 25 Nov. 1730.   [97] Ibid. 110, 25 Nov. 1745.

the Kings Scholars as it may contain to sit at Sermon time.'[98] Schoolchildren assisting in the singing of psalms became a frequent sight in town churches in the eighteenth century.

The transition from traditional practice to reading the service in the parochial manner was not always accomplished smoothly. A Dean and Chapter order in Gloucester Cathedral for the service to be read rather than chanted created a specially rancorous controversy. The old prejudice against chanting because of its Roman Catholic origins was just one of the issues recorded in rather frank entries in the Chapter Acts. The initial order was rescinded less than a year after it was issued.

30 November 1782 – Ordered that in future all the Morning & Evening Prayers & the whole Litany and Communion Service be read in this Cathedral Church in the same manner as in Parish Churches & not chaunted except the Psalms Hymns & Anthems which shall continue to be chaunted and sung with the Organ as heretofore. And whilst the Officiating Clergy are retiring from the Communion table a short Voluntary shall be played or a Psalm or Portion of a Psalm sung accompanied with the Organ at the discretion of the Dean or Resident Prebendary for the time being.

 [marginal comment] a low-Church System, and contrary to the very spirit of
 Cathedral Institution, which should be kept distinct from Parish forms.

23 June 1783 – Whereas the Dean and Chapter had ordered some months ago that the Exhortation Confession Absolution Prayers Collects Responses Creeds and Litany – should be read in a solemn and devout manner according to the nature of the case and the reason of the thing and in conformity to the usage of all Parochial Churches throughout the Realm – also of all his Majesty's Chapels Royal and even of – Cathedrals themselves both at the Communion Service and at early Prayers & in consequence thereof had abolished the mode of chaunting (a mode of recitative in Divine Service first introduced by Italian Ecclesiastics into England the better to conceal their foreign accent and pronunciation – from the observation of the People and in order to colour their usurpation of the richer benefices in Cathedrals – granted to them by the Pope under the pretence of their great adroitness in plano canti also to devise some excuse for using Prayers in an unknown tongue) But whereas – diverse persons through an attachment to old customs – appear to be much prejudiced against this alteration or rather this Restoration of Divine Service to its primitive simplicity and propriety, the Dean and Chapter influenced by the superior motives of charity and condescension – towards weak brethren (which require the sacrifice of private opinion regarding the Forms of Public Worship – where the essentials of Religion are not at stake) and being also supported by the authority of the Lord Bishop their Visitor actuated by the same good motives do now revoke their late order for parochial Prayers and hereby establish the former mode of Recitative or Chaunting.

A Copy of the Bishop's Approbation of the above.

[98] Ibid. 141, 14 June 1749.

I very much approve of the above Contents but think that all reasonable Persons must be contented if the Cathedral Service were restored on Sundays and Great Festivals and that the present mode of parochial Prayers be continued on the Week Days. And I do not approve the way of chaunting the Litany in the middle of the Choir.

S. Gloucester

[marginal comment] Dr. Hallifax was not much acquainted with Cathedral Services or Customs, ab origani. His friend, Bishop Hurd, thought much otherwise; and in Worcester Cathedral caused to be restored the mode of service by Chanting – The Litany is still performed in the middle of the Choir.[99] [marginal comment in another hand] This may be all very ingenius; but the real fact seems to be, that the Service being performed by ourselves as a Choir, Company, or Bands of persons, independent of Aliens, Visitors, or Strangers, some regularity of measured movement for performing an united Service seems to be desirable, for the sake of preventing straggling voices & dissonant responses: in the same principle as Soldiers are required to move in Uniform Steps.[100]

The issue of uniformity and the means of achieving a proper observance of liturgical tradition concludes the record of this part of the Gloucester controversy. Officials such as William Mason, precentor of York Minster, who favoured reading creeds rather than chanting them on theological grounds, conceded that the 'unaccompanied chaunt used in the versicles and responses' was preferable; 'its long prescriptive use is its best defence' and 'in very large Churches it serves to make the voice more audible.'[101] Anselm Bayly agreed that chanting was 'wisely ordained for spacious cathedrals' on the same grounds.

The daily services at Gloucester continued to be said in parochial fashion until the early nineteenth century, when chanting was restored, with the approval of the Bishop:

30 November 1808 – The Dean and Subdean having lately caused the Service to be chaunted on Weekdays in the same manner as on Sundays and having since received the Approbation of the Bishop of Gloucester for so doing desire to express to the Chapter their reasons for this deviation from the former orders on this head, in the Bishop's own Words, as contained in a Letter from him of the date of the 23d November instant.

I prefer chaunting in Cathedrals for these reasons –

1. The Service of Cathedrals was always intended to be 'sui generis' and equally different from Parochial Service as the Buildings themselves are different from parochial Churches.

[99] The Bishop of Gloucester, Samuel Hallifax (1733–91) and the Bishop of Worcester, Richard Hurd (1720–1808) were both in office from 1781. Hurd's predilection of choral service is evident in his correspondence with William Mason.

[100] Gloucester Cathedral, Dean and Chapter Act Book 4, 97, 105–6.

[101] William Mason, 'A Critical and Historical Essay on Cathedral Music', p. li. The essay was published as part of *Essays on English Church Music* (York, 1795).

2. From the immensity of Cathedrals there is a flatness in reading which there is not in chaunting so that the prayers go on in a manner dull and heavy—

3. For one Man, who can be well heard in Cathedrals when reading, twenty can be found who will be better heard when chaunting—

4. By continual chaunting the Voices of all the Choir are kept in better force and tune.

All this I know by experience of very many Years and therefore I am decidedly against that Innovation which made Cathedral Service less interesting and less striking than parochial –

G. J. Gloucester[102]

The parochial versus cathedral argument in terms of music and liturgy, it is abundantly clear, was conducted along the same grounds in the early nineteenth century as it was at the end of the seventeenth century. Yet compromises in form and practice were a regular feature of the choral service in many places around the turn of the century. They were not necessarily welcomed by those concerned for its future:

It is to be much lamented that the regular cathedral service seems to be rapidly declining, which may chiefly originate in the too prevalent custom of omitting to chant, as formerly, the prayers and responses; . . . Indeed the discontinuance of the whole service has made an opening for every species of innovation, and our Cathedral Music, instead of being, as formerly, one uniform and dignified *concord of sweet sounds*, is now almost reduced to a level with the rude performance of Psalm singing in our Country Parish Churches.[103]

Lord Torrington visited Winchester in 1782 and reported that the service was 'more irregularly perform'd, than I ever remember to have heard it; and to a most shabby congregation, none but the Winchester boys, and a few wanderers being present; the belief after the communion service was chaunted to a tune like God Save the King'.[104] The Creed was the focus of criticism elsewhere as well, partly for being chanted and not sung to a composed service, just the opposite of the way Roger North had thought it should be sung, in plainsong.

In the Cathedral of Norwich, contrary to the practice which I believe obtains in every other Cathedral, the Nicene Creed is *chanted*, not sung, to this I should raise no objections if it were properly chanted . . . after a Dean or a Prebendary has finished the Gospel, instead of a single note on the choir organ, merely to give the choir a certain pitch, comes a most terrific blast of three octaves on the full organ, and off start the

---

[102] Gloucester Cathedral, Dean and Chapter Act Book 5, 10.
[103] John Clarke-Whitfeld, *Cathedral Music* (4 vols.; London, 1800–37), ii, preface.
[104] John Byng, *The Torrington Diaries*, ed. C. B. Andrews (4 vols.; London, 1934–6, 1938), i. 80.

boys with more indecent speed than the Nicene Fathers scampered at the sound of the dinner-bell . . .[105]

The writer counted himself among the 'lovers of Choir Service, and real friends of Cathedral Establishments', who, 'year after year, feel increasing uneasy sensations at the rapid decline of this most interesting part of the service, as far as it differs from parochial service, and the manner in which services and anthems are performed, and the wretched voices and style of singing.'[106]

Decorum and correct attention to duty were seen to be lacking in 'the late entry & talking of some of the singers & their almost all going out as soon as ye anthem ended without staying for ye remainder of ye prayers and sermon.'[107] Many entries in cathedral chapter acts ask for better attendance or levy fines against singing men for various offences and neglect of responsibilities. The general education and training of choristers was also reported to be at a low ebb in many places. Clarke-Whitfeld held up the practice at Oxford colleges as the desired course:

At Christ Church Cathedral, and (as I can assert with more confidence) at Magdalen and New Colleges, there are regular Schools for the choristers, who are classically educated by Clergymen belonging to those societies; and when their voices are no longer serviceable as trebles, they are not discarded for being unable to render their assistance in the Choir, but are admitted on the foundation as Lay Clerks; and after taking their degrees, and entering in holy orders, are appointed Chaplains, and for the most part Minor Canons of St. Paul's and other Cathedrals. During my residence at Oxford, Clergymen and Gentlemen did not consider it as in the least degrading to place their children as choristers in the different Choirs, from which, if their conduct merited it, they obtained a sure reward.[108]

The value of a chorister's training was obviously not held in the high regard it is now.

The generally perceived decline in choral service prompted even staunch believers to discouragement and John Marsh set to work during one of his wife's confinements, 'beginning a work I had for some time projected, viz., "Some thoughts on the abuse of Cathedral Service, as now commonly perform'd in England" '.[109] Yet as F. C. Mather has observed, 'eighteenth-century cathedrals varied a good deal in their attainments, according to their past experiences and the energy and inclinations of their bishops and chapters.'[110] Marsh himself recorded a range of quality in choral service from very

[105] *The Gentleman's Magazine*, 82/1 (1812), 222–3, letter from C. J. Smyth, 17 Feb. 1812.
[106] Ibid.   [107] HM 54457, xxix. 47–8.   [108] Clarke-Whitfeld, *Cathedral Music*, ii, preface.
[109] HM 54457, ix. 152–3.   [110] Mather, 'Georgian Churchmanship', 262.

good to very poor. In some places, Worcester Cathedral, for instance, choral service was revived in the 1780s, and the service at York Minster was reported to be well sung from the 1760s onward.[111] Robert Forbes, the musically knowledgeable minister of a nonjuring congregation in Scotland, visited the Minster in 1764 and was favourably impressed:

Just as we were walking out of the Minster, we spied a Clergyman in his Surplice going to read prayers; upon which Dr. Burton asked, if we would stay to hear the Music. Agreed accordingly, and after standing to hear the Chanting of the Gloria Patri, of the 95th Psalm [Venite], I proposed going up to the Organ-Loft, where we stood, & joined in the Chanting of the Psalms, the *Te Deum*, & the *Benedictus*, and then came off. The officiating Churchman had a most musical Voice in reading, & the other Clergymen & the singing Boys had charming, harmonious Voices in carrying on the music.[112]

The excellent choir and choir service at Lichfield Cathedral in 1817 received Marsh's highest praise.[113]

John Clarke-Whitfeld noted that 'the Chanting of prayers and responses, which had long been out of use at New College, Oxford, was (shortly after I had the honour of taking the duty at that college and at Magdalen) revived in its ancient purity.'[114] At Cambridge, a Scottish student at St John's College reported that in his college chapel 'on surplice days [Saints' days and eves, Sundays and eves] several singing men and little Boys attend and sing all the psalms in the service along with the organ—they all appear in surplices . . .'. At King's College, he reported that 'the service here is all sung—the Priest singing the Prayers and the singers answering . . .'. The service in 'Trinity Chapel is elegant and simple with an incomparably sweet organ and the music here is admirably solemn . . .'.[115] The Chapter Books of Christ Church Cathedral record a number of special ceremonial services, such as installations, when the service was chanted.[116]

Until the picture of cathedral performance in the late eighteenth and early nineteenth centuries is more complete, a definitive judgement about the real extent of the perceived decline will be at best tentative. Certainly the compromises in conduct of the liturgy, dwindling congregations, poor attendance, and the low economic state of cathedral musicians took a heavy toll. An

[111] Ibid.; Dorothy M. Owen, 'From the Restoration until 1822', in G. E. Aylmer and Reginald Cant (eds.), *A History of York Minster* (Oxford, 1977), 260–3.

[112] SRO:RSEC, CH 12/4/18/183, Robert Forbes Journal, 27 Sept. 1764.

[113] HM 54457, xxi. 154.

[114] Clarke-Whitfeld, *Cathedral Music*, ii, preface. He was at Oxford in the late 1780s.

[115] SRO:RSEC, CH 12/30, 20, James Walker (Bishop of Edinburgh 1830–41) to Alexander Jolly (Bishop of Moray 1789–1838), 30 Nov. 1789.

[116] Christ Church Chapter Books, 1754–99.

example of the worst possible state of affairs is documented for Lincoln Minster, partially due to the long tenure, fifty plus years, of the same incompetent organist and master of the choristers.[117] But even there it would prove to be a temporary situation. One important, possibly even the most important, factor in the eventual rebirth of cathedral choral service everywhere was its firm foundation in the English ancient music canon. The primitive church and its early traditions were discovered anew with the growth of Romanticism, and in music this meant the cathedral music of the sixteenth century and the liturgical chant of the old Latin rite. The 'ancient' choral service had been placed firmly in the canon of 'ancient music' long before, beginning with the writings and musical activities of three of the central figures in the early development of the idea of ancient music—Henry Aldrich, Thomas Tudway, and Arthur Bedford, all of whom have been discussed here in connection with some aspect of choral service.[118]

The groundwork was also being laid for the type of service that would combine elements of parish and cathedral practice in a new relationship. The suggestion had been made in the first half of the eighteenth century that 'instead of the Choir Way being ordered to dwindle into the Parochial, it would be highly useful and much more serviceable to Minister and People, for the Parochial Way, especially in the great churches, to be raised up, in some measure, to the Choir'.[119] The publication of liturgical music in many parish church music books from 1718 onward, to be examined next, shows that attempts were made to do just that.

---

[117] Thistlethwaite, 'Music and Worship', in Owen, *Lincoln Minster*, 88–98.
[118] Weber, *Rise of Musical Classics*, 25; ch. 2.   [119] *Rubrick of the Church of England*, 17.

6

Chants and Chanting in Parish Churches c.1710–1820

> Parish-Churches should as much as possible conform to the customs of
> the Cathedral Churches which are as the Mother-Churches to all the
> Parish Churches within the Diocese, and should give the rule to them.[1]

THE musical performance of responses, prose psalms, and canticles in parishes
was part of a wider reform movement in parish music. While the revitaliza-
tion of congregational psalm-singing was its initial aim, the formation of
choirs and the performance of more elaborate music soon followed. The new
personal prosperity fostered by a thriving commercial economy in the eighteenth century contributed directly to the movement to improve the standard of church music, especially in London and outlying market towns. An
important aid to reform in town churches was the installation of an organ,
obtained through a subscription or donated by a parishioner of means, for
whom an organ was an impressive and visible sign of wealth, and of a generous public conscience. The growth of charity schools was another important
aspect of the changes in town church music. The children were taught to sing
as part of their general education and eventually took their places in the choir
for Sunday services. Special music was composed for the annual charity sermon at which the children sang to help raise funds for the school. Later in the
century, the music sometimes included hymns and chanted prose psalms. In
country churches, where the financial means were not as readily available for
the purchase of an organ, newly formed choirs of volunteer singers assumed
the leadership role.[2]

Improvement in congregational singing was brought about in large measure by men who filled the ranks of a new cadre of singing masters, also called
psalmodists. They taught vocal and music-reading skills to parish singers,
enabling them to add other kinds of part music to their repertory of traditional

---

[1] Thomas Bisse, *Beauty of Holiness*, 95. For the influence of Bisse and other prominent clergymen, see
Temperley, *MEPC*, i. 97–105; Weber, *Rise of Musical Classics*, 114–19.
[2] Temperley, *MEPC*, i. 97–105.

metrical psalm tunes. They also compiled and published music books of metrical psalm tunes, anthems, and service music, most of which contained intro-
ductions on rudiments of music theory. The singing master often wore a
number of hats: teacher, compiler, arranger, engraver, printer, publisher, and
salesman of his books. The spread of musical literacy was given a push and a
steady stimulus by the activities of these new entrepreneurs, aided by 'the lapse
of the licensing of printed material and the rapid adoption of engraving as the
premier method of music printing in England.'[3] The skills involved in engraving music could be learnt quickly and 'the techniques of engraving and
rolling-press printing lent themselves admirably to musicians such as the country psalmody-book compilers who wanted to control the development of their
books and who had the time and interest to print for themselves.'[4] Many,
nonetheless, continued to produce their books using the typesetting process.

A fair number of parish church music collections included musical settings
of texts from the liturgy, chants, and chant settings, including a few complete
orders for Divine Service. The publisher of one of the most enduring parish
music books, the curate of Skipton, Yorkshire, John Chetham, expressed the
philosophy of all his fellows (and was universally quoted in nearly the same
words) when he stated: 'the design of this undertaking is to better and improve
this excellent & useful part of our Service, to keep up an uniformity in our
Parish-Churches, and bring them as much as may be to imitate their Mother-
Churches the Cathedrals.'[5]

The idea that parishes should imitate cathedrals was contrary to the conventional wisdom and usual interpretation of church history of the time. The
disparity between the two was more often highlighted, particularly in terms of
musical practice. Did the Book of Common Prayer offer a clear choice? Many
thought not. One clergyman spoke for others when he said: 'the rubrics
indeed say sung or said, by which I do not suppose be intended a *discretionary*
power to do either at pleasure, but that in Choirs, and places where they sing,
they should be sung, and said in Parish Churches, where they do not sing.'[6]
The dichotomy between cathedral and parish music was as precisely perceived
at the end of the century as at the beginning, despite a growing challenge to
their complete separation:

According to the usage of the Church of England, Music is either Cathedral or
Parochial.

[3] David Hunter, 'English Country Psalmodists and their Publications, 1700–1760', *JRMA* 115 (1990), 220.
[4] Ibid. 225, 229.   [5] John Chetham, *A Book of Psalmody* (London, 1718), preface.
[6] Richard Banner, *Use and Antiquity of Musick*, 23.

1. Cathedral Music being scientific, is confined to those only who are masters of the science.

2. Parochial Music is designed for the people at large; it is therefore simple, intelligible, and easily attainable by ear.[7]

There were many ways that a closer interchange might be effected, nevertheless. The suggestion was put forward 'for the Parochial Way, especially in the great churches, to be raised up, in some measure, to the Choir.'[8] This was also the message preached by the widely read and influential Thomas Bisse, Chancellor of Hereford Cathedral, whose words urging parishes to imitate their mother churches may have been John Chetham's direct inspiration. Bisse made many suggestions in his sermons for changes in parish worship that would bring them closer to cathedral practice, for instance, the proposal that parishes should sing the metrical psalm in the same place in the liturgy that the anthem is sung in cathedrals.

Some parish musicians took Bisse's advice and imitated cathedrals in the kinds of music they published and by adopting musical ideas, such as the standard four voice-parts of the cathedral choir to 'make up that fullness of consonancy which cannot be expected in two or three.'[9] Entries in glossaries from parish music books reflect cathedral practice, for example; choral music: 'music sung by turns by two opposite Choirs';[10] choir: 'signifies a chosen set of singers that answers one another by turns in any of our Mother Churches, or Cathedrals';[11] recitative: 'to sing in a tone like grave chanting';[12] and chant: 'to sing as practised in the cathedrals'.[13] John Ivery's glossary contained quite a few cathedral references:

canto-ferme—Church-tune, or chant.
Note ferme—the reading-tone in chants.
Plain-Chant, or Plain Song—the church-tune.
Choral Musick—Is eight parts, which are sung by turns, &c.
Services—Church hymns, &c. set to musick.
Te deum—A famous church-hymn or service, composed by St. Ambrose; and frequently sung as a national Thanksgiving for a victory.
Trisagium, or Trisagion—A church hymn with three holies.[14]

The reform in parish church music reputedly had already achieved some success by the end of the first quarter of the century:

[7] William Vincent, *Considerations on Parochial Music* (London, 1787), 2.
[8] *Rubrick of the Church of England*, 17.   [9] Chetham, *Psalmody*, preface.
[10] John Arnold, *The Compleat Psalmodist* (London, 1741), 31.
[11] John Buckenham, *The Psalm-Singer's Devout Exercise* (London, 1741).   [12] Ibid.
[13] John Crompton, *The Psalm-Singer's Assistant* (London, 1778), p. cxx.
[14] John Ivery, *The Hertfordshire Melody* (London, 1773).

It is evident from experience, that singing in our Parish Churches and Chapels, may be improved to a great degree, and that where is a competent number to learn, and due encouragement given, they may in a short time become masters of the greatest part of this book and perform the Te Deum, Jubilate &c. as in several Churches they do now, to the great satisfaction of all those that understand Divine Music, and indeed of the audience in general.[15]

The liturgical music in publications for parishes was most often arranged in a special section of the book under the collective title *Chanting-tunes*, broadly meaning music to be sung in imitation of cathedrals. This special section included both chant tunes and through-composed settings. In the latter half of the century cathedral terminology largely replaced the generic title *Chanting-tunes*, except in a few editions of country collections. The 1811 edition of Chetham's psalmody still used it. John Arnold's new sectional title, 'A Set of Services, commonly called Chanting-Tunes', in the 1753 edition of *Compleat Psalmodist*, anticipated his forward-looking edition of 1779.

The service music in parish books published after mid-century was drawn from diverse sources. Some pieces came directly from cathedral repertories, but single or paired canticles were also specially composed for parish choirs. At least a dozen books contain selections of chants in the new standard notation by cathedral composers. In the main, this service music reflects changing tastes in town churches where organs, choirs, and trained musicians could better imitate cathedral style and performance practice. In country churches, volunteer choirs could choose from the same kinds of music, but instead of organs, accompaniment for the singers was often provided by wind or string instruments. After 1790 some churches had mechanical barrel organs and many barrels contained chants as well as metrical psalm tunes.[16]

Parish music books often claimed to be adaptable to any type of church and frequently advertised this intention on their title-pages. Thomas Jackson, organist at Newark on Trent, published a collection of church music in 1780 with the following title:

Twelve Psalm Tunes and Eighteen Double and Single Chants with a new Species of Chant to the Benedicite, the Psalm Tunes may be adapted to the Old or New Version and are very proper for Cathedral, Collegiate, Parochial & Country Choirs: the whole Composed for four Voices.

Early in the century, however, music for chanting in town and country churches was a new phenomenon.

[15] Chetham, *Psalmody* (3rd edn., 1724), preface.
[16] N. Boston and L. G. Langwill, *Church and Chamber Barrel-Organs* (Edinburgh, 1967), 20–30; K. H. Macdermott, *The Old Church Gallery Minstrels* (London, 1948), 39–42; Temperley, *MEPC*, i. 234–9.

Robert Barber, psalmodist of Castleton in Derbyshire, published in 1733 the first complete order of service expressly for a parish choir in *A Book of Psalmody*. The new music and style of singing for chanting-tunes is advertised in Barber's title: '. . . with chanting-Tunes for Te Deum, Jubilate Deo, Magnificat, Nunc Dimittis; likewise the Order of performing Divine Service by Way of chanting, after the Cathedral Manner, suitable for our Country Churches . . .'. John Arnold, psalmodist of Great Warley, Essex published another order of service in 1741. Both are adapted from John Playford's 'Order of Performing the Divine Service in Cathedrals and Collegiate Chapels' in the seventh edition of *Introduction to the Skill of Music*. Between nine editions of Playford (1674 to 1730), two of Barber (1733, 1753), and six of Arnold (1741 to 1769), a choral service for Morning Prayer, the Litany, and Communion was readily available to parochial musicians who wanted to try out chanting in their churches. Some did so, for example in Selby Abbey in Yorkshire, where Bishop Pococke saw that 'they chant all their service, except the litany; and the clerk goes up to the communion table and stands on the epistle side to make the responses, and they sing well not only the psalms but anthems.'[17]

Playford's cathedral choral service was arranged differently in the publications in which it appeared. John Arnold copied the opening monotone recitation for the Lord's Prayer and Preces and Responses without alteration, but Robert Barber set these parts for three voices moving in octaves and fifths, ending with a V–I Amen. A more extended cadence closes the doxology (Ex. 6.1).[18] Barber's Venite exultemus is arranged in the alternatim fashion much favoured by parochial composers. The first verse is sung by tenor and bass with recitation on C, and the next to a different melody, by countertenor and bass reciting on G. Barber set the second phrase of the doxology, 'as it was in the beginning', for four voices with a short closing amen. In contrast, Arnold's Venite imitates the older form of psalmody indicated by Playford's rubric, 'Venite is begun by one of the Choir, then sung by sides'. The chant tune is Turner in A (see above, Fig. 1, no. 14) and the first verse of text is set out on the tenor clef for 'the Priest'.

Arnold copied Playford's monotone recitation for the remaining chanted portions of the liturgy, the Apostle's Creed, Suffrages, and Litany, while Barber continued on with his three-voice arrangement. Arnold's response for the Commandments in the Second Service, the English Kyrie, is the most unusual chant in any of the parish orders of service. The music is in two parts,

---

[17] Richard Pococke, *The Travels through England of Dr. Richard Pococke*, ed. J. J. Cartwright (2 vols.; London, 1888–9), i. 173. There was no organ in the Abbey, only a volunteer choir and some instruments (Temperley, *MEPC*, i. 169).
[18] Responses transcribed in Temperley, *MEPC*, ii. 166, ex. 65a.

Ex. 6.1. Barber's 1733 Preces and Responses from Playford

Priest and Choir

Our fa-ther, which art etc.   for ev-er and ev-er A - men.

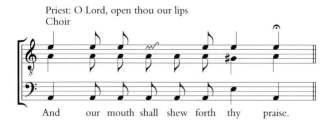

Priest: O Lord, open thou our lips
Choir

And   our mouth shall shew forth thy   praise.

Priest: O God, make speed to save.   Choir: O Lord, make haste to help us.
Priest: Glory be to the Father, etc.
Choir

As   it was in the be-gin-ning etc.   - - out end A - men.

the melody for the choir and a lower part labelled 'organum', presumed to be for the organ or lower voices. Is it too fanciful to suggest that Arnold portrays here the same type of performance that Roger North described as an example of 'plainsong practice'?

There are certain grave airs to be found, or composed for the purpose, and some used in the cathedral services very proper, as the versicle between the Commandments and as a pattern I have shadowed a consort part . . . set for a lower part, but the same methods serve for the superiors, the notes being disposed accordingly.[19]

North's consecutive sixths between voices in the second phrase and fifth and octave at cadences do hint at an older kind of improvisation. The melodies of both the Arnold and North Kyries have some similarities in contour, for example, the descending second phrase of the upper parts (Ex. 6.2).

---

[19] Wilson, *North on Music*, 237–8.

Ex. 6.2. Response to Commandments: (*a*) Arnold, 1741; (*b*) North, early eighteenth century

(*a*)

(*b*)

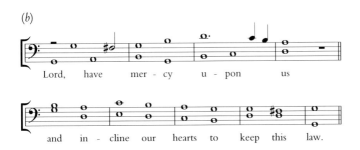

The Commandments and the Epistle and Gospel were part of the ante-Communion portion of the liturgy, and therefore heard more often than the full Communion service. It is not altogether unexpected to find music for the Commandments and for the traditional response to the naming of the Gospel in parish collections. William Tans'ur, for instance, composed a 'New Response, or Answer to the Ten Commandments' similar to cathedral settings in its extension of the last response, but the rough harmonization and voice-leading betray an unfamiliarity with the idiom. One of the most popular responses in cathedrals and parishes was William Mason's Kyrie in D, a miniature verse anthem with a pretty melody and the customary graces, the brief solo phrases sung by trebles in thirds. The traditional Gospel acclamation was usually set in a simple, syllabic style, whether for parish or cathedral. Richard Langdon's typical four-part response in *Divine Harmony* (1784) carries an alla breve time signature, but the tempo direction indicates that the response was sung slowly.

The Sanctus, when sung, was more often used as an introit to Second Service than in its normal position in the liturgy, and special settings were composed for this purpose. Even though many of these pieces set an entirely unrelated text, they were all called 'Sanctus'. Richard Wainwright, the organist at Manchester, composed a typical 'Sanctus' with the text 'I will wash my Hands in Innocency O Lord and so will I go to thine Altar.'[20] Another popular type of setting added a final Hallelujah chorus to the liturgical Sanctus text. In parishes, a new custom of singing a metrical psalm in the place the Sanctus was sung in cathedrals came into use, and Ralph Thoresby noted the beginning of this practice in Leeds Parish Church early in the century. He confirmed that it was already known in the capital and elsewhere:

3 Oct. 1708: . . . a new order of [singing] was begun this day in the parish church, to sing a stave betwixt the daily morning and communion service (as has been long done at London, &c.) and is more agreeable, making a greater distinction, as there ought to be, betwixt the several parts.[21]

The Arnold and Barber orders of service were minimally altered in later printings. Barber (1753) added a four-part doxology to his Preces and Responses and omitted the Second Service, while Arnold (1761) replaced his plainsong-like Kyrie response with Barber's original four-part response. How often responses or prose psalms may have been chanted in parish churches remains a matter for considered speculation. The Barber and Arnold musical services were the only ones published, besides Playford's, for either parish or cathedral use in the eighteenth century. The editions specially arranged and published for parishes at least show what was probably sung in London and in the regions outside of London in which these books were used—South Yorkshire, Derbyshire, and Essex.

The parish music books published between 1718 and 1820 that contain formulaic chants, the alternatim chant settings excepted, are catalogued in Appendix B. The entries are listed in order according to date of publication with a brief summary of the chants in each. The formulaic chants for parishes early in the century were less often paired with canticle texts than with the Venite exultemus, and a number of compilers copied Chetham's directions to fit any of the prose psalms to the same music. While psalm chanting must have been tried out, there is no verifiable evidence to suggest that the printed music and text signalled widespread psalm chanting. A single chant often made a one-time appearance in an otherwise metrical psalm and hymn book, although a few chants were reprinted in many successive editions. The total number of chants is not large compared with the repertory of alternatim canticles, but the sample is sufficiently varied, even so, to demonstrate some of the processes of adaptation common to functional music.

---

[20] Manchester Public Record Office, Music MS 341 Cr 71.
[21] Ralph Thoresby, *The Diary of Ralph Thoresby*, ed. Joseph Hunter (2 vols.; London, 1830), ii. 10.

The melodic phrases sometimes recall the old psalm-tone melodies, while others are immediately recognizable as faithful copies or altered versions of composed cathedral chant tunes. A clear legacy from the Sarum psalm-tone system occasionally turns up, such as the tone 5, third ending cadence in the second phrase tenor of John Bellamy's Venite in *A System of Divine Musick* (1745). Of the several William Turner chant tunes that made their way into parish use, the tune in A major (see above, Fig. 1, no. 14) was most widely copied. It appears in its chant form in nearly twenty parish collections, and in many more in the arranged version of the Chetham Te deum. Francis Timbrell's 'Chant for Singing the reading Psalms as it is sung in Cathedral Churches' is so far the first known parish printing of the Turner chant.[22] Except for transposition a tone lower, the notation is the same as Turner's seventeenth-century autograph. Timbrell has observed cathedral practice in leaving the melody in the treble, whereas the tenor was the customary melody part in parish music of that time. The first verse of Venite exultemus is underlaid and verses 2 through 11 are printed below the music. Timbrell added a doxology in 1722, and in later editions reduced the four voice-parts to three by omitting Turner's tenor. There were some alterations in key and voice-parts in other parish printings, and one compiler changed the text to Cantate domino, the choice of Scottish and American psalmodists. These various changes are collated in Table 6.1.

A few other chants are paired with Venite in parish music collections, such as Chetham's four-part chant in his second edition (1724). The general directions for chanting any of the 'reading psalms' to the same music was an invitation to parishes to try out psalm chanting, and quite possibly a response to the progress in chanting he reported in the preface.

This, or any other Tune of this kind, may suit the whole Book of Psalms, commonly called the Reading Psalms: Due regard being had to the Points, (i.e.) by observing to proceed upon the same that (&c.) is fixed or, be the Verse long or short, 'till one comes to those notes that are before the Points in the Middle, and before the End of the Verse. The Amen may fit any other that is in the same Key.

These instructions, worded slightly differently, accompany a minimally altered version of Chetham's Venite chant in James Green's 1730 *Book of Psalmody* (Ex. 6.3). There are a few changed pitches and chord voicings at the beginning of the first phrase and in the second, and in the Amen, a dominant chord intervenes between Chetham's subdominant and tonic final. Green's second recitation is also on the dominant, whereas Chetham's recitations in both

---

[22] Francis Timbrell, *The Divine Music Scholars Guide* (London, *c.*1720), British Library shelf mark A.1232.1.

TABLE 6.1. *Pre-1800 parish sources of Turner in A*

HTI code[a]	Editor and title	Key	Parts	Tune	Text	Alterations
PlayJL_7	J. Playford, Introduction to the Skill of Musick, 1674	A	4	Tr	Ve	Ct has E in 1st chord in termination
TimbFDM_b–d	F. Timbrell, The Divine Musick Scholar's Guide, 1720, 1723, 1724	G	4	Tr	Ve	T G♯ omitted in mediant
BettEISM	E. Betts, Introduction to the Skill of Musick, 1724	A	4	Tr	Ve	Copied from Playford
BrooMCCP_b	M. Broome, A Choice Collection of Psalm-Tunes, 1730	G	4	Tr	Ve	Same as Timbrell
BrooMMBC_b–d	M. Broome, Michael Broom's Collection of Church music, 1726–9	G	4	T	Ve	T and Tr interchanged
GreeJBP_8, 9	J. Green, A Book of Psalmody, 1734, 1738	C	4	T	Cd	Tr and Ct altered in mediant
SreeJOH3	J. Sreeve, The Oxfordshire Harmony, iii, 1741	G	3	Tr	Ve	B has 7th in 1st chord in termination
BeesMBP_c–h	M. Beesly, A Book of Psalmody 1743–52	G	4	Tr	Ve	Dotted rhythms both phrases
ArnoJCP_1–5, 7	J. Arnold, The Compleat Psalmodist, 1741–79	C	4	T	Ve	Copied from Green
TimbFDM_o, r	F. Timbrell, The Divine Musick Scholar's Guide, 1737, 1748	G	3	Tr	Ve	T omitted
TansWRM_1–3	W. Tans'ur, The Royal Melody Compleat, Book III, 1755, 1760, 1766	C	4	T	Ve	Music as in Green

[a] See p. xvi above for an explanation of HTI source codes.

Ex. 6.3. Parish chants for Ve and psalms: (*a*) Chetham, 1724; (*b*) Green, 1730

(*a*)

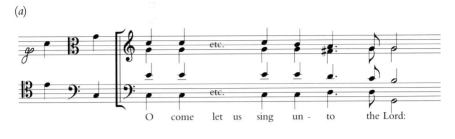

(*b*)

phrases are on the tonic. Green's penultimate tenor D♯ is evidently a mistake and has been omitted in the example.

Chetham's chants assigned to the Benedicite, alternate canticle to Te deum in Morning Prayer, and Nunc dimittis in Evening Prayer are, according to present dating, the earliest chants printed in a parish collection. His choice of text appears unusual and may well indicate that the chants were for special use. On the other hand, both were popular in metrical form. The Benedicite was sung in Rogationtide processions when the parish boundaries were perambulated, the 'processioning' led by the clergy and choir:

the Sacrist, resident prebendaries, and members of the choir, assembled at morning-prayers on Monday and Tuesday in Rogation week, with the charity-children, bearing long poles cloathed with all kinds of flowers then in season, and which were afterwards carried through the streets of the town with much solemnity, the clergy, singing men, and boys, dressed in their sacred vestments, closing the Procession, and chanting, in a grave and appropriate melody, the Canticle, Benedicite, omnia opera, etc.[23]

The chants for Benedicite in parish collections in the latter half of the century may have been intended to be sung on these or other special occasions rather than in liturgical order in Morning Prayer. The second phrase of the Benedicite text repeats in each verse, making possible a verse and choral refrain approach to its performance. The refrain is very often set in triple metre, as for example, in Thomas Jackson's 'new Species of Chant to the Benedicite'.

Chetham's chant for the Nunc dimittis by itself may indicate an early beginning to the custom of singing the Nunc dimittis as a dismissal hymn, although some parish collections simply selected one canticle from Morning Prayer and one from Evening Prayer. The tenor melodies in both chants show close affinities with psalm tones, Benedicite with tone 8 and Nunc dimittis with tone 1. The first verse of text is indicated and cadential syllables placed beneath their notes (Ex. 6.4). The hold sign over the mediant cadence chords takes the place of a barline between phrases. Chetham closed each chant, as he did the Venite chant, with an Amen sung to two chords in the harmonic progression of subdominant to tonic, for which there are few precedents. Cathedral chant tunes and canticle and psalm settings characteristically closed on dominant–tonic progressions.

Amen is the last word in the doxology prescribed by rubric to be sung or said after each psalm and canticle. It is possible that Chetham was imitating here the way these final chords sounded in cathedral chanting, which suggests that final cadences were sung more slowly than the cadences in verses of the

---

[23] Stebbing Shaw, *The History and Antiquities of Staffordshire* (London, 1801), ii. 165, quoted in Legg, *English Church Life*, 230, app. II.

Ex. 6.4. Chetham's 1718 chants: (*a*) Bte; (*b*) Nd

(*a*)

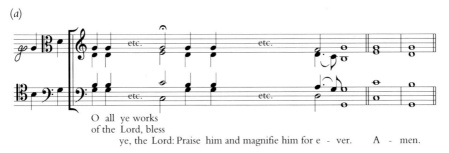

O all ye works
of the Lord, bless
ye, the Lord: Praise him and magnifie him for e - ver.   A - men.

(*b*)

Lord now lettest
thou thy servant
de - part in   peace: ac-cor-ding   to   thy word.   A -   men.

psalm or canticle text. The only obvious precedent for separate chordal Amens in notated form are those which follow the recitation of each Collect in Morning or Evening Prayer, when the responses in the rest of the service are sung in four parts. The Amens to the Collects in Tallis's setting of the Responses are IV–I, V–I, and IV–I chords in F. Since Tallis's Responses were those most commonly heard, they could have been the model for the separate Amens in Chetham's chants.

Chetham's use of the subdominant–tonic final cadence, in any case, extends beyond imitation of the short Amen. His alternatim canticles also have final subdominant–tonic progressions, even though verses alternating dominant and tonic harmonies are an important feature of their structure. Chetham frequently uses V–I–IV–I chords in extended Amens (Ex. 6.5(*a*)), a sequence also present in the chordal Amen to his Cantate chant, in which the verse ends inconclusively on a dominant rather than tonic chord (Ex. 6.5(*b*)). The Cantate chant is an interesting version of John Blow's cathedral chant tune in E minor, transposed up a tone to F sharp minor, the melody kept in the top voice. Blow's final resolution to the tonic is held over the double bar, when the countertenor sings the F♯ and the treble moves up to C♯. The F♯ is then held over into the last bar while the harmony changes to the subdominant, resolving finally on the tonic.

Ex. 6.5. Chetham's plagal Amens: (*a*) in Td, 1718 and Mg, 1724 (extended); (*b*) in Cd adapted from Blow in E minor

(*a*)

(*b*)

At the least, the plagal cadences in parish chants and written-out alternatim canticles indicate an environment in which subdominant harmony was acceptable, even conventional. Improvised parts to metrical psalm tunes yielded octaves, fifths, and fourths, especially in rhythmically strong parts of the music.[24] Up to the early eighteenth century and in some rural parishes into the latter part of the nineteenth century, metrical psalms were sung in the old

---

[24] W. H. Tallmadge, 'Folk Organum: A Study of Origins', *American Music*, 2, (1984), 61.

style of unaccompanied unison singing. An example of this 'Old Way of Singing' for Ps. 4 can be found in the first edition of Chetham's psalmody collection, published when he was already 53 years of age.[25] Other parish compilers also had experience of the 'Old Way of Singing' and of improvised harmony to psalm-tune melodies. In the nineteenth century, a short plagal cadence was commonly attached to hymn and psalm tunes and became known as the 'Amen cadence'. The Amen which comes at the end of parish chants and alternatim canticles must surely be considered as an important precedent.

In the first half of the eighteenth century, chant arrangements of the morning and evening canticles, written out with full text underlay, were the choice of the majority of parish compilers. These are alternatim settings in the form of alternating vocal textures, with an appropriate key change in each verse of the text. In their formal structure, they imitate the cathedral choir practice of singing some or all verses of a text, whether a composed setting or chant tune, in a sequence alternating decani and cantoris sides. The spatial and musical effect of chanting a prose psalm antiphonally, or singing a verse service with alternating choir and solo verses, most likely inspired the parish alternatim canticle setting. The antiphonal effect had to be created in some other way, however, for the divisions of the cathedral choir were rarely within the bounds of practical consideration for new parish choirs. The formation of voluntary parish choirs was a relatively young development in the early eighteenth century and their separation from the congregation in a special pew, or singing gallery, was quite new. Even if a parish choir was seated in a separate gallery they would still be performing in a body, since the 'singing seats' would be together.[26]

The paradigm for all alternatim canticles was a Te deum published by John Chetham in the first edition of *Book of Psalmody* (1718). This Te deum on the melody of Turner in A, as well as Chetham's other chants for Nunc dimittis and Benedicite, appears to have been taken down from a performance, both by written form and internal structure. Alternately, Chetham or someone else made this special arrangement expressly for parishes. At first glance, the dotted rhythms of the Te deum suggest a very different kind of performance than the flexible recitation and slow cadence of the cathedral chant tune. But it must also be remembered that many notated versions of the Turner chant in cathedral manuscripts have dotted-note articulations in both mediant and terminal cadences, and these may have been ornamented and extended to produce a more definite metrical feeling. From later cathedral sources, we know that the cadences of a chant were directed to be sung in stricter metre than the

---

[25] Nicholas Temperley, 'The Old Way of Singing: Its Origins and Development', *JAMS* 34 (1981), 527.
[26] Temperley, *MEPC*, i. 151–62.

recitation. It is not impossible that Chetham actually heard a performance that sounded like the two phrases he printed.

Chetham made one structural pitch alteration in Turner's melody by keeping the second recitation on the third of the mediant cadence chord. The first verse is sung by tenor and bass, and the second by countertenor and bass singing the melody a fifth higher in the key of the dominant (Ex. 6.6). Succeeding verses have small variations. The vocal duos alternate verses until the last and the closing doxology is sung in four-part harmony, the melody remaining in the tenor. The Chetham plagal amen, with some slight decoration in the inner voices, concludes the piece.

Chetham has written a different bass line for verses 5, 17, and 21 (Ex. 6.7(*a*)). In verse 21, an alternate for six other of the tenor and bass verses, the first recitation chord is changed to E minor. The tenor part is marked 'sung as before'. These verses strongly suggest another potential influence on the Te deum, that it imitates some form of verse service rather than a chant performance. The alternate verses for countertenor and bass present even more compelling evidence. A florid second phrase with a running semiquaver pattern is suggested for alternate versions of verses 7 and 8 (Ex. 6.7(*b*)). These verses together are introduced with the note, 'for further variety, these verses may be sung thus'. Their use is therefore optional and their source a matter of great interest.

Melodic decoration of this kind was not unfamiliar in cathedral or parish music. Organ preludes and interludes for both prose and metrical psalm tunes, for instance, used small-note figures in sequential patterns. Florid melodies can be found in solo verses in the cathedral verse service and anthem and in the chanting service. One of Henry Aldrich's services, his setting of the morning and evening canticles in A major, opens with a melody having the same pitches as Turner's chant tune, in nearly the same organization. This service was copied in many cathedral music manuscripts around the turn of the century and the possibility of it being the service imitated in the Chetham Te deum is intriguing. Other verses of the Aldrich Te deum are similar in phraseology and contour, with small-note figures suspiciously like those in Chetham's verses 7 and 8, and cadences are frequently enlivened with dotted rhythms (Ex. 6.8).

The answer at the fifth in the dominant key in the Chetham Te deum formalizes a tonic–dominant relationship that is often found in the phrase structure of cathedral canticle settings. Hawkins's Chanting Service in D major, for example, follows a dominant–tonic harmonic scheme throughout. Cathedral double chant tunes also frequently cadence on the dominant at mid-point and begin their second half recitation in the dominant key. Arthur Bedford noted

Ex. 6.6. Chetham Te deum, 1718: (a) odd vv. 1, 3, etc.; (b) even vv. 2, 4, etc.; (c) final verse in four parts

(a)

We praise thee O   God: we acknow-ledge-thee to be   the Lord.

(b)

All the earth doth wor - ship thee: the Father   a - ver-last - ing.

(c)

O   Lord   in thee have I trus - ted   let me ne-ver be   con -

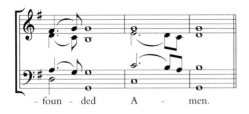

- foun - ded   A -   men.

Ex. 6.7. Alternative verses: (*a*) bass lines; (*b*) second phrase, vv. 7 and 8

(*a*)

v. 5 first phrase

Ho - ly Ho - ly Ho - ly, etc.

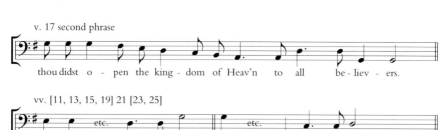

v. 17 second phrase

thou didst o - pen the king - dom of Heav'n to all be - liev - ers.

vv. [11, 13, 15, 19] 21 [23, 25]

Make them etc. with thy saints: in glo - ry e - ver-last - ing.

(*b*)

The glor-ious a - po - stles: prai - - - se thee.

The good-ly ... pro - phets: prai - - - se thee.

that in single chants 'the middle close at the colon is usually made in some other place of the Gamut, differing both from the full close of all, and also from the chanting part, (the Base usually closing in the fifth above the key)'.[27] The Chetham Te deum amplifies this contrast by alternating the tonic and dominant harmonic scheme at each complete verse, and by assigning alternate verses to different vocal combinations.

[27] Bedford, *Temple Musick*, 162.

Ex. 6.8. Aldrich's Te deum in A, first and last verse

We know-ledge thee to be the Lord: all the

earth doth wor - ship thee thou art the Fa-ther e - ver-last - ing.

O Lord in thee have I trus - ted let me ne ver-be con-foun - ded let me

ne-ver ne - ver be con-foun - ded let me ne-ver be con - foun - ded

The Chetham Te deum was reprinted almost immediately in Green's *Collection of Psalm Tunes* (1718), where it is transposed to F major. An alternate verse with the semiquaver sequential figures has been added for four more of the countertenor and bass verses. A fully written-out version appeared in Robert and John Barber's *A Book of Psalmody* in 1723.[28] It follows Chetham's in most details, though a harmonic alteration omits the bass C♯ in the verses on the dominant. Most subsequent printings are also fully written out, with the notable exception of Chetham's own short formula in his second edition (1722). In this chant tune in B flat, the first two verses are set for four voices with the melody in the treble. Gone are the florid melodies for alternate verses, and in their place a simple direct symbol at the end of the line shows that remaining text verses are to be fitted to the same music. Rhythmic articulations remain, but the chant seems a pale shadow of its former self.

Chetham repeated the four-part Te deum chant in his third edition (1724), but returned the melody to the tenor voice. Now in C major, this even plainer chant is the one found in Chetham editions for the rest of the century. The psalm tunes in this third edition are also fewer and simpler, but the severity of the collection may have been unpopular with the public, for the fourth edition (1731) brought back the old preface and more ornate tunes.[29] For some practical reason or local circumstance, perhaps, the original Te deum, with its rhythmic vitality and alternating duos singing ornamented melodies, was not revived.

Other parish compilers obviously preferred the rhythmic piece first published by Chetham in 1718, since an overwhelming number of the total repertory of alternatim canticles is based on its form and structure; fifty-six of seventy-six pieces belong in the Turner in A melodic group. Although small variants in pitch and rhythm are found in the most faithful copies of the Chetham Te deum, and more extensive alterations appear in the many adaptations, the original melodic contour is always recognizable and shows how quickly the chant-tune melody became common property (Ex. 6.9). Unusual in parish collections is the simultaneous printing of two different but musically related Te deum settings, seen in the second and third items. Israel Holdroyd, from the Halifax area, printed the first in the part of his book he claimed to be entirely of his own composition, the second with a name possibly related to its rhythm. The lineage of both is, of course, unmistakable.

The general preference for Chetham's original Te deum is evident in the changed, but consistently dotted note-values of Robert Barber's successive editions. Dotted rhythms are also preserved in an adaptation of the Chetham

---

[28] See complete transcription in Temperley, *MEPC*, ii. 80, ex. 31b.
[29] Table of editions and contents ibid. i. 183.

Ex. 6.9. Chetham Td melody in parish alternatim canticles: (*a*) Jd, Barber 1723; (*b*) Td, Holdroyd 1724; (*c*) 'French' Td, Holdroyd 1724; (*d*) Mg, Green 1730; (*e*) Nd, Green 1730; (*f*) Td, Bellamy 1745; (*g*) Td, Davenport 1755; (*h*) Td, Street 1785

Te deum published by Ralph Harrison in *Sacred Harmony* (1788). He regularized the note-values of the reciting portion and turned the chant setting into a long metre tune called Sterling (Ex. 6.10).

Ex. 6.10. Sterling Tune adapted by Harrison from the Chetham Td

Two other melodic groups can be isolated in the alternatim canticle repertory, one in the minor mode and one with a variant of Imperial Tune in the opening phrase. Compared to the overwhelming number of canticles based on Chetham's original Te deum, the thirteen settings using the minor mode melody occupy a distant second place. The first of these is James Green's Magnificat (1718), which appears to be arranged from Chetham's chant for the companion evening canticle, Nunc dimittis. Green has copied the Nunc dimittis, and the Te deum and Benedicite as they appear in Chetham. For the Magnificat, Green's top voice, written in the treble G clef, is made up of Chetham's first-phrase treble, with an added upward inflection, and second-phrase tenor. The alternating verse closes on the dominant, but the melody, now in the tenor C clef, consists of C, B, C with mediant cadence in C major, and second phrase of C, D, E twice (Ex. 6.11). The four-voice Amen is the usual plagal cadence.

The number of settings in the third melodic grouping is relatively small in English sources, but the same variant can be found in a widely reprinted Scottish Te deum. The opening phrase of a triple chant first printed by James Dallas, a singing master in Edinburgh, also has the variant Imperial Tune, which has accrued a downward inflection to the seventh scale degree (see below, Ex. 7.3). The Dallas Te deum may be an arrangement of the English parish alternatim canticle, or it may be of Scottish origin (these details are explored in the next chapters). Robert Bremner's printing of the Dallas triple

Ex. 6.11. Green's Magnificat chant (1718), vv. 1 and 2

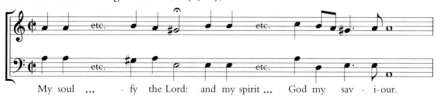

My soul ... - fy the Lord: and my spirit ... God my sav - i-our.

For he hath re - gar-ded the low-li - ness ··· hand - mai - den. A - men.

Te deum launched it on a new and long-running career, both in Scotland and in the United States. It was paired with Te deum and Gloria in excelsis by William Smith, an American clergyman of Scottish descent, in an 1809 collection. The Gloria in excelsis version has been sung in American Episcopal churches since the early nineteenth century and is still in the repertory. Coincidentally, this first-phrase Imperial Tune variant is the same melody, leaving out the intonation, that John Merbecke used for Gloria in excelsis.

During the course of the eighteenth century, the proportion of alternatim canticles in parish collections gradually declined in favour of chants in standard notation and single canticles borrowed from cathedral settings. Henry Hall's Te deum in E flat, Benjamin Rogers's Kyrie in D, Hine's Jubilate deo in E flat, and a Nunc Dimittis by John Alcock are among the pieces published in parish collections. These 'set tunes', as John Chetham called them, included canticles, responses, and doxologies. Some of the arrangements seem to be intended for special uses or to be sung as anthems, for example, Chetham's Gloria (1724) from Henry Purcell's Service in D. Another Gloria, 'A Canon Four in One by the late Dr. Blow', from the Jubilate deo in Blow's Short Service in G, was published by Edward Betts in *Introduction to the Skill of Musick* (1724). The canticles specially composed for parish or country choirs are mostly homophonic in texture, with accompaniments in some pieces written for wind instruments. Thomas Billington's paired morning and evening canticles on the Chetham Te deum melody, for instance, are set for three voices and bassoon and cello.[30]

---

[30] Thomas Billington, *The Te deum, Jubilate, Magnificat, and Nunc dimittis . . . Instructions to the Performers* (London, [1784]).

The number of chants published in general collections for parish use increased dramatically towards the end of the century and in the first two decades of the nineteenth. These publications are described in the annotated catalogue of parish music books with chants from 1718 to 1820 in Appendix B. Two publications contained only chants, Dixon's *Canto Recitativo*, a pointed psalter and matching chants in Dixon's own system of short notation, and Philip Knapton's *A Collection of Chants used in the Church of St. Saviour, York*, one of the earliest chant books for a specific parish church. The chant repertories range in size from one piece in William Jones's *Ten Church Pieces for the Organ* to the large repertory of over seventy single and double chants in Ralph Harrison's *Sacred Harmony*. The majority of the collections contain a dozen or less chants, some from the cathedral chant books that were just beginning to appear in print and others newly composed by cathedral and parish musicians.

Chants in parish music books were initially intended for choirs, but towards the end of the century the idea that congregations should chant parts of the liturgy gained ground. The theological basis for this idea was the desirability of congregational participation in all parts of public worship. The idea that chanting is a technique easily acquired by anyone was broadcast early in the century by William Law, a nonjuring high church man and the most effective writer, though not a formal member, of the early Evangelical movement.[31] Evangelical thinkers urged chanting prose psalms in private devotions and William Law gave them a reasoned argument for its spiritual advantages.

I do not mean, that you should read over a psalm, but that you should chant or sing one of those psalms, which we commonly call the reading psalms. For singing is as much the proper use of a psalm as devout supplication is the proper use of a form of prayer; and a psalm only read is very much like a prayer that is only looked over. Now the method of chanting a psalm, such as is used in the colleges, in the universities, and in some churches, is such as all persons are capable of. The change of voice in thus chanting of a psalm is so small and natural, that everyone is able to do it, and yet sufficient to raise and keep up the gladness of our hearts. You are therefore to consider this chanting of a psalm, as a necessary beginning of your devotions, as something that is to awaken all that is good and holy within you, that is to call your spirits to their proper duty, to set you in your best posture towards heaven, and tune all the powers of your soul to worship and adoration.[32]

Now chanting in the privacy 'of the closet' is a long way from a congregation chanting in prose together, but the notion of chanting being accessible to

---

[31] Abbey and Overton, *English Church . . . Eighteenth Century*, i. 575–88.
[32] William Law, *A Serious Call to a Devout and Holy Life* (London, 1729), 263. I wish to thank the Revd Alan Luff, Westminster Abbey, for this reference.

any learner was appealing to church music reformers. 'Reading in an even tone
is the first step to Chaunting', wrote Edward Hodges, and

if after reading *steadily* through some verses, a slight deflection of voice (the half tone
of musicians) be made on the penultimate syllable, there will be produced a very
agreeable musical effect. Hence originated the old Ecclesiastical Chaunt, which consisted of but few notes, and was sung of the whole congregation in unisons. This is
music of the simplest description, but such as is capable of association with the true
sublime. What is much to be regretted, it is rarely now heard, excepting in some parts
of the Cathedral service, and there but very sparingly . . .[33]

A belief that the ancient method of chanting involved the congregation was
one of the prevalent ideas in the renewed emphasis on liturgy in the late eighteenth and early nineteenth centuries. The important reason for using prose
translations of the psalms from the original Hebrew was the conception of such
texts being closer to the practice of the primitive church, and to the true
meaning of the Bible Psalms, than metrical versions. Granville Sharp's notes
on chanting reflect this Evangelical view: 'a Congregation may go through a
whole Psalm *with understanding*, in the time that would be required for singing
a mere detached stave or two, of the Metre Psalms in the common way.'[34]

Congregational chanting was tried out in a few places before the end of the
century, according to William Vincent, rector of All Hallows, London, who
proposed several reforms in parish music:

The first is, that adopted by some few chapels* in London and other places, where a

*Portland Chapel, the Octagon Chapel in Bath; and some Churches, if I am rightly informed,
in Lancashire.

band is appropriated to chant the Psalms, Te Deum, &c. and who are competent to
perform an Anthem with sufficient accuracy. This is a system which partakes more of
Cathedral, than Parochial service. But as the instruction of the performers is not so scientific as to give it all the advantages of the former, it would perhaps be wiser, if they
could be brought to lead the congregation in the performance of a Musical service
which all might partake in, than to assume a distinct share to themselves. A common
chant* is easily attainable by the ear; and if the same was always used, would soon

*For this purpose, no chant is better calculated than that which the charity children sing at
the conclusion of each psalm at St. Paul's.—It is composed by Mr. Jones, and has been
adopted in one congregation with success.

become familiar to the audience, and all be insensibly led to join in it.
A chant of this kind might not only become congregational, but national; . . . if such
a band as this could be made subservient to this purpose, it would contribute much

[33] Minimus [Edward Hodges], 'Church Music No. X', *The Bristol Mirror*, 12 May 1821.
[34] Granville Sharp, MS annotations, *Fifty Double and Single Chants*, British Library shelf mark E.487; see
App. E.

more to edification, both in the service, and the Psalms, than their own separate performance; and might point out the means of commencing and establishing a mode of public service at once consistent with reason, and the practice of the primitive Church.[35]

It was largely through the example and teaching of Evangelical clergymen that congregational chanting was pioneered in Yorkshire.[36] Jonathan Gray reported in 1821 that chanting had been revived within the last thirty years in parishes in 'many of our principle towns':[37]

the Congregations join in chanting the Venite Exultemus, the Te Deum, and Jubilate, the Magnificat, (or the Cantate Domino,) and the Nunc Dimittis, (or the Deus Miseratur,) with a happy and devotional effect. In proportion as the usage of the primitive ages is copied; in proportion likewise as the rites of the Church are respected, the structure of her poetry attended to, and her music duly appreciated, this mode of singing will be preferred above Metrical Psalmody.[38]

Edward Hodges reported in the same year that 'the practice of the legitimate style of Church Music is reviving. In many Parochial Churches, the hymns following the lessons are regularly chaunted, and the congregations begin to take a part in the performance.'[39] Matthew Camidge, organist of York Minster, printed the following note on the title-page of *24 Original Psalm and Hymn Tunes* (1823): 'as chanting is becoming general in Parish Churches the Author has subjoined Twenty four of his own Double Chants'. In one parish collection, L. B. Seeley transposed Turner's popular chant from A to C for Ps. 117:1, the first phrase marked for the choir and the second for the congregation.[40] John Beckwith put forward the thought that 'it is hardly possible not to admit the idea that a congregation may join in the antiphonal singing of the psalms in an undervoice, without injury to the choir'.[41] At the least, then, the congregation might be expected to be singing along in the psalms as well as the canticles.

Congregational chanting, and parish choir chanting as well, created a need for straightforward methods of teaching amateur singers how to allocate text syllables to their music. John Marsh was one of the first musicians to discuss this matter in print and to recommend marking prose texts with a stroke at the

[35] Vincent, *Parochial Music*, 10. Vincent was also Dean of Westminster 1802–15. The Jones chant covers a wide vocal range, but the first and third phrases are sung in unison, which makes it less difficult for amateur singers than it first appears (see below, n. 44).

[36] Temperley, *MEPC*, i. 215–23; id., *Jonathan Gray and Church Music in York, 1770–1840*, Borthwick Institute of Historical Research Publications, 51 (York, 1977).

[37] Jonathan Gray, *An Inquiry into Historical Facts relative to Parochial Psalmody* (York, 1821), 9.

[38] Ibid.   [39] Minimus [Edward Hodges], 'Church Music', 12 May 1821.

[40] L. B. Seeley, *Devotional Harmony*, ii (London, 1806).

[41] Beckwith, *First Verse of Every Psalm*, preface.

beginning of the cadence, or printing cadential text syllables in italics.[42] Since parish singers were for the most part inexperienced in cathedral chanting practices, more detailed information about assigning text syllables might have been expected in earlier parish publications, but very few have details beyond the often-copied general explanation John Chetham printed with his prose psalm tune in *Book of Psalmody* (1724). There is only a little more information, mainly for the organist, in William Tans'ur's 1755 directions for his 'Chanting-Tune, To the Reading Psalms'. The music is a version of Turner in A with the customary first verse of Venite exultemus underlaid, the last four notes matched in the old way with sal-va-ti-on. The organist was expected to lead the chanting:

To perform this Kind of Singing well, is of great Art; which being accompanied with an Organ, no Part of the Service is more grand: For, by observing these Points (:) in every Verse of the Psalms, you may perform any Psalm to the same Tune; by observing the Reading-Tone, and Cadence; especially, if the Organist is a good Hand, and has good Regard to the Length of every Verse; who may use Forte, or Piano at Pleasure; and perform all Verses of Importance, and Doxologies, with a Full Organ, &c.[43]

A few compilers early in the eighteenth century printed chants with at least one text verse aligned vertically underneath its music (see Exx. 6.3–5). Michael Broom laid out the complete text for Cantate domino underneath Edward Finch's eight-part chant, with the cadential syllables clearly shown (Ex. 6.12). This method was not pursued to its logical conclusion until the next century in America. In the texts that were printed for the canticles in parish books, it is clear that the conventional *rule of 3 & 5* was generally followed.

Fully written-out canticle chants with text and musical accent adjusted verse by verse were Benjamin Jacob's answer to the problem of correct accentuation.[44] His brief suggestions for performance of the chants suggest that by the early nineteenth century a different style of chanting was desired than early parish chants and alternatim canticles indicate was the common practice. The goal seemed to be to approximate the cathedral ideal more closely:

The Pause over certain words in the Recitative or speaking part of the Chants, is intended to shew the emphatic word which gives sense to the whole, and which should be forced and dwelt upon a little; it is also recommended, that this Recitative be not hurried, but every word pronounced distinctly.[45]

[42] John Marsh, *New Chants*, preface.
[43] William Tans'ur, *The Royal Melody Complete* (Book III, London, 1755), 140.
[44] Jacob's Jubilate deo to Jones's octave chant is transcribed in Temperley, *MEPC*, ii. 128, ex. 49.
[45] Benjamin Jacob[s], *National Psalmody* (Lambeth, 1817), preface.

Ex. 6.12. Broom's text underlay in chant by Finch from *Michael Broom's Collection of Church Musick*, 1725–9

O	sing	etc.	Lord a	new	song:	For	he hath done mar - vel - lous things.
The	Lord	etc.	his sal - va - tion:	his	etc.	sight of	the	heath - en.
Shew	your	etc.	Lord all ye	lands:	sing	re - joice and	give thanks.
With trumpets	etc.	and al - so	shawms:	O	shew ...	fore the Lord	the	King.
Let	the	etc.	be-fore the	Lord:	for	he is come to judge	ye	earth.

With his	etc.	ho - ly	arm:	hath he etc.	-self the	vic - to - ry.
He hath	etc.	Is - ra - el:	and	all the etc. -va - tion	of	our	God.
Praise the	etc.	on the	harp:	sing to the etc. psalm of	thanks - gi - ving.
Let the	etc.	there in	is:	the round	etc. they that dwell	there - in.
With	etc.	judge the	world:	and the peo - ple with	e - qui - ty.

The reformers of the next generation, who were responsible for the recovery of older chant traditions and ceremonial usages, would find the ground already prepared by the changes of the eighteenth century. Only country churches in remote areas remained unaffected by the movement to reform the Old Way of Singing and the trend towards performance of more elaborate service music. The psalmodists had served their clientele well and choirs in many outlying parishes were well established. All kinds of music was available in print for large town churches and small village churches, and a foundation had already been laid for a blend of influences and musical styles in service music. The music of the choral service was no longer the exclusive property of cathedrals and collegiate churches and chapels. Even the first efforts to emulate the physical aspects of cathedral music in parishes had already taken place. Leeds Parish Church accounts for 1818 record payments for salaries for choristers and the purchase of linen for surplices, a step that had been taken before 1800 in an Episcopal church in Scotland.[46]

The configuration of various styles of church music that came to be practised in parish churches turned out to be attractive to many denominations of Christians. The parish church could select freely from different musics practised by non-Anglicans, since it was not bound by a particular liturgical musical tradition, or by the historical expectation of a concomitant performance standard. It even became possible at the end of the eighteenth century to select music from Roman Catholic chapels without incurring the usual instantaneous censure of 'popery'.[47] The custom of singing metrical psalms was generally held to be the traditional parish music, but it was always legally separate from the Book of Common Prayer liturgy, and a number of writers on church music, for example Jonathan Gray in England and William Smith in America, debated the question of prose versus metre anew at the beginning of the nineteenth century.

The kind of service in which the canticles and doxologies were chanted, a metrical psalm sung before or after the sermon, with organ accompaniment, and an organ voluntary played before and after the service, turned out to be highly exportable. It was mainly this sort of parish musical practice that was imitated in eighteenth-century Scotland and in the new United States in the early nineteenth century.

---

[47] For the influence of the music sung in embassy chapels in London, for example, that by Samuel Webbe, George Paxton, and Samuel Webbe, Jr., see Temperley, 'Music in Church', 395–6; J. Vincent Higginson, 'Hymn Tunes from the Embassy Chapels', *The Hymn*, 1 (Oct. 1949), 5–12, and many other articles in 1969–76 issues of *The Hymn*. For plainsong, see Bennett M. Zon, 'Plainchant in the Eighteenth-Century Roman Catholic Church in England (1737–1834)', D. Phil. thesis (Oxford, 1994).

7

Music and Liturgy in the Episcopal Church of Scotland

> While we were indulged the more publick Exercises of our Ministry, many of the Established Communion, some for Curiosity, others, perhaps, with worse Design, came frequently to our chapels. They can tell what we said & taught, & to them appeal, whether at any time, even the most trying & critical, our Sermons have not been intended, & our Labour employed, in affirming & indicating the fundamental Truths of Religion, the essential Doctrines of the Gospel, in Opposition to Heresies & Innovations of whatever kind, & to the evident dreadful Growth of Deism & Infidelity? . . .
>
> As for our *Solemn Devotions*, they were no other than the Common Prayers & Liturgy of the Church of England, pure, & unmixed with any Addition of ours. And, it is humbly conceived, this could occasion no Jealousies, nor give any Offense, at least, not till that excellent Liturgy has, once again, had the same hard Fate in England, that Episcopacy has had in Scotland, which, I pray God, may never happen.[1]

THE main outlines of the history of the Episcopal Church in Scotland in the eighteenth century are well known, but the relationship between episcopalian parties is less clear. For over a century, Episcopalians in Scotland were divided by a physical and jurisdictional 'Schism'. Neither body conducted its public worship under the concurrent sanction of both church and state. The nonjuring congregations were governed by the remnant of Scottish Bishops descended from the pre-Reformation church, and they met for most of the eighteenth century under the threat of a series of Penal Laws, which outlawed their public and private worship. The qualified chapels belonged to no episcopal jurisdiction, although they were allowed by the government to worship publicly, if they used the English Book of Common Prayer and prayed for the Hanoverian royal family. The liturgies of these separate bodies, except for the Communion office, were in many respects the same. Nonjuring clergymen also used the English Book of Common Prayer, altering passages to suit their

---

[1] SRO:RSEC, CH 12/18/5, 118, 18 Aug. 1752, copy of a letter from the Revd William Harper, sen., to George Drummond, Esq., Lord Provost of Edinburgh.

needs. After the repeal of the Penal Laws in 1792, tentative moves towards reunion of congregations from both parties accelerated. The formal process began in 1804, when a convocation of clergy met in Laurencekirk and agreed to subscribe to the Thirty-Nine Articles of the Church of England, thus paving the way for the legal union of separated congregations as the Episcopal Church in Scotland.

The musical practice of the qualified chapels and the nonjuring chapels provided more contrast than similarity, however, due as much to circumstance as to theological belief. Episcopalians were not opposed, as a general rule, to other music besides metrical psalms in public worship, nor were they against the use of organs, as were the Presbyterians. Even so, the congregations worshipping underground, so to speak, especially after 1745, were restricted in resources and circumscribed by law. The qualified chapels could worship openly, and many installed organs and hired musicians, following the practice of the English parish church, singing music in the liturgy as well as metrical psalms. When the separate congregations of Episcopalians began to come together in the 1790s, the basic canon of liturgical music used in qualified chapels was quickly assimilated into the practice of the unified church.

Early in the eighteenth century the Schism deepened in the wake of the Toleration Act, strange as it may seem. *An Act to prevent the Disturbing of those of the Episcopal Communion in that part of Great Britain called Scotland in the exercise of their Religious Worship and in the use of the Liturgy of the Church of England* was passed by the Parliament of Great Britain in 1712.[2] It was the outcome of the 'Greenshields affair', when a clergyman ordained by the deprived Bishop of Ross opened a meeting house in 1709 near St Giles in Edinburgh and used the English Book of Common Prayer. James Greenshields refused to cease officiating when ordered to do so by the Presbytery of Edinburgh, and was put in prison. He appealed unsuccessfully to the Court of Session and then took his case to the House of Lords, where the action of the Court of Session was reversed.[3]

The Toleration Act secured the right of episcopalians to meet and worship following Anglican forms, if they agreed to use the English liturgy. Many English prayer books were sent to Scotland and the Book of Common Prayer was printed in Edinburgh in the same year, though it had been in use in Scotland since it was approved by the Privy Council in 1680 for use in private chapels.[4] Also, the 1637 Scottish prayer book was reprinted in 1712 by George

[2] 10 Anne, Cap. 29.

[3] Summary in Henry Sefton, 'Revolution to Disruption', in D. B. Forrester and D. M. Murray (eds.), *Studies in the History of Worship in Scotland* (Edinburgh, 1984), 65–6.

[4] John Dowden, *The Scottish Communion Office of 1764*, ed. H. Wilson (London, 1922), 38.

Seton, the fifth Earl of Winton, for the use of Scottish Episcopalians who refused the oaths and prayers for the ruling dynasty.[5] The Communion Office was printed separately, beginning in 1722, in a series of 'wee bookies'.[6]

A few qualified chapels were established following the passage of the Toleration Act and although the English liturgy was used, the congregations were more Scottish than English. 'Scottish episcopalians of the time tended to have a curious "love–hate" relationship with the Church of England. Many of them were inordinately proud of their native heritage and had no wish to be considered as mere Anglicans *in partibus*.'[7] The historian of St Paul's Church in Aberdeen went to great lengths to explain that in 'so founding S. Pauls' there was no withdrawal from the Scottish Episcopal Church'.[8] An English visitor to St Paul's about 1730 wrote about 'the peoples disaffection to the present government' there:

Being there, one Sunday morning, with another English gentleman, when the minister came to that part of the Litany where the king is prayed for by name, the people all rose up as one, in contempt of it, and men and women set themselves about some trivial action, as taking snuff, &c. to show their dislike, and signify to each other they were all of one mind; and when the responsal should have been pronounced, though they had been loud in all that preceded, to our amazement there was not one single voice to be heard but our own, so suddenly and entirely were we dropped.[9]

The legal position of the nonjurors did not improve under the Toleration Act, but 'it tended to protect the whole body from the arbitrary prosecutions to which they had been subjected'.[10] The nonjuring clergy profited indirectly from a changed climate in which it was deemed prudent to show less harshness towards Anglicans in general.[11] The new option for Episcopalians to set up their own chapels and thereby escape the Penal Laws was bound to affect adversely the number of those willing to maintain their allegiance to the nonjuring bishops. The greatest threats to their survival came in the aftermath of the Jacobite risings of 1715 and, especially, 1745. After the first, an Act was passed by Parliament (1719) ordering that no person be permitted to officiate in any Episcopal meeting house or congregation where more than nine persons beyond household members were present, without praying for King

[5] Alan C. Don, *The Scottish Book of Common Prayer 1929* (London, 1949), 21.   [6] Ibid. 35–9.

[7] William Ferguson, *Scotland: 1689 to the Present* (1968; repr. Edinburgh, 1994), 110.

[8] A. Emslie Smith, *S. Paul's Episcopal Church, Aberdeen* (Aberdeen, 1901), 10–11.

[9] Edward Burt, *Letters from a Gentleman in the North of Scotland to his Friend in London* (1754; 5th edn. 1822), 212. Burt was an officer of engineers sent to Scotland as a contractor about 1730. His letters are undated, except for one on military ways begun in 1726, so the visit to St Paul's can only be provisionally dated around 1730.

[10] George Grub, *An Ecclesiastical History of Scotland* (4 vols.; Edinburgh, 1861), iii. 364.

[11] Dowden, *Communion Office*, 46.

George and the royal family and without having taken the oath of abjuration required by the Toleration Act.

In the wake of 'the Forty-Five', more severe penalties were levied against Episcopal clergy and lay people and at the time of the battle of Culloden many meeting houses in the north were burnt down by arriving or departing troops. Another Act in 1746 required all Episcopal clergy to take the oaths and register their Letters by September 1st, or face six months' imprisonment for the first offence and transportation to the American colonies for life for the second or subsequent offence. Lay people, too, faced fines and imprisonment if they were caught attending a prohibited meeting. Any meeting house where an unqualified clergyman presided was shut up or destroyed.[12] In England, the reactive backlash after the Jacobite risings fell most heavily on Roman Catholics, but in Scotland it affected mainly the nonjurors. Yet despite restrictive legislation and vigorous actions taken to dispose of the nonjuring Episcopalian presence in Scotland, once and for all, the church survived, led by a small band of clergymen who conducted services at gatherings of the faithful in their homes, or in the open fields.

The years from 1745 to 1775 were the most difficult. The Penal Laws served as an encouragement to Episcopalians to leave their congregations and join the established Presbyterians, or to organize new meeting houses legalized by use of the English liturgy. The surviving correspondence between nonjuring ministers is full of the practical day-to-day affairs of a church operating against all odds to keep congregations supplied with clergymen and services read according to the church calendar. It is not altogether surprising to find only a few descriptions of actual services in nonjuring congregations, or rare references to the music sung. Even so, a few have come to light, such as the Revd Robert Forbes's report in the year before the 1745 uprising, that 'as of late our Church-musick has been much improv'd, & several Members of this Congregation have interested themselves to obtain the Offering of a Sunday for the Encouragement of the pr[ecentor]'.[13]

After 1745, a segment of Forbes's congregation established a qualified chapel and Forbes continued ministering to a separate nonjuring congregation. He described one memorable service in his new chapel at Leith, opened in 1763, when the local gendarmerie paid a visit:

5 August 1764. 7th Sunday after Trinity, just as I was near the End of the First Lesson, Morning Prayer, 2 Sam. 21. at verse 15. narrating the flaying of the Giants, there Stept

---

[12] Frederick Goldie, *A Short History of the Episcopal Church in Scotland* (Edinburgh, 1976), summary of 1715 and 1745 events in chs. 5 and 6.

[13] SRO:RSEC, CH 12/23/1486, 3 June 1744, Forbes to Alexander. The offering was taken on 3 June and 'amounted to five pounds sterling'.

into the Chapel about 20 Dragoons, a Serjeant at their Head, . . . They were shown to Seats, & joined in the Worship with great Decency . . . No sooner had they made their Appearance, than I read with a more elevated & determined Tone of Voice than usual, as much as to say to my good Folks, who could not fail to be frightened, *Courage! Courage!* And indeed it had a notable Effect upon them; for they all behaved with much Composure, though a great variety of Emotions arose in their Breasts at the Appearance, no less formidable than unexpected, as they afterwards acknowledged to me. Some of them became blind for a short Time; others said, their Hearts dunted [dialect for palpitation of the heart]; a third Sort trembled, insomuch, that they were afraid their legs would not bear them up in Time of Singing the Te Deum; a Fourth shed some Tears, but very privately; & a Fifth Sort declared, that their Mouth became as dry as Horns, . . . The Precentor was struck with such a Panic & Tremor, that in singing the Introit, Ps. 119.49 [Brady & Tate] to it's own proper Tune, he failed in the very first Line with a faltering Voice & Notes altogether wrong. Most luckily I struck the Note right, and roared it out above all the Congregation, Stamping with my Foot, & rapping upon the Pulpit, as much as to say, *Thou poor Soul, be not terrified!* This set him to Rights, & then he went on very well. . . . After sermon, I desired all those who were not to communicate, to withdraw; upon which the military Gentlemen went off very discreetly . . . Then we sung Ps. 73.1 and proceeded to the Altar-Service; &, God be thanked, 87 communicated.[14]

With the accession of George III in 1760, less attention was paid to the activities of the surviving nonjuring congregations, and gradually the zeal with which the Penal Laws were enforced abated. They were finally repealed in 1792 in 'An Act for granting Relief to Pastors, Ministers, and Lay Persons of the Episcopal Communion in Scotland'. The Repeal Act required that any minister of an Episcopal chapel 'take and subscribe the Oaths of Allegiance, Abjuration, and Assurance, in such manner as all Officers, Civil and Military, in Scotland, are now by Law obliged to take and subscribe the same, and shall also subscribe, at the same time and place, a Declaration of his Assent to the Thirty-nine Articles of the Church of England'.[15] The prayers for the royal family were required to be read in public worship in all places.

In episcopal congregations, liturgical forms had been disused for many years before the Commonwealth. Episcopacy was re-established in Scotland at the Restoration, although 'when the king came back, in 1660, there was no governmental action in respect of worship to parallel the change made in administration by the restoration of episcopacy'.[16] The attempt to impose uniformity and the 1637 prayer book had met with disaster and the experiment was not

---

[14] SRO:RSEC, CH 12/18/765–864, Journal of Robert Forbes. Shortly after this incident, Forbes took a brief leave in England while the situation at Leith 'settled down'.

[15] 32 Geo. 3, Cap. LXIII.

[16] Gordon Donaldson, 'Covenant to Revolution', in Forrester and Murray, *Studies in . . . Worship*, 56.

repeated. Some tentative steps towards the reintroduction of liturgical forms were taken, such as reviving the office of reader, whose function was to read a 'set form of prayer' comprising psalms and lessons from Scripture. Readings were to include the Lord's Prayer, the Doxology at the end of the Psalms, and the Commandments.[17] It was only the use of these texts, according to several contemporary accounts, that separated Episcopalians from Presbyterians in the late seventeenth century.

Bishop Thomas Rattray recorded his own observations, and although they are written from the point of view of a nonjuring liturgical scholar, they tally with other more neutral observations in regard to the music sung:

The method in our ordinary assemblies on the Lord's day was almost the same as with that of the Presbyterians: beginning with singing a stanza or two of the Metre Psalms, after which followed an extemporary Prayer, during which, as well as at singing of the Psalms, most of the congregation sat irreverently on their breech, only they were uncovered. Then came a long Sermon, the text of which was no sooner read, but most of the People put on their hats or bonnets. After the Sermon followed another extemporary Prayer, at the Conclusion of which they said the Lord's Prayer; then another stanza or two of the Metre Psalms, which they concluded with a Doxology, but the people sat likewise during all the time of this last Prayer and Psalms, in the same manner as in those before the Sermon, only they rose up at the Doxology, though some thought even that too superstitious (whether they generally stood up at the Lord's Prayer I am not so certain). After the Doxology the congregation was dismissed with the blessing . . .[18]

During the reign of Queen Anne, the gradual restoration of liturgical services was accelerated, encouraged for a time by the passage of the Toleration Act. The Book of Common Prayer had been used at Glasgow in 1703 by clergymen who took the oaths to Queen Anne, and in the North the liturgy had been introduced in 1709 at Montrose, Aberdeen, Elgin, Inverness, and many other places.[19]

Chapels licensed by the state were organized in the main urban centres where they might be expected, such as Edinburgh, Glasgow, Dundee, Perth, and Aberdeen, but they were also established in more remote places, for example, Banff, Montrose, and Inverness. Many congregations traced their history from the Reformation or early seventeenth century through the seesaw changes in establishment. Others were newly founded in 1712, many more after 1745, in legal meeting houses with qualified clergymen. There were two or more Episcopal congregations in many communities, especially

---

[17] Ibid.
[18] Dowden, *Scottish Communion Office*, 39, quoting a MS in the library of the Diocese of Brechin.
[19] Grub, *Ecclesiastical History*, iii. 358–9.

in the north-eastern part of the country, and their relationships and interactions were frequently complicated. Bishop Pococke reported on his visit to Portsoy and Banff in 1760, for example, that 'there are a great number of the Church of England here, the wife often going one way and the husband another'.[20] Brief descriptions of a sample of churches and chapels in the cities of Aberdeen, Edinburgh, and Glasgow, and the more remote town of Banff, on the coast north of Aberdeen, will give some idea of the complicated history of Episcopalians of whatever party in eighteenth-century Scotland.[21]

Aberdeen was the centre of Episcopal leadership throughout most of the nonjuring period. Three main Episcopal congregations survived the 'troubles' of 1715 and 1745, two nonjuring and the qualified chapel, St Paul's, described by Bishop Pococke in 1760 as

built on the London model, with galleries supported by Doric pillars, the pillars above are of the Ionick order, there is a Cupola or small Dome in the Middle, it is decently furnished, and they have a congregation of 1000 people, the other [Trinity Hospital] being about 500. At St. Paul's two ministers have £60 a year each; which the people make up by the collections as at most other places in Scotland.[22]

The chapel was founded in 1720 when a group of 130 'Burgers, Merchants, Tradesmen, and Inhabitants of Aberdeen "met for settling ane Episcopal Meeting House by a qualified minister in the terms of law" '.[23] An organ was purchased before 1726 and an English visitor around 1730 reported that St Paul's had 'an organ, the only one I know of, and the service is chanted as in our cathedrals'.[24] Andrew Tait was the organist from sometime before 1737.[25] Tait and his successor, John Ross, a composer of church and keyboard music, were both organists of the Musical Society in Aberdeen.

The congregation of St Andrew's Church, now the Cathedral, began in a meeting house established 'at the back of the Tolbooth' by Andrew Jaffray, after he was turned out of his charge at Alford in 1716.[26] William Smith, minister from 1735, introduced the use of the English prayer book for morning and evening service and followed the customary practice of using the Scottish Communion liturgy. The place of worship changed a number of times in these

[20] Richard Pococke, *Tours in Scotland*, ed. Daniel W. Kemp (Edinburgh, 1887), 194.

[21] John P. Lawson, *History of the Scottish Episcopal Church from the Revolution to the Present Time* (Edinburgh, 1843), app. 1, pp. 485–514. A decided majority of congregations surveyed in the Commission Reports of 1836–9 traced their history to the late 17th c., some to the early 17th c.

[22] Pococke, *Tours*, 202.   [23] Smith, *S. Paul's . . . Aberdeen*, 3.

[24] Burt, *Letters*, 212, also quoted in David Johnson, *Music and Society in Lowland Scotland in the Eighteenth Century* (London, 1972), 170.

[25] Henry Farmer, *A History of Music in Scotland* (London, 1947), 272; Aberdeen University Special Collections, Records of the Scottish Episcopal Church, Aberdeen and Orkney, Section 5, no. 2.

[26] *Sketch of the History of the Congregation of St. Andrew's Church, Aberdeen* (Aberdeen, 1846), 12.

years and it was probably the chapel in Concert Close that was destroyed in
1746. The congregation then met in various places and private houses until
two years after John Skinner replaced Smith in 1774, when a new chapel was
fitted up in Skinner's house in Longacre. It was there in November of 1784
that Samuel Seabury, from Connecticut, was consecrated the first Bishop for
the Episcopal Church in the United States. The new St Andrew's Chapel was
built on the site of the house-chapel after the repeal of the Penal Laws in 1792
and service was performed there for the first time on 13 September 1795. An
organ was installed the next year.

By 1760 there were three qualified chapels and three nonjuring meeting
houses in Edinburgh.[27] The congregation of the first qualified chapel met
from 1708 in a house in Half Moon Close under the rector, Robert Blair, who
was licensed by the Bishop of Aberdeen. After Blair's death in 1718, it is
reported that the church became a collegiate charge.[28] A new chapel was built
in 1722 on land purchased by John Smith, Chief Baron of the Court of the
Exchequer. The Patronage Act passed in 1712 had restored a patron's power
to present a nominee to a living and Smith's wishes regarding public worship
in the new chapel are set forth in the records:

Whereas I have purchased in the Name of John Vicaridge, (But in trust for my selfe)
the Inheritance of a piece of Ground lying at the Bottom of Black-ffryers Wynd in
Edinburgh, and have built thereupon a Chappel, (which is to be called the New
Chappel) for the more convenient carrying on the Worship and Service of God,
according to the Liturgy and Usage of the Church of England . . . And my Will and
Intent further is that no Minister shall be capable of Officiating in the said Chappel
who is not conformable to the Said Liturgy and Usage of the Church of England, and
who is not qualified by takeing the Oaths to the Government, and who shall not
Expressly by Name Pray for the present Majestie King George and those who shall
Succeed him to the Crown of Great Brittain according to the Settlement thereof in
the Protestant Line, by the Acts of Parliament relative thereto. I desire the
Communion Service when there is no sacrament, may be read in the reading Desk as
is at present used; And that the Ministers will in their Sermons avoid Contraversial
Points, as far as may be, and Endeavor by their Lives & Preaching to recommend to
their Auditors, Solid and Substantial Piety. . . . John Smith, Lord Chief Baron.[29]

The need to avoid arousing suspicion is apparent, also Smith's aversion to the
Laudian practice of reading ante-Communion at the altar. Smith made further

---

[27] Pococke, *Tours*, 302–3.
[28] John Steele, 'Edinburgh's Fourth Cathedral: The Church of St. Paul and St. George, York Place',
typescript, 3.
[29] Edinburgh, Records of Old St Paul's in care of the Rector of St Paul's and St George's Church,
Sederunt Book No. 1, 1726–1810.

provision for the chapel after his death (1726) by leaving enough money to the trustees to pay £40 salary yearly to ministers.[30]

There is record of an organ purchase in 1735 and regular payments to the Clerk of the Chapel as leader of the singing.[31] In the 1770s negotiations were conducted to merge the New Chapel with two other Episcopal chapels, Old St Paul's in Skinner's Close and St Andrew's in Carubber's Close. A new building, still standing, was constructed in the Cowgate and the united church went by the name of Cowgate Chapel until the congregation moved to the New Town in 1818. Old St Paul's had an organ built by Snetzler and given by Queen Anne in 1712, but it was removed in 1716.[32] A second Snetzler organ was purchased sometime later. St Paul's called a qualified minister after 1747 and Mr Pescatori was the organist from about 1750, relinquishing his post in 1774.[33] St Andrew's organist in the 1780s was Alexander Campbell.

In the unified Cowgate Chapel the organist was Stephen Clarke, whose son, William, succeeded him at his death in 1797. William Clarke was the editor of *A Collection of Chaunts* (1817). The clerk in the 1780s was famous Scottish musician Neil Gow's son, William. Two organists were paid up to 1797, Mr Clarke in the new building and Mr Butler in Blackfriars Wynd, where part of the old New Chapel congregation continued to meet until about 1800. According to a manuscript history written in 1820, 'on removing from the Cowgate Chapel, the Congregation brought along with them the Altar table which had been used there, and placed it in the new Chapel; the Organ, which had been originally built by Snetzler, and to which considerable additions have been made; and the Bell which had been used in the Cowgate Chapel'.[34]

The Episcopal congregations in Glasgow also represented both parties of Episcopalians. Bishop Pococke visited there in May 1760 and reported some dissenting churches, a small nonjuring congregation, and the qualified chapel, St Andrew's Church, founded 1750, where he preached and confirmed candidates:

The English Licensed Episcopal congregation have built a very handsome oblong square church near the Green, in the model of the churches in London, for galleries which are not yet built. It cost about £1100. The minister has about £60 a year from the collections . . . they perform divine service in a most decent and solemn manner,

[30] Steele, 'Edinburgh's Fourth Cathedral', 3.
[31] Records of Old St Paul's, New Chapel Blackfriars Wynd Sederunt Book 1726–1810, No. 1.
[32] David A. Stewart and David A. R. Thomson, *A Survey of Edinburgh Organs* (Edinburgh, 1975), 14; private correspondence from David A. Stewart, June 1980.
[33] Scottish Guardian, Jan.–Feb. 1933.
[34] Records of Old St Paul's, Sederunt Book 1806–50, No. 2.

chanting the hymns and singing the psalms extremely well insomuch that I think I
never saw divine offices performed with such real edification.[35]

St Andrew's musical establishment consisted of an organist, choir, precentor, and musical committee, which shared responsibility with the minister for
the choice of music and oversight of personnel. Alexander Reinagle was chapel
organist in 1782 and John Fergus, jun. was appointed to the post in 1784.
About 1785 the chapel decided to fit up seats in the organ gallery for 'singing
boys'; purchases that year include six prayer books for the singing boys and
nineteen copies of music books, and James Rea was paid for 'teaching the children, 18 boys in all'.[36] John Banks was elected 'Clerk & Teacher of the Music
Boys' in December 1787 and the chapel's own *Collection of Sacred Music* was in
print earlier in that year.[37]

In the following months, some disagreements surfaced about the choice of
music and its performance that affected several parts of the public worship over
the next few years. There were complaints that

many of the new pieces of Music introduced lately into the Chapel did not meet with
the approbation of a great part of the Congregation being too complicate for the
greater part of the Hearers, & it was recommended to give the preference in generall
to those simple & solemn tunes that have been formerly used & those of the new
pieces that are in this strain being more suitable to devotion then those pieces that are
more difficult of execution and which the Congregation in generall cannot so easyly
join in.[38]

The 'Clerk and Teacher of the Musical Band', Mr Banks, was the target of
some of the dissatisfaction, for the Managers and members present at the
December 1788 parish meeting found it necessary to give Mr Banks a vote of
complete confidence 'with respect to his Duty performed in the Chapel and as
an orderly Member of the Congregation'. Banks eventually resigned and a new
Precentor, Robert Cock, was hired in 1790. He was allowed £5 over his salary
in December 'for his exertions in teaching & bringing to the Chapel a new sett
of Singers to officiate in place of the Boys who had mostly left the Chapel'.

In October of 1791 the chapel 'agreed to postpone singing the responses to
the Communion till such time as a Committee should determine on what days
it ought to be sung', and in December notified the Superintendent of Music
'to order the Responses to the Commandments to be sung upon the first
Sunday of every month; and also upon each of the four Festivals, if not disagreeable to the Clergymen officiating at these Festivals'.[39] But there were

[35] Pococke, *Tours*, 50–1.
[36] Strathclyde Record Office, Records of St Andrew's Church, TD 423/1/1, 13, 20, 33.
[37] Ibid. 51–5.   [38] Ibid. 58.   [39] Ibid. 115.

clerical and congregational objections and the issue was taken up at a general meeting in March 1792. A resolution was passed that 'in time coming the Responses to the Commandments shall not be sung or chanted'. There was also a vote to discontinue the Music Committee, but the December meeting again asked

the managers to appoint a Committee to conduct the music of the Chapel and to procure a proper band of singers, they preferring always such of the Members of the Congregation as may offer their services. It being understood that Mr Falconer or the officiating Clergyman shall as usual have the appointment of the Psalms, Hymns & Anthems to be sung, and that in other respects the arrangement of the Music shall be under the direction of the Committee.[40]

The music budget continued to rise over the next twenty years, with payments for personnel, music, and some music-copying in addition to the Chapel's own printed music book. Expenditures related to making and washing of surplices for the choir first appeared in the accounts in 1795, about twenty-three years before the notice of a surpliced choir at Leeds Parish Church in 1818.

St Andrew's Episcopal Church in Banff traces its official history to the building of a chapel in 1723, but before that the congregation was part of the parish church, whose minister was deprived by the Synod in 1716 for Episcopalian and Jacobite sympathies. The agreement for purchase of the lot for the chapel states that the house will be 'ane Chappell for ane Episcopall Minister to preach and administer every part of the Ministeriall function therein till in all time comeing Debarring all Dissentors and Presbitereans from the use of thes House'.[41] The organist's salary is mentioned in the minutes of 1732 and Mr Shoneman named in 1734. The 'Musick Book belonging to the Chapel', purchased in 1738–9, is unfortunately not further identified. John Geddes became the organist in 1743, but for a brief tenure. The chapel was believed to be the one burnt down by the Duke of Cumberland's army in April 1746.[42] A new chapel was built in 1752 and the minister sent to London for orders. A new organ was purchased in 1759 and in preparation, James Shand was sent to Aberdeen the year before to study the organ with Andrew Tait, organist of St Paul's Church. Shand was then sent to London to help in choosing the new instrument. He was last paid as organist in 1784. The Revd Charles Cordiner, from Peterhead, was instituted in 1769, and the next twenty-five years were prosperous years for St Andrew's.

There was another Episcopal congregation in Banff, presumably nonjurors from the pre-1745 congregation, who did not join the new qualified chapel in

[40] Strathclyde Record Office, Records of St Andrew's Church, TD 423/1/1, 133.
[41] Banff, St Andrew's Church, Records vol. beginning 3 Oct. 1723.
[42] St Andrew's Episcopal Church, Banff, typescript.

1752. In the year the Penal Laws were repealed, their chapel was at Braehead in Banff and their minister was John Skinner, son of Bishop Skinner. In 1792 they united with St Andrew's to form a collegiate charge. The earlier history of the nonjuring congregation is of particular interest, because the first resident minister of the chapel at Braehead, built in 1778–9, was William Smith, whose career as clergyman, liturgical scholar, teacher, and musician in America after 1784 is described in the next chapter. Smith was born in Portsoy, the seaport town next along the coast to the west from Banff, and was educated in Aberdeen, graduating from King's College in 1774. He taught school in Speymouth (now Urquhart) before deciding to pursue studies for the ministry with the nonjuring Episcopal Bishop of Brechin, George Innes. Smith was 'newly come over from the Presbyterian Party' and this caused him some difficulties in fulfilling his mission.[43] The Primus, Bishop Robert Kilgour, wished him to return to the nonjuring congregation in Portsoy, but they did not relish the idea. He supplied elsewhere in the diocese, and after his ordination in March 1780 he was given official charge in Banff. In November 1781 the Braehead chapel was vandalized, and Smith wrote to a colleague, 'if the altar & pulpit had been spared, we could have more easily pardoned the rest, these are destroyed beyond expression. The villians are openly named, and Banff rings with the horridness of their crime . . .'.[44] In the year that Seabury was consecrated in Aberdeen Smith 'made for America', and among his belongings must have been a number of music publications. One of them was Robert Bremner's *Rudiments of Music*, with its *Collection of the best Church Tunes, Canons, and Anthems*, a source Smith used for his own publications of music for the Episcopal service.

The liturgical music in church music collections published in Scotland in the 1740s and 1750s may be presumed to have been published for and sung in the qualified episcopal chapels. Nevertheless, the use of this music by other Episcopalians cannot be entirely dismissed, and in the 1780s, and especially after the repeal of the Penal Laws in 1792, the increasing number of music collections with chants and special hymns points to wider usage. The introductory remarks in *A Collection of Hymns and Anthems for the use of the Episcopal Church of Scotland* are worth quoting in this context:

The improvement of singing in our christian worship has of late been regarded as an object worthy of some attention from those who can join in that animating part of the divine service: and several attempts have been made to introduce a few hymns and anthems, better adapted to the genius and spirit of our religion, than any of the present poetical versions of the psalms of David. The following collection is now offered as a help in that way, till something of the kind more perfect make its

---

[43] SRO:RSEC, CH 12/14/146, correspondence of Bishop Jolly.
[44] SRO:RSEC, CH 12/30/7, Smith to Jolly 24 Nov. 1781.

appearance. It is principally designed for the service of the Episcopal Church of this kingdom; and care has been taken to procure for each of the solemn festivals and fasts observed in that church, two suitable hymns, one of which may be used at morning, the other at evening prayer. A few more are added for ordinary Sundays, and some other occasions . . .[45]

There were no theological restrictions on service music and instrumental accompaniment in the Episcopal Church. The prejudice that does surface occasionally in clerical correspondence is directed less at the presence of the organ than at the qualified chapel as rightly belonging under their episcopal jurisdiction. Several clergyman, for example, Patrick Torry, assistant to Robert Kilgour at Peterhead in 1789 and later Bishop of St Andrew's, Dunkeld, and Dunblane, were known to be knowledgeable about music.[46] Torry was reported to be proficient on several instruments, besides being an organ-builder. One of his instruments was in the church in Inverness around 1800 and another, 'formerly in his own drawing room, and afterwards in the church at Elgin, is still used in that of Forgue'.[47] It is quite apparent that Episcopal chapels without organs and new chapels built in the 1790s were quick to pre-pare for their use, when they were at liberty to worship in public without interference from the authorities.

An unexpectedly large number of Scottish psalmody collections contain chant tunes for the hymns (that is, the canticles) of the Episcopal service. Only St Andrew's *Collection of Sacred Music* was published for a specific congregation before 1800. The others were intended for more general use by both Episcopal and Presbyterian churches. These music books are listed in Appendix C with imprint, Hymn Tune Index code where applicable, and chant content, and as the imprints show, the publishers came from many urban and outlying areas. *A Short and Useful Psalmody* (Edinburgh, 1742) by James Dallas, a singing mas-ter who lived 'within the Head of Peebles Wynd', is the earliest book with Episcopal music presently known. The accounts of the Edinburgh Musical Society record payments to Dallas for 'writing musick' in 1734–5, 1742, 1754–5, 1757–8, and from 1755 through 1758 for teaching the boys of the Heriot Hospital to sing in the oratorio performances.[48] Dallas's dedication to the Governors and Members of the Musical Society comes as no surprise.

---

[45] *A Collection of Hymns and Anthems* (1779), introduction. Later editions contain fold-out pages of music.

[46] See, for example, letters from Robert Forbes to Bishop Alexander discussing a letter about a Descant sent to a colleague from the clerical musician and theorist William Jones. Forbes also mentions consulting Playford's 4th edn. (1664) of *Brief Introduction to the Skill of Musick*. SRO:RSEC, CH 12/23/1204, 1209.

[47] J. N. Neale, *The Life and Times of Patrick Torry, D.D.* (London, 1856), 44–5. John Skinner corre-sponded at length with Torry in 1795 about purchasing one of his instruments for the new St Andrew's Chapel, Aberdeen, SRO:RSEC, CH 12/12/2314–16, 2318.

[48] Edinburgh City Library, Music Room q YML 28 MS A 41026–8, Minutes of the Edinburgh Musical Society, i. 1728–47, ii. 1747–67.

Dallas advertised his psalm and hymn tunes as 'used in the Churches of Scotland and England', and his music bears him out. Some of the chant tunes are easily recognized, although their immediate source, other than manuscript copies in use in one of the qualified chapels, can only be suggested. In the second category of music in the book, 'the usual Hymns, &c. with Tunes proper to them', Dallas gives two chant tunes for the Te deum, with text incipits, and seven numbered chant tunes in two parts, without text but intended for 'the Hymns of the Prayer book'. The Te deum and Magnificat texts are printed with the metrical hymn texts at the end of the book and both are designated for William Turner's familiar chant in A major. Dallas's version is in three parts, the melody with passing tones and trills in the middle or tenor voice, and the first verse of text underlaid. The presence of the Turner tune might be expected, given its widespread use and the large number of English parish sources that contain it.

Two other old friends from the seventeenth-century royal chapels generic repertory found their way to Scotland, Edward Purcell's chant tune in D minor, Dallas no. 4 (Fig. 1, no. 10), and John Blow's chant tune in E minor, Dallas no. 5 (Fig. 1, no. 4), both in their original keys. Tracing the remaining five tunes is complicated by Dallas's basic notation, and by traditional alterations in transmission of chant tunes, especially in the melody. Although final cadence tones are usually stable, the contour of cadences often changes, most frequently by ornamentation, added grace notes, and filled-in intervals. In the case of the Dallas chant tunes, all are written in common time with a single barline between the two phrases. Recitations are represented by a single semibreve, and most have cadences of varying crotchet values, with a minim or semibreve final (Ex. 7.1).

Some of these chant tunes must have been transmitted in manuscript, but English parish music books that were in print may also have been used in Scotland. A number of sources could be suggested for the no. 7 tune, for example (Ex. 7.2). Paired with Venite by Bremner, the melody is strikingly similar to the Venite chant tune in Edward Betts's *Introduction to the Skill of Musick*, published in 1724 when he was organist at Manchester Collegiate Church. (Ralph Harrison, also of Manchester, reprinted this chant in *Sacred Harmony* in the 1780s, and attributed it to Tallis.) The Venite in Robert Barber's version of the Playford cathedral choral service is also very similar, except for the mediant return to the reciting tone. One other source that might tentatively be put forward is James Green's alternatim Magnificat (Ex. 6.11 above), in which the first verse tune, if sung in A major rather than A minor, is the same. While a change of mode might seem to preclude any relationship between these two tunes, the same chant was sometimes sung in

Ex. 7.1. Dallas chant tunes: (*a*) no. 1; (*b*) no. 3; (*c*) no. 4 by E. Purcell; (*d*) no. 6

major and minor keys. Adding the C♯ in the second-phrase melody is, in any case, a quite reasonable alteration.

Dallas's triple chant for Te deum (Ex. 7.3) is especially intriguing, partly because of its musical features and partly due to its transmission and long history as a congregational chant in the American church. It is, in addition, the earliest triple chant sung in Britain. Part A begins with an altered phrase from the Imperial Tune melody in which a mediant inflection to the leading-note, F♯, has become part of the tune. The same phrase can be found in English parish alternatim canticles. Part B combines a rising phrase leading to a repeat of the second phrase of part A, intervals adjusted, at the fifth above the tonic. Such a sequence was also a common feature in parish alternatim canticles. In part C, the treble close on F♯ makes a natural bridge back to part A. Notice

Ex. 7.2. Suggested sources for (*a*) Dallas tune no. 7 and (*b*) Bremner version: (*c*) Bett's Ve chant; (*d*) Barber Ve chant

Ex. 7.3. Dallas's Te deum triple chant

We praise etc.   Holy etc.

Thou art the King etc.   Vouchsafe etc.

also the second phrase in part C, this time identical with the second phrase in part B. The melodies move mostly by step and stay within the range of a sixth, making the complete chant easy to sing and to remember. In older plainsong Te deums, certain verses required a traditional change of mode, a convention followed in the triple Te deum, where two of the component chants succeed one another at the same places; verse 14, 'Thou art the King of Glory', and verse 26, 'Vouchsafe O Lord'.[49] The rising phrase in the part B chant, at 'Holy, Holy, Holy', bears some resemblance to an intonation for a plainsong Sanctus. Many of these features show the mark of a knowledgeable trained musician.

No earlier printing or manuscript copy of the triple Te deum has come to light, and unless such a copy with an attribution appears, all possibilities must be considered. Yet the obvious relationship between the Dallas triple Te deum and English parish alternatim canticles does indicate that the musical ideas had a common origin. The first two phrases strongly suggest that the Dallas piece is a reworking of the Chetham Te deum or one of its versions, perhaps by an organist in one of the qualified chapels. The triple Te deum is presumed to have been sung often enough, before Dallas printed it, to be called a 'proper tune'. The juxtaposition of Turner in A with Dallas's note assigning the text to it, and the triple Te deum on the next page, both 'proper tunes', could also indicate that the occasions on which they were sung were different, or that the Turner chant is the proper English tune and the triple chant was specially arranged for a Scottish chapel.

All but one of Robert Bremner's chant tunes were printed first by Dallas. They are part of *A Collection of the best Church-tunes, Canons and Anthems*, the last part of Bremner's treatise, *Rudiments of Music* (Edinburgh, 1756). The importance of this publication in the 1750s reform of psalmody in the established church, and the support of the Committee for improving Church Music in the city of Edinburgh, has been pointed out before.[50] Little notice has been taken of the other types of music in the *Collection* that were designed for a wider audience, or for social and educational use.[51] The presence of the 'Chants or Tunes for particular Hymns' for episcopal chapels, in an authoritative publication such as Bremner's, contributed in large measure to their dissemination as the official chant tunes for the Episcopal liturgy. They included Venite exultemus and its alternate text prescribed by rubric for Easter, 'Christ our Passover is sacrificed for us', and the Morning and Evening canticles and their alternates. Bremner's chant for Benedicite is not in Dallas and Dallas's

[49] John Aplin discusses this and other features of early English Te deums in 'The Survival of Plainsong in Anglican Music'.

[50] Millar Patrick, *Four Centuries of Scottish Psalmody* (Oxford, 1949), 161–3; Farmer, *Music in Scotland*, 267–8; Johnson, *Music and Society*, 178–9.

[51] Farmer, quoting William Cowan, did point out the Anglican connection in *Music in Scotland*, 264.

sixth numbered tune is not in Bremner, but the rest are: Dallas numbered tunes 1–5 and 7, the triple Te deum, and Turner in A, which Bremner assigned to the alternate evening canticle, Cantate domino.

Bremner's method of laying out the first verse of the text for each chant tune, and adding notes of smaller value between the main tones of Dallas's melody, provide some clues about where the chant was adjusted to accommodate the variable number of text syllables. In the Te deum, filled-in intervals are indicated by small grace notes (Ex. 7.4(*a*)). Bremner's dominant harmony in the mediant of the second part, the C♯ leading to D, became a permanent feature of the triple Te deum. In the Magnificat, his procedures were similar, with more of the small notes filling in intervals and functioning as symbols for different word accents or quantities (Ex. 7.4(*b*)).

The Benedicite, alternate text to Te deum in Morning Prayer, was offered in two versions, one in metre and one in prose. The music for these versions is clearly related and since the metrical tune was published by Dallas, it obviously came first. Bremner may have arranged this chant by using the refrain from the metrical tune as a second phrase (Ex. 7.5). The metrical tune was almost always placed with the other Episcopal music in later Scottish music collections, although less than half reproduced Bremner's prose chant.

Before 1762, when Bremner brought out the official second edition of *Rudiments of Music*, he reprinted the *Collection* in various editions with the 1756 *Rudiments* title-page and index. In these intermediary printings of the *Collection*, the chant tunes were recast in three voices, with the melody in the middle voice, and remained so in all subsequent printings. The two- and three-part arrangements may be compared in John Blow's E minor chant for Deus misereatur (Ex. 7.6). The upper two voices were probably sung by tenors and altos an octave lower, but either part could be sung by the treble as written. William Taas was of the opinion that in two- or three-part music, the countertenor could sing the bass part an octave higher to create a 'very good effect'.[52]

The Dallas/Bremner canon of chants for morning and evening service forms the basic repertory in every currently known Scottish collection containing music for the Episcopal liturgy up to and beyond 1820. In terms of transmission and liturgical authority, the Dallas/Bremner canon assumed a position similar to the twelve official metrical psalm tunes sanctioned for Presbyterian use by the established Church. This is apparent in the comments of the Revd John Skinner, jun. to the Revd Patrick Torry regarding the purchase of a barrel organ for the Revd Skinner's chapel:

[52] William Taas, *The Elements of Music* (Aberdeen, 1787), p. vi.

Ex. 7.4. Bremner editions of Dallas chant tunes: (*a*) Td in two parts; (*b*) Mg melody only

(*a*)

We praise thee O God we ack-now-ledge thee to be the Lord etc.

Ho - ly Ho - ly Ho - ly Lord God of Sab - baoth etc.

Thou art the King of glo - ry O _____ Christ etc.

Vouch - safe O Lord etc. to keep us this day with-out sin etc.

(*b*)

My soul doth mag-ni-fy the Lord and my spi-rit hath re-joi-ced in God my sav-i-our.

Ex. 7.5. Scottish Benedicite in two forms: (*a*) Dallas in metre; (*b*) Bremner in metre; (*c*) Bremner chant tune

(*a*)

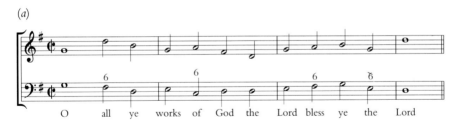

(*b*)

(*c*)

Ex. 7.6. Blow in E minor in Scottish sources: (*a*) Dallas chant tune no. 5; (*b*) Bremner edn. for 2 voices; (*c*) Bremner edn. for 3 voices

(*a*)

(*b*)

God   be   mer - ci - ful   to   us   and   bless   us: and   shew   us   the   light

of   thy   coun - te - nance   and   be   mer - ci - ful   un - to   us.

(*c*)

Inchgarth, 18 April 1812 . . . Our Chapel Treasurer Mr. Scott is now in London. I had a letter from him this morning, most anxious for the Managers to conclude a Bargain for a Barrel-Church-organ, which he says would answer our house to a T. The price is 45 Guineas, but he says, as a Chaunt Barrel would be necessary to complete the Instrument, the expense of that & of freight &c. might make the purchase money in all £60. As he requested an answer in course of post we have written him to secure the Organ and I take this opportunity of requesting your advice about the Chaunts –

were we to order a Barrel with them, they would send us their Chaunts, which differ materially
from ours – It strikes me therefore, that we ought to get correct Music to send them – and as I
know no one more capable of directing us to where these are to be found, than your-
self, I request your speedy information on this head. . . . The Chaunts are only 7 in
no., so that we can have on the same barrel with them 3 additional tunes – for every
additional barrel they charge 4 guineas.[53]

   The chants in the Dallas/Bremner canon are organized in Table 7.1 on the
basis of Dallas's music with Bremner's text–tune pairings. The only prose texts
indicated by Dallas were Te deum, for the triple chant and for the Turner single, and Magnificat, also for Turner, which makes it impossible to be certain
whether Bremner's other choices were based on customary use. Given the
nature of his publication, it might be safe to assume that some of the Bremner
text underlay was traditional. The most stable text–tune pairings in subsequent
music collections were for Venite exultemus, Te deum, Benedicite, Nunc
dimittis, and Deus misereatur. The Magnificat was sung to one of two tunes,
the tune in C major (Ex. 7.4(*b*)), or alternatively Turner in A, the latter in
accordance with Dallas's note next to the prose text. Bremner's association of
Turner in A with Cantate domino was copied by the nine other compilers
who included the text. Not surprisingly, the majority of compilers chose one
or the other text for the tune Bremner assigned to Benedictus and, alternately,
Jubilate deo. The tune for the Proper Anthem for Easter Day was paired with
Jubilate deo in two collections and Nunc dimittis in five others.

   The progression of text–tune choices can be followed in Table 7.1 under a
separate heading for each text and its tune. The Dallas tunes are editorially
assigned according to the Bremner arrangement, even though these choices
may not all have been Dallas's. They would seem to be supported by the relative stability of the repertory. The names of compilers and date of publication
appear in the left-hand column; the titles of these music books published
between 1742 and 1820 can be found in the annotated catalogue in Appendix
C. The number of voice parts, key (m = minor), and text, where it differs from
Dallas and Bremner, are also given.

   The music underwent little substantive change from the Bremner version
in three voices, with the melody in the middle or tenor voice. There are some
exceptions, besides the usual small alterations which crept in naturally in the
course of reprintings. The dotted rhythms of the Chetham Te deum, copied
in so many English parish music collections throughout the century, turn up
in Laurence Ding's Te deum and in his version of the Turner single chant, to
which he set Cantate domino and Magnificat. The final cadence in his

---

[53] SRO:RSEC, CH 12/12/2334. Italics mine.

TABLE 7.1. The Dallas/Bremner canon

	Ve	Td	Bte	Bn/Jd	Mg	Nd	Dm	Cd	Easter
Dallas 1742	G 2v	G 2v	—	D 2v	C 2v	D m 2v	E m 2v	Mg A 3v	A 2v
Bremner 1756	A 2v	G2v	F 2v	D 2v	C 2v	D m 2v	E m 2v	A 3v	A 2v
1758	A 3v	G 3v	F 3v	D 3v	C 3v	D m 3v	E m 3v	A 3v	A 3v
Campbell 1784	A 3v	G 3v	—	C 3v	C 3v	D m 3v	E m 3v	A 3v	A 3v
Taas 1787	G 2v	G 2v	F 2v	Bn D 2v	Dm C 2v	—	Nd E m 2v	Mg A 2v	Jd G 2v
Sacred Music 1787	A 3v	G 3v	F 3v	Jd F 3v	Bn/Jd C 3v	—	—	Mg A 3v	Nd G 3v
Church Tunes 1790	A 3v	G 3v	F 3v	D 3v	C 3v	D m 3v	E m 3v	A 3v	A 3v
Ding 1792–1806	G 3v	G 3v	G 3v	Bn D 3v[a] Jd G 3v Jd F 2v[a]	C 2v[a] Bn C 3v	D m 3v[a] Dm D m 3v	E m 2v[a]	G 3v Mg G 3v A 2v[a]	Nd G 3v
Thomson 1793–6	G 3v	G 3v	G 3v	Bn D 3v[b] Jd G 3v Jd F 3v[b]	C 3v[b] Bn/Jd C 3v	D m 3v[b] Dm D m 3v	E m 3v[b]	A 3v Mg G 3v	Nd G 3v
Peat 1801	A 3v	G 3v	—	D 3v	C 3v	D m 3v	E m 3v	A 3v	A 3v
Smith 1805–10	A 3v	G 3v	—	D 3v	C 3v	D m 3v	E m 3v	A 3v	A 3v
Sivewright 1805–15	A 3v	G 3v	G 3v	Jd G 3v	Bn C 3v	—	E m 3v	Mg A 3v	Nd G 3v
McDonald, P., –1809	A 3v	G 3v	—	D 3v	C 3v	D m 3v	—	A 3v	—
Anderson 1810	A 3v	G 3v	—	D 3v	C 3v	D m 3v	E m 3v	A 3v	A 3v
Davie 1815	A 3v	G 3v	G 3v	Jd G 3v	Bn C 3v	—	E m 3v	—	Nd G 3v
Clarke 1817	A 4v	G 4v	G 4v	F 4v	C 4v	D m 4v	G m 4v	A 4v	—
McDonald, A. 1819	A 3v	G 3v	F 3v	Bn D 3v	Dm C 3v	D m 3v	—	Mg G 3v	Jd A 3v

[a] 2nd Sett
[b] Modern Set

Benedicite chant is decorated with a semiquaver turn and a penultimate articulation.

Ding's *Beauties of Psalmody* offered two concurrent sets of chants, one called
the 'second sett'. James Thomson copied this format and content in *A
Collection of the Best Church Tunes, Catches, Chants* published the next year
(1793), but his second set is supposedly a 'modern set'. The only new chant,
however, is the second tune for Venite, again copied from Ding. The close
concordance of the content from the canon in these two books can be seen in
the Ding and Thomson entries in Table 7.1.

According to William Taas, music teacher in Banff and the compiler of *The
Elements of Music* (1787), 'it is clear to every intelligent observer, that our
Church Music in many places of this country is evidently on the decline, and
fast approaching to that state wherein it was about thirty years ago, when very
few, if any, in most congregations, knew any thing either of time or concord'.
That would have been the 1750s, when Robert Bremner first published his
reform publication, the *Rudiments of Music* and the collection of official music
printed with it. Taas brought up several causes for the reversal: (1) 'the want
of care in parents to have their children instructed in this part of education';
(2) 'the custom that prevails in many places of the country, of reading every
line before it is sung'; and (3) 'there is generally no proper place in the church
appointed for the singers'.[54]

Taas laid out a plan for reform which recommended a rather large choir:

Let as many seats be fitted up, adjoining to the precentor's desk, as will contain from
fifteen to twenty persons, to be allotted for the tenors; and let as many seats be
appointed in the middle of the church, before the precentor's desk, as will contain
from twenty to thirty trebles, and from fifteen to twenty basses: And if proper voices
can be had for the counter tenor,* three or four of them to sing along with the bass
will have a fine effect. This proportion of tenors, is by far too weak for the other parts;
but as the generality of the congregation always sing tenor, this will make them fully
an equal match.

    * The counter tenor should be sung with a fine smooth voice, between that of a tenor and
    treble; for if it is sung with a strong rough voice, it is very disagreeable. In tunes which are
    only composed in two or three parts, the counters may sing the bass part in the octave above,
    which will have a very good effect.[55]

[54] Taas, *Elements*, pp. [iii]–v. The copy in the Taylor Collection, Special Collections, Aberdeen
University, contains James Beattie's manuscript copies of the Dallas/Bremner chants in three parts. In *A
Letter to the Reverend Hugh Blair, D.D. One of the Ministers of Edinburgh: On the Improvement of Psalmody in
Scotland* (Aberdeen, 1778), 6, Beattie wrote 'nay, I am in doubt whether Church-musick would not have
more energy, if we were to sing our psalms in prose, according to that form of Recitative, which in England
is called *Chanting*. However, being no friend to innovation, I willingly submit this opinion to the authority of the Church, and to the general voice of the people'.

[55] Tass, *Elements*, p. vi.

Besides additional remarks about performance in his long preface, Taas cited some of the sources he drew upon. In addition to the *Encyclopaedia Britannica*, he took 'such hints from Bremner, Tansure, and others, as we thought necessary for our purpose'. The chants from Bremner are all for two voices, and five of the eight Dallas/Bremner canon tunes are assigned to different texts (see Table 7.1). The second chant for Nunc dimittis, in A minor, was published by Tans'ur as a double chant in *The Royal Melody Complete* (1755). Taas has copied only the first two phrases. This is the minor-mode melody from the alternatim canticle settings of the Magnificat and Nunc dimittis published by Green, mentioned above as a possible source for the Venite tune in Dallas and Bremner (see Ex. 7.2). There were other printings of the minor-mode tune by Tans'ur for the Magnificat in *A Compleat Melody* (1736) and *Melodia Sacra* (1772).

The number of new chants in Scottish publications increased after 1800, but the Dallas/Bremner canon continued to hold its primary place. William Clarke labelled chants from the canon 'old chaunt' in his 1817 collection, to distinguish them from the new repertory of chants of his own composition and others from English cathedral sources. In *A Complete Collection of the Psalm and Hymn Tunes, Anthems, and Chants, as used in St. Andrew's Chapel, King Street, Aberdeen* (1829), the Venite, Te deum, Benedicite, Benedictus, Jubilate deo, Magnificat, and Nunc dimittis are still the canon tunes, written out in full in order 'to adopt the Musical accent to the rhetorical emphasis'. The canon tunes outnumber the few other chants from English cathedral sources, such as a Battishill double chant and the Robinson double chant from Boyce.

The majority of chants published for the Episcopal Church in Scotland before 1820 are paired with canticle texts, and although there are no specific directions for prose-psalm chanting, the Venite chant could have served the prose psalms as well. Alternatively, the Venite was chanted, the psalms for the day read, and the doxology, Gloria Patri, sung or chanted, as was done in some English churches. A first verse of text was usually underlaid, leaving the remaining verses to be fitted to the music in another way. Many of the chants printed in Scotland came from English parish and cathedral sources, but some were composed or arranged by Scottish musicians. In the next chapter, a similar pattern of transmission will be found in the music of the first overseas branch of the Anglican Communion, the Protestant Episcopal Church in the United States of America.

8

Early Episcopal Music in America

> But when in the course of Divine Providence, these American States
> became independent with respect to civil government, their ecclesiastical
> independence was necessarily included; and the different religious
> denominations of Christians in these States were left at full and equal lib-
> erty to model and organize their respective Churches, and forms of wor-
> ship, and discipline, in such manner as they might judge most convenient
> for their future prosperity; consistently with the constitution and laws of
> their country.[1]

THE formal process by which remnants of colonial Anglican ecclesiastical
societies were welded into an autonomous American church began its most
important phase in Philadelphia in 1785. With the working out of a trial
liturgy, the stage was set for the next step, a few years of experimentation
with the Proposed Book in episcopal congregations. Representatives of the
churches within the states then came together in 1789 to hammer out a final
settlement, and by 1790 the important elements of the Anglican Church were
in place: a united episcopate, a federal system of government, and a liturgy.
The revised liturgy authorized for use on 1 October 1790 adhered to the general outline of services in the 1662 English prayer book, but, as might be
expected, there were substantial changes in the text. Also, part of the
Communion liturgy of the Episcopal Church in Scotland was adopted
according to suggestions made by the Scottish bishops to the first American
bishop, Samuel Seabury, at the time of his 1784 ordination in Aberdeen.
When the sum of substantive revisions are considered, however, the similarities between the American liturgy and the English liturgy outweigh the differences. As the church fathers pointed out, they were 'far from intending to
depart from the Church of England in any essential point of doctrine, disci-
pline, or worship; or further than local circumstances require'.[2]

Local circumstances, as it turns out, produced a liturgical practice similar to
but not identical with that of the mother country. The Episcopal Church in

---

[1] *The Book of Common Prayer and Administration of the Sacraments and other Rites and Ceremonies of the Church according to the Use of the Protestant Episcopal Church in the United States: Together with the Psalter, or Psalms of David* (1789), preface.

[2] Ibid.

Scotland had already led the way in shaping a liturgy and organizing a church along national lines. The American church was the first overseas member of what would later be known as the Anglican Communion, churches with liturgies in close alignment with the Anglican liturgy and with episcopal governments in communion with, yet independent of, the see of Canterbury.

The musical practice of the American church in the first quarter century of its independence offers a unique opportunity to study the development of Anglican liturgical music in a social and cultural environment far removed geographically from its origins. The most influential organists and composers in the early American churches were British émigrés, some of them church musicians trained in cathedrals, or former occupants of posts in town churches. They emigrated to America in the late 1780s and 1790s to take up similar posts in cities along the eastern seaboard, bringing with them their music and their practical skills. The professional environment in American city churches was not unlike the one they had left, for the 'mixed' practice of the English parish church in the late eighteenth century was the model for early American churches. The widespread imitation of the performance practice and physical setting of the English cathedral choral service came much later.

The religious settlement worked out in convention amongst representatives of diverse regions in the Protestant Episcopal Church is evident in the prayer book, whose outline of liturgical musical practice reflects colonial experience. At the same time, the prayer book follows the general framework of the English prayer book in the order of contents, order of reading psalms and lessons, the calendar, and tables of Feasts and Fasts. The holy days were adopted in the main from the 1662 prayer book, although special observances such as the American Thanksgiving Day replaced irrelevant English state occasions.

The rubrics of the 1789 American prayer book were even less precise than those of its model, the English 1662 Book of Common Prayer, in the amount of music they prescribed. Further, a different collective experience informed early Episcopalians when they interpreted the rubrics in terms of liturgical language and action. The long history of the English cathedral choral service impinged only peripherally on the American liturgy and its participants and practitioners in the colonial period, and then only in the person of an occasional visitor or émigré, such as cathedral-trained William Tuckey, parish clerk of Trinity Church in New York in the 1750s. To conclude that colonial Anglicans were not conversant with English cathedrals and their traditions would be incorrect, however, especially in the southern and middle states where the Anglican church was the established church. The choral service, nonetheless, was not a living tradition in colonial Anglican worship in southern, middle, or New England states. Consequently, the liturgical terms used in the rubrics were initially taken literally, that is, texts coupled with *read* and *say* were delivered in the ordinary spoken voice and those with *sing* were translated into musical tone.

In the American revision, the rubric preceding the psalms in Morning and Evening Prayer, 'then shall be said or sung the following Anthem', referred to the proper prefaces, the invitatory psalm, Venite exultemus, and the proper psalms in course, inclusively. The doxology was not obligatory after every psalm or canticle, but only after the last psalm, and the Gloria in excelsis was allowed as an alternative to Gloria patri. In these particulars, the rubric in the American prayer book differed from its English model:

Then shall follow a PORTION of the Psalms, as they are appointed, or one of the SELEC-TIONS of Psalms set forth by this Church; and at the end of every Psalm, and likewise at the end of the Venite, Benedicite, Jubilate deo, Benedictus, Cantate Domino, Bonum es Confiteri, Deus Misereatur, Benedic Anima Mea—MAY be said or sung the GLORIA PATRI; and, at the end of the whole Portion, or Selection of Psalms for the day—SHALL be said or sung the GLORIA PATRI, or else the GLORIA IN EXCELSIS, as followeth . . .

The psalmody rubric reveals the extent of the changes in canticle texts from their English counterparts.[3] Magnificat and Nunc dimittis in Evening Prayer were replaced by their alternates from the English prayer book, Cantate domino and Deus misereatur. The new alternate texts are Bonum est confiteri, Ps. 92:1–4 and Benedic anima mea, Ps. 103:1–4, 20–2. The Venite exultemus was shortened to seven verses and verses 9 and 13 of Ps. 96 were added to create a new conclusion. The Morning Prayer canticles, Benedicite and Benedictus, were also shortened, the latter to four verses.

The Psalter, of which only selections had been included in the Proposed Book, was restored in its entirety in the 1789 prayer book. The customary punctuation between the phrases of binary psalm verses, the colon or 'musical pointing' of the English prayer book, was in many psalms changed to a comma or semicolon, with presumably variable results on the singing or reading of the text. Bishop White of Philadelphia described the new policy authorizing the metrical or 'singing' psalms: 'In the old book they were no part of the common prayer, but were only used by the royal permission. With us, as I conceive, they are to be part of the liturgy.'[4] Accordingly, the *New Version of*

---

[3] A summary of content and changes may be found in Marion Hatchett, *The Making of the First American Book of Common Prayer* (New York, 1982), ch. 10.

[4] Horace W. Smith, *Life and Correspondence of the Rev. William Smith, D.D.* (Philadelphia, 1880), ii. 175. This William Smith (1727–1803) was Provost of the College of Philadelphia and a key figure in prayer book revision. He should not be confused with William Smith, the younger, editor of *The Churchman's Choral*

Psalms (Tate and Brady, 1696 and later editions) was appended to the prayer book with the title 'The Whole Book of Psalms, in Metre; with Hymns Suited to the Feasts and Fasts of the Church, and Other Occasions of Public Worship'. Twenty-seven of the hymns from the Proposed Book were authorized for singing in church.

There is no mention of music in the rubrics for the Creeds or the Litany, 'to be used after Morning Service, on Sundays, Wednesdays, and Fridays'. The rubric in the 1662 prayer book allowing an anthem to be sung after the collects was not repeated. Among the alterations in the Communion liturgy was the official status given to the customary response to the naming of the Gospel, 'Glory be to thee, O Lord', not prescribed by rubric in the English liturgy. The first mention of music in the Communion comes after the general prayer for the state of the church. The proper Prefaces and Sanctus are directed to be 'said or sung by the Priest and People'. The rubric for the hymn added after the Oblation states 'Here shall be sung a Hymn, or Portion of a Hymn, from the Selection for the Feasts and Fasts &c. of the Church'. The Gloria in excelsis follows the prayer of thanksgiving at the end of the Communion service, according to the rubric 'Then shall be said or sung, all standing, Gloria in Excelsis, or some proper Hymn from the Selection'.

A measure of flexibility regarding the music to be heard in public worship was built into the wording of the rubrics of the American prayer book. The minister and vestry had the task of coordinating the wishes of the congregation and the financial resources of each church in determining the details of ceremonial and ritual in liturgical practice. The minister, however, carried the primary responsibility of the choice of psalms and hymns. These hymns were not the canticles of the liturgy, but composed texts set in metre, to be chosen from the official selection:

This Translation of the Whole Book of Psalms into Metre, with Hymns, is set forth, and allowed to be sung in all Congregations of the said Church, before and after Morning and Evening Prayer, and also before and after Sermons, at the discretion of the Minister.

And it shall be the duty of every Minister of any Church, either by standing directions, or from time to time, to appoint the Portions of Psalms which are to be sung.

And further, it shall be the duty of every Minister, with such assistance as he can obtain from persons skilled in music, to give order concerning the Tunes to be sung, at any time, in his Church: And, especially, it shall be his duty, to suppress all light and unseemly music; and all indecency and irreverence in the performance; by which, vain and ungodly persons profane the service of the Sanctuary.[5]

Companion to his Prayer book (1809). Both clergymen were born and educated in Aberdeenshire and emigrated to America from Scotland.

[5] *Book of Common Prayer*, rubric preceding the Psalms and Hymns.

The diversity that led to a different shape for the liturgy as it was performed in rural and town parishes in England was also at work in colonial parishes in America. Yet the standard for public worship was set by town churches in major cities—Boston, New York, Philadelphia, Baltimore, and Charleston—where choirs and organs made it possible to provide as little or as much music as the rubrics allowed and custom might dictate. The example of town churches in England provided the type of service Francis Hopkinson outlined to Bishop White in his description of appropriate service playing: an organ voluntary before the first lesson; chanted canticles accompanied on the organ; the metrical psalm sung before and after the sermon, with proper prelude and interludes between verses; and a concluding voluntary at the end of the service.[6]

The same type of service is outlined in the schedule of responsibilities drawn up in February 1803 for the organist of St. Michael's Church in Charleston, South Carolina. It is a summary of the practical application of clerical oversight and choice of service music:

The Organist: Shall perform the duties of his office, which shall from time to time be directed by the ministers, in the mornings & evenings of every Sabbath day in the year; also on such Festivals or Holy-Days, as now are, or shall hereafter be established by the said Church, and at such other periods as shall be appointed by Authority: He shall perform on the Organ, at all times preceding the services of the day the tune usually adapted the 36 Hymn, or any other solemn piece of music; to begin at the exact time the clergyman enters the desk, and to continue the music for one verse only or for a reasonable time. He shall chaunt the 'venite exultemus' and te Deum, on alternate Sundays; and shall play a solemn & well adapted Voluntary preceding the first lesson, and shall receive from the Clerk such psalms or hymns as the ministers shall appoint for the day, in order to adapt them to suitable tunes. He shall not only accompany the clerk with the Organ, in such psalms and hymns as may be appropriated by the ministers; but shall join the Clerk in the Gloria Patri, which shall invariably be sung after ev'ry Sermon: He shall also perform at all funerals, to which he may be invited, accompanying the Clerk with the Organ in the Gloria Patri, which shall always be sung at the conclusion of funerals, psalms or hymns: He shall in conjunction with the clerk, instruct such youth as choose to attend & who shall be particularly placed under his charge in the rules and practise of psalmody; and he shall command and require of them, a serious & decent deportment during the time of divine service: And at the conclusion of the morning & evening service, the Voluntary, which he shall play, shall be some piece of sacred music, of rather slow time, such as will tend to cherish the

[6] Francis Hopkinson, 'A Letter to the Rev. Doctor White, Rector of Christ Church and St. Peter's on the Conduct of Church Organs', *Miscellaneous Essays and Occasional Writings*, ii. 119–26, quoted in O. G. T. Sonneck, *Francis Hopkinson, the First American Poet-Composer (1737–1791) and James Lyon, Patriot, Preacher, Psalmodist (1735–1794): Two Studies in Early American Music* (Washington, DC, 1905), 59–62.

solemn impressions made by the pious exercises of prayer and exhortation. And lastly, it is fully understood & required that he shall be under the direction of the clergymen of the said Church for the time being, in all things appertaining to its religious services.[7]

The music used in the formative years of the Episcopal Church was selected largely from English music publications for cathedral, parish, and nonconformist churches and chapels. It was an eclectic repertory and extended to music of other liturgical denominations, particularly Roman Catholic, Moravian, and Lutheran. The first two decades of the nineteenth century saw the beginning of a steady increase in the composition of chants, responses, doxologies, and liturgical anthems, such as sentences to serve as introits and settings of proper prefaces and other texts for special use. Gradually, an indigenous repertory of service music for all parts of the liturgy was built up.

In form and content, the Episcopal music books printed in America in the early years, listed with their contents in Appendix D, established the pattern for such publications for several decades to come. The first printed music for the liturgy, however, was a promotional venture, an outgrowth of the singing school conducted by the compiler, Andrew Law, in St. Peter's Church in Philadelphia early in 1783. In this respect, Law's was the first of a long line of general tunebooks which catered for all Protestant denominations and carried a supplement or section of Episcopal liturgical music, including chants, responses, and short anthems. All but one of Law's chants came from the Scottish publication he encountered at St. Peter's, Robert Bremner's *A Collection of the best Church Tunes, Canons, and Anthems*, bound with his treatise, *The Rudiments of Music*, the title Law chose for his own publication.[8] Law's *Rudiments* also contained the Chetham Te deum, in an edition from Uriah Davenport's *Psalm-Singer's Pocket Companion* (1755).[9]

Law arranged his chants for four voices from Bremner's three, keeping the tune in the tenor voice and copying the same notation. The recitation occupied a minim followed by crotchets for the required number of syllables for each text, and minims and a final semibreve served both mediant and terminal cadences. As a general rule, Law copied the lower two voices and put Bremner's top voice up an octave, adding a new alto part or a new treble. The texts for all Law's chants were printed on separate pages. Since this was a pio-

---

[7] George W. Williams, *Jacob Eckhard's Choirmaster's Book of 1809* (facs. edn., Columbia, SC, 1971). The schedule is entered in the vestry minutes and in Eckhard's MS organbook. Hymn text 36, no. 10 in the organbook, is 'Before Jehovah's Awful Throne', set by Martin Madan to the tune Denmark.

[8] Robert Bremner's brother, James, was organist of St. Peter's Church in 1767 and again in the 1770s. See Oscar G. Sonneck, *Francis Hopkinson and James Lyon*.

[9] Richard Crawford, *Andrew Law, American Psalmodist* (Evanston, Ill., 1968), 28–9 and 136. Law owned a copy of Davenport's first edition.

neering venture, a description of the new type of music and brief directions for its performance were offered:

Chanting is a simple kind of prose singing, similar to the common method of verse singing by plain Psalm tunes. The difference between Chants and Anthems is the same as between Old Hundred and Denmark. In Anthems and such tunes as Denmark every verse of the words is sung to different music; but in Chants and such tunes as Old Hundred every verse is sung to the same music.

In chanting, observe, there are two lines of the music, the words to the colon, are sung in the music to the first semibreve; from that to the period, to the end of the Chant.

Most of the words are sung on the same key with the first note, and about as fast as they are naturally spoken in conversation. The whole book of Psalms as they stand in the Bible, may be chanted; for more or less syllables may be sung in the same tune, as the verse requires.[10]

Further details of fitting text syllables to recitation and cadence for succeeding verses of text would not appear in print for another twenty years, and then the authors would be Episcopal musicians.

The next publication of Episcopal music was an official one, the music supplement to the Proposed Book of 1786, prepared by Francis Hopkinson. The inclusion of four chants with the metrical psalm tunes was due to his insistence, according to Bishop White, the rector of St. Peter's and Christ Church: 'Mr. Hopkinson had so fitted his tunes as to occupy an half sheet on both sides; besides which, he is desirous of inserting a page of chants; and if I comply with this, it will be to gratify him, as he has taken so much trouble in the matter'.[11] When the final edition of the music supplement was ready, only four chants were fitted in on the bottom staves of two of the music pages. Blow in E minor and Turner in A had been in circulation since their appearance in the Restoration royal chapels repertory. Kelway in G and a double chant by Garret Wesley were eighteenth-century chants.[12]

Their notation suggests that the Turner and Blow chants were copied from Bremner, but a printed source for the other two chants may not have been involved at all. The Kelway chant was published in Granville Sharp's *Fifty Double and Single Chants* about the time Hopkinson visited London (1766–7) or shortly thereafter, but the Wesley chant circulated only in manuscript. Hopkinson's notation suggests that these chants were taken down from a performance heard during his attendance in one of the cathedrals he visited. The

[10] Andrew Law, *Rudiments of Music* (Cheshire, Conn., 1783), intro.

[11] H. W. Smith, *Life . . . W. Smith*, ii. 175.

[12] Garret Wesley (1735–81), Earl of Mornington, was Professor of Music at the University of Dublin, 1764–74. See *New Grove*, xii. 586.

treble of the second phrase recitation in the Kelway chant is on the third rather than the fifth. In 'Lord Mornington in E flat', one of two Wesley chants in the same key, there are interesting variants from English manuscript sources, especially in melodic accent (Ex. 8.1). Both the Blow chant and the Kelway chant are transposed a third higher, perhaps to accommodate the choristers of Christ Church and St. Peter's Church.

The four chants in the Proposed Book, which was widely available during its trial period, provided a small repertory of chant tunes for any congregation that might wish to try out chanting in their services. Some surely did so, judging by reliable accounts and by music books perpetuating the Proposed Book repertory. Only one of these from the late eighteenth century is known at present, a small oblong tunebook from Philadelphia. It contains five chants,

Ex. 8.1. Lord Mornington in E♭: (*a*) Tr (Ob Tenbury MS 805); (*b*) Tr (DRc Music MS A 18); (*c*) Tr and B copied by Hopkinson

three reprinted from the Proposed Book (Blow, Kelway, and Mornington) and two reprinted from Law (Law no. 6, Turner in A for Cantate Domino, and no. 8, the Dallas/Bremner tune for Magnificat).[13] No texts were listed in the index or underlaid in the chants, but those usually tried out in initial experiments with chanting were the Venite or the canticles. Hopkinson described chanting as 'speaking musically':

The chants form a pleasing and animating part of the service; but it should be considered that they are not songs or tunes, but a species of recitative, which is no more than speaking musically. Therefore, as melody or song, is out of the question, it is necessary that the harmony should be complete, otherwise chanting, with all the voices in unison, is too light and thin for the solemnity of the occasion. There should at least be half a dozen voices in the organ gallery to fill the harmony with bass and treble parts, and give a dignity to the performance. Melody may be frivolous; harmony never.[14]

The choir of St. Michael's Church in Marblehead, Massachusetts chanted the canticles in Christmas services in 1787.[15] This was admittedly one of the main festivals of the year and customarily called for special music, but the choir continued to chant on ordinary Sundays, too. The rector wrote to his brother about the new practice the following February:

Will it give you any pleasure to learn that our choir at St. Michael's do constantly chant the Venite, the Te deum & in the afternoon the Cantate & Nunc dimittis to great acceptation. This I assure you is the case & I believe mine is almost the only Church on the Continent in which this is done.[16]

The word 'almost' is the crucial one in this account, for another New England church also claimed to be the first to chant.

It was said of St. Paul's Church in Narragansett, Rhode Island 'that in the Church at Narragansett, the Venite was first chanted in America'.[17] If this is so, the innovation would surely have taken place during the tenure of William Smith, rector from 1787 to 1789. Chanting the prose texts of the liturgy was one of Smith's central ideas for improving church music, for he believed that prose psalmody was closer to the practices of the primitive church than metrical psalms. He may well have been responsible for the Episcopal music

---

[13] *A Collection of Church Music, II* (1787). No copy of I, indexed in II, is known at present.

[14] Hopkinson, 'Letter to Doctor White'.

[15] Massachusetts Historical Society, Oliver Family Papers, Box 192, Folder 1785–1789; Marblehead, Mass., Saint Michael's Church Archives, 'Records of St. Michael's Church 1716–1784'.

[16] Thomas Fitch Oliver to Dr B. Lynde Oliver, 11 Feb. 1788, Oliver Family Papers, Box 192. Oliver was rector 1786–91.

[17] Wilkins Updike, *A History of the Episcopal Church in Narragansett, Rhode Island*, ed. Daniel Goodwin (Boston, 1907), ii. 19.

published in New Haven, Connecticut by Stephen Jenks and Israel Terril during the first few years of the nineteenth century. Jenks's tunebook has two liturgical items and these, like Law's, were undoubtedly included for commercial reasons, since there are no other such pieces in his large output of tunebooks. Terril's *Episcopal Harmony* (*c.*1802) was no doubt also a commercial venture, but it includes music for Morning and Evening Prayer and Communion arranged in liturgical order, a format that William Smith and John Cole would develop fully in their later works for the Episcopal church.

Terril, a relatively obscure Connecticut psalmodist, admitted that he had 'been requested by the Bishop, and a number of the Clergy and other friends of Christianity, to publish an edition of this kind'. William Smith was Principal of the Episcopal Academy in nearby Cheshire at the time, and his imprint can be seen in a typical Smith dictum in Terril's preface, 'it is a matter of regret that the ancient mode of singing, viz. by Chants and Anthems, has been so much neglected'. The music for Morning Prayer includes chants for Venite and Jubilate deo and through-composed settings of Gloria in excelsis, Gloria patri, and Te deum. The Venite is the Kelway chant from the Proposed Book, but here it is set in triple metre with instrumental interludes. Chants in this rhythm appear very rarely in printed books of similar vintage, though there are a few in John Aitken's later *Collection of Divine Music* (1806). The only obvious exception is the special Benedicite chants in which the second phrase, 'Praise him and magnify him forever', is set in triple metre as a choral refrain. Triple-metre chants, however, were apparently a fad in England at the time, for John Marsh roundly condemns them in his discussion of English chant in *Twenty four new Chants*:

The last innovation upon the plain Chant I shall notice, is a species I have lately met with in *triple* time, by which the single Chant, and each division in a double one, is lengthened out from ten to thirteen or fifteen notes. Should this deviation be allowed to pass, and become adopted, there is no knowing to what it may lead, as any alteration of the cadence may afterwards be made, and Chants for three or more verses may be introduced, by which means, what was originally intended to be simple and easy to a common congregation, will become a complicated system, attainable only by professed musicians.[18]

The Venite in Terril's psalmody is a good illustration of this sort of chant, which is neither fish nor fowl, falling somewhere in between a chant tune and a set liturgical anthem of the kind to be met with further on. The triple metre does change the underlying rhythm of the binary phrase dramatically, and it is easy to see why Marsh would be opposed on grounds of altering the traditional

---

[18] Marsh, *New Chants*, p. v.

Ex. 8.2. Terril Venite chant

chant formula. The chant is transcribed in Example 8.2 as it appears in Terril's book, the melody on the staff above the bass, inner parts on the top staff. The instrumental interludes written out in the current fashion only add to the un-chant-like feeling of the piece, although a note directs that 'the Symphonies or parts of music set for Instruments, are to be omitted when performed with voices only'. The *rule of 3 & 5* also makes its appearance in Terril's prefatory instructions for the first time in an American music book: 'in the performance of the chants, three syllables are sung in the first part of the verse and five in the last'. Smith is a likely source for this information, too.

Terril's Communion music includes the first American printing of William Mason's English Kyrie, the responses to the Commandments, and a setting of the Trisagion, that is, the Sanctus with its proper preface. The only Evening Prayer items are Turner in A for Cantate domino, a standard text–tune pairing in Scottish and American sources, and another chant for Deus misereatur or its alternate, Benedic anima mea, with the latter text. Jenks's versions of Turner in A and the Mason Kyrie show only minor differences from Terril, but the attributions are to Blake for Turner in A and Langdon for the Mason Kyrie. Richard Langdon's *Divine Harmony* is the first printing of the Mason setting and it was available in America, since other compilers used it. George Blake's *Vocal Harmony*, however, was published in Philadelphia about 1810.[19] Unless its date is much earlier than now supposed, Jenks's source lay elsewhere.

Two important tunebooks followed Jenks and Terril almost immediately from publishers in Baltimore and Philadelphia, John Cole and John Aitken. Cole's second edition of *The Beauties of Psalmody* was one of his many music books that carried a separate section of music in liturgical order for Morning Prayer, Evening Prayer, and Communion. Cole's repertory of chants and responses, some arranged by himself, come from a selection of manuscript and printed sources identified in Table 8.1. The Episcopal service music of Rayner

TABLE 8.1. *John Cole's 1805 service manual for Christ Church and St. Paul's*

Text	Music	Rubrics and notes
Morning Service		
Ve	Dbl chant Davis; pr Vandernan, *Divine Harmony*, 1770	'Venite, Exultemus. To be omitted on the 19th of the Month.' 1st pr Taylor arr as changeable chant
Glx	Sgl chant W. Turner; 1st Am pr Law, *Rudiments of Music*, 1783	'After the Psalms for the day—Gloria in Excelsis. The Gloria Patri, may be sung in place of this, to the same Chant.' 2nd recitation on 3rd of chord
Jd	Sgl chant Richard Woodward; pr Woodward, *Cathedral Music*, 1771	'After the second lesson—Jubilate Deo'
Bn	Dbl chant Thomas S. Dupuis; pr Boyce, *Cathedral Music 2*, 1768	'or the Benedictus.'
Evening Service		
Glx	same music as Morning Service	'After the Psalms for the day, sing the Gloria in Excelsis, as in the Morning Service.'
Cd	Dbl chant Jonathan Battishill; pr Vandernan, *Divine Harmony*, 1770; ?copied from Marsh, *Twenty four New Chants*, [1804]	'After the 1st lesson—Cantate Domino— To be omitted on the Nineteenth day of the Month.' tr. to D, new 3rd phrase
Bc	same music as Cd	'Or this. Bonum Est Confiteri to the same Chant.'
Dm	Sgl chant Henry Aldrich; pr Boyce, *Cathedral Music 1*, 1760	'After the 2nd Lesson—Deus Misereatur. To be omitted the 12th of the Month.'
BnA	Sgl chant Thomas Jackson; pr Jackson, *Twelve Psalm Tunes*, [1780]	'Or this. Benedic, Anima Mea.'
Communion Service		
CoR	Setting William Mason; pr Langdon, *Divine Harmony*, 1774	'Response after the Tenth Commandment.' Mason's last response only
Glt	Setting John Cole	'Doxology before the Gospel.'
Glp	Setting ?John Cole	'Doxology, after Sermon.' Metrical text; adagio close.

[19] A. P. Britton, I. Lowens, and R. Crawford, *Sacred Music Imprints 1698–1810: A Bibliography* (Worcester, Mass., 1990), 188–9.

Taylor, one of the important church composers in this period, first appears in print here. Taylor was formerly organist of St Mary's Church, Chelmsford (now a cathedral church), a large market town north-east of London, from about 1772 to 1783.[20] He returned to London for about ten years and emigrated to America in 1792. He was organist of St. Peter's Episcopal Church in Philadelphia from 1795 to about 1813. According to colleagues, Taylor was generous with copies of his liturgical pieces. Benjamin Carr noted that his own *Collection of Chants and Tunes* 'consists of old chants and tunes that were then in use—the former are by Mr. Taylor and arranged by him—and whenever I doubted the genuineness of a tune I applied to Mr. Taylor who furnished me with a correct copy'.[21]

Taylor's arrangement of a double chant for Venite, printed by Cole, was one of the most often reprinted chants in the early years of the Episcopal Church. Taylor set the ninth verse in the tonic minor key as a variation, with a repetition of the text in the first two bars. The first and last phrases of the original chant are combined, and each is extended by one measure (Ex. 8.3). The doxology is then sung in the major key of the first eight verses. This is one of the early chant arrangements that fall stylistically somewhere between a formula and a miniature set piece, the kind of short liturgical anthem that was widely imitated. Taylor's Philadelphia colleague, Benjamin Carr, printed this piece in his later *Collection* with the characteristic Carr expressive touch, a dotted minim and a hold over the rest in the first bar of the ninth verse. In the organ-book used at St. Peter's Church, every verse is introduced with a brief interlude or trill, usually on the pitch below the reciting tone (see below, Ex. 8.9).

Cole's service music supplement has another important feature, its systematic ways of coordinating text syllables with their music. The allocation of a full text and music for each chant is determined by the layout of the page, but in each case text syllables are matched to notes in one way or another. The text in the Taylor Venite is underlaid, and the syllables to be sung to the cadences are italicized, as shown in Ex. 8.3. The Gloria in excelsis is laid out below and spaced to fit the music, making italics unnecessary. The Jubilate deo and Benedictus texts are printed beside or below their music, and again the cadential syllables are italicized. Cole could have worked out these methods of showing syllable placement in the course of his own service playing, but he

---

[20] Essex Record Office, Chelmsford, Records of St Mary's Church, D/P94/11/2; Norwich Public Record Office, A. H. Mann MS 448; *Chelmsford Chronicle* (9 July, 3 Sept. 1773; 22 July, 26 Aug. 1774). Taylor (1747–1825) was an unsuccessful candidate for the organist's post in two London churches in 1785 and 1790 (Dawe, *Organists of the City of London*, 29, 44), and this may have had some influence on his decision to emigrate in 1792.

[21] University of Pennsylvania, Van Pelt–Dietrich Library Center, Special Collections, Parker Papers, Box 4, Folder 10, Benjamin Carr to John R. Parker, 4 Oct. 1821.

Ex. 8.3. Davis double chant arranged by Taylor

1. O come let us sing un - to the Lord:
3. For the Lord is a great _____ God:
5. The sea is his and he made it;
7. For he is the Lord our God;

let us ... our sal - va - - tion.
and a great King a - bove all Gods.
and his hands pre - pared the _____ dry land.
and we are the people ... and the sheep of his hand.

[Gloria patri in major]

2. Let us come before ... with thanks - giving;
4. In his hand are ... of the earth;
6. O come let us ... and fall down;
8. O worship the Lord ... hol - i - ness;

and shew ourselves glad in _____ him with psalms.
and the strength ... hills is _____ his al - so
and kneel before ... Lord our _____ Ma - - ker.
let the whole earth stand in awe of him

may also have been familiar with John Marsh's dissertation on chant in *Twenty four New Chants*, published the year before, in which Marsh demonstrated his idea of italicizing cadential syllables.

John Aitken's early sacred music was published for the Roman Catholic service in 1787, but the *Collection of Divine Music* (1806) cast a wider net, catering for the service music needs of Episcopalians with about twenty chants for Episcopal texts. These were copied on odd staves throughout the book and were chosen mainly from English publications, but a few new chants by Rayner Taylor and George K. Jackson were also included. There did not seem to be any proscription about juxtaposing chants with Latin texts used in Roman Catholic churches with English chants for Episcopal churches, a phenomenon, perhaps, of the New World. The subscribers to Aitken's 1806 collection included Bishop White, Rayner Taylor, Alexander Reinagle, and John Cole.[22] A number of Aitken's chants are part of the modest eclectic repertory George Blake compiled in *Vocal Harmony* from collections already in print, including a triple-metre version of Lord Mornington in E flat, printed earlier in the Proposed Book.

The most ambitious early Episcopal service manual was the Reverend Dr. William Smith's *The Churchman's Choral Companion to his Prayer Book*, 'designed to furnish the Protestant Episcopal Churches in the United States,

---

[22] Britton, Lowens, and Crawford, *Sacred Music Imprints*, 89.

with a form of services in prose, and . . . to hold a medium between the volu-
minous and difficult service of the Cathedral, and that which is unadorned,
and merely parochial'.[23] Single and double chants, responses and doxologies,
and liturgical anthems make up the music for daily and weekly services, and
holy days in the church calendar. Smith applied to a new committee on sacred
music appointed at the New York Diocesan Convention in October 1809 for
official adoption of his manual. At the New York Convention meeting a year
later, the committee was able to report: 'With regard to Chants, they recommend the collection of the Rev. Dr. William Smith, so far as that collection
comports with the Rubrics of the Church in the United States of America.'[24]

No further action was taken in regard to Smith's manual, nor is there any
evidence that he was able to find out what objections there might be on rubri-
cal grounds. However, Smith's direction to the priest to intone the opening
phrase in each chant was innovative in terms of Episcopal liturgical practice,
and may have seemed radical at the time. His use of Latin titles for some items
could have been a problem, and there were statements in the preface which
seemed to prejudice the long-standing custom of singing metrical psalms.
Bishop White explained the rejection of Smith's subsequent application to
General Convention in New Haven in May 1811:

> The book is well esteemed; and it was not from dissatisfaction with it, that the appli-
> cation was rejected; but because the request to enjoin the use of chants and tunes
> exclusively of all others, was thought unreasonable. The expectation of the applicant
> has been misunderstood by some; who have supposed, that he included in his demand
> the prohibition of the singing of psalms in metre.[25]

The discussion of this issue must have been quite heated and Smith's
thoughts on psalmody were evidently well known, although his major theological and theoretical treatises on the subject had not yet been published.[26]
He preached that 'without chanting, our services are destitute of vocal
psalmody; for the appointed psalms and hymns of public worship, when *read*,
become verbal scriptures addressed to the human understanding, rather than
vocal praises offered up to Almighty God'.[27] He believed, along with the
English Evangelicals, that chanting could be easily learned, and was within the
capabilities of volunteer choirs and congregations.

---

[23] William Smith, *Choral Companion*, preface.
[24] *Journals of the Annual Conventions of the Diocese of New York* (1810), 9, 19, quoted in K. W. Cameron, *Samuel Seabury among his Contemporaries* (Hartford, Conn., 1980), Part One, 83.
[25] William White, *Memoirs of the Protestant Episcopal Church in the United States of America*, ed. B. F. deCosta (New York, 1880), 285.
[26] These were *The Reasonableness of Setting Forth the Most Worthy Praise of Almighty God* (New York, 1814) and *An Assistant to the Evangelical Psalmodist* (New Haven, 1816).
[27] William Smith, *The Reasonableness of Setting Forth . . . Praise*, p. vi.

Choral Companion was dedicated to and recommended by Henry Moore, Bishop of New York, and despite its failure to receive the General Convention's stamp of approval, it was adopted in many churches. Among them were St. George's and St. John's, chapels of Trinity Church, New York, where Smith's colleague Peter Erben was organist.[28] Jacob Eckhard used the *Choral Companion* at St. Michael's Church in Charleston, South Carolina. Smith's rubric for the performance of the Benedicite is copied in Benjamin Carr's organbook (New York Public Library, Drexel 5843, discussed below), indicating that Smith's book was used in Philadelphia churches. The music offered a balanced choice between traditional items and new pieces arranged and composed expressly for the publication, and the layout of text and music across facing pages was easily comprehended.

The rubrics, attributions, sources of the music, and the pieces themselves make the *Choral Companion* well worth exploring as a significant and representative repertory of early Episcopal service music. This information is brought together in Table 8.3 (at the end of this chapter) and makes it possible to see very quickly the diversity and wide range of clerical and musical contributors. In Smith's words, 'of these Chants, Responses, and Anthems, some are derived from English Cathedral services, others from anonymous books of celebrity, and most of the Harmonies have the names of the authors prefixed, when they could be ascertained with certainty.' All but a few pieces are attributed, although the name that is given is not always synonymous with the original composer. The printed sources are some of those that provided English parish and cathedral churches, and dissenting chapels, too, with their service music. Some pieces are from the music publications of other liturgical denominations, for instance, the United Brethren. The manuscript sources include new pieces from composers and copies of chants that circulated mostly in manuscript. Smith stated that pieces by Rayner Taylor and Benjamin Carr were provided through the good offices of the Revd James Abercrombie, D.D., of Philadelphia.

Functional music is traditionally regarded as common property and therefore adaptable to local needs, and *Choral Companion* follows the customary procedures. In the more routine adaptations, four-part chants are arranged for two or three voices, or the tenor is transcribed for first or second treble in a four-part texture of two trebles, alto, and bass. Smith observes the conventions of early nineteenth-century notation: 'the alto and second treble are frequently set in the upper stave; the first treble or cantabile, is always set directly over

---

[28] Erben was at St. George's 1807–13 and St. John's 1813–20. He and Smith worked together in the Society for Cultivating Church Music, supported in part by Trinity Church. See Trinity Church, New York, Minutes of the Vestry, vols. i, ii.

the bass, and has the harmony filled up with small notes for the benefit of amateurs and young performers on the organ and piano forte'. The lower two staves thus serve as the keyboard score, with figured bass given for most chants, but since the accompaniment is also written out, they do not appear in examples from the collection quoted here. Smith was of the opinion that 'for Chanting, the swell and the choir organ ought to be used in general, and the full organ in doxologies', and for choral forces, he suggested that 'a choir of twenty good singers are quite sufficient to direct and give a proper tone to the singing of any of our largest congregations'.[29] These were best arranged with eight singing bass, six on first treble, four on second treble, and two on counter or alto.

Besides adapted chant formulae, *Choral Companion* contains a sample of the many new chant arrangements and small settings of responses, doxologies, and texts for Litany, Communion, and special holy days. One of Benjamin Carr's short chant-derived settings, for example, the Agnus dei with which Smith begins his section of 'Litany Chants and Anthems', was first published with Latin text for St. Augustine's Roman Catholic Church, where Carr was organist.[30] It is a good example of his approach to functional liturgical anthems, and resembles the style of William Mason's responses for the Commandments. The chorus begins 'Lord have mercy' and a solo treble enters for just over half a bar at 'that takest', followed by a three-bar duet in thirds for two trebles at 'away the sins of the world'. Two chorus statements of 'grant us', separated by whole-bar rests, culminate in the last, 'grant us thy peace', and this chorus is then sung again. The same music accommodates the final statement of the text, closing with 'have mercy upon us', the rhythm adjusted to the words (Ex. 8.4). The composer explained the reason for three parts: 'It is very difficult to find Counter Tenors in all the Choirs I have anything to do with . . . the best reason I can give you for 3 instead of 4 parts, is an old proverb "cut your coat according to your cloth".'[31]

There are eleven pieces by Rayner Taylor in *Choral Companion*, about as many as he contributed to Carr's *Masses, Vespers, Litanies . . .* for the Roman Catholic service. The short settings and chants are written in a comfortable vocal range and easy harmonic style, with melodies made memorable by a

[29] William Smith, *The Reasonableness of Setting Forth . . . Praise*, 164–74.

[30] Benjamin Carr, *Masses, Vespers, Litanies . . .* (Philadelphia, 1805). Carr (1768–1831) was organist of St. Augustine's Roman Catholic Church, 1801–31, and concurrently organist of St. Peter's Episcopal Church for an undetermined tenure. It is reasonable to assume the degree of coordination of music and performance practice indicated in Carr's own publications, but the subject of Roman Catholic–Episcopal relationships in terms of liturgy and music is an extended separate inquiry.

[31] University of Pennsylvania, Special Collections, Parker Papers, Box 4, Folder 10, Carr to Parker, 30 June 1821.

Ex. 8.4. Carr setting of Agnus dei

moving passage, triplet, or other small gesture. One of Taylor's arrangements, his version of the Scottish triple chant Te deum known as 'Old Scottish Chant', is still sung in several Protestant denominations in the United States (see above, Exx. 7.3 and 7.4).[32] Taylor added a fourth voice to Robert Bremner's version in three, and regularized rhythmic values into semibreves and minims. This new arrangement was used by Smith for both Te deum and Gloria in excelsis (see Fig. 7). The Gloria was sung more frequently in American churches than the Te deum, since it could be sung as an alternate doxology in Morning and Evening Prayer, in addition to its prescribed place in the Communion service. Whether for this reason or for its musical features, the Gloria in excelsis to the Dallas/Bremner chant in Taylor's arrangement had become a standard item in the liturgy by the mid-nineteenth century. Indeed,

---

[32] See the list of denominational music books with the Old Scottish Chant in Wilson, 'The Old Scottish Chant', *The Hymn*, 31 (1980), 174–82.

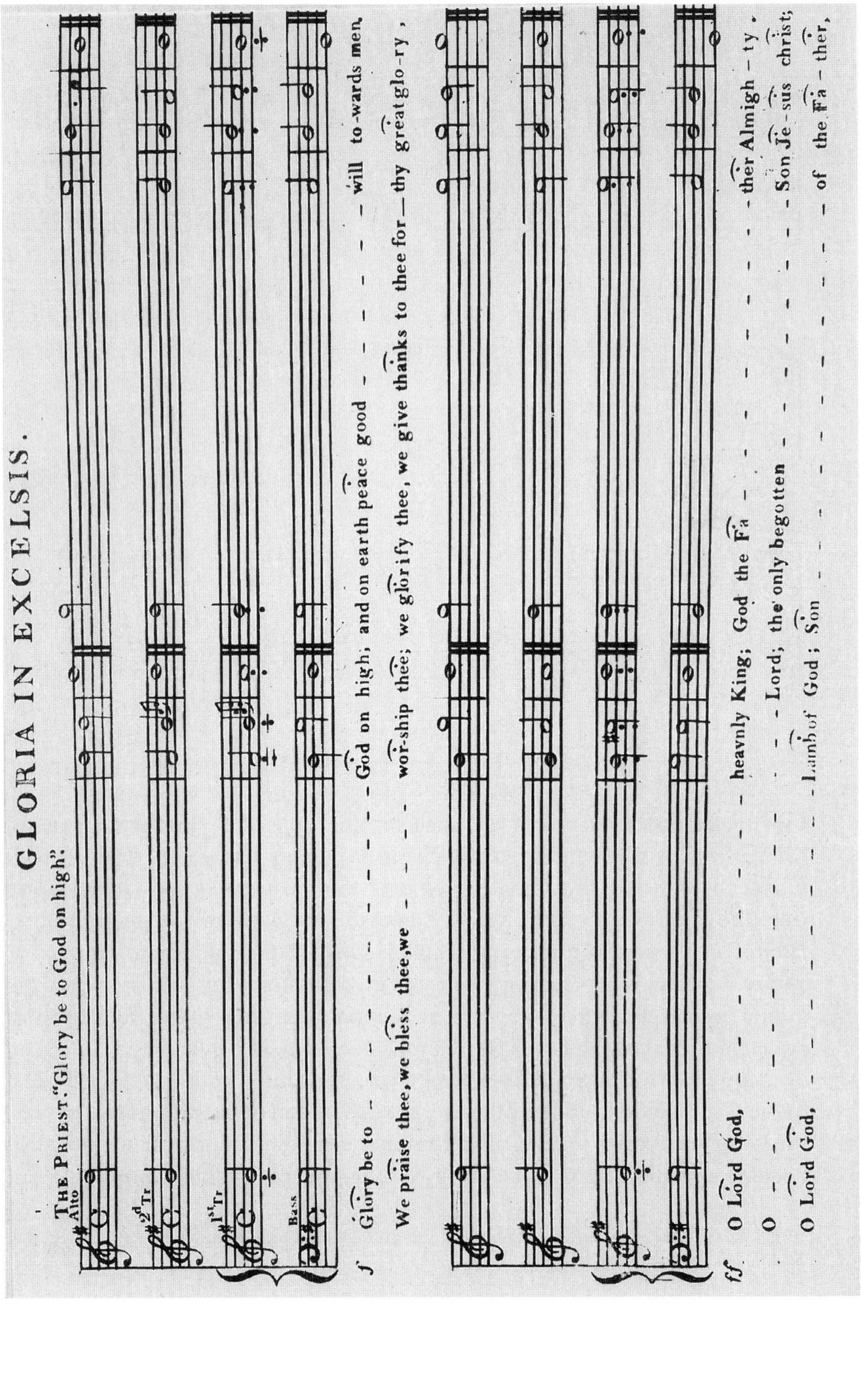
GLORIA IN EXCELSIS.
THE PRIEST: "Glory be to God on high."
Alto
2d Tr
1st Tr
Bass
f
Glory be to God on high; and on earth peace good will to-wards men,
We praise thee, we bless thee, we wor-ship thee; we glorify thee, we give thanks to thee for thy great glo-ry,
ff
O Lord God, heavnly King; God the Fa-ther Almigh-ty.
O Lord; the only begotten Son Je-sus christ;
O Lord God, Lamb of God; Son of the Fa-ther,

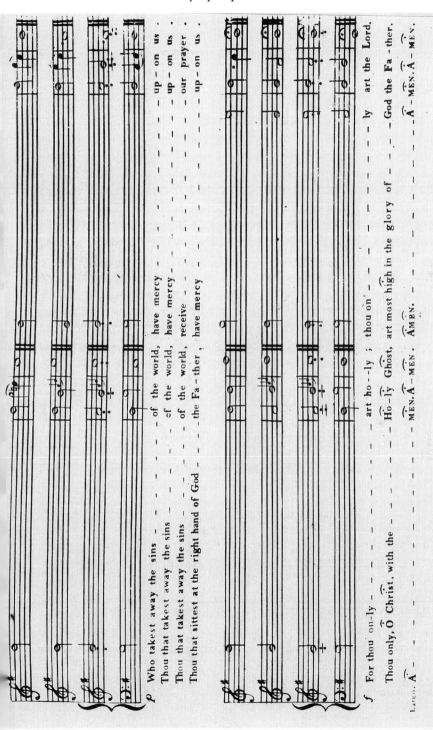

FIG. 7. Gloria in excelcis, William Smith, *The Churchman's Choral Companion to his Prayer Book* (New York, 1809), 32–3

one publisher maintained that 'excepting "the old *Gloria in Excelsis*" there is hardly a fragment of our service that has its own music'.[33] The 'Old Scottish Chant' was usually sung by the congregation in unison, the organ filling out the harmony, the minister singing or intoning the first phrase in accordance with Smith's rubric.

Perhaps the most influential Episcopal musician represented in *Choral Companion* was Dr George K. Jackson, and Smith gave him special mention in his preface: 'a few Chants were revised, some years since, by Dr. Jackson, of this city, with a view to publicity—and the favour is not forgotten'. Jackson occupied an important place among his colleagues, for he was generally recognized as the leading authority on English cathedral music. He was reported to have received his training in the Chapel Royal under James Nares and was organist of St Alban Wood Street in the city of London from 1774 to 1790.[34] He was awarded a doctorate in music from St Andrew's University in Scotland in 1791 and emigrated to America sometime before 1797. Smith knew him during the years he was active in New York in the first decade of the nineteenth century. He was organist of St. George's Chapel from 1802 to 1807, an acknowledged contributor to several publications of Episcopal service music, and, in the latter years of his life, adviser to Lowell Mason in Boston. The Revd Jonathan Wainwright's remarks about Jackson in the preface to *A Set of Chants* (1819) are a typical accolade:

With respect to the music, the Compiler can speak with greater confidence, than with regard to the arrangement of the words, because, in this part of the work, he has been able to avail himself of the important assistance of Dr. G. K. Jackson, whose profound knowledge of the science of harmony, and long acquaintance with Cathedral music, render him in every way competent to the task. Dr. Jackson has not only corrected the harmony of the chanting tunes, which have been selected from the most approved ancient masters, but he has furnished the work with several of his own valuable compositions.

One of Jackson's chants in *Choral Companion* is the only one in Smith's collection in which the customary interludes are written out. The first four verses of Venite are sung in the major key and the next four to the same chant in the tonic minor key. It was routine in changeable chants to return to the major key in the doxology. Jackson's original chant is set for treble, alto, tenor, and bass, while Smith has changed the tenor to a treble part. The different voicing produces an interchange of treble parts and places the melody in the midst of the texture rather than on top, a procedure that would seem to obscure the

[33] George Rider, *Plain Music for the Book of Common Prayer* (New York, 1854), preface.
[34] Guildhall Library, MS 1264/3, Vestry Minutes, St Alban Wood Street, 110, 320. Jackson was born in 1757 and died in Boston in 1822.

original tune, unless the number of voices singing it overwhelmed the other parts. Only the first verse of text is shown in Ex. 8.5; the holds over certain words are Smith's way of indicating what words should be emphasized.

One of Smith's more successful editing techniques produced a good practical solution to problems of text underlay. The full text for each chant is printed beneath its music, the notes carefully spaced out according to the desired placement of each syllable in the cadences. The *rule of 3 & 5* is quite strictly observed, but Smith later moved to a more flexible system of pointing, explaining that he had thought it necessary in 1809 'to compliment the ear of our people accustomed to syllabic singing [metrical psalms] only'.[35] John Cole carried Smith's text layout a step further in *Episcopalian Harmony* (1811). He extended the musical barline down the page through the text below, to separate and enclose syllables with the portion of the chant they were to be sung to, a legible format which easily accommodated variable verse lengths and verbal accentuation. It is easy to see why this way of laying out text and music was adopted almost exclusively for chants in Episcopal collections for many years to come. It is equally easy to see why more complicated directions for coping with the coordination of word accent and musical accent, such as William Bull's method of chanting designated text to *supposed notes* in unison to the one printed and 'after *y*, proceed syllibically', were short-lived.[36]

Publications containing Episcopal service music from the second decade of the century continued the trends set by their predecessors. The *Chants, Occasional Pieces and Plain Tunes* published in Salem, Massachusetts, for example, was largely a reprint of music from Smith's *Choral Companion*. John Cole in Baltimore repeated his tried-and-true formula for a service-music section in liturgical order in several general collections. A close relationship between manuscript and print continued, and two tunebooks that came out in 1816 contained music from organbooks of Benjamin Carr and Jacob Eckhard. The Episcopal Church was growing rapidly in this period and creating an increased demand for special service-music publications with directions for chanting. Eventually, individual churches supported the compilation of liturgical music for their own use, as was done in the old country. An early example is *Chants of the Morning and Evening Prayer and Communion Service as sung at St. James's Church, Philadelphia* (1820).

A few music publications were unusual for the times. George K. Jackson brought out the first large American collection devoted almost exclusively (except for one 'Sanctus') to chants, at least half of these of his own composition.

---

[35] William Smith, *An Assistant to the Evangelical Psalmodist*, 6. Cf. Broom's early 18th-c. Cantate domino for parish use in Ex. 6.12.

[36] William Bull, *Music, Adapted to Language* (Greenfield, Mass., 1819, copyright 1813), 29.

Ex. 8.5. Jackson's double chant adapted by Smith

The Priest, 'O come let us sing unto the Lord.'

A Choice Collection of Chants for Four Voices . . . As used in Cathedrals, Churches & Chapels is a small oblong volume in the style of English cathedral chant books, which in this period rarely included text or specific directions. In Jackson's chant book, however, an exception had to be made to accommodate uninitiated participants. As he pointed out, 'experience teaches us that the Art of Chanting requires good Judgment, nice Discernment, and great Practice. Tho' Chanting is confined only to General Rules yet these properly applied will be found both Useful and Necessary.' The *rule of 3 & 5* is familiar, but Jackson's system of assigning a number to each note of the chant is unique:

To Number 1. is Chanted the first part of the Verse, Ending at the Colon Stop, excepting the Three last Syllables, which are sung to the Numbers 2. 3. & 4. If any small word, or article, should ocurr in the three last Syllables, it is generally sung to No. 3. and if the word immediately preceeding the Colon Stop, consists of Two Syllables, it is generally sung to No. 4.

To Number 5, is Chanted the second part of the Verse, Ending at the Period Stop, excepting the Five last Syllables, which are sung to the Numbers 6. 7. 8. 9. & 10. If any small words, or articles, should occur in the Five last Syllables they are generally sung to the Numbers 7. & 9. and if the Verse Ends with a word of Two Syllables it is generally sung to No.10.

N.B. The above refers to the Metrical No's of the Chant.

The next year Jackson published a companion volume, *The Choral Companion and Elucidation of Dr. G. K. Jackson's Chants*, in which eight of the pieces in the first collection are joined by a Communion Office with Kyrie, Trisagion, Gloria tibi, 'Sanctus', and Gloria in excelsis. The Sanctus, so called, was not a setting of the liturgical text at all, but another text intended to be sung as an introit between the sections of Divine Service. The music in this companion is presented in the Smith/Cole format with full text underlay and barlines extended to enclose text syllables with their notes. Gone are the numbers giving the 'metre of the chant'. In his first chant book, Jackson laid out the music in the usual manner, the treble and bass on the lower two staves, which are also the 'organo' part with figured bass, and the alto and tenor on their separate upper staves. In the companion volume, the four voice-parts are written in choral score, treble on top, still with figured bass written in. The chants are numbered according to the original collection and some have revoiced inner parts and small alterations. Chant no. 26, for example, published first by Smith and then by Jackson as a changeable chant, appears in the companion volume as a single chant in D major for Deus misereatur, all verses and the doxology sung to the same music.

Among the many compositions Jackson has left in manuscripts are some of

his chants and Episcopal service settings.[37] While these copies provide authoritative readings, more specific information relating to performance practice of
the period can be found in the surviving organbooks from Episcopal churches
in Charleston and Philadelphia. Jacob Eckhard prepared a large collection of
psalm and hymn tunes, anthems and service music for the parish choir of St.
Michael's Church in Charleston soon after taking up his duties there in 1809.[38]
Besides his own organbook, he copied out books for the choir and placed in
each a printed notice: 'The Members of the Choir are particularly requested
not to write in, turn over the backs, or otherwise deface the Manuscript
Books—They were made with much cost of time, labour and expense, and
belong exclusively to the Organist.' Choir members were allowed to borrow
the books for practice at home during the week. St. Michael's vies with
St Andrew's in Glasgow for first honours in maintaining a surpliced choir in a
parish church. In the last decade of the eighteenth century, under the aegis of
the Reverend Henry Purcell, rector from 1782 to 1802, choirboys were
recruited from the Charleston Orphan House, where Eckhard conducted the
annual children's concert. A twelve-voice male vested choir was in existence
in 1791, and the boys were singing until about 1801. The next few years were
without a choir, for the vestry designated the parish clerk and the organist to
work together to recruit and teach boys psalmody and chanting. In the minutes, notice was taken of the 'well-supported choir' in St. Philip's Church, and
additional funds and guidelines for rehearsal schedules were set out, and a minimum number of twelve boys requested.[39]

The music in Eckhard's organbook is written in short score with figured
bass, and graces and interludes are sparingly used. Sources and previous
American printings are listed in Table 8.2 (the letter designations are those
used in the facsimile edition). The majority of the chants come from Smith's
Choral Companion, which came out early in 1809, and was thus available to
Eckhard when he moved in the late spring from his post at St. John's Lutheran
Church to St. Michael's Episcopal Church. Half of Eckhard's twenty chants
have no text underlay and no specific text designated, while all verses are written out for the Venite, Deus misereatur, and Benedic anima mea. Chants a
through g, k, m, and s vary from the standard Anglican chant formula in having six bars each, twelve in doubles. The terminal cadences are two bars long
rather than three, and in some chants part of the first cadence bar is placed at
the end of the recitation.

In 1816 Eckhard published a smaller collection of music containing selec-

---

[37] Illinois State University Library, Special Collections, M 1. A1 J3, & v. 4.

[38] See above, n. 7.

[39] George W. Williams, *St. Michael's Charleston, 1751–1951* (Columbia, SC, 1951), 206–13.

TABLE 8.2. *Jacob Eckhard's organbook: service music*

Facs. no.	Music	Source and notes
a	Sgl chant T. Purcell	tr. D to A
b	Sgl ch in C	anon.
c	Dbl ch John Jones	Smith (1809); see k
d	Turner in A	Cole (1805), Blake (c.1810); see m; 2nd recitation on third of
chord		
e	Sgl ch Turner	from Boyce 1 (1760)?
f	Turner in A, original tune	Law (1783), Proposed Bk (1786), Smith Terril (c.1802), Jenks (1804), Cole
g	Sgl ch Kelway	Proposed Bk, Terril, Blake, Smith
h	Sgl ch in C	Ve written out, 4 bars each phrase
i j	Changeable, G. Jackson	Smith, D/D m, Ve
k	Dbl ch John Jones	Smith, BnA written out; see c
l	Chant setting	Jd by ?Eckhard
m	Turner in A	Dm written out; see d
n	Sgl ch H. Aldrich	Dm alternate, Cole, Smith
o	Dbl ch John Robinson	Smith Proper Christmas Day, 'Sing we merrily'
p	Dbl ch T. Dupuis	Smith Proper New Year's Day, no text
q	Sgl ch from Td, Latrobe, *Hymn Tunes*, 1806	Smith
r	Grace from Latrobe	arr Smith, marked Largo, note-values halved
s	Sgl ch, arr. from Dallas/Bremner Mg	Law, Glx chant setting, 2nd phrase variation
t	Setting ?Eckhard	Gospel acclamation
u	Setting Taylor	Gospel acclamation

tions from his manuscript books for the Episcopal service, and hymns authorized by the Evangelical Lutheran Synod of New York. In the chants for Venite exultemus, Benedic anima mea, Gloria in excelsis, and Easter Day, complete texts are set out under the music in the Smith/Cole format. The method of syllable placement adheres closely but not rigidly to the *rule of 3 & 5*. The text of the 'Chant for Easter Day', for example, departs from the rule in the terminal cadence of most verses, and indicates that Eckhard's shortened terminations are text-related (Ex. 8.6). The melody will be familiar to Episcopalians, for it is the 'Old Scottish Chant', arranged as a changeable chant. In the hymn section of the book for Lutheran use, Eckhard has rewritten the music for the Episcopal chants at the beginning of the book, without text, to allow Lutheran readers to chant the texts appropriate to their own liturgy. The voice parts in these chants in short score are arranged in modern fashion, treble on top.

Two organbooks used in St. Peter's Church in Philadelphia contain a number of chants by Rayner Taylor and Benjamin Carr, in which interludes, embellishments, and performance directions are written out. 'Chaunts, Psalms & Hymns for St. Peter's Church' is either a preparation copy for Carr's 1816 *Collection of Chants and Tunes*, or a manuscript copy of it, since it is indexed in

Ex. 8.6. Eckhard arrangement of 'Old Scottish Chant' for Easter

1. Christ our passover is sacrifi   -   ced   for   us;
3. Christ being raised from the dead di - eth   no   more;
5. Likewise reckon yourselves dead indeed un   -   to   sin,
7. For since by   man   came   death,

Therefore let   us   keep   the   feast.
Death hath no more domi   -   nion   o - ver   him.
But alive unto God. through Je - sus   Christ   our   Lord.
By man came also the resurrec - tion   of   the   dead.

2. Not with the leaven of malice and wick - ed   -   -   ness;
4. For in that he died, he died un - to   sin   once;
6. Christ is risen   from   the   dead,
8. For as in A   -   -   dam   all   die,

But with the unlearned bread of sincer - i - ty   and   truth.
But in that he liveth, he li   -   -   veth   un - to   God.
And become the first fruits   of   them   that   sleep.
Even so in Christ shall all   be   made   a - live.

the same order.[40] The 'Collection of Sacred Music' contains autographs of many liturgical compositions by Benjamin Carr and later additions in the hands of Joseph Taws, W. H. W. Darley, and J. C. Standbridge, who followed Carr as organists of St. Peter's Church.[41] These organbooks are extremely valuable for recreating performance practice of their time, for very few printed tunebooks show the style of chant accompaniment. They also record pieces whose structure, source, and transmission are of great interest.

'The Foundlings Chant from recollection' in Drexel 5843 was arranged by Carr from its performance in the chapel of the Foundling Hospital in

Ex. 8.7. 'Foundlings Chant (London) from recollection' (NYp Drexel MS 5843)

[40] Philadelphia Free Library, 783.9. C 23c. A collation of Carr's MSS and publications can be consulted in Ronnie L. Smith, 'The Church Music of Benjamin Carr', SMD diss. (Southwestern Baptist Theological Seminary, 1969).

[41] New York Public Library, Special Collections, Drexel 5843, 'Collection of Sacred Music', labelled 'B. Carr's Library, 287, Organo'.

Ex. 8.7. *cont.*

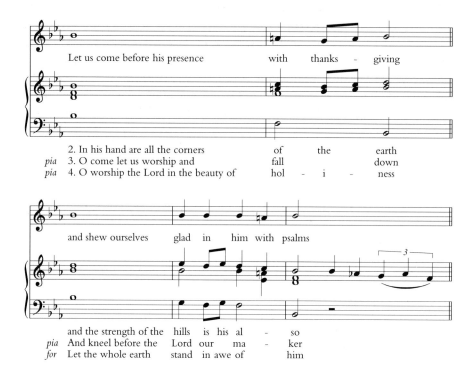

London.[42] The text is the Venite exultemus and the music is a double chant version of the Chetham parish alternatim Te deum. The third and fourth phrases are on the dominant as they are in the original Te deum, in which alternate verses are sung on the tonic and the dominant by different vocal duos. Short organ interludes connect the halves of the chant, and lead the singers up to the reciting tone on the fifth, and back to the tonic at the beginning of the next verse (Ex. 8.7). The triplet figures are both functional and ornamental. Note that in the ninth verse (labelled 5 in the example), the text of the recitation is repeated, and holds placed where they occur in the Taylor arrangement of Davis's double chant (Ex. 8.3 above).

Carr has written out in Drexel 5843 the interludes and special instructions for the final verses in Rayner Taylor's double chant for Te deum; they do not

[42] The Hospital for the Maintenance and Education of Exposed and Deserted Children, otherwise the Foundlings Hospital, was founded by Thomas Coram in 1714. The chapel, built in 1747, was a proprietary chapel, not consecrated but licensed for Anglican worship by the Bishop of the diocese. See Temperley, *MEPC*, i. 206–7.

appear in the copy in the Philadelphia organbook. The first chant statement, an intervening sequence, and the final verses of the Te deum are reproduced in Example 8.8. The arpeggiated-chord technique is described in the preface to Carr's 1805 *Masses, Vespers, Litanies*, where he tells the novice organist 'at the close of each piece to take his fingers off the chord one by one, beginning at the top note and pausing awhile on the lowest or last note'. The diatonic or chromatic preparation for the choir to begin the next verse was used for the Responses in case the officiant ended the recitation in the wrong key. Taking the officiant's last pitch, Carr wrote, 'may bring some of the notes, especially

Ex. 8.8. Taylor Td chant, select verses in organ score written out by Carr (NYp Drexel MS 5843)

Ex. 8.8. *cont.*

in the bass, below the usual pitch, and otherwise derange the parts', and he recommended 'a diatonic or chromatic assent, with a shake on the last note'.

The Philadelphia organbook from St. Peter's Church contains organ scores for several chants with interludes written in, none with the full directions Carr wrote out for the Te deum, but interesting examples nonetheless (Ex. 8.9). The diatonic ascent with a shake on the top note before the reciting tone can be seen in the Jubilate deo, also the chromatic interlude and shorter ascending

Ex. 8.8. *cont.*

vv. 26–29

scale between verses. Preparatory trills in both treble and bass clefs are a feature of Taylor's Venite chant, while his setting of the Trisagion as a liturgical
anthem is introduced with the ascending arpeggio. The Amen is reminiscent
of the parish alternatim canticles examined earlier.

All these accompaniment techniques are discussed, either historically or in
instructional terms, in a later publication by Thomas Loud. In a note 'of taking and leaving a chord on the organ', he directed the organist to 'take the

Ex. 8.9. Organ scores (PHf 783.9.C23c): (*a*) Jd; (*b*) Ve; (*c*) Trisagion

(*a*)

O be joyful all ye lands
in the Lord

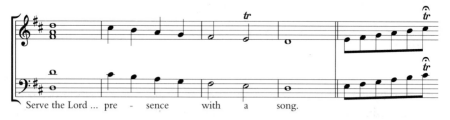

Serve the Lord ... pre - sence with a song.

(*b*)

O come let   let us
us sing un - to the Lord   heartily...

our sal - va - - tion   Let us come
before...

(*c*)

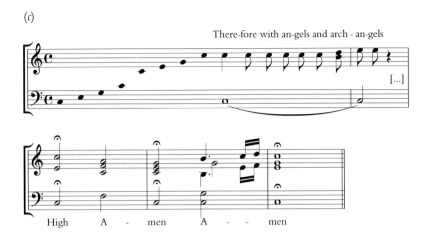

There-fore with an-gels and arch - an-gels

[...]

High   A - men   A - - men

notes one by one, beginning at the bottom note, and leave them in the same way, beginning at the top note . . . the first half of it should be used for the commencement of a Chant or Tune where no preparatory shake is given.'[43] This is described as the 'method now used' (1845), but it had already been part of Carr's practice:

It has been usual to lead into Chants and Psalm and Hymn tunes, by what is called the introductory shake, that is, a shake either on the note below or above the note to be first sung; this, however, is in a great measure abandoned; the method now used is, to close the prelude or interlude with the final chord, and then lead up, from the bass note the first chord of the tune, (the voices falling in when the chord is full), following on the rest of the tune in the ordinary way, so also between the different lines of a verse or chant, a slight leaving off of the upper parts of the last chord, after its time has passed and then filling up the first chord of the next movement will be sufficient to call the voices to their parts, and is much better than any shake or running about of the right hand.[44]

Loud's reference to a slight leaving off of the upper notes of the chord between the lines of a chant would produce the same pedal bass William Smith had recommended earlier, as a device for marking the main divisions of a chant for singers:

At the time of each half verse, the upper part ought to rest the time of a minum, but the bass should continue; and at the end of each verse, a rest of one semibreve is advisable, not only to relieve the singers from continued exertion, but also that a proper distinction may be made between one verse and another.[45]

[43] Thomas Loud, *The Organ Study: Being an Introduction to the Practice of the Organ* (Philadelphia, 1845), 5.
[44] Ibid. 14.   [45] William Smith, *Choral Companion*, preface.

Carr recommended to the organist 'pausing awhile on the lowest note' before leaving the final chord.

Loud's directions for playing Rayner Taylor's changeable chant to Venite exultemus involve accelerating the tempo in the ascending arpeggios, depending on their position in the chant:

At the commencement of a chant or tune in the division of the chord the first and lowest note should be made rather long and the chord should be taken slowly upwards accelerating its rapidity as you approach the upper note but afterwards in the repetition of the commencement of the succeeding verses it should be played quicker. So also of the leaving of the chord between the verses it should be done with more rapidity than at the final close of the piece which is always done slowly sustaining the last or lowest note.[46]

These refinements may well come from the secular world of harpsichord technique, taken over into liturgical organ performance through the medium of extempore playing and improvisation on a given theme, both popular with audiences. Rayner Taylor, for instance, had a reputation for excellence in organ improvisation, and his keyboard style was one of the talents most admired by his younger colleague, Benjamin Carr. Since chant and psalm-tune accompaniments were mostly improvised, the details of style and method recorded in the few organbooks that survive from the early nineteenth century become all the more significant. Few English chant collections have much to say about the organ accompaniment, but there is one mention of an appropriate place for the arpeggio in chant accompaniment. In *Canto Recitativo*, J. Dixon states that 'whatever may be the length of the preloquium [recitation], the organ will, of course begin with the voice; and all verses beginning with unaccented words or syllables should be played arpeggio; but in all verses beginning with an accented word or syllable the chord should be struck in the plainest and most distinct manner . . .'.[47]

Benjamin Carr wrote a number of extended chants to texts from both ordinary and extraordinary parts of the liturgy. The settings of texts for special uses, as might be expected, are farthest away from the basic psalmodic form of a chant in phrasing, harmony, and embellishment. Carr often added a complementary chant to pieces already in the general repertory, adding brief diatonic interludes, with a trill on the minim between verses. He routinely set phrases in certain texts in the minor key to express such words as death and die. Ornamental and harmonic affective gestures are what make his 'semi-chaunt' for the Lenten season especially appropriate. The 'Miserere' is a setting of Ps. 51:1–3 and 9–11 to a single chant for three voices and organ, with

---

[46] Loud, *Organ Study*, 16.   [47] J. Dixon, *Canto Recitativo*, (London, 1816), p. xviii.

a four-bar introduction and two-bar interludes. The unusual harmonic plan, placing the first recitation on the dominant, repeats with each statement of the chant. In the second phrase, a 'pathetic' Db embellishes the melody. The introduction creates an appropriate penitential mood by means of repeated grace notes over a pedal Bb (Ex. 8.10). The piece is surprisingly effective in performance and achieved a measure of popularity in its day; it was reported to have been performed at Carr's own funeral.[48]

The 'Miserere' and several other Carr church compositions were published separately in numbers of the *Musical Miscellany*, and in a compilation of 'Chants

Ex. 8.10. Miserere 'semi-chaunt' by Carr

---

[48] The Miserere by Carr was performed as part of my paper on 'Early Episcopal Music, 1789–1850' for the conference on American Music at the University of Illinois, 29 Sept. 1990.

& Melodies adapted to the Psalms and Hymns of the Episcopal Church', inscribed to the 'Ladies and Gentlemen forming the Choral Association of St. Peters Church', published as *The Chorister*.[49] Carr's thanks for a good review give another glimpse of the esteem in which George K. Jackson was held by Episcopal musicians: 'Accept my best thanks for your truly kind & favourable notice of "*The Chorister*" and that it has found some favour in the opinion of Dr. Jackson is truly gratifying—especially from a Man of his high talent.'[50]

The first piece in the *Chorister* is a favourite text for the opening of morning service, the Sentence 'the Lord is in his holy temple', to be sung 'slow and solemn'. In the chants, Carr has printed certain of the preludes and interludes, and suggested registrations to the organist for particular verses. The Venite exultemus, for example, is John Jones's octave double chant, the full text written out for treble, tenor, and bass, with some of the octave phrases sung as solos. The first statement of the double chant is straightforward, with a short ascending connecting figure leading to the fourth phrase. Verses for full organ are marked, with the trumpet stop added at 'for he cometh' in verse 9. The Gloria patri which follows is in the key of A to different music. The Benedicite is the Scottish metrical version from Bremner, marked 'trio', and prefaced with an explanatory note:

Some apology is requisite for publishing this Canticle in a form not used by the Church—but tho' not suited to the words as they stand in the Book of Common Prayer, yet it is inserted for the gratification of those who may possess this work, on account of the beauty and simplicity of the Music. NB: This is copied from an Edinburgh Prayer Book, being the way it is Sung in the Episcopal Churches in that City.[51]

It should be clear, after surveying the Episcopal service music printed in America before 1820, that the initial repertory of chants and short liturgical anthems, copied and reprinted from English sources, was quickly increased by new composition. This body of music included a variety of pieces besides chants, from three-bar doxologies, short responses, and opening sentences to cantata-like canticles. The survival of manuscript organbooks illustrates the complementary role of print and manuscript in the dissemination of this large body of functional music, as well as the ways in which church musicians improvised and arranged music to suit their immediate needs.

[49] *The Chorister* and *Musical Miscellany* are published in facsimile in the series Recent Researches in American Music (Madison, 1977–).

[50] University of Pennsylvania, Special Collections, Parker Papers, Box 4, Folder 10, Carr to Parker, 30 June 1821.

[51] Benjamin Carr, *The Chorister* (Philadelphia, 1820), 8. The Edinburgh publication quoted was probably Bremner, although many other current music books contained the same metrical Benedicite (see Ch. 7).

This Episcopal service music and its performance conventions are an unmistakable legacy from antecedents in the Church of England. As Horton Davies has observed, the 'strong element of tradition in the Anglican cultus', which contributed to the widespread adaptation of the English liturgy for the use of churches in other countries, also ensured the maintenance of a commonality among them.[52] The founders of the Protestant Episcopal Church in America were quite firm in their intention to alter the English liturgy only in so far as needed to reflect their new independent status. Similarly, the musical practice that has traditionally been part of the English liturgy, in all its diverse forms, has never lost its appeal, nor its authority, for Episcopal musicians in the United States.

[52] Horton Davies, *Worship and Theology in England* (5 vols., Princeton, 1961–75), iii. 21.

TABLE 8.3. *William Smith*, The Churchman's Choral Companion to his Prayer Book (1809): *musical sources*

Text	Smith rubrics and attributions	Sources and notes[a]
Morning Prayer		
Se	Costellow	Intro. repr. from Thomas Costellow, *Sunday's Amusement* (1801), for Bedford Chapel, London; setting Hab. 2:20
Glp 1	Revd Wm. Jones	Sgl ch in F; org sc, inner parts in small notes
Glp 2	unattributed	Setting George Jackson, 4v, from MS; pr Cole (1811) and Jackson (1817)
*Ve 1	Edin. Collec.	Sgl ch from Robert Bremner, *A Collection of the Best Church Tunes* (c.1758); Tune in 2nd Tr, Ct in 1st Tr, 3v
Ve 2	Arranged by R. Taylor	Davis dbl ch arr Taylor, 4v; 1st pr Cole (1805)
Ve 3	unattributed	Sgl ch George Jackson, 4v, vv. 6–9 tonic minor, Dx major; from MS; pr Jackson (1816)
Td	R. Taylor, Edin Collec; 'N.B. This is read on Ash wedens day, and on Good-Friday; sung one note lower in Lent, and one note higher on the Festivals.'	Arr Rayner Taylor, 4v, from Bremner, c.1758
Bte	Revised by Dr Jackson; 'N.B. The priest and people may, in responses, read this Canticle unto the versicle, wherein the children of men are mentioned, and then the Choir, may perform their part, when the Priest shall have pronounced the words 'O ye children of men, bless ye the Lord!'	Sgl ch from Bremner, c.1758; arr Jackson, 4v (A, 2T, B)
Jd	Arranged by R. Taylor from Dr Nares	Dbl ch arr Taylor, 4v
Jd	Composed by R. Taylor	Sgl ch Rayner Taylor, unison
Bn	Composed by R. Taylor	Sgl ch Rayner Taylor, 4v
Jd	'Kent's Favorite Jubilate'	Morn Service James Kent; repr. from Costellow (1801)
Evening Prayer		
Se	Barthelemon; 'The Lord is in his holy temple'; called Introduction	Setting F. Barthelemon from J. W. Calcott, *The Anthems, . . . sung at the Asylum Chapel* (c.1800); transp F to E♭, vv. 1st and 2nd choirs, full final repeat
Glp	Revd W. Jones	Sgl ch F
*Glp	B. Carr	Verse setting G, Benjamin Carr, duets and chorus, 3v; 1st pr Carr, *Masses, Vespers, Litanies . . .* (1805)
Cd 1	Arranged by P. Erben	Octave dbl ch, 4v

Cd 2	Arranged by R. Taylor	Sgl ch William Turner, 2nd recit. moved to third of chord
Bc	Arranged by R. Taylor	Sgl ch Thomas Kelway, 4v; pr *Fifty Double and Single Chants* (c.1769); 1st US pr Proposed Book (1786)
Dm	Dr Boyce's Collec.	Sgl ch Henry Aldrich, 4v; pr Boyce, *Cathedral Music 1* (1760); Boyce notation copied
BnA	R. Taylor	Sgl ch Rayner Taylor, 1st pr

Litany

Ag	B. Carr; Anthem	Setting Benjamin Carr
Ag	Unit. Frat.	Arr dbl ch, 1st part Latrobe, 2nd Purcell transp to A m; from Litany ch, Christian Latrobe, *Hymn-Tunes sung ... United Brethren*[b] (1806) and T. Purcell G m ch, pr Boyce 1
Ky	B. Carr; Anthem	Setting Benjamin Carr, 3v response 'Lord have mercy upon us'
Sd	Unit. Frat.	Arr from 1st two vv. Td ch, 2v, from Latrobe (1806)
*Dx	Webbe; Anthem	Arr from 1st v., duet Quia fecit, bass solo of Mg by Samuel Webbe, *A Collection of Motetts or Antiphons* (1790)
Dx	R. Taylor	Titled dbl ch but music repeats second half

Communion

Cr	'Kyrie Eleison' Responses to the Commandments	Setting William Mason, 2v, Tr and B, duets 2 Tr; 1st pr Richard Langdon, *Divine Harmony* (1774)
*Cr	B. Carr; 'Kyrie Eleison proper for high Festivals'	Setting Benjamin Carr, prelude, Tr and B solos, chorus
Glt	R. Taylor	Short response to naming Gospel, Rayner Taylor
Glt	Pleyel	Last 4 bars of German Hymn, Ignace Pleyel
Sa	R. Taylor; preface included	Setting Taylor of Trisagion, solo recit. and Sanctus, 4v cho
*Ben	Unit. Frat.; 'Gratia domini to be sung after Pax Dei'	Short hymn from Latrobe (1806); org sc, inner parts small notes
Glx	unattributed	Music Td above, adapted to Gloria text by Smith

Propers

Christmas Day; Dr Boyce; 'Sing we merrily unto God our strength'	Dbl ch John Robinson; pr Boyce 1; T in 2nd Tr
New Year's Day; Revd W. Jones; 'Praise ye the Lord'	Dbl ch T. S. Dupuis; pr Boyce 2 (1768), 2v, Tr and B Dupuis
Epiphany; B. Carr; 'We have seen his star'	Sgl ch Benjamin Carr, 3v
Ash-Weden's Day; 'O hear in heav'n the voice of our calling'	Sgl ch Michael Wise; transp to F#m, melody altered

TABLE 8.3. *cont.*

Text	Smith rubrics and attributions	Sources and notes[a]
Propers		
Good Friday; Dr Boyce; 'Behold the Lamb of God'		Sgl ch John Blow; pr Boyce 1; 1st US pr Law, God' *Rudiments* (1784)
Easter Day Morning Prayer; Revd W. Jones; 'Christ our passover'; To be sung on Easter Day instead of Venite exultemus		Dbl ch John Jones; pr Jones, *Sixty Chants* (1785); 2v, Tr and B from Jones
Easter Day Evening Prayer; Revd W. Jones; 'O Sing unto the Lord'; To be sung on Easter Day before the reading Psalms at Evening Prayer		Dbl ch John Robinson, 2v Tr and B, final cadence altered; pr Boyce 1
Ascension Day; 'Thine, O Lord, is the greatness'		Dbl ch Nares arr Taylor, see Jd above
*B. Carr; 'O Christ, thou art the head of the Church'		Sgl ch Turner arr Carr; 3v, melody C2, high tessitura for boys or women
Whitsunday; Dr Boyce; 'O give thanks unto the Lord'		Dbl ch Robinson, pr Boyce 1; melody altered with contour per original in 2nd and 4th phrases some chords revoiced
Trinity Sunday; Dr Boyce; 'There are three that bear record in heaven'		Dbl ch Richard Langdon; pr Langdon *Divine Harmony* (1774); 4v
All Saints' Day; 'Blessed are the poor in spirit'		Dbl ch Dupuis, pr Boyce 2
*Benedicentur Sancti; [same text]		Sgl ch Turner arr from Law by ?Smith; 4v, melody 2nd Tr
General Thanksgiving; 'Praise the Lord'		Dbl ch Davis arr Taylor, see Ve above
*Laudate Dominum; Revd W. Smith; [same instead of the Venite		Dbl ch Smith; 3v, 1st phrase like Davis; 2nd and 4th phrases same music, voices interchange

text]; Proper for the Feast of Thanksgiving,
*Music added second printing in same year

[a] Sources: 1st printing New Haven, Beineke Library; 2nd printing Emory University, Pitts Library, Smith's copy, autographed
[b] Unit. Brethren items identified by D. McCorkle; see facs., *Eckhard's Choirmaster's Book*, ed. G. Williams

9

Per Retro et Recte

> The earliest chant or however the most taken notice of in church history is that said to be introduced by St. Ambrose, Archbishop of Milan, in the latter end of the fourth century, thence called the Ambrosian: in the next century, Pope Gregory, the Great, introduced another, named the Roman or Gregorian. Both these seem to be kinds of singing in mere unisons, similar to our chanting the prayers, not in harmony as we sing the psalms, a practice prevailing since the reformation; the oldest and most simple chant with us is that of Tallis.[1]

WITHIN this broad outline, the history of Anglican chant and chanting takes shape, from its roots in the pre-Reformation Latin rite to the early nineteenth century. The essentially unbroken development of liturgical practice in the English liturgy of the Book of Common Prayer has continued under the aegis of the 'one use', which replaced the complex ritual of the pre-Reformation Latin Offices and Mass. The 'one use', however, did not establish uniformity in interpretation of the rubrics of the Common Prayer across the spectrum of institutions subsumed under the jurisdiction of the national church. The performance of the same liturgy varied historically from parish to cathedral to collegiate chapel and church, and from town to country and south to north.

The imprecision of the rubrics in the Book of Common Prayer, containing all the services of the English rite in one volume, left many details of performance to be worked out in traditional ways and customary procedures, and thus the liturgy and its music evolved in practice from the mid-sixteenth century to the twentieth with, until recently, only occasional liturgical revision. While the absence of precise directions seems to impart a haphazard appearance to Anglican chanting over the centuries since the Reformation, there are discernible broad patterns of consensus. In the old Latin liturgy, order was imposed by the complex musical canon governing ordinary and extraordinary worship. A more simplified canon replaced it, but the strength of the central body of liturgical music still brought order to the processes of transmission and inherited custom. Even the dramatic upheavals of the Civil War did not obliterate this fundamental store of liturgical musical knowledge, for the

---

[1] Anselm Bayly, *Practical Treatise*, 74–5.

Restoration was just that in musical terms, a conservative resuscitation of former ways of conducting the choral service. A new order then began its development and a new canon of melodies in plain and harmonized form brought
some stability to Anglican liturgical forms.

It is useful in attempting to assess the state of the choral tradition in the early
nineteenth century to recapitulate the highlights of the history of Anglican
chanting. Anselm Bayley cites Tallis as the oldest composer of chant for the
English service, and so he was—at least he was the most prominent of the
cathedral musicians writing for the new English liturgy in the sixteenth century. Tallis was honoured in the late eighteenth century as the 'most excellent
Composer of Church Music, at least equal to any Contemporary, either of his
own Country or of Foreign Nations',[2] and in the first decade of the nineteenth
century William Crotch honoured this position again with his publication of
the Tallis setting of the English Litany, this time with Latin text. Crotch perhaps drew some of his inspiration for his views about the sublime qualities of
ancient liturgical chant from his study of the music of the Tudor age. He
broadcast these ideas in a series of well-attended lectures on music history and
practice given in London.[3] The nearly universal use of Tallis's service music in
the seventeenth and eighteenth centuries, particularly the Litany and Preces
and Responses, reinforced his high standing in the canon of ancient music, an
idea formulated and disseminated in eighteenth-century England.[4] One of its
central components, the legacy of the cathedral choral service, would inspire
one of the most important reprintings of Reformation service music in the first
half of the nineteenth century, John Merbecke's *Book of Common Praier, Noted*,
adapted to the form of the 1662 liturgical review and presented in a beautifully
decorated volume imitating the old Sarum red-letter service books.[5]

From the Reformation era came also the fundamental musical materials with
which the services of the church are clothed. The discarded ritual of the Latin
rite left behind some of its underpinnings in the form of methods and procedures from the plainsong system of improvisation and composition. Its basic
treasure of melodic material was not out of fashion, nor were the ways of harmonizing in the faburden technique. And so chanting the daily prayers and the
psalms continued in a more simplified way than before. The Reformation

---

[2] William Boyce, *Cathedral Music*, i, p. vii.

[3] Nicholas Temperley, 'William Crotch', *New Grove*, v. 65–7.

[4] Weber, *Rise of Musical Classics*, ch. 2, especially pp. 25–32.

[5] William Dyce, *The Order of Daily Service, the Litany, and Order of the Administration of the Holy
Communion, with Plain-Tune, according to the Use of the United Church of England and Ireland* (London, 1843).
Dyce (1806–64) was a painter, musical amateur, and professor of fine art at King's College, London. Besides
Merbecke, he consulted the 1544 Litany and a number of Latin rite service manuals, from which he made
up a table of Sarum psalm tones for recitation of the prose psalter.

principle that the text must be presented in a clear and straightforward manner dominated liturgical performance and composition. The differentiation between daily service and holy days and festivals continued, however, and the special sets of preces and responses and psalms written out for these occasions increased in numbers and complexities. The earlier pieces in this repertory, composed on plainsong tenors, became in turn a source for the arrangement of homophonic formulae for chanting the psalms in harmony. Psalms were still chanted to plainsong melodies during the week, and the use of these melodies resumed after the complete cessation of cathedral worship from the 1640s to 1660.

From the Restoration onward, chanting the psalms in harmony became the more accepted custom, though chanting the prayers, responses, creeds, and the psalms to single melodies continued on into the early eighteenth century. As Anselm Bayly noted nearer the end of the century,

much easier is it, and more agreeable to chaunt the service at the altar in one tone, than to read it in a variety of dissonant sounds. For the chaunt, though a monotony, is capable of all the graces of accent, emphasis and pause; it is also more audible and more striking, and upon the whole, produces a greater effect than can the best cadences of speaking.[6]

Thus the influences of secular music, expressiveness, and the eighteenth-century passion for the study of language and grammar infused Anglican chanting with variations on the old theme. Even the actor David Garrick was noted for his reading of the Common Prayer.[7]

The publication of single and harmonized plainsong melodies in the Restoration era began the new trend of writing out some of the functional music that was formerly sung by rule. The four-part tunes restored to use in the 1660s were the models for a new genre of psalmodic formula for chanting prose psalms or canticles, and so the chanting tune, or chant tune, began its history as a deliberately composed piece by a recognized composer. The new chant tune differed from the earlier harmonizations of plainsong melodies mainly in the position of the melody in the top voice, and the shift to cadences

[6] Bayly, *Collection of Anthems*, preface, p. xv.
[7] Richard Cull, *Garrick's Mode of Reading the Liturgy of the Church of England* (London, 1840). Cull prefaces this work with an acknowledgement to MS notes of a friend, J. W. Anderson, 'The Common Prayer as read by the late Mr Garrick' (1797). Among the discussions of body posture, vocal tone, and punctuation are such suggestions as marking the declarations at the beginning of the Litany with a downward movement of pitch, because it expresses uncertainty, and giving prayer an upward pitch movement in a minor key expressive of entreaty (p. 101). This approach to the liturgy was considered excessive by William Mason, causing him to recommend the 'unaccompanied chaunt' for 'this one great merit, that it prevents all affectation of what is called modern *fine* Reading, a thing almost as misplaced in the Church Service as old curious Music' ('Essay on Cathedral Music', (1782), p. l). Note, also, John Marsh's disapproval of Mr Courtial's (Canon of Chichester) fine reading in App. F.

harmonized in major and minor tonalities. New repertories of chant tunes were created for the use of organists and choirmasters in many places.

The earliest of the new repertories was especially significant as a harbinger of things to come in the development of the English chant tune. Compiled in the late 1660s or very early 1670s, the 'royal chapels repertory', distributed from the capital to outlying cathedrals and collegiate churches and chapels, served simultaneously as a model for new composition and an authoritative generic repertory. Some of the pieces in this new canon are still sung today. Adaptability to a prose text of any length was one of the reasons the chant tune became the generally accepted vehicle for chanting psalms and canticles. It also developed its own standard notation and performance conventions in a format derived from the unbalanced phrases of the first verse of the invitatory psalm, Venite exultemus, sung before the psalms in Morning Prayer.

In the eighteenth century the maintenance of choral service traditions was affected by the same general conditions which prevailed in the mid-sixteenth century, with a very important exception, the changed position of the national church. The challenge of Puritan theology and the difficulties of retaining well-trained musical personnel in seriously reduced choral establishments were old problems.[8] The position of the Church of England, as one among competing Protestant denominations, was largely a development of the Glorious Revolution and the eighteenth century. The once monolithic state church found itself challenged by nonconformists of many colours and many 'enthusiasms' in a climate of increasing religious diversity. As the century wore on, the success of the Methodists and the 'chapel' movement made substantial inroads into the membership rolls of the Church of England. The cathedral choral service, originally intended for worship in a closed community, seemed of little relevance for those outside it in relation to the new industrial and commercial age. Of a visit to Lincoln Minster in July 1791 Lord Torrington wrote,

this was a decent and honourable performance, but, unluckily for us, no anthem, as that is perform'd on Wednesdays, and Fridays, at evening service. How few people attend! Any attendance will soon cease: and I shall live to see when none will be present at a cathedral service, but a reader, a verger, and 2 singing boys; who will gallop it over in a few minutes.[9]

On another occasion two years previous, Lord Torrington had visited Southwell Collegiate Church and found an establishment of '16 Prebends, 6 Vicars, Six singing men, and 12 Singing Boys, besides Vergers, an Organist, etc.':

---

[8] See case study in Joseph Pring, *Papers, Documents, Law Proceedings, &c. &c. respecting the Maintenance of the Choir of the Cathedral Church of Bangor* (Bangor, 1819).

[9] Byng, *The Torrington Diaries*, ii. 400.

At most Cathedrals, under the Eye of a Bishop, Six o'clock Prayers are left off; Here they are Continued, and there is Regular Service performed 3 times a day all the year round.

The Bell now ringing for Evening Service carried me to the Church, where I was met by Dr. Marsden, a Prebend, who offer'd me, as a Stranger, every civility, as a Choice of Anthem etc., and I then enter'd a Stall. If I commonly find fault, I shall seldom be wrong; and if I sometimes praise, you may suppose it right: Therefore let me now express my Astonishment of Pleasure at hearing this Service. The Prebend was attended in due Form; The Prayers were read most leisurely, and devoutly, by Mr Houlson, one of the Vicars; the Organ was excellently play'd; and four Singing Men, and Eleven Boys, sang as carefully as if at the Antient Concert! The Anthem of 3 parts, 'Sing O Heavens,' by Mr. Kent was capitally perform'd; and I was told that one of the Boys was reckon'd to have the finest voice in England . . .[10]

The adverse reports of rudimentary attention to preservation of liturgical form and substance in many places were clearly not the whole story. There were other institutions—York Minster, for one—where the choral service was chanted to an acceptable standard, and the cathedral ideal was still held up as a desirable goal. The picture of decay and degeneration in the English Church and the portrayal of 'something of a "Dark Age" in English music', heretofore accepted as historical truth, are beginning to be challenged by a new generation of scholarship.[11] The eighteenth century can no longer be seen as a long blank space between the glorious Tudor age and the liturgical revival of the Oxford Movement. Revivals by their nature imply a preceding period of decline and the strength of the revival seems to influence adversely the perception of the depth of decline. While it would be irresponsible to imply that there was little reason for revival, a balanced picture of the years leading up to the Oxford Movement will eventually show a less black-and-white image. In many ways, it was a time of great ferment in religion as well as society in general, and the music of the church was not isolated from its milieu.

Against the background of many cross-currents in the new urban and industrial society of early nineteenth-century England, with its growing multiplicity of religious denominations, the critical question concerning Anglican chant and chanting must be: had chanting practice changed over the course of the eighteenth century? Were different methods and music available to church musicians in the early nineteenth century than in the late seventeenth? The answer in regard to new music can be found simply by consulting the annotated catalogues of manuscript and printed music in this book. The answer in

---

[10] Ibid. iv. 141. This visit took place during the earlier career of the organist Thomas Spofforth. Cf. John Marsh's comments in App. F on later visits, when the state of the music had declined.

[11] See H. Diack Johnstone, Preface, in Johnstone and Fiske, *The Eighteenth Century*, p. xiii; also the proliferation of recent dissertations cited in Walsh, Haydon, and Taylor, *Church of England*.

terms of methods and performance practice requires a bit more circumspect examination, and one very important underlying principle must be borne in mind. Liturgical chant and chanting, although it had moved from the realm of memory and improvisation into the modern era of printed music and written instruction, retained a certain measure of its customary extempore performance. This makes it incumbent upon the outside observer to take into consideration both theory and expectations of what practical applications should, or did, produce. The ideal of the cathedral choral service in terms of its fundamental musical material, recitation and response in liturgical musical speech, was essentially unchanged. It might even be said that the 'cathedral ideal' was kept alive by remembered tradition and reinforced by Romanticism's re-emphasis on ancient history and tradition, until the Commission Reports of the 1830s and renewed attention to the state of the nation's cathedral foundations brought new resources to the performance of the choral liturgy.

   Some of the same expectations of cathedral chanting practice that were published in the early eighteenth century can be read in the early nineteenth. Roger North wrote about the singers all pronouncing the syllables of the text together, 'the verse as well as the close in distinct counterpoint time, with respect to long and short syllables', and closing each psalmodic phrase with an appropriate cadence, all together.[12] He and others also wrote about the preferred sound of chanting in large cathedrals and the position of the organist as the ruler of the chanting, to keep the recitation in time with the sense of the text and quantity and accent of the words. As for the harmonized chant to which the Venite, psalms for the day, and sometimes the canticles were sung, the ideal performance followed the general rule for any musical recitation governed by a prose text, that the words should be understood and the chanting be paced in balance with all performing forces. Looking back from 1821, it was Edward Hodges's opinion about chant and chanting that 'the addition of Harmony, of course rendered it somewhat more complicated; but still the principal part, or Melody, was such as might be sung with the greatest ease. With some slight modification, both the name and the thing are still retained.'[13]

   John Beckwith, organist of Norwich Cathedral, gave his own history of English chanting in 1808, and the familiar ideal principles emerge. Psalm chanting, he wrote,

should be very decent, grave, and uniform; the choir attentive to their several parts; the organ not too loud; the length of the concluding semibreve never exceeded, a pause being disagreeable, unnecessary, and distracting; no hurrying in the longer

---

[12] Wilson, *North on Music*, 269.   [13] [Hodges], *Bristol Mirror*, 12 May 1821.

verses; the organ should not clog the voices by hanging on the note of recital a moment after the words are finished.[14]

Prefaces to chant collections began to include such statements as 'chanting is but another name for reading to a tune', 'with regard to the time of performing a chant, it may be said that a psalm should occupy, in chanting, very little more time than a good reader would take to pronounce it', and 'the best rule is to be guided by the sense of the words, attend to expression and effect, and pay little or no regard to the restraints of time'.[15]

Imbalances similar to those implied by Beckwith were probably legion in the chanting of choirs where the old ways were still followed. J. Dixon refers to the 'tiresome adagio with which some choirs conclude the last half verse of every hymn or psalm they chant', also 'the abruptly cutting short of concluding notes' and 'the extreme of either quick or slow playing'.[16] An actual performance might be as Beckwith thought it should be, or as he sometimes observed it, for example:

it is possible to hear a chant where the men and children are trying which can sing the loudest, which can recite fastest, and which can fairly get to the last note first: but with all this irreverent clatter, the grand object is not gained, as the organ contrives to be either behind or before them all the way. If this grand object be saving two or three minutes, they are on the contrary lost. I can assert from long experience that the same chant, and the same psalms, take up more time in a confused performance, by two or three minutes, than they would consume in the decent consent of the organ with the choir, and the choir with its several members.[17]

The number of recorded suggestions for regular choir practice sessions in the late eighteenth and early nineteenth centuries are sufficient testimony to the awareness of the need for coordination, and of at least one basic practical approach to achieving it. It still seems incredible to present-day church musicians that the regular practice we take for granted was a 'sometime thing' then. The choice of anthem being left to the last minute and offered to important visitors is another procedure that is hard to imagine, but John Marsh's many references to 'putting up' not only the anthem, but also the music for canticles, Sanctus, and Responses to the Commandments at the time of the service, recorded throughout his journals from the 1760s to the 1820s, give a first-hand inside view of the process.[18]

[14] John Beckwith, *The First Verse of Every Psalm of David*, preface.

[15] Jonathan Wainwright, *A Set of Chants Adapted to the Hymns in the Morning and Evening Prayer* (Boston, 1819), 'General Directions for Chanting', preface; *Chants of the Morning and Evening Prayer and Communion Service as Sung at St. James's Church, Philadelphia* (1820), preface.

[16] Dixon, *Canto Recitativo*, p. xviii.

[17] Beckwith, *First Verse of Every Psalm*, preface.

[18] HM 54457; selected entries in App. F.

The search for a widely applicable practical method of producing uniform chanting focused primarily on the coordination of text syllables with notes of the chant, and on this front there were new developments in the early nineteenth century. The idea of marking a psalter to indicate text underlay, now known as pointing, began in 'some choirs' at some time before John Marsh mentioned it in 1804, and his suggestion that the last syllable of the recitation should be marked in the text to indicate cadence syllables was wholeheartedly endorsed by Beckwith, and many successors. Marsh's example of the correct way to chant the Venite, with cadential syllables in italicized script separated from the recitation portion of the text, was one of the most easily comprehended ways of marking texts and turned out to be a long-term favourite. In Baltimore, Maryland, John Cole introduced this method to Episcopal musicians in America.

Another solution was laying out the complete text, with cadence syllables separated in groups of three and five to match the cadence tones of the Anglican chant in standard notation, and this method led to the commonly accepted chant printed in America through the mid-nineteenth century. It is not altogether surprising to find this system in sources for amateur choirs, where chanting was a new practice, and a full text printed underneath the chant can be found in a few parish music books published in England by parish psalmodists early in the eighteenth century. The Revd Dr Smith presented his chants in this fashion in *The Churchman's Choral Companion to his Prayer Book* in 1809 and John Cole promptly published his *Episcopalian Harmony* in 1811 with musical barlines extended down the page through the text below, to organize syllables by recitation and cadence tones.

In England, experiments continued with marking prose texts, and J. Dixon established a timely precedent with *Canto Recitativo* (1816), the earliest complete psalter pointed for chanting. It was doomed to be assigned to the shelf, however, since the system he devised was tied to his own form of short and long chants, hence not applicable to the standard written form of the Anglican chant, by then irreversibly established in general use. In 1821 Jonathan Gray printed a Te deum 'pointed to be conveniently chanted in Churches' as part of *An Inquiry into the Historical Facts relative to Parochial Psalmody*, in which the text was laid out as Marsh had shown in the sample Venite from 1804, with final syllables for mediant and terminal cadences separated and italicized. Gray's acknowledgement was to Dr Camidge, organist of York Minster, and it is not clear whether this was Matthew, organist at the time, or his son John Camidge, who succeeded him in 1842.[19] In either case, it was John Marsh's

---

[19] Nicholas Temperley points out that Matthew Camidge, who published chant repertories of his own, was certainly a friend of Gray's, but he was not a doctor and was not usually referred to as such. John's doctorate was from Cambridge, 1819. See Temperley, *Jonathan Gray*, 18–19.

system which Gray used in the Te deum, and Marsh's system which was published by J. E. Dibb in the first fully pointed psalter, *Key to Chanting*, in 1831.[20]

The complete musical psalter of the later nineteenth century, with chants selected for each psalm in morning and evening service throughout the month, was a logical extension of these ideas, and of the practice of matching chants to specific psalm texts according to their message. It was a development that owed its inception and implementation to a number of musicians working in both cathedral and parish churches. In a sense it was the child of the new synthesis between cathedral and parochial practice, worked out gradually from its beginnings early in the eighteenth century. By the 1820s the groundwork had already been laid for the 'choral revival' and the kind of 'mixed service' often attributed mainly to the Oxford Movement and the Victorian era.

It is a remarkable development of the Victorian period that

cathedral music came to be regarded as the normal music of the Anglican Church as a whole, not just the preserve of the choral foundation. . . . While it was impractical, even undesirable, for all parish churches to adopt the cathedral idea wholesale, it was this ideal that had the potential for public enthusiasm, as adopted in the diocesan choral festivals [see Weber on their inception in the early eighteenth century], and as the cathedrals themselves raised their musical and devotional standards. Elements of the cathedral ideal found their way into the typical parish churches of the land to produce that varying mixture of congregational and choral worship that had become the norm by the end of the Victorian era . . .[21]

The active promotion of the 'cathedral ideal' resulted in exchanges of liturgical music and performance customs, and even the formation of surpliced choirs in a few urban churches in England, Scotland, and America before 1820. In theory, if not in exactly the same practice as in earlier centuries, the English cathedral tradition was maintained according to the historical imperative of partly oral and partly written traditions. It is more difficult, of course, for a tradition that is supposed to have well-defined characteristics to preserve its purity than for a new tradition to evolve in a less restrictive framework. In parishes any form of music might be adopted according to local preference and resources, and parish churches were thus in a position to absorb many influences, from the practices of cathedrals or collegiate churches and chapels to those of Roman Catholic chapels in London, or to other Protestant denominations that were flourishing, especially in the capital.

The existence of fertile ground for the musical ideas associated with the Oxford Movement, in terms of liturgical chant and chanting, must be

---

[20] A sample verse from this psalter is printed in Temperley, ibid. 20. Now very rare, there is a copy in the British Library. See also Temperley, *MEPC*, i. 220–3.

[21] William Gatens, *Victorian Cathedral Music in Theory and Practice* (Cambridge, 1986), 15.

credited in large measure to the Evangelical ideal of congregational worship and its corollary: the 'old Ecclesiastical Chaunt, which consisted of but few notes, and was sung of the whole congregation in unisons . . . is music of the simplest description, but such as is capable of association with the true sublime.'[22] The idea that the true ancient chant was sung by the congregation and ministers in unison was attributed to the primitive Fathers and underlay attempts to promote congregational chanting in the late eighteenth and early nineteenth centuries. This, too, came out of the parish–cathedral interchange that began in the early 1700s. As Nicholas Temperley has written, the period of reform and rediscovery of tradition, from about 1760 to 1850,

is perhaps the most important one in the history of parish church music, with the exception of the Reformation itself. It was in these years that the modern concept of Anglican worship was evolved, as were many other aspects of modern English life. The Oxford movement, though its contribution was important and distinctive, was not in the end the decisive factor in the evolution of the new style of Anglican church music.[23]

The 'mixed service' was increasingly exportable, and the lineage of its music in the first churches of the future Anglican Communion is unmistakable. The historical continuity of an intrinsically conservative theology and liturgy fostered a commonality between English, Scottish, and American Anglican and Episcopal churches. Tradition and custom, the things commonly done but not needing to be written down, have always been constant elements in the process of transmission and adaptation of functional music for chanting liturgical texts. Repertory and performance in any one place in the early nineteenth century depended as much as ever on a balance of local and regional factors: the presence or not of a choir and instruments, the availability of professional musicians or trained amateurs to sing and play, the degree of clerical control and congregational participation, the wider cultural and social environment, and the strength of regional or national traditions. The 'last word', for the moment, goes to the liturgical scholar and church musician from Aberdeenshire, the Revd William Smith, written from his perspective of the second decade of the nineteenth century:

From numerous and credible testimonies it appears that the usage of chanting the psalms and hymns of public worship obtained in the times of the apostles, and continued to be common to all Christian nations, until about two hundred and sixty years since, when it was, in several parts of Europe, more or less interrupted by the struggles of the reformation. It does not appear from any of the histories or tracts relative to the Church of England, that there was any difference between the psalmodic usage

---

[22] [Hodges], *Bristol Mirror*, 5 May 1821.   [23] Temperley, *MEPC*, 244–67.

of the Cathedral, Collegiate, and Parochial Churches, until the year 1549, when some of the parish-churches began to discontinue the practice of chanting the psalms and hymns, and others to reject the use of music altogether in public worship. But notwithstanding a temporary interruption, occasioned by adversaries to primitive truth and order, prosaic psalmody was re-established after the lapse of a few years, and continues to be estimated as one of our mother-church's brightest ornaments.[24]

[24] William Smith, *The Reasonableness of Setting Forth . . . Praise*, p. v.

APPENDIX A

English Chant Tunes: Manuscript Sources 1635–1750

Left column: repository and manuscript, page or folio nos., type, date, (EECM no.).
Right column: contents, date of tunes if different, text, voice parts, provenance if different than location.

Abbreviations not on page *xviii*:

rc	royal chapels repertory	TD	tenor decani
MC	medius cantoris	TC	tenor cantoris
MD	medius decani	BD	bass decani
CD	countertenor decani	BC	bass cantoris
CC	countertenor cantoris		

Bodleian Library

MSS Mus. Sch. B. 7, page pasted to cover, Sc; 1698–1716
5 ch tunes copied ?Charles Badham; Ve; Tr, Ct, T, B

MSS Mus. Sch. C. 42, fos. 17–19; Sc; *c*.1676
2 rc ch tunes with full text underlay; Ve, Td; Tr, B

MSS Mus. Sch. D. 217, fo. 19ᵛ; Sc; 1690s
Isaack dbl tune, Purcell rc tune; Ps; Tr, Ct, T, B

British Library

Add. MS 5327, fo. 127b; Sc; 18th c.
M. Greene tune; Tr, Ct, T, B

Add. MS 9073, fo. 6, 6b; Sc; early 19th c.
4 rc tunes copied by V. Novello from older Westminster Abbey Orgbk; Tr, Ct, T, B

Add. MS 17784, fo. 177, 177b; B; 1670–77 (127) — Nos. 1–21 rc tunes; Ps; Tr, Ct, T, B; St George's Chapel, Windsor

Add. MS 31559, fos. 46, 49, 63, 73; Sc; 18th c. — 4 Ps tunes to Blow short services; copied J. C. Smith; Tr, Ct, T, B

Add. MS 36268, fo. 85b; Sc; 1721 — Tudway Ps tunes Wimpole Service; Tr, Ct, T, B

Add. MS 37027 (fos. 47–55), fos. 50–2; Sc; 1720s — 10 rc of 13 tunes; hand John Church; Ps; Tr, Ct, T, B; Chapel Royal or St George's, Windsor

Add. MS 39868, fo. 100r–v; O; c.1728 — 'Chappel Tunes' in liturgical order, Morning and Evening Prayer, 5 rc Tunes; Tr, B

Cambridge University Library

ELY CATHEDRAL

EDC/Music Mss./4, pp. 2, 183; O; c.1625 (95) — 2 tunes (Imperial, hand John John Ferrabosco), c.1670; Td, Mg

EDC/Music Mss./9, fo. 1r; O; 1680s — Imperial tune; Tr, B

EDC/Music Mss./11, p. 164; Sc; 1720s — Tudway Ps tunes for Wimpole Service, 1721; Tr, Ct, T, B

EDC/Music Mss./27, pp. 114–20; B; late 17th c. (96) — Repertory with 6 rc tunes, early 18th c.; Ps; Tr, Ct, T, B

EDC/Music Mss./28, pp. 26, 128; T; mid-17th c. (97) — 7 rc tunes, late 17th c.; Ps; Tudway Wimpole tune, 1721; Mg; T

EDC/Music Mss./29, p. 24; B; mid-17th c. (98) — Tudway Wimpole tune, 1721; Ve; B

EDC/Music Mss./32, pp. 1–10, 5, 6; Sc; early 18th c. — Repertory MS 27 with add's, early 18th c.; 8 rc tunes; Ps; Tr, Ct, T, B

PETERHOUSE COLLEGE

Music MS 479, p. 92; MC; c.1635 (33) — 5 tunes, psalm tone tenor; Ve; Tr, T

Music MS 485, fo. W3v; MD; c.1635 (36) — Lincoln tune, 1660s; Ct

Music MS 486, fo. A2v; CD; c.1635 (37) — 6 tunes, ps. tone T; Ve; Lincoln tune, Woorthy tune, last p., 1660s; Mg; Ct, T

Music MS 487, fo. B3v, last p.; T; c.1635 (38) — Canterbury tune 4 parts, hand Henry Loosemore; rc tunes; Lincoln tune inside cover, Woorthy tune; Ve; T; 1660s

Music MS 488, last p.; BD; *c*.1635 (39)   Lincoln tune, 3 notations, 1660s; Nd; B

Music MS 489, last p.; MD; *c*.1635 (40)   Lincoln tune, 1660s; Nd; Tr

Music MS 490, last p.; TC; *c*.1635 (41)   Lincoln tune, 1660s; Nd, Mg; T

Canterbury Cathedral

Music MS Barnard; H 82, W; *c*.1660   Finch and Nalson tunes, early 18th c.; Imperial tune, hand John Fenn, 1660s; Ve; Tr

Music MS 2 A, pp. 211, 212; TD; *c*.1680   Finch and Nalson, sgl ch Raylton, early 18th c.; Ve; T

Music MS 3 A, p. 76; TC; *c*.1680   Same as MS 2 A

Music MS 4 A, p. 197; BD; *c*.1680   Same as MS 2 A; B

Music MS 5 A, p. 203, BC; *c*.1680   Finch 8 parts: 2 Raylton, early 18th c.; Ps; B

Music MS 7 A, pp. 151, 194; CC; *c*.1680   1 rc tune: Finch 8 parts; early 18th c.; J; Ct

Music MS 8 A, pp. 50, 109; TC; *c*.1680   1 Daniel Henstridge, rc tunes, *c*.1700 Ve; T

Music MS 9 A, pp. 12, 19; O; *c*.1700–10   12 tunes, sgl ch Henstridge, G. Cooper; Tr, B

Music MS 11 A, fo. 35, fo. 39; O; 1699–1715   8 tunes, sgl ch Raylton; Tr, B

Music MS 13 A, p. 182; CD; 1699–1715   Finch and Nalson; Ve; Ct

Music MS 15, p. 178; TD; 1699–1715   7 Finch and Nalson; Ve, T

Music MS 16, p. 134: TC; 1699–1715   8 Finch and Nalson; Ve; T

Chichester Cathedral

Music Ms. Kelway 4, pp. v–viii; anth word bk; –1725   14 rc of 23 tunes; Bass part on 1st pp. of canon's anthem wordbk

Christ Church Cathedral, Oxford

Music MS 46, fo. 11ʳ⁻ᵛ, 12; Sc; after 1682   3 rc ch tunes, prelude to Canterbury tune; Td, J, Mg; Tr, Ct, T, B

Christ Church (cont.)

Music MS 48, pp. 171, 181–6; Sc; *c.*1700 — sgl tune in Litany Service; Ve; 'Proper Tunes', H. Aldrich autograph, 10 rc tunes; Ps, Ath Cr; Tr, Ct, T, B

Music MS 49, pp. 44–7; Sc; late 17th c. — 16 chant tunes, W. Turner autograph; some rc tunes, 1 Purcell; Ve; Tr, Ct, T, B

Music MS 437; O; *c.*1675 (348) — fo. 2ᵛ, Isaack tune; Tr, B
fo. 4ᵛ, Isaack dbl tune; Ve; Tr. Ct, T, B
fo. 9, Imperial (Windsor); Tr, Ct, T, B
fo. 16, R. Watton; Ve; Tr, Ct, T, B
fo. 29, R. Watton; Tr, Ct, B
fo. 50ᵛ, short version of fo. 29 tune; Ve; Isaack dbl tr.; Tr, Ct, T, B

Music MS 1220, p. 362; Ct; *c.*1640 (400) — 6 rc tunes, Isaack dbl tune; late 17th c.; Ve, Ct

Music MS 1223, pp. 332, 331; B; *c.*1640 (403) — 6 rc tunes, Isaack dbl tune; late 17th c.; Ve; B

Music MS 1224, pp. 332, 331; B; *c.*1640 (404) — 6 rc tunes, Isaack dbl tune; late 17th c.; Ve; B

Dulwich College, London

Music MS 92B, pp. 39–41; O; 1720–30 — 5 rc of 8 tunes, hand J. Reading; Tr

Durham Cathedral

Music MS B 1, fo. 1ʳ; O; late 17th c. — Turner rc tune; Ve; B

Music MS C 12, fos. 273–275ʳ, 88; TC; *c.*1670 (73) — Nos. 1–20 rc tunes; 1670–4; 2 James Heseltine tunes; T

Music MS C 28, pp. 507f–h; B; 17th c. — Nos. 1–25 rc tunes; 1670–4; B

Music MS C 21, p. 48; T; early 18th c. — T. Davis tune; Ve; T

Music MS C 26; B; late 17th c. — 9 rc tunes; B

Music MS E 32, pp. 76, 87; Cpl; early 18th c. — Tunes by B. Lamb, T. Tudway, W. Fuller, Nd, J; Tr, B

Music MS B70, p. 1; Cpl; early 18th c. — Finch tune autograph, 6 Parts
Music MS M170; B; late 17th c. — John Tomlinson tune inside cover; Tr, B
Music MS M200, pp. 1, 2; Sc; early 18th c. — Finch 6 parts, 2 versions

Fitzwilliam Museum

MS 116, p. 77; Sc; 1707 (4) — Tune to Blow in A; Ve; Tr, B

Gloucester Cathedral

Music MS Organbk. p. 1; c.1670 (110) — Charles Wren autograph tunes; Tr, B

Hereford Cathedral

Music MS 30. A. 30, fo. 30ᵛ, fo. 126; late 17th c.–early 18th c. — 8 rc of 12 tunes; Tr, B; M. Green tune; Tr, Ct, T, B
Music MS R. 14. iii, fo. 24; 1720s — 8 John Travers autograph tunes; Ve; Tr, Ct, T, B

Manchester Public Library

MS 340 Rb 15, p. 82; O; 18th c. — 3 ch tunes copied by Wm. Raylton; Tr, Ct, T, B

Rowe Music Library, King's College, Cambridge

MS 9, fo. 1s; O; 1660s (9) — Ch tune repertory to 1720, some rc tunes; Ps; Tr, B: Repertory 1720–49; Norwich Cathedral

Royal College of Music

Music MS 673, fo. 43; O; 1674–88 (244)					'Welles Tunes A 4 Voc.', 1 rc tune; Ve; Tr, Ct, T, B; Wells Cathedral; John Jackson ?autograph

St John's College, Oxford

Music MS 315, fos. 100ᵛ–101; O; c.1660 (407)					5 rc of 9 tunes; Ve; B

St Paul's Cathedral

Mus. MS A.1.8vo; Psalter; 1670s					Bass of 12 rc tunes

Music MS Ct II, p. 160; Ct; 1670–90 (259)					Ch tune W. Turner autograph, 1706; Tr, Ct, T, B

Mus. MS Organbook 10, pp. 171–95; early 18th c.					Large repertory of Thomas Sharp, 17 rc tunes; add's Granville Sharp; Ps; Tr, B

University of California, Berkeley

MS 173, pp. 136–8; O; early 18th c.					7 dbl, 2 sgl; Ps; Tr, Ct, T, B; Oxford

University of California, Los Angeles

Music MS 627, pp. 95–7; Sc; 18th c.					Finch and Nalson set ch tunes per Canterbury Cathedral ptbks; Tr, Ct, T, B

Wells Cathedral

BCP, MS add's; back p.; c.1680					Tunes by J. Jackson, J. Blow, Ely and Lincoln tunes; Ve; Ps; Tr, Ct, T, B

Westminster Abbey

Music MS Set 3; TD; 1712–60

Tone 1.4 psalm tune with Tallis Responses, copied John Church c.1720

Wimborne Minster

Music MS P10, fos. 6ᵛ, 7; O; c.1670 (475)

9 rc tunes; Ps; Tr, Ct, T, B

Worcester Cathedral

Music MS A. 3.2, p. 107; Ct; 1670–85

4 W. Turner rc tunes; Ct

Music MS A. 3.3, pp. 129S, 78; T; 1670–1710

7 rc tunes, 1670; Ps; T: Ps Ch to Davis Service in G minor; T

Music MS A. 3.4, pp. 129S, 138; Ct; 1670–1702

7 rc tunes, 1670s; Ve: Ct: Ps Ch to Davis Service in G minor; Ct

Music MS A. 3.5, pp. 175, 183; B; 1670–85

4 W. Turner rc tunes; B: 7 rc tunes, 1670s; B: Ps Ch to Davis Service; B

Yale University

Filmer MS 21; choir bk leaves; 17th c.

2 ch tunes; J; Ct

York Minster

Music MS 1/5s, page pasted to back cover; MD; 1668–97 (492)

8 rc ch tunes copied Stephen Bing, c.1675; Ve; Ps; Tr

Music MS 1/6s, page pasted to back cover; CD; 1668–97 (493)

8 rc ch tunes as above; Ct

Music MS 1/7s, page pasted to back cover; TD; 1668–97 (494)

8 rc ch tunes as above; T

York Minster (cont.)

Music MS M 1/8s, page pasted to back cover; BD; 1668–97 (495) — 8 rc ch tunes as above; B

Music MS M 11s, pp. 14–33; Cpl; 1712–18 — York composers tunes, some rc tunes, hand Wm. Knight; Ps; Tr, Ct, T, B

Music MS M 40; Sc; 1700–39 — Dbl, sgl tune (2 versions); Tr, Ct, T, B

Music MS M 47, fo. 5ᵛ; Sc; early 18th c. — 2 Ps ch; Tr, Ct, T, B

Music MS M 164/J 1s, pp. 1–12B; CC; late 17th c. — Repertory tunes nos. 1–42, some rc tunes; Ps; Ct, B in Ct ptbk

Music MS M 164/J 3s, pp. 1–10B; BC; late 17th c. — Repertory nos. 1–42 as above; Tr, B in B ptbk

Parish Music Books with Chants 1718–1820

HTI Code	Title and editor*	Notes
ChetJBP_1–8	A Book of Psalmody, 1718–52; John Chetham	Td; Bte, Nd in 1 and 2, Ve and Cd added in 3 (1724)
GreeJCPT_4	A Collection of Psalm-Tunes, 1718; James Green	Td, Bn, Mg, Nd ch at end of bk
TimbFDM_b–d, o, r	The Divine Musick Scholars Guide, 1720–4, c.1737, 1748; Francis Timbrell	Turner sgl, Ve; Dm ch in c, 1st v.; text under music, rest below
LangWBPT_2	A Book of the Choicest . . . Psalm-Tunes, 1723; William Langhorne	Chetham's Bte in 4 pts
BettEISM	Introduction to the Skill of Musick, 1724; Edward Betts	6 4-pt ch tunes from Playford, Ve and psalms
BrooMMBC_a–d	Michael Broom's Collection of Church Musick, Birmingham, 1725–9; Michael Broom[e]	Turner Ve; Finch 8-pt ch in b, c, d, Cd text
BrooMCCP_b	A Choice Collection of Psalm-Tunes, Birmingham, 1727, 1730; M. Broom[e]	Turner Ve, 1st v. text under music, rest below, cf. Timbrell
AnchWCC_a	A Choice Collection of Psalm Tunes, 1726; William Anchors	Sgl ch 2 pts, Tr and B, Ve; Dbl ch 3 pts, Tr, Ct, B, Ve, G m
BircJCCPT	A Choice Collection of Psalm Tunes, 1728; John Birch	Bn, Bte from Green, full text below the music
GreeJBP_6, 8, 9	A Book of Psalmody, 1730, 1734–51; James Green	Ve in 6 arr from Chetham, Blow in 8 and 9, transp A m; Mg ch, text Bn; Cd to Turner
SmitBHC	The Harmonious Companion, 1732; Benjamin Smith	Ve from Green (arr from Chetham); chanting directions from Green
BarbRBP_2, 3	A Book of Psalmody, 1733; 1753; Robert Barber	Order of Service; Ve, canticle ch
TansWCM_3	A Compleat Melody, 1734; William Tans'ur	'A Chanting-Tune to the Reading-Psalms', arr from Turner, Ve

HTI Code	Title and editor*	Notes
SreeJOH3	The Oxfordshire Harmony, 1741; John Sreeve	Turner Ve
ArnoJCP_1–5, 7	The Compleat Psalmodist, 1741–61, 1779; John Arnold	Last is reform edition in new format
BeesMBP_c–h	A Book of Psalmody, 1743–52; Michael Beesly	Turner Ve; A m Ps. 136
BellJSDM	A System of Divine Musick, 1745; John Bellamy	Ve ch, 1st phrase Turner, 2nd Psalm tone 5
WattJCCCM	A Choice Collection of Church Musick, Fennycompton, 1749; Joseph Watts	Jd from Turner; Mg dbl ch
TansWRM_1–3	The Royal Melody Compleat, Bk III, 1755, 1760, 1766; William Tans'ur	Turner Ve; Nd to Green Mg
WainJCPT	A Collection of Psalm Tunes, Anthems, Hymns, and Chants, [c.1767]; John Wainwright	4 sgl,2 dbl ch; familiar phrases in some melodies
AlcoJPSHE	The Pious Soul's Heavenly Exercise, 1756; John Alcock	Ch for Td, Jd by Alcock
—	Six and Twenty Anthems in Score, 1771; John Alcock	10 sgl,2 dbl ch, florid style of *Divine Harmony* (1752)
TansWMS_2	Melodia Sacra, 2nd 1772; William Tans'ur	Dbl ch evening canticles, full text vertically aligned
LangRDH	Divine Harmony, 1774; Richard Langdon	20 ch; Ky, Sa; Reform publ 'to introduce into Parish Churches that chaste and perfect Harmony which is most suitable to Divine Worship'
RoomFHS_a	The Harmony of Sion, 1778; Francis Roome	Sgl ch for Td, Jd by Alcock from AlcoJPSHE
JackTTPT	Twelve Psalm Tunes and Eighteen Double and Single Chants, [1780]; Thomas Jackson	Adv as own composition; special Bte ch, 2nd phrase in 3/2
MarsJVA	A Verse Anthem in Four Parts . . . Five Chants . . . , 1785; John Marsh	3 dbl, 2 sgl ch for parish/cathedral use by Marsh
HarrRSH	Sacred Harmony, 1788; Ralph Harrison	Over 70 sgl, dbl ch from parish and cathedral sources, several ps tunes adapted from ch

JoneWTCP	*Ten Church Pieces for the Organ* . . . , 1789; William Jones	Td dbl ch by Jones
HeroHPMC	*Parochial Music Corrected*, 1790; Henry Heron	For charity children, sgl ch Td; Jd octave ch by Jones, text of 1st v. laid out over 4 phrases of ch
CostTSPH	*A Selection of Psalms* . . . *Use of Bedford Chapel*, 1791; Thomas Costellow	Dbl chant, 4 texts given (Td, Jd, Mg, Nd)
*AFOC_B_a, c	*The Hymns and Psalms Used at the Asylum* . . . *for Female Orphans*, 1785, 1792, 1795; William Gawler	6 sgl ch by Savage, Calcott, Humfrey, 3 dbl ed. c by Jones, Robinson, Dupuis
BeauJFA	*Four Anthems* . . . , 1793; John Beaumont	4 sgl ch; 1st a version of Turner in A
RandJC_a, b	*A Collection of Psalm and Hymn Tunes*, 1794, 1800; John Randall	1 dbl, 3 sgl (2 rc), 2 shortened Td ch
CookMSPP	*Select Portions of the Psalms of David*, 1795; Matthew Cooke	12 dbl ch 'for use of all Cathedrals, Churches, and Chapels, as perform the same'
JoneWMES	*A Morning and Evening Service*, 1795; William Jones	Dbl ch from JoneWTCP
WillRSH	*Sacred Harmony in Parts*, 1799; Robert Willoughby	4 ptbks, orgbk, ch by Barrow, Purcell, Humfrey, Willoughby
MarsJFNPT	*Fourteen New Psalm Tunes*, [1790]; John Marsh	5 dbl, 2 sgl (from MarsJVA), for charity children
BeauJNHM	*The New Harmonic Magazine*, 1801; John Beaumont	Ch from BeauJFA
StevRSM3	*Sacred Music*, III, c.1802; R. J. S. Stevens	6 sgl, 6 dbl ch, for the organ
CrotWTL	*Tallis's Litany* . . . , 1803; William Crotch	Adapted to Latin, with Henry Aldrich second suf frages; 2nd edn. 1807
SeelLDH_2	*Devotional Harmony*, 1806; L. B. Seeley	Turner transp C for Ps. 117:1, 1st phrase choir, 2nd congregation
WardJCPHT	*A Collection of Psalm and Hymn Tunes*, [1810]; J. Wardle	Nos. 1–9 dbl, 10–17 sgl ch, rc ch, Langdon, Davis, Dupuis; 2 Glt; Bte in 3/2
ChetJSM	*Sacred Music: . . . New Book of Psalmody*, 1811; John Chetham, rev. Thomas Stopford	'Chanting tunes' section; Nd, 4 dbl, 4 sgl ch, some shortened to 2 bars per phrase

HTI Code	Title and editor*	Contents
HowgJSM	Sacred Music, 1813; John Howgate	4 sgl, 4 dbl ch; 2 resp (Ky)
TomlTPT1	Psalm Tunes, Chants &c., 1813; Thomas Tomlins	2 dbl, 4 sgl ch, own comp; 2 Ky
ClarTSPT5	A Fifth Set of Psalm Tunes, c.1813; Thomas Clark	2 sgl, 2 dbl ch
—	Canto Recitativo, [1816]; J. Dixon	Large coll sgl and dbl ch in Dixon shortened notation; pointed psalter with new system
JacoBNP	National Psalmody, [1817]; Benjamin Jacob	Canticle ch written out in full; selection dbl and sgl no text
—	A Collection of Chants used . . . St. Saviour, York, 1817; Philip Knapton	18 ch selected and arr by Knapton; one of 1st chant coll for a specific parish church
ClarTSPT6	A Sixth Set of Psalm Tunes, c.1818; Thomas Clark	sgl, dbl ch; Ky resp; Sa
GreaTPP	Parochial Psalmody, 1820; Thomas Greatorex	4 dbl ch Ebdon, Battishill, Cooke, Henley; Ky, Sa
HolmJPH	The Psalms, Hymns and Miscellaneous Pieces . . . [1820]; J. S. Holmyard	Selection dbl ch; Ky, Glt by Walmisley
RideCPB1	Psalmodia Britannica, c.1820; Charles Rider	16 dbl ch; 8 Ky; 3 Sa
CratWSM	Sacred Music . . . used at St. Mary's Chapel, Hammersmith, 1820; William Crathern	Selection ch and responses

*Place of publication is London unless otherwise indicated.

APPENDIX C

Scottish Music Books with Chants 1742–1820

HTI Code	Title and compiler	Notes
DallJSUP	A Short and Useful Psalmody; James Dallas (Edinburgh, 1742)	Td, Mg (Turner, 3v); Td (Old Scot Ch); nos. 1–7 Tr, B for canticles
#CBCTCA_a	A Collection of the Best Church Tunes, Canons and Anthems; Robert Bremner, bound with Rudiments of Music (Edinburgh, 1756)	Ch from Dallas 2v; Bte, Cd added
#CBCTCA_c	A Collection . . . [1758]; bound with Rudiments, [c.1757]	Ch from 1756 arr in 3v
#CBCTCA_d	A Collection . . . [1758]; bound with Rudiments, [c.1758]	Ch 3v as [1758]
*SCT_F_g	A Collection . . . ; bound with 2 edn. Rudiments (Edinburgh, 1762)	Ch 3v as [1758]
*SCT_F_h	A Collection . . . ; bound with 3 edn. Rudiments (London, 1763)	Ch 3v as [1758]
*SCT_F_e	A Collection of Canons, Anthems and Chants; bound with Psalms of David, (1772)	NYp copy and Mitchell 51751 have no chants
*SCT_F_i	A Collection of the Best Church Tunes [Bremner]; J. Brysson (Edinburgh, 1790)	Ch 3v as [1758]
CampJC	A Collection of the Best Anthems, Tunes and Chants; John Campbell (Edinburgh, [1784])	Ch as Bremner [1758]
TaasWEM	The Elements of Music; William Taas (Aberdeen, 1787)	Ch D/B, 2v

HTI Code	Title and compiler	Notes
#CSMEC_a	A Collection of Sacred Music. Published for the use of the Episcopal Chapel in Glasgow. By the Managers (Glasgow, 1787)	7 ch D/B
#CSMEC_b	A Collection . . . (Glasgow, 1800)	Ch 1787; 9 sgl, 2 dbl added
#CCTEC	A Collection of Church Tunes, in Three and Four Parts, together with The Chants, Used in Episcopal Congregations (Aberdeen, [1790])	9 ch D/B
DingLBP_a	The Beauties of Psalmody; Laurence Ding (Edinburgh, 1792)	Ch D/B; 2nd Sett added
DingLBP_b	The Beauties of Psalmody (Edinburgh, [1800])	Ch content as 1792 edn.
DingLBP_c	The Beauties of Psalmody (Edinburgh, [1806])	Ch content same
ThomJCCT_3	A Collection of the Best Church Tunes, Catches, Chants, Hymns Anthems &c.; James Thomson (Leith, 1793); Part 2, Rudiments of Music	Ch D/B; Modern Set added
ThomJCCT_3b	A Collection . . . (Edinburgh, 1796)	Ch as 3rd edn.
#CTFP	Church Tunes in Four Parts; David Peat (Perth, 1801)	Ch D/B
SmitACCT_a	A Collection of Church Tunes Hymns and Canons; Alexander Smith (Edinburgh, [c.1805])	Ch D/B
SmitACCT_b	A Collection . . . [c.1810]	Ch as [1805]
SiveJCCTA	A Collection of Church Tunes & Anthems in Three Parts; John Sivewright (Turriff), (Edinburgh, [c.1805])	Ch D/B, in 'Addition to the Former Collection'
—	A Collection of Church Tunes & Anthems in Three Parts . . . A New Edition, Enlarged; Sivewright (Fordoun)	Described by Love, Scottish Church Music (1891) as 'now very scarce', presumed 2nd edn., no copy known

SiveJCPT_4	*A Collection of Psalm Tunes Hymns & Anthems in Three Parts*; Sivewright (Old Deer), 4 edn. (Edinburgh, [1814])	Ch as [c.1805]
SiveJCPT_5	*A Collection of Psalm Tunes . . .*; Sivewright (Turiff), 5 edn. (Edinburgh, 1815])	Ch as [1805]|
McdoPP	*A Psalmody, Consisting of Psalm Tunes, Anthems, Chants, Canons &c.*; Peter McDonald [~1809]	Ch D/B
AndeJPP	*The Perth Psalmody*; John Anderson (Perth, [c.1810])	Ch D/B; plates nearly same as #CTFP
DavijSPHT	*A Selection of Psalm and Hymn Tunes, Ancient and Modern*; James Davie (Aberdeen, [1813])	Ch D/B; additions
ClarWC	*A Collection of Chaunts, Psalm Tunes & Hymns, set to Harmony in Four Parts*; William Clarke Edinburgh, [1817]	Ch D/B called 'old chaunt', new repertory English ch arr Morning and Evening
McdoAES_3	*The Elements of Singing*; Alexander McDonald, 3 edn. (Edinburgh, [~1819])	8 Ch D/B

APPENDIX D

Episcopal Liturgical Music Printed in America 1783–1820

HTI Code	Title and Compiler	Notes
LawARM_1a	*Rudiments of Music*, Cheshire, Conn., 1783; Andrew Law	Chetham Td arr Davenport; 8 sgl ch; text pr separately; C353[a]
LawARM_2	2nd edn. 1786	same items; C354
*TS_Com	Tunes, suited to the Psalms and Hymns of the Book of Common Prayer . . . Revised and Proposed to the Use of the Protestant Episcopal Church, 1786; [Francis Hopkinson]	1 dbl, 3 sgl ch; C409
#CCM2	*A Collection of Church Music* I, Philadelphia, 1786	advertised; no copy known
	A Collection of Church Music II, Philadelphia, 1787	1 dbl, 4 sgl chants, 4 *TS_Com; 3 copied in 2 pts; 2 copied from Law in 4 pts
TerrIEH	*The Episcopal Harmony*, Newhaven, [c.1802] Israel Terril	4 sgl ch, 4 liturgical anth; C483
JenkSDH_a	*The Delights of Harmony*, New Haven, 1804; Stephen Jenks	sgl ch; Ky by William Mason; C287
JenkSDH_b	2nd edn. [after 1804]	same 2 items; C288
CoopWBCM	*The Beauties of Church Music*, Boston, 1804; William Cooper	Chetham Td per Law; C161a
ColeJBP_2	*The Beauties of Psalmody*, 2nd edn., Baltimore, 1805; John Cole	8 pp app. of service music sung at Christ Church and St. Paul's; C143
AitkJAC_a	*Aitken's Collection of Divine Music*, Philadelphia, 1806; John Aitken	15 sgl, 5 dbl ch; Mason Ky; Dx; 3 plainsong ch; C15

Code	Title	Description
—	*Hymns . . . Use of Trinity Church*, Boston, 1808	Chetham Td per Law
—	*The Churchman's Choral Companion to his Prayer Book*, New York, 1809; William Smith	Ch and liturgical anth for Morning, Evening, Communion, Litany, Propers; C473; 5 pieces added 2nd pr 1809; C473a
CoopWSM	*Sacred Musick*, Boston, 1810; William Cooper	Ch to Ps. 150 by George Sweeny
BlakGVH_b	*Vocal Harmony*, Philadelphia, [1810]; George Blake	12 sgl, 3 dbl ch, pp 198; C116
ColeJEHH	*Episcopalian Harmony*, Baltimore, 1811; John Cole	Ch, responses for Morning, Evening, Communion
—	*Chants for Public Worship*, 1814; William Smith	no copy known; catalogued by Warrington, *Short Titles*
#COPPT	*Chants, Occasional Pieces and Plain Tunes*, Salem, 1814	Service music repr mainly from Smith
ColeJDMPT	*Devotional Harmony*, Baltimore, 1814; John Cole	Service music per 1811, some additions
#MSCPT_1	*Musica Sacra*, Utica, 1815; [Thomas Hastings]	12 plus ch for Prot Episc Ch
#MSCPT_2	*Musica Sacra*, Utica, 1816	2nd edn. rev, ch content same
CarrBCC	*A Collection of Chants & Tunes for the use of Episcopal Churches*, Philadelphia, 1816; Benjamin Carr	2 dbl, 5 sgl for Ve, Glx, Td, Jd, Dox, Bc, BnA; Trisagion Glt, Preparatory MS
EckhJCB	*Choral-Book used in the Episcopal Churches of Charleston, South Carolina*, Boston, 1816; Jacob Eckhard	1 dbl, 3 sgl Ve, BnA, Glx, Ch for Easter; Ve arr; 4 ch repr in short score on later pp. without text underlay
SeymLNS_2	*The New-York Selection of Sacred Music*, New York, 1816; Lewis and Thaddeus Seymour	Ve, Davis dbl ch arr Taylor, repr from Smith
—	*A Choice Collection of Chants for Four Voices*, Boston, 1816; George K. Jackson	Dbl and sgl ch nos. 1–38; 'Sa' setting
—	*The Choral Companion and Elucidation of Dr. G. K. Jackson's Chants*, Boston, 1817; George K. Jackson	8 of above repr in Cole/Smith format; Comm Ky, Trisagion, Glp, 'Sa', Glx
—	*Sacred Music For the Use of Churches . . .*, n.d.; George K. Jackson	Sgl, dbl ch, 'Sa', Glp, from his other publications
#SZ	*Songs of Zion . . . as sung at St. Paul's and other Churches*, [1818]; John Cole	Ch for ps, canticles, resp, 1 liturgical setting
HastTMR_a	*The Musical Reader*, Utica, 1817,	BnA sgl ch Taylor, full text
HastTMR_b	1819; Thomas Hastings	below music; ex syllable placement

HTI Code	Title and Compiler	Notes
HastTSUC_1 HastTSUC_2	*Musica Sacra: or Springfield & Utica Collections United*, Utica, rev 2nd edn. 1818, 1819; Thomas Hastings and Solomon Warriner	'Select Chants for the Protestant Episcopal Church', Morn, Eve, Glx, Glp
ReedEMM_a	*Musical Monitor, or New York Collection*, Utica, 1817; Ephraim Reed	Ch, canon
SoutCHS	*Harmonia Sacra*, New York, 1818; Charles Southgate	1 ch
BullWMAL	*Music, Adapted to Language*, Greenfield, 1819; William Bull	Copyr 1813, 8 ch; own system for chanting any prose text
—	*A Set of Chants adapted to the Hymns in the Morning and Evening Prayer . . .* , Boston, 1819; Jonathan Wainwright	Chants in liturgical order; harmonies by Jackson; Communion service Jackson 1817
ColeJTFPT	*Thirty Four Psalm Tunes*, Baltimore, 1820; John Cole	ch from his other publs; additions
CarrBC	*The Chorister*, Op XII, Philadelphia, 1820; Benjamin Carr	Sentence; Jones dbl Ve written out; Glp; Bte; Bn; Cd; Dm; Miserere
AdamBES_2	*The Evening Star*, Utica, 1820; Benoni Adams	Cd, Bn ch from Reed, Glt Cole
ReedEMM_b	*Musical Monitor*, Ithaca, 1820; Ephraim Reed	'Select Chants' from *Musica Sacra*; sgl in G by Reed
—	*Chants of the Morning and Evening Prayer and Communion Service as sung at St. James's Church, Philadelphia*, Philadelphia, [1820]	Ch directions preface, ch Carr, Taylor, sel from Episcopal bks in print; first separate ch collection for one church

[a] C nos. from Britton, Lowens, and Crawford, *Sacred Music Imprints*.

APPENDIX E

Performance of Choral Service: Selected Documents 1668–1791

1. Orders of Bishop Anthony Sparrow on his primary visitation to Exeter Cathedral in 1668; Dean and Chapter, D & C/VC/Book I, Vicars Choral Ordinances and Statutes

(1) That the priest vicars reade & singe the divine service att morninge tenn of the Clock and afternoons according to the Rubrick without addinge or dimishinge [*sic*] or alteringe.

(2) That none of the Hyms [*sic*] appointed after the Lessons be Justled out by any Anthem.

(3) That after praise the Lord the Answeare the Lords name be praised be said or sunge.

(4) That as soone as the preist [*sic*] hath begun the Creede the rest of the Quire join with him.

(5) That upon Holy dayes the preacher come down after his Sermon ended in the Quire, and that the preist who officiates the Communion service (if the Bishopp be not present) give the Blessinge.

(6) That the former use of Choristers singinge in the tyme of the participation of the holy Eucharist, be henceforth omitted, it being presented to us as a disturbance to the Communicants.

(7) That all persons belonginge to the Quire behave themselves reverently in tyme of divine service standinge upp at gloria patri, Creed, & Hyms, kneelinge at prayers quietly, attendinge to heare & marke & understand that which is read preached or ministred sayinge or singinge in their due places audibly with the Minister the Confession Lords prayer & Creeds & makinge such Answeare to the publique prayers as are appointed in the Common prayer Booke.

(8) That all vicars petty Cannons Singingmen & all others of the ffoundation receive the Holy Eucharist in the Cathedrall ffower tymes a yeare at the least according to the 24: Cannon of 1603. . . .

2. 'Copy of a Paper hung up in the Vestry at York Minster', autograph of Granville Sharp (original paper 1760s; copy sometime later); Gloucestershire Record Office, Lloyd-Baker Collection, D 3549, Box 33b.

Forasmuch as it was one End of the Foundation of the Cathedral and Collegiate Churches, that whilst Divine Service was performed with more than ordinary

Decency and beauty, the Devotion of the People might also be excited in some greater degree: and for this reason it was appointed that the Service of the Church of England should be sung there in a solemn manner, and Hymns and Anthems composed so as might be most affecting to the End that those Distractions in Prayer which do but too often disturb even the best, might in some measure be remedied, and the Devotion of others assisted by that influence which Experience shews Grave and Solemn Musick hath most often on those who are in any measure disposed to be serious and devout, and inasmuch as the same Experience shews that if that Musick which is appointed, be slightly or carelessly performed it is so far from helping their devotion, that it rather causes distraction and Irreverence in the People; to the end that the Godly and pious designs of our Founders may be persued with better effect to the Glory of Almighty God and the Benefit and advantage of his People, We have thought fit for the regulation and improvement of the singing and Chanting in this Choir to make these Orders following.

First that in Chanting the Psalms, for the avoiding that confusion which arises from some Persons going before others, Every Member of this Choir do endeavour to Speak or Chant the same Syllables at the same time, by which means the Words themselves will not only be heard more distinctly, than they can be in Parish Churches where they are read alternately by the Minister and People, but likewise it will highly contribute to the Harmony, or rather indeed necessary for it; for all Psalm tunes being Counterpoint, unless this method be observ'd the Harmony will be much lessen'd, if not too often spoiled, and therefore we do Order that the Choir do meet together frequently to practice this way of Chanting till they are perfect in it, and agree among themselves which of them shall set the time for each side whom the rest are to listen and attend to, so as that they may the more easily and effectually keep together.

Second that in Chanting the Lord's Prayer and the Creed a like Method be observed: only with this difference, that the Minister who officiates shall here be always the leader of the Choir, and therefore that he do Elevate his Voice, and Endeavour to be louder than the rest of the Choir, and for this reason that they do not only attend to him, and Endeavour to keep his time Exactly as to the Pronunciation of each Syllable, but also that they do this in a lower Voice, that the Minister may be heard more distinctly without too much straining himself.

Third that in Chanting the Litany the singing man who assists the Vicar be careful to keep his time exactly in the pronunciation of the several Words and Syllables, which being so near him he may more easily observe; for otherwise it makes such Confusion as renders it scarce intelligible by the People and thus in fine that they endeavour to do in all responses, and every part of the Service, where the Choir are to Joyn either altogether or alternately by sides.

Fourth that in all their actions and behaviour during Divine Service they Endeavour to Express all imaginable reverence and Devotion toward Almighty God, as well for their own Sakes that they themselves may be Affected, as for the sakes of others whose Devotion may be Excited thereby.

Fifth that the several Services that are already in the Bookes or hereafter shall be ordered to be pricked into them be practised by the Choir meeting together till they are able to perform their several parts readily, and that these bè performed in the Church in their turn, i.e., that they may be sung each so often as that the several members of the Choir may be ready at their parts, whenever any of them, shall be appointed to be sung. And because it is hardly possible that the several Members of the Choir should be perfect in their parts, when they come to perform them in the church, unless they have practised them together in all the parts, we do therefore

Order that notwithstanding some may be ready and perfect in their parts they do yet come to these private practises and that this Method be likewise observed for Anthems and Chorus's of Anthems, that so each Member contributing what he can for the perfecting of the rest, the whole Service of the Church may be rendered more perfect and compleat. And therefore that there be one Day fixed upon in every week when they are to meet together for this End; which if they shall not among themselves agree upon one more convenient for all, we do hereby appoint to be every Monday from the Ending of Morning prayer till 12 O Clock, and that such as neglect or refuse to come to these meetings be noted by the senior Vicar or senior Singingman there present, and the note of their absences delivered the next Morning to the Dean, Precentor or Major in Choro.

Article Seventh That a full Anthem be sung every morning, unless when the Litany is appointed, and that these be performed according to the table hereunto annexed, beginning at the first and so proceeding to the next till all be performed, and then beginning again with the first go on in the same order.

Article Eighth That a verse Anthem be sung every Evening, and that they be performed in the order prescribed in the table annexed, but insomuch as through Sickness or any other reasonable cause of absence or inability to perform, it may sometimes happen that the Anthem appointed by the table to be sung cannot be performed, it is ordered that in such a case they are to proceed unto the next in course according to the table which can then be performed, and what was omitted must be sung the Evening following and so proceed on to the end of the table, only omitting that in its course which is sung in the stead of another which could not be performed in its prescribed order; and that this method be constantly observ'd, unless the Dean, Precentor or he who is Major in Choro, shall upon any occasion think fit to appoint any other Anthem, which however shall not be reckoned a repealing or altering these orders, but the same method shall still be observ'd the next Evening, as if there had been no such interruption in the course.

Article Ninth Whereas it may happen that the Anthem which is thus appointed to be sung, may be capable of being performed several ways, we do hereby order, and our meaning is, that the Anthems be always sung by the best voices present who are able to perform them.

Article Tenth Whatever Anthem shall hereafter be added to this table that they be plac'd in such order, as that there may never be any single Anthem where one sings by himself, above once a week at the oftenest, and that of this sort none be put into the table, or admitted to be sung, unless there be 2 or more Choruses belonging to it of four parts which the rest of the Choir can perform, which Chorus's must be also the best and most substantial part of the Anthem in which the composer endeavours to shew his skill in Musick.

Article Eleventh Forasmuch as it is so difficult a matter, to find persons fitly qual-ify'd by their skill in Musick and their voices to supply the places of singing Men of this Choir upon any vacancy: we do order and require the Master of the boys for the time being, to do his endeavours so to teach the boys the art of Musick, that if it shall happen that their voices prove good, when they become men, they may be qualifyed by their skill for any such place, so that indeed the Statute of the Church may thereby be fulfilled, which gives the preference to such as have been educated in it if they are duly qualify'd. And therefore that in order to this the Master do teach them by notes, so as that in a reasonable time they may be able to sing readily, any easy thing which can be laid before them in true time and Tune. And that he may lose his time and labour upon them, that such boys who by their voices are unable to serve the Choir, or shall refuse or neglect so to learn, upon complaint to the Dean, Precentor, or Residentiaries; be removed and other of better hopes and qualifications put into their places.

Article Twelfth Whereas these or whatever other orders shall hereafter be made for the regulation and improvement, of the performances in this Choir, can have no effect unless the several members of it do pay a diligent and constant attendance. We do therefore order that for this end the Statutes of the Church on this behalf be duly observed; and the accustomed penalties on such as shall without just cause fail in their attendance be constantly exacted. And therefore that the Camerarius Sive custos Vicariorum do take care that the Absences and failures of each member be duly and faithfully noted. And (as indeed his Oath doth require) that he do Bonafide without any collusion keep back so much of their profits as each one shall by their failures have thus forfeited by the accustomed penalties, we mean those which by the consent of the Dean and Chapter, and with the agreement of the Vicars themselves, some years since were allow'd to be such Viz: 4^d for each failure on Sundays and Hollidays, and 2^d on every other day.

3. Granville Sharp's directions for chanting, entered in his copy of Fifty Double and Single Chants *(London, C. & S. Thompson, [1769]); Lbl, shelf mark E. 487.*

Chants are Tunes adapted to the Prose Psalms, whereby any Psalm may be distinctly sung by a Congregation, without being tortured into *Metre*: the true sense & spirit of the Psalms are thereby retained, as nearly as they can be rendered in a literal transla-tion from the original Hebrew; & a Congregation may go through a whole Psalm *with understanding*, in the time that would be required for singing a mere detached stave or two, of the Metre Psalms in the common way.

The Words of each Verse ought to be solemnly & distinctly read (tho' they are too often hurried over in so slovenly & indecent a manner as to occasion inveterate pre-judices in many well meaning persons against Chanting) in the pitch or Tone of the *first Note* of the Chant, throughout all the 4 parts of Treble, Contratenor, Tenor & Bass; making thereby a solemn Chord of Harmony to be continued as far as the 4th or 3rd Syllable preceding *the Colon* or *double point* (:) or : in the middle of the verse; to which 3 or 4 Syllables, the 2nd, 3rd & 4th Notes of the Chant are to be applied: And the remainder of the Verse must be distinctly pronounced in the pitch of the *first Note* after that Double Bar, continuing the same Tones or Chord as far as the 6th, 5th or 4th Syllable preceding the end of the Verse, on which & the following syllables the remainder of the Tune must be formed according as the expression or accenting of the Syllables may seem to require, at the discretion of the Singers; who by a little attention in practice may easily acquire a very just & proper mode of expression; which, however, is more easy to be imitated, (when sung by a skillful Musician) than to be described in words. . . .

4. *Funeral of Dr Boyce, 16 February 1779, St Paul's Dean and Chapter Library, John Pridden Collection, v. 2.*

Minutes of what was proposed at a Meeting of the Gentlemen of St. Pauls choir (this Morning 15th February 1779) for conducting, in the most solemn manner the performance of the Funeral Service (tomorrow Morning) at the Interment of the Remains of Boyce, Doctor of Music.

The Gentlemen of the 3 Choirs are desired to meet in the middle Aile [*sic*] at the West End of the Church at 10 o'Clock. The Corpse is to be brought in at the South Door, & to be carried down the South Aile to the West end of the Church, where it will be met by the 3 Choirs, which will then face about & move slowly in Procession before the Corps along the middle Aile towards the Choir.

As soon as the Procession (with the 3 Choirs) begins to advance along the middle Aile, as above, the Organ is to begin a few Bars of the Funeral Service to give the proper Pitch to the Voices, & then to *cease* but the Voices are to continue singing (without the accompanyment of the Organ) till they arrive at the Grate *in the centre of the Dome* when the Voices are to stop at the first full period or double Bar; & are *not to pass the Grate* till the Revd Mr. Wight has made a Signal for the Organ to begin the Funeral-Service again 'I am the Resurrection' &c. in the proper Pitch, which the 3 Choirs are immediately to join, & to advance, singing, to the Choir: & when they arrive at the Centre of the Choir, they are to range themselves on each side of the middle Aile (still singing) till the Corpse is placed in the Centre; around which they are to stand till they proceed in the Service as far as the words 'Blessed be the name of the Lord'

Then the Gentlemen of the Choirs are to retire to their Seats, & the usual Morning Service of the Church is to be performed, except the Psalms & Lessons, which are agreed upon to be as follows.

A Solemn Chant by Mr. Purcell [Thomas] in the Key of G. Minor 3d. to the 95th
  Psalm or Venite.

Proper Psalms 39th & 90th.

1st Lesson XIV Job to the 16th Verse.
Te Deum – Patrick
2d Lesson I Cor. XV.
Benedictus – Patrick

The rest of the Service continued as usual & in the proper place the Anthem 'If we believe that Jesus died' &c Dr. Boyce.

After the Morning Service is ended the Corpse is to be carried down to the Vault; during which time Mr. Jones will perform with the Organ a solemn March composed by Dr. Boyce.

Whilst they are placing the Corpse under the Grave in the Centre of the Dome (around) which some dry Earth from the Grave will be previously laid, & the proper Sextons ordered to attend it, to prevent its being trampled on & dispersed) the officiating Minister & Gentlemen of the 3 Choirs are to proceed to the Grate before the solemn March is concluded.

When the 3 Choirs have formed a Circle at a proper distance round the Grate & as soon as it is placed under the Grate the Officiating Minister is to make a Signal for the Organ to begin the proper part of the Service that is usually performed at the Grave, vizt. 'Man that is born of a Woman' which the 3 Choirs are to sing as far as the words 'for any pains of death to fall from thee'.

Then the officiating Minister is to read the Exhortation 'Forasmuch as it has pleased Almighty God of his Mercy &c' ending 'to subdue all things to himself.' After which the Choirs (with the Organ after the usual Signal) are to sing 'I heard a Voice from Heaven &c' & go on to the end of the Choral Service. The Remainder of the Service is to be read by the Officiating Minister.

5. *John Marsh,* Eighteen Voluntaries *(London, 1791), preface on the organ and service playing, summary prepared by H. Diack Johnstone, private correspondence, 1995.*

Marsh deals at great length with the various stops, as also the ways in which they might best be combined and used. Having first defined a 'complete Organ' as one which 'has usually Three Sets of Keys': the Swell ('which seldom extends lower than F or G below middle C'), the Great, and the Choir, he next lists the five most important stops to be found on the Great Organ. These five (Open Diapason, Stopt [*sic*] Diapason, Principal, Twelfth, and Fifteenth), he says, 'form a proper Mixture [by which he means a proper (i.e. tonally homogeneous) chorus] to accompany the Choral Parts of the Services in Cathedrals . . . and to accompany a small Congregation in the Psalms in Parish Churches'. Next comes the Sesquialtera, a compound stop 'which must never be used without the Five preceding Stops, or at least the Diapasons and Principal to qualify it', and 'this Mixture is sufficient whenever the Full Organ is directed to be used, and to accompany the Choral Parts of Services and Anthems in Cathedrals on Sundays, or a common Congregation in the Psalms in a Parish Church'.

'Where however the Church or Congregation is pretty large', Marsh continues, 'the Chorus may be made one Degree louder by drawing the Mixture or Furniture [*sic*]', but as this is shriller than the Sesquialtera, it 'should only be used in addition to that Stop'. The Trumpet is regarded by Marsh as an alternative to the Furniture, and 'this Stop, when it does not render the Organ too Powerful for the Voices, always improves as well as increases the Chorus, as by being in unison with the Diapasons, it strengthens the foundation, and thereby qualifies the 3ds and 5ths in the Sesquialtera, &c. by rendering them less prominent'. This particular combination of stops 'should however only be used to accompany Voices in Cathedrals, in the Chorusses of Verse Services or Anthems (which should be very full in order to make the greater Contrast to the Verse) and in Gloria Patris, Hallelujahs, &c., where the drowning of the words is of no great consequence; and in Parish Churches, only for a single Verse or two by way of contrast; or where the Congregation and Church are very large; or where some Score of Charity Children add their voices to the Chorus'. In this latter case, 'the deep and powerful Bass of the Trumpet serves to qualify the shrillness of the Children's Voices; the whole therefore forming as grand and as powerful a Chorus as can be made without the help of other Instruments: this may however be further augmented and also improved, (where the magnitude of the Church and Congregation permits) by the addition of the Furniture also'. When used as solo (as opposed to chorus) stop, the Trumpet is best combined with the Diapasons. To all these stops, the only possible addition is the Clarion or Octave Trumpet which 'where the Church and Congregation are very large, improves the Chorus by rendering it more brilliant. This Stop however must never be used but in addition to all the foregoing, the force of which altogether, will be too great to accompany Voices even in the Gloria Patris, &c., except on particular festivals or times when the Church is much crowded, or the Voices exceedingly numerous, for which purpose it should be reserved'.

Thus there are five different kinds of Full Organ: (1) Great to Fifteenth plus Sesquialtera, (2) the same with the addition of the Furniture, (3) the same with the Trumpet instead of the Furniture, (4) the same basic five stops plus Sesquialtera, Furniture, and Trumpet, and finally, (5) the same combination as (4) with the addition of the Clarion. 'I have been the more particular in mentioning these gradations', he says, 'because in Scores and Organ parts of Church Music, it being usual to put only in general terms, the Words Full Organ, too much is left to the discretion of the Organist, many of whom (especially young people) are apt to be too ambitious of being distinguished above the Voices, thereby making the Organ a Principal instead of an Accompaniment'. According to Marsh, the Tierce and Larigot (or Octave Twelfth) 'only incumber an Organ, and consume wind to little or no purpose', and being put in, he maintains, by organ builders 'merely to make a shew of Stops to draw, at a small Expence', they 'can only be properly used in the Full Organ'. The Cornet, likewise on the Great, is 'a compound Stop . . . tuned something like the Sesquialtera, but as it is only a half, or treble Stop, it ought never to be used in the full Organ, but only with the Diapasons, in Voluntaries, giving out Psalm Tunes, Symphonies of Anthems, &c.'

The three basic stops on the Choir Organ are the Stopt Diapason, Dulciana, and

Principal [4′], and these three together, Marsh maintains, make 'the proper Accompaniment in full Services, where the Sides sing alternately, and not together (when the Full Organ should be used) or during the Chanting on week days'. To these, the 4′ Flute may be added ('especially if there is no Dulciana'), but this particular stop, 'frequently used alone, (as an imitation of the common Flute or Flageolet) . . . is more properly joined with the [Stopped] Diapason, which two Stops (with the Dulciana at pleasure) are the proper accompaniment in Solo or Verse parts of Anthems, the Principal being too loud for that purpose, except where the Voices are unsteady, and require to be led'. The Choir Twelfth and Fifteenth may also be added 'to accompany the Chants on a Sunday, and in full Services (except when the two sides sing together), when the Congregation is large, or the Singers numerous; and also in Parish Churches in some of the middle Verses of a plain Psalm tune by way of relief'. Not many organs had a Bassoon stop (on the Choir), but where there was one, this too, says Marsh, might occasionally be added 'for the same Purposes'. When used 'as a fancy Stop in Voluntaries', it was normally drawn in conjunction with Stopped Diapason and Dulciana. Other organs had a 'Vox Humane, or Cremona (or Cromhorn, as it is sometimes called) instead of a Bassoon', but, unlike the Bassoon, these 'should only be used with the Diapason . . . and not in the full Choir Organ' as their bass notes were 'very rough and disagreeable'.

According to Marsh, the usual stops on the Swell Organ were 'the two Diapasons' [presumably one Open and one Stopped], Principal, Hautboy, Trumpet, and Cornet, all six of which together 'makes what is called the *Full Swell*'. The Hautboy and Trumpet 'may be used either singly or both together, but always with the Diapasons'. 'The Swell is frequently used in accompanying Voices instead of the Treble of the Choir Organ, for which it may be sometimes more convenient, as the Sound may be increased or diminished so as to accommodate such Voices as may require such asistance; but it's [*sic*] principal use is in Voluntaries, giving out Psalm Tunes, &c. . . .'.

Next, 'a few hints on the manner of giving out, and accompanying the Psalms' . . . 'All Tunes of a lively and joyful nature, may be given out on the Cornet, and those of a plaintive kind on the Diapasons or Swell; and though the modern practice seems to be, to give out the whole on one Stop, yet I must own, I think the old custom of playing the alternate lines of plain Psalm Tunes on different Stops (using the Swell for the 2nd and 4th lines) has it's use, especially in tunes that are not universally known, as it more easily enables the unlearned to adapt the Tune to the Metre. For the same reason they should be given out quite plain, or with no other graces or embellishments than a good Singer would naturally apply; except at a Close, when a short, neat Cadence on the Swell, may not be improper.' . . .

'As for those little Voluntaries or Interludes between the Verses of the Psalms, I shall only observe that the shorter they are, and the more they coincide with the style of the Psalm tune the better. Of course the Cantabile style is proper, though now and then for variety's sake, a neat flourish, or point taken upon the full Organ may not be improper. But long Interludes, in which two or three sets of keys are alternately used, are impertinent to the subject (and mischievous in effect), as they tend only to discompose the devout Psalm singer, instead of merely giving him breath. Nothing also can be more impertinent than those long Shakes *constantly* between each line, without regarding whether there be a pause in the version or not, on which account it might not be amiss for the Organist to put the word of the Psalms, as well as the Music before him (if he conveniently can) or at least, to look them over first.'

APPENDIX F

Autobiography and Journals of John Marsh: selected representative entries 1769–1820, the Huntington Library, MS HM 54457, 37 vols.

volume and page number follow each entry

[Winchester, 14 June 1769 – met James Kent] He also was so good as (at my desire) to write me out a few Chants and send over to Romsey, with ye practice of which on Mrs. Daman's Spinnet I was then much pleased.   (ii. 132)

[Chichester, October 1770] – At Prayer time this morning . . . Mr Moore & I took the opportunity of going to the Cathedral, where, it being St. Luke's Day, we had the compleat Service, with a Voluntary before the 1st Lesson & another after church, the Organ being play'd by the Rev. Mr. Tireman a Prebendary, as we thought in a very good church style. The Organist then was a Mr. Hall, a young Man of but indifferent character & rather wild.   (iii. 88)

In the Afternoon therefore I had full leisure to go to the Cathedral again, which I did with Mr Blagden, and sat in the Organ Loft, where we found young Hall the Organist to whom Mr Blagden introduced me. Having been practising chants much lately, I felt a great desire (especially as there were not above 3 or 4 people in the Church besides those concern'd in the Service) to try & play the Chant myself, which indeed Mr. Hall offer'd me to do, but, thinking I might make some mistake I did not venture it. Just however at the concluding Gloria Patri, I could no longer refrain but as I stood behind Mr. Hall, put my hand round him down upon the Keys of the Great Organ & thus made my *first attempt* in this way. . . . Having now broke the Ice, I determin'd the next Morning, should we stay, to play the whole Chant.   (iii. 92–3)

The next day we bade adieu to Chichester . . . As we set out about the time of the Cathedral's beginning I had not the opportunity I had wish'd of playing the whole Chant & lamented that I had not introduc'd myself sooner to Mr Hall.   (iii. 96)

[Salisbury, October 1773] – The next day (Sunday) I went to ye Cathedral both Morning and Afternoon & was much pleased with ye whole Service & particularly in ye Afternoon with an Anthem of Dr. Stephen's, the Organist 'Thy Mercy O Lord reacheth unto ye Heavns' sung principally by Norris & Parry, in which was a Verse for ye latter which shew'd the Depth & Compass of his Voice to great advantage.   (iv. 110–11)

[Salisbury, December 1776] – Dr Stephens being engaged to spend the thirtieth instant at a friend's in ye Country, and wishing to take his apprentice Wellman & 2 of the choristers with him, to make up a little party for catches and glees, ask'd one day, if I thought I could not manage to acompany the choir in a plain Chant on the Cathedral Organ; which if I could do and would undertake for him, he could settle that there should be no Anthem put up, and have the Services only chanted, by which means I should enable him to take Wellman with him. Having readily agreed to this, on the 26th I, by way of trial, played ye Grand Chant (in C) in which I succeeded so well, that the Dr. thought he might venture to leave ye Organ to me for that day, though it was ye 1st time I ever attempted anything of the kind. (v. 111)

The next day I went again to the Cathedral in the afternoon (which Service on week days began at a quarter past 2) & played Felton's Air in C for a Voluntary at going out, 2 of which I should have to play when I officiated for Dr. Stephens, it being there customary always to play a Voluntary after Service, except on Sunday Morning, when there was always a Sacrament. (v. 112)

The 30th now arriving, I as I had undertaken to do, attended the Cathedral twice, and did the whole Duty, which I got through without any mistake at which I was not a little elated, though in ye Chant in the morning I had got on a verse too forward for want of being able distinctly to hear the Boys (the 2 principal of whom were gone with Dr S.) but luckily got right again, before I came to the end. To prevent this from happening in ye afternoon, I got young Waterlane, one of the Boys, to come into the Organ Loft and chant out of the book with me, in which he had like to have led me into another mistake, as he got wrong himself, so that instead of his being of Service to me, I was forc'd to correct him. This being a remarkably cold, snowy day, the Bishop of Bath and Wells (who was in residence and whom ye Dr. had informed of my doing the Duty) did not come in the Afternoon, in consequence of which Mr Trickey ye vicar, sent up young Hall (who still remain'd a Chorister, tho' of little use, his voice being quite gone) to put up the Anthem 'Call to remembrance' on which I sent to desire him to call to remembrance that the proper organist was absent and therefore he must do without an Anthem. I however played a voluntary after each service, viz. Corelli's Pastoral in the morning, and a slow Italian Air by Porpora in the Afternoon. Having done this business for the doctor, he afterwards told me that I was now *free of the Organ Loft* and might in future sit there whenever I pleas'd. (v. 114–15)

[Salisbury, February 1777] – Having now occasionally play'd the Chant at the Cathedral, my next Musical attempt was to compose a few new ones, of which I played a double one there on ye 6th after which I now and then introduced another, with Dr S's permission. (v. 120)

[London, 9 February 1777 – there to be admitted Solicitor in Chancery] On the next morning (Sunday ye 9th) I walked to Dr Nares's, one of the Organists & Masters of ye Choristers of the King's Chapel, at Pimlico, with a Note of introduction from Mr Corfe of Sarum, in order to be admitted into the Organ Loft of that Chapel, which I accordingly was, where I had ye pleasure of seeing their Majesties, hearing a verse Anthem well sung, & Mr Dupuis (the other Organist) on the Organ, a great player on that Instrument tho' not a better Musician than Dr Nares — As soon as the Service & concluding Voluntary were over I wish'd Mr Dupuis good Morning . . . (v. 121)

[Salisbury, May 1777] – It having been always usual at Salisbury Cathedral (as in many others) for ye Congregation after Morning Prayers on Sundays to adjourn for the Sermon from the Choir to the Nave or Body of the Church, which for that purpose was filled up with Pews &c. and which were a great Dissight to that Building; the Dean & Chapter at length came to a resolution of putting into execution a scheme that had been often propos'd, of enlarging the Choir by building Closets, Galleries &c. carrying the Altarpiece farther back, after which they meant to erect a Pulpit there & lay open the Nave, by removing the Pulpit & pews therefrom. At the same time they agreed also to new face the Stalls, all which together, it was expected would take up a considerable time in putting into execution. Accordingly on Monday May the 12th the alterations began in consequence of which the Service was stopt on the week days, & on Sunday June the 1st the Canons began attending St. Thomas's church instead, where they read the Communion Service and a sermon was added by the cathedral preacher (of which there only used to be one in ye Afternoon) but there being no Chanting &c. there, ye Choir were not required to attend.   (v. 135–6)

[Salisbury, 7 June 1778] – On Sunday, the 7th, Mr Corfe being in London (to put his Son into the King's Chapel under Dr. Nares) I went into the Organ Loft at St. Martin's in the Afternoon & play'd the 1st Voluntary & 2 Psalms, being the 1st time of my ever doing Parochial Duty.   (vi. 30)

[Exeter, June 1779] – It being now about the time of Service at the Cathedral I made (as usual in a city) my 1st visit there, where I found myself in high luck, it being the time of a Visitation of the Clergy, when ye Service was done in the best manner with a Verse Anthem &c. in the Morning. . . . finding it to be the time of Afternoon Service, I again went to the Cathedral with Mr Ridout, where the Chant was just began, but he seeming not inclin'd to stay, I told him I only wish'd to hear the effect of ye Full Organ with the Double Diapasons at the west end of ye Church, which would be used at the 1st Gloria Patri. As however we waited full 10 minutes & no Full Organ was used, I told him I was sure it must be the 15th day of the Month with ye long Psalm of 73 Verses, which turning out upon reflection to be the case, it was not 'till after Mr Ridout had fidgeted about & shewn much impatience, before I was gratified with what I wanted to hear; on which we immediately resum'd our Walk. (vi. 101–2)

[Canterbury, Monday, 13 August 1781] – . . . we went to ye Cathedral at 5 when they were so good as to put up a good Verse Anthem for me to hear, which was very well sung & accompanied on the organ by a Mr Brown a much better player than Porter, the Organist.   (vii. 90)

[Bath, March 1782] – This week I went every Morning to ye Abbey Church, which was very well attended, particularly on Good Friday, when the Congregation being very large & number of Communicants great, the Sacrament was administer'd by 4 Clergy-men.   (vii. 160–1)

[Canterbury, Thursday, 8 July 1784 – new cathedral organ opened] As to the Choir Organ it was entirely new & likewise too soft, even when Full, to accompany the Chants and Services on a Sunday, or when the Congregation was large. There was however a very pleasing Dulciana in it, which was afterward frequently used in Voluntaries before the Anthem, & gave much satisfaction. (ix. 54)

[Canterbury, 2 October 1785] – The next morning after going to Barham church I went to Canterbury . . . Cathedral, where I for the 1st time play'd the whole Service, viz., Bishop's Verse Service in D (which with some other easy Services, of which young Porter had written me out Organ parts, I had been some time practising) my Anthem—'Oh, praise God!'—, the Chant, & concluding Voluntary. (x. 22)

[Chichester, 25 December 1785] – . . . went to the Cathedral where I went into the Organ Loft & played the 2d voluntary and 104th Psalm before the Sermon; and in the Afternoon, went there again, when Mr Walond told me that it being Christmas Day, the Pastoral Symphony in the Messiah was desired for a Voluntary immediately after which he said we could play my Fugue in C for 2 performers, which however I thought we had better do for the concluding Voluntary but as Walond said people would be then going out of Church and would not hear it, he desir'd it might be played after ye Pastoral Symphony, which therefore having played myself, Walond join'd me in the Fugue, just as we finished which nothing would serve but we must have it over again (tho' I remonstrated as much as I could against it, thinking it would altogether make the Voluntary too long) which we accordingly played. (x. 48–9)

[Westminster Abbey, 1 July 1786] – On Saturday July the 1st the Te Deum & Jubilate [by Marsh] were perform'd (accompanied on ye Organ by myself) before the Archbishop, & Bishop of St. David's, almost all the Prebendaries & Clergy of ye Cathedral & a great concourse of other people, & seem'd to go off very well, all the Minor Canons singing & exerting themselves in it to the utmost. . . . This day being that of the Cathedral Visitation, the Archbishop was receiv'd at the great West door by the Dean, 12 Prebendaries, Archdeacons, Six Preachers, 6 Minor Canons, 10 Lay Vicars & 10 Choristers, who sang a Full Anthem accompanied by the Organ during the procession to the Choir; (& there being no Communion Service), an Anthem of Crofts was sang before the Sermon (which was preach'd by the Dean) in which the Verses were sang by the Minor Canons in their best manner. In the Afternoon my Evening Service was done with my Anthem 'Oh praise God in his Holiness! (x. 106–7)

[Chichester, July 1787] – As to the state of this Choir & of the Chapter of Chichester &c. when we came first to settle there, it was as follows — The Bishop, Sir Wm Ashburnham, was an old Man of near 4 score & the oldest Bishop on the bench, being the only one then remaining of the late King's appointing. He was then reckon'd a fine Preacher & used to ascend the Pulpit at the Cathedral always once a year; but tho' he could move the Passions by his Oratory, & pathetic manner of preaching (which in the later period of his life was enforc'd by a little tremor in his voice) yet with regard to his private Character he was reckon'd a very cold hearted Man, as well in respect to ye Poor, as in his conduct to his own Son & 3 Daughters, the former of whom from some family disagreement was dismiss'd with a paltry Annuity of £50 a Year & was I believe principally supported by Lord Ashburnham & the latter he allowed so very little, that they were much stinted in doing any charitable Acts that might otherwise naturally have been expected of them, as Daughters of the Bishop.   [discussion of the 3 daughters]

The Dean at this time was Dr Harward, a Man much fitter to be at the head of a Regiment, than of a Chapter, being a very headstrong, passionate Man & much given to *Swearing*; dealing out his Oaths to ye Virgers whenever he had the least excuse of Complaint. He was also a very litigious Man, & was remarkably irreverant in his behaviour at Church, frequently talking during ye Lessons &c. & sometimes amusing himself on Week Days with a Pencil & Paper &c.   [description of second wife and two daughters]

The Precentor (the next in Dignity) was then (& is now) W. Ashburnham, younger Brother to the Bishop, a little deform'd, infirm Man, so very nervous & whimsical (tho' a sensible Man in other respects) as at times to amount to a species of Mental Derangement. As from his Infirmity, he was incapable of exerting himself in his Office, he appointed Mr Toghill [one of the vicars] as his Deputy—[on influence of Mrs Ashburnham] who by some used to be term'd the real Bishop of Chichester. [details of son and daughter]

As to the Canons Residentiary forming the Chapter of Chichester, there were then only 3 viz. Mr. Courtial, Mr. Webber & Mr. Miller, of whom the former, an elderly Man, was reckon'd to know more of the Statutes & ecclesiastical matters in general than either of the others & had therefore the greatest sway of any in the Chapter. He was then & still is a remarkably good looking Man of his age, but under the idea probably of fine Reading, had so uncommon & unpleasant a delivery that it was disagreeable to hear him.

Mr. Webber was also an elderly Man & ye only one of the 3 that resided constantly at Chichester. He was himself much of a Valetudinarian & lived very retired, [description of wife and two sons] . . . The remaining Canon was Mr. Miller, Brother to Sir Thomas Miller of Hampshire, who resided mostly at a Living he had in Suffolk. When in residence at Chichester he enter'd very little into ye common run of visiting there, having no taste for Card playing, which was so far from being ye case with Mrs. Miller that it seem'd to be her principal delight—The reason of there being then but 3 Canons instead of 4 (the proper number) was from the Chapter having ever since a Vacancy that happened 2 or 3 Years before, been divided in their choice of another to fill it up; the Dean & Mr. Webber being for Dr. Buckner & Messrs. Courtial & Miller for Mr. Metcalfe, Chaplain to Lord Pelham, so that (the Dean not having ye casting vote) they could come to no decision, but kept it open & received ye Emolument of ye vacant Canonry amongst them in return for the consequent additional Duty of keeping 4 Months residence instead of 3 — In fact this was no particular concern of ye Gentlemen of ye Chapter, who probably cared but little which of the 2 were chosen (they being both very unexceptionable Men) but was a struggle between the Duke of Richmond, who by means of the Dean & Mr. Webber, wish'd to bring in his friend Dr. Buckner & Lord Pelham, who with ye influence of the Bishop & the other 2 Gentlemen of ye Chapter wish'd to bring in Mr. Metcalfe.

The four vicars were Messrs. Toghill, Walker, who had an exceedingly good con-

tralto voice, and, when well and in spirit sang with great energy, but was so very nervous, that he seldom chanted the service, or attended it, but on an afternoon Mr.
Moore was also another counter-tenor singer, though his voice was naturally a tenor,
or bass. The remaining vicar was Mr Middleton; a young man, then lately recommended by Dean Horne of Canterbury, president of Magdalen College, Oxford, a
very moderate tenor-singer, who had been lately appointed in the room of Mr
Shenton, who died a few months before we came to settle at Chichester. Besides these
gentlemen the choir only consisted of four singing men instead of six, the proper
number, and six boys, so, that it would have been much smaller than that at
Canterbury, had the four vicars been in the habit of all generally attending the service;
instead of which there seldom was more than one at church at a time, and as to these
lay-vicars, one of them was good for little; Prince, a bass-singer, who pleaded a stom-
ach complaint, that prevented his making the least exertion in singing, and another,
Silverlock, an old man, the only tenor-voice, was worse than none at all, every note
he sang being so flat and out of tune as to mar the general effect, so, that the only two
efficient singers were Barber, a pretty good, but weak counter-tenor, and Luffe, a
good choral bass. The strength of the choir seemed therefore to consist almost wholly
of trebles, the six boys bawling, and making all the noise they could, as if by that means
to remedy the deficiency of men. These boys were then very badly taught by Walond,
who seemed to take very little pains with them. As to Walond himself, he was certainly a very good harpsichord player, and might be equally excellent upon the organ,
would he but consider that instrument in its general use in cathedrals, as an accompaniment only, and not a principal, and therefore confine himself to the music before
him; instead of which he never played a chant, service, or anthem without interlard-
ing it with flourishes, unmeaning embellishments, making variations, and accompanying the verse or solo voices too loud and full, and playing in short without discretion
and judgment; for which reason even his voluntaries, where he of course might be
allowed a little more scope, are frequently light and trifling, though neatly executed,
from his paying less attention to style than execution.   (xi. 89–98)

[London, 18 November 1798] – My Cousin Charlotte having told me that young
Pring, Organist of Aldersgate Church was reckon'd one of the best then in that line,
I on the next Morning (Sunday ye 18th) went to that church, where the Service was
also very well performed, & where one or 2 of ye Sentences before the Exhortation
at the opening of ye Service were sung by ye Charity Children instead of being read,
which had a good effect.   (xix. 112)

[London, May 1799] – The next day being Whitsunday I went to St. Paul's in ye
morning, at which as usual on these Festivals the Organ was used in all the Responses
& Amens, & also in ye Responses of ye Litany.   (xix. 168)

[Oxford, 20 July 1800] – At 2. we went to St. Mary's Church again with Dr. Cooke
[president Magdalen College], when I sat in the Organ Loft with Dr. Crotch & played
my Fugue in C for the last Voluntary & At 5. we went to Christchurch, after which
Service Dr. Crotch at my desire played the Hailstone Chorus, immediately after which
we accompanied the Dr. to St. John's when I again sat with him where I heard an

Anthem of his admirably accompanied by himself. He now telling me it was *my turn* to play ye last Voluntary, I played part of my Concerto in G, just as I had finish'd which Mr Silvester (who with Dr Cooke & his party had been there) came up to thank the Dr. for his Voluntary, who saying it was not his performance, I got more credit than I expected.

On the next morning (Monday 21st) I called on Mr Vicary & got the keys of Magdalen Organ which I played on at 1.

On the Afternoon of the following day I went to Magdalen chapel where I played the Chants & last Voluntary.   (xx. 170–1)

[Southwell, 10 August 1801] – Having attended the choir-service, which was performed in as bad a manner as I ever heard, we went into the chapter-house . . . & at 4. went to ye Afternoon Service, when I went into ye Organ Loft & played the Chant & Voluntary, the rest of ye Service being played in a slovenly manner by a Boy, the apprentice to Mr. Spofforth ye organist.   (xxi. 150)

[Winchester, 20 September 1808] – In ye evening I called & left a copy of my Cathedral Chant book at Mr Chard's ye Organist, & on the following morning we immediately after breakfast went to the Cathedral, where I saw Mr Chard in ye Organ loft, who promised to shew my publication to the Dean & Chapter there, & recommend its adoption in ye choir. . . . just staid to hear the chant, which was a very pleasing one of Dr. Randall, not in my collection, & very well performed . . .   (xxvii. 63)

[Chichester, April 1810] – On Sunday ye 15th & on the Sunday after Easter Day, 2 very unusual circumstances happened at Chichester Cathedral, on the afternoon of the first of which days there was *no singing man present*, & on Easter day, Mr Moore the Vicar (there being *no residentiary*) was obliged, besides chanting the Morning Service & Litany, to read the Communion Service, preach afterwards & administer the Sacrament alone to a great many communicants. The cause of the latter circumstance was owing to their being, in fact, *no residentiary* for ye Spring quarter, the Bishop of Exeter (Pelham) ye junior residentiary, having procured a dispensation, & Mr. Marwood who, to keep up appearances frequently attended for him on Sundays &c was now laid up with the gout.   (xxviii. 16–17)

[London, 28 April 1811] – On the next morning (Sunday ye 28th) I looked in at St. James's church at 11. but finding it very full, & not being asked into any pew, I went on to St. George's, Hanover square, which began later, but that being still fuller, I went to the King's chapel at 12 where I heard the Service very well performed, & meeting with Mr. Goss at coming out was asked by him to dinner at 4. to meet Mr. Welch the singer, which I did, & at tea we were joined by a Mr. Van— who succeeded my friend Mr. Champness as Minor canon of St. Paul's & Westminster Abbey & joined with Mr. Goss, his brother & Mrs. Goss in some anthems, Glees, &c.   (xxviii. 122–3)

[London, April 1812] – At 3. we went to St. Paul's, where Edward [Marsh's son] was much disconcerted with ye slovenly manner in which the Service was performed, the late entry & talking of some of the singers & their almost all going out as soon as ye anthem ended without staying for ye remainder of ye prayers and Sermon.   (xxix. 47–8)

[Southwell, 14 September 1817] – The next day (Sunday the 14th) I went twice to the Cathedral, or Minster, where the Singers were sadly overpowered by the organist, Mr. Spofforth, an old, deaf man, who, to make matters worse, used the Cornet besides ye sesquialtera in ye full organ. In the morning a Sanctus and Commandments of mine were put up by Mr Becker, the vicar general and one of the residentiaries . . .   (xxxi. 148)

[Marsh loaned a copy of his Service in D for John Becker, son of the vicar, to copy for the choir] without the Creed, which they did not sing at Southwell . . . . on the next morning I played my changeable double chant in E at church . . .   (xxxi. 150)

[Lichfield, 27 September 1817] – I went to the afternoon service at the cathedral, after which I tried over my double chant in G with the boys,

which I wished to have done the next morning. As Mr Spofforth, ye organist (nephew to Mr S. of Southwell) was not himself at church, I next called on him, who told me he was invited to meet me the next day at dinner at Dr. Muckleston's the sub-chanter who had heard of my being coming that way from Mr Brown of the choir; late of Chichester, who called on me soon after my return to the Inn, & afterwards acquainted Dr M of my arrival, on which he immediately sent me an invitation to their family dinner on the next day, Sunday the 28th — I therefore on that day, called & introduced myself to him about 10 o'clock when he told me my Te deum, Jubilate & my printed Verse Sanctus in D were appointed for that morning, & which I accordingly heard most admirably performed with my chant in G by that celebrated choir. Indeed, as I afterwards observed to the Dr., there was there every requisite there could be for giving effect to cathedral service, namely a venerable & most beautiful building, kept in the highest state of repair & neatness, an excellent choir, & a fine Organ judiciously played.   (xxxi. 154–5)

[Carlisle, August 1818] – On the next morning I went to the cathedral when it being the Assize Sunday, the service was opened by one of the prebendaries, & an anthem (The Lord's Prayer) by Dr. Clarke, was sung before the Litany. The choir consisted of 8 men & 6 boys whose singing would have been fair enough, had it not been for a stentorian counter-tenor, whose harsh voice overpowered all the rest. (xxxii. 140–1)

[Manchester, 29 August 1819] – On Sunday the 29th I went to the collegiate church, the largest parochial one I think I ever saw, with an Organ of suitable magnitude with a double front, & a regular choir of singers with surplices.   (xxxii. 144)

[Hereford, September 1819] – . . . to the cathedral, where there was a Sermon for the Charity by Dr Clutton ye Canon in residence, in the course of which service were introduced the Overture to Esther, Dettingen Te deum, an anthem of Dr. Boyce's & the coronation anthem, & the chanting performed by the 3 united choirs in a fine style!   (xxxii. 150)

BIBLIOGRAPHY

Other music sources are listed in appendices A–D and Tables 3.3, 6.1, and 8.3. Code numbers are given for sources in *HTI*.

Manuscripts

Aberdeen University, Special Collections, Records of the Scottish Episcopal Church, MS 3320/1, 6–8, 37, 47; Taylor Collection.
Bodleian Library, Oxford, Music MSS Tenbury 805, 810–26, 827–40, 863–4, 1504–5.
—— MSS Mus. Sch. b.7; c.42; d.155; d.217; e.420–22.
—— Tanner MSS 133, 134, 138, 401.
Borthwick Institute of Historical Research, York, York Minster S 3/4 b, e, Subscription Books; H8 5, 6, Acts Books.
Bristol Cathedral, Canon's Vestry, Music MSS 1–5 (Tom I, II, V, VII, VIII), MSS 6–10.
Bristol Record Office, Bristol Cathedral DC/A/B/1, Minutes of Dean and Chapter; DC/A/11/1/1, Records of Lay Clerks and Choristers.
British Library, London, Additional MSS 4911; 5327; 9073; 14341; 17784; 27750; 28864; 30392; 31420; 31445; 31559; 33239; 34609–10; 34998; 36268; 37027; 39868; 50202; 50888–9; 70481–2.
—— Arundel 130.
—— Harley 3782; 7337–42.
—— RM.27.g.3, Set 7.
—— Royal Appendix 74–6.
Cambridge University Library, Additional MSS 2960–2; 7757 (Books 4–15).
—— Ely Cathedral EDC/2/1/2–4, Dean and Chapter Act Books; EDC/10–12; EDC/Music MSS 1–9, 11, 13, 15, 18, 19, 23–33.
—— Peterhouse College MSS 479, 485–90.
Canterbury Cathedral, Dean and Chapter Library, Music MSS 1–9, 11, 13, 15, 16, 53; Act Books AC/3–9.
Chichester Cathedral, Cathedral Library, Music MS Kelway 4.
Christ Church Cathedral, Oxford, Music MSS 9, 45, 48–9, 88, 437, 1220–4, 1226, 1229; Chapter Books.
Dorset Record Office, Dorchester, Wimborne Minster P 204/CW 42, Church-warden's Accounts.
Dulwich College, London, Music MS 92B.
Durham Cathedral, Dean and Chapter Library, Additional MS 110, Minutes relating to Services of the Church; Music MSS A7, A8, A18, A29; B1, B17, B26, B28, B35, B36, B70; C8, C10, C12, C21, C26, C28, C29, C35; E32; M170, M200.

Edinburgh City Library, Music Room, q YML 28, MS A 41026–8, Minutes of the Edinburgh Musical Society.

Edinburgh General Register House, Scottish Record Office, Scottish Episcopal Church, CH/12/12–18, 20, 23, 30.

Edinburgh, Records of St Paul's and St George's Church, Sederunt Books 1, 2.

Essex Record Office, Chelmsford, St Mary's Cathedral D/P 94/11/2, Records.

Euing Library, Glasgow University, MSS Rd 23, 39, 84, 88.

Exeter Cathedral Library, D&C 3787–91, Extraordinary Solutions; D&C 3561– 76, Dean and Chapter Act Books; D&C VC/5349, Accounts Book I, Vicars Choral Ordinances and Statutes; D&C 6077/1, Miscellaneous Letters; Music MSS MUS/2/1–19, 28.

Fitzwilliam Museum, Cambridge, Music MSS 116, 735.

Free Library of Philadelphia, MS 783.9.C 23c, St. Peter's organbook.

General Theological Seminary, New York, St. Mark's Library, Samuel Seabury MS, 'Occasional Prayers and Offices'.

Gloucester Cathedral Library, Dean and Chapter Act Books 1–4; Music MSS 1, 2, 11, 12, 27, 58, 110.

Gloucestershire Record Office, Lloyd-Baker Collection, Boxes 21, 28a, 30–3, 37, 52, 54, 56, 58, 77–8, Papers of John, Thomas, and Granville Sharp.

Guildhall Library, London, St Alban Wood Street, MS 1264/3, Vestry Minutes.

—— St Paul's Cathedral, MS 25663, Visitations; MS 25650, Acquittance Books 1–8; MS 25746, Account Book; MSS 25738/1– 5, Minute Books.

Hereford Cathedral Library, Dean and Chapter Act Books, vols. 3–5; Vicars Choral Act Books B, C; Visitations 1565, 1568–9, 1571, 1574, 1577, 1579; Music MSS 30.A.30; 30.B.vi; R.14.iii.

Huntington Library, San Marino, California, MS HM 54457, John Marsh Autobiography and Journals, 37 vols.

Illinois State University Library, Normal, Special Collections, George K. Jackson MSS M1.A1.J3, vol. 4.

King's College, Cambridge, Rowe Music Library, Music MSS 9–17, 127, 265, 416; A. H. Mann Notebooks; Skeleton Collegii Regalis Cantab; Mundum Books, vols. 45–7; Lay Clerks File, Margaret Cranmer and Andrew Parker.

Leeds Parish Church, Vestry, Minute Books, Churchwarden's Account Books.

Lichfield Cathedral, Library, Music MSS 1, 65.

Lincoln Cathedral, Library, Dean and Chapter A/3/11–13, Acts Books; Music MSS 48, 61, 108, 126, 136.

Manchester, Cathedral Library, Minute Books.

Manchester Central Public Library, Henry Watson Music Library, Music MSS 340 Cr 71; 340 Rb 15; 341 Cr 71.

Massachusetts Historical Society, Oliver Family Papers Box #192, Folder 1785–9.

National Library of Scotland, Edinburgh, Dep. 251/II/23.

New York Public Library at Lincoln Center, Library and Museum of the Performing Arts, MSS Drexel 1022, 5843.

Norfolk and Norwich Record Office. A. H. Mann MSS 427–52; Norwich Cathedral DCN/R 229/A 3–6, Chapter Act Books; DCN/Q 231/A, B 1–16, Audit Books; DCN/Q 232/D, Box 1, Choir School; DCN/Q 228/C, Subscription Book; DCN/Q 230/A–C and Q 231/C, D, Audit Papers Boxes 2–9; DCN Papers relating to Visitations.

Norwich Cathedral, Brian Runnett Memorial Library, Music MSS 1–16.

Peterborough Cathedral, Dean and Chapter Act Books; Subscriptions, vol. 1713–1804; Music MSS 1–10; Small Folio no. 7.

Public Record Office, London, PRO 28,1 Cheque Book Chapel Royal, 1592–c.1736.

Royal College of Music, Parry Library, Music MSS 673–5; 1045–51; 1053; Cooke Collection MSS 807–19; Frost Collection MSS A,V,10, A,VI,22.

Saint Michael's Church Archives, Boston, Records of St. Michael's Church (Marblehead, Mass.) 1716–1784, 2 vols.

St Andrew's Cathedral, Aberdeen, Minute Books of the Diocese of Aberdeen, vol. I (1783–1840).

St Andrew's Church, Banff, Vestry, Records, Accounts.

St George's Chapel, Windsor, The Aerary, Audit Books XII.B.6, 7, 11; Attendance Books V.B.3–5; Chapter Acts VI.B.3–8; Accounts XI.B.35–8, 53–4, 57, 59.

St George's Chapter Library, Music MSS 1–4, 21–6, 89, 90.

St John's College, Oxford, Music MS 315.

St Paul's Cathedral, Dean and Chapter Library, Vicars Choral Account Books A/1–3; John Pridden Collection; Case B2, B13 Special Services; Maria Hackett Collection; Music MSS Chant Books I–V, Organ Books 1–10; Music MSS Partbooks Sets A–G, Music MS A.1.8vo.

Strathclyde Regional Archives, Glasgow, MS TD 423/1/1, St Andrew's Church, Minutes and Accounts.

Trinity Church Archives, New York, Minutes of the Vestry, vols. i–ii.

University of California, Berkeley, Music Library, MS 173.

University of California, Los Angeles, William Andrews Clark Memorial Library, MS A 627.

Wells Cathedral Library, Book of Common Prayer 1681 with MS chant tunes.

Westminster Abbey, The Muniment Room and Library, Dean and Chapter Acts Books 5–13; MSS 61228 B, C, Precentor's Books; MSS 33694–33798, Treasurer's Accounts; Music MSS 1, 7, Set 3, Organ 20.

Wimborne Minster, Wimborne Minster Library, Music MSS P10, P46, P47.

Worcester Cathedral, Cathedral Music Library, Music MSS A.3.1–6, A.2.5, A.2.13–14, B.2.1.

Yale University, New Haven, School of Music Library, Filmer MS 21.

York Minster Library, Add. MS 157/1; Music MSS M1/5–8s, M2/1–11s, M8s, M11s, M40, M47, M83, M87, M90, M103, M116, M164/H1, 2s, M164/J1, 3s; Mason Correspondence; VC 1/1, 2, VC 2/1–3, VC 4/1, Vicars Choral Archives.

Papers and Theses

ALLWARDT, A. PAUL, 'Sacred Music in New York City, 1800–1850', SMD diss. (Union Theological Seminary, 1950).

BRADSHAW, MURRAY, 'The History of the Falsobordone from its Origins to 1750', Ph.D. diss. (University of Chicago, 1969).

CUTHBERT, JOHN A., 'Rayner Taylor and Anglo-American Musical Life', Ph.D. diss. (University of West Virginia, 1980).

DORAN, CAROL A., 'The Influence of Rayner Taylor and Benjamin Carr on Church Music in Philadelphia at the Beginning of the Nineteenth Century', DMA diss. (University of Rochester, 1970).

FORD, ROBERT, 'Minor Canons at Canterbury Cathedral: The Gostlings and their Colleagues', Ph.D. diss. (University of California at Berkeley, 1984).

—— 'Some Notes on John Barnard and his *The First Book of Selected Church Musick*' (unpublished manuscript, 1979).

HORTON, PETER, 'The Music of Samuel Sebastian Wesley (1810–1876)', D.Phil. thesis (University of Oxford, 1983).

JENNINGS, KENNETH L., 'English Festal Psalms of the Sixteenth and Seventeenth Centuries', DMA diss. (University of Illinois, 1966).

JOHNSTONE, H. DIACK, 'The Life and Work of Maurice Greene (1696–1755)', D.Phil. thesis (University of Oxford, 1967).

LINDSLEY, CHARLES, 'Early Nineteenth Century American Collections of Sacred Choral Music, 1800–1810', Ph.D. diss. (University of Iowa, 1968).

MAKELEY, RONALD A., 'Recitation Practices in Early Anglican Church Music, 1544–1676', Ph.D. diss. (University of California at Santa Barbara, 1975).

MARR, PETER, 'The Life and Works of John Alcock (1715–1806)', Ph.D. thesis (University of Reading, 1978).

MARSHALL, PERRY D., 'Plainsong in English: An Historical and Analytical Survey', SMD diss. (Union Theological Seminary, 1964).

MARTENS, MASON, 'Organs in Colonial Anglican Churches', paper read at the meeting of the American Musicological Society (Washington, DC, 1976).

MOREHEN, JOHN, 'The Sources of English Cathedral Music c.1617–c.1644', Ph.D. diss. (Cambridge University, 1969).

QUIST, EDWIN A., Jr., 'John Cole: Music Publisher, Compiler of Sacred Music and Composer', paper read at the meeting of the Sonneck Society (Baltimore, 1980).

'St Andrew's Episcopal Church Banff', typescript.

SMITH, RONNIE L., 'The Church Music of Benjamin Carr', SMD diss. (Southwestern Baptist Theological Seminary, 1969).

STEELE, JOHN, 'Edinburgh's Fourth Cathedral: The Church of St. Paul and St. George, York Place', typescript.

SWANSON, JEAN P., 'The Use of the Organ in the Church of England (1660–1800)', Ph.D. diss. (University of Minnesota, 1969).

THOMPSON, James W., 'Music and Musical Activities in New England, 1800–38', Ph.D. diss. (George Peabody Institute, 1962).

WILSON, RUTH M., 'Anglican Chant and Chanting in Britain and America, 1660–1811', Ph.D. diss. (University of Illinois, 1988).

—— 'Music and Musicians of Norwich Cathedral', typescript, Brian Runnett Memorial Library, Norwich Cathedral, 1988.

WINDEATT, MICHAEL, 'A Handlist of Vicars Choral Wells AD 1592–1935', Wells Cathedral Library, 1979.

ZON, Bennett M., 'Plainchant in the Eighteenth-Century Roman Catholic Church in England (1737–1834)', D.Phil. thesis (University of Oxford, 1994).

Books and Articles

ABBEY, CHARLES J., and OVERTON, JOHN H., *The English Church in the Eighteenth Century* (2 vols.; London, 1878).

ADDLESHAW, G. W. O., and ETCHELLS, F., *The Architectural Setting of Anglican Worship* (London, 1948).

AHLSTROM, SYDNEY E., *A Religious History of the American People* (2 vols.; New York, 1975).

ALCOCK, JOHN, *Divine Harmony* (Birmingham, 1752; facs., ed. Peter Marr, London, 1980).

Annexed Book. See Church of England, *Facsimile of the Original Manuscript.*

APLIN, JOHN, 'Anglican Versions of Two Sarum Invitatory Tones', *MR* 42 (1981), 182–91.

—— 'Cyclic Techniques in the Earliest Anglican Services', *JAMS* 35 (1982), 409–35.

—— ' "The Fourth Kind of Faburden": The Identity of an English Four-part Style', *ML* 61 (1980), 245–65.

—— 'A Group of English Magnificats "Upon the Faburden" ', *Soundings,* 7 (June 1978), 85–100.

—— 'The Survival of Plainsong in Anglican Music: Some Early English Te-Deum Settings', *JAMS* 32 (1979), 247–75.

ARKWRIGHT, G. E. P., *Catalogue of Music in the Library of Christ Church Oxford* (Oxford, 1915; repr. 1971).

ARNOLD, JOHN, *The Compleat Psalmodist* (London, 1741). Arno JCP.

ARNOLD, SAMUEL, *Cathedral Music* (4 vols.; London, 1790).

ASTON, PETER, *The Music of York Minster* (London, 1972).

AYLMER, G. E. (ed.), *The Interregnum: The Quest of Settlement* (London, 1972).

—— and CANT, REGINALD (eds.), *A History of York Minster* (Oxford, 1977).

BALDWIN, DAVID, *The Chapel Royal* (London, 1990).

BALLEINE, G. R., *A History of the Evangelical Party in the Church of England* (London, 1909).

BANNER, RICHARD, *The Use and Antiquity of Musick in the Service of God* (Oxford, 1737).

BARBER, ROBERT and JOHN, *A Book of Psalmody* (London, 1723). Barb RBP.

BARNARD, JOHN, *The First Book of Selected Church Musick* (London, 1641; repr. Farnsborough, 1972).

BARROW, JOHN, *A New Book of Psalmody* (London, 1730; *The Psalm-Singer's Choice Companion*, [1740]). BarrJNBP, BarrJPSC_2.

BARRY, JONATHAN, 'Cultural Patronage and the Anglican Crisis: Bristol c.1689–1775', in Walsh, Hayden, and Taylor (eds.), *Church of England*, 191–208.

BATTELL, RALPH, *The Lawfulness and Expediency of Church-Musick, Asserted, in a Sermon Preached at St. Brides-Church, Upon the 22d. of November, 1693* (London, 1694).

BATTISHILL, JONATHAN, *Six Anthems and Ten Chants*, ed. John Page (London, 1804).

BAYLY, ANSELM, *A Collection of Anthems Used in His Majesty's Chapel Royal* (London, 1769).

—— *A Practical Treatise on Singing and Playing with Just Expression and Real Elegance* (London, 1771).

BEATTIE, JAMES, *A Letter to the Reverend Hugh Blair, D.D. One of the Ministers of Edinburgh: On the Improvement of Psalmody in Scotland* (1778).

BECKWITH, JOHN, *The First Verse of Every Psalm of David* (London, 1808).

BEDDARD, R. A., 'The Restoration Church', in Jones (ed.), *The Restored Monarchy*, 155–75.

BEDFORD, ARTHUR, *The Great Abuse of Musick* (London, 1711).

—— *The Temple Musick* (London, 1706).

BELLAMY, JOHN, *A System of Divine Musick* (London, 1745). BellJSDM.

BERRY, MARY (Mother Thomas More), 'The Performance of Plainsong in the Later Middle Ages and the Sixteenth Century', *PRMA* 92 (1965–6), 121–34.

BESANT, WALTER, *London in the Eighteenth Century* (London, 1902).

BEST, WILLIAM, *An Essay on the Service of the Church of England* [1746] (London, 1808).

BETTS, EDWARD, *Introduction to the Skill of Musick* (London, 1724). BettEISM.

BILLINGTON, THOMAS, *The Te Deum, Jubilate, Magnificat, and Nunc Dimittis, Set to Music for Three Voices, with Instructions to the Performers*, Opera XI (London, [1784]).

BISSE, THOMAS, *The Beauty of Holiness in the Common-Prayer: As Set forth in Four Sermons Preach'd at the Rolls Chapel* (London, 1716, 1721).

—— *Decency and Order in Public Worship Recommended in Three Discourses, Preached in the Cathedral Church of Hereford* (London, 1723).

—— *Musick the Delight of the Sons of Men* (London, 1721).

—— *A Rationale on Cathedral Worship or Choir-Service* (London, 1721).

BLEZZARD, JUDITH, *The Tudor Church Music of the Lumley Books* (RRMR 65; Madison, 1985).

BLUME, FRIEDRICH, *Protestant Church Music* (London, 1975).

BLUNT, JOHN H., *The Annotated Book of Common Prayer* (2 vols.; London, 1903).

BOND, HUGH, *Twelve Anthems* (London, [1789]).

BOSHER, ROBERT S., *The Making of the Restoration Settlement 1649–1662* (2nd edn.; London, 1957).

BOSTON, NOEL, *The Musical History of Norwich Cathedral* (Norwich, 1963).

—— and LANGWILL, L. G., *Church and Chamber Barrel-Organs* (Edinburgh, 1967).

BOWERS, ROGER, 'Music and Worship to 1640', in Owen, *Lincoln Minster*, 47–76.

—— COLCHESTER, L. S., and CROSSLAND, ANTHONY (eds.), *The Organs and Organists of Wells Cathedral* (7th rev. edn.; Wells, 1979).

BOYCE, WILLIAM, *Cathedral Music* (3 vols.; London, 1760, 1768, 1773; vol. ii, London, 1788).

BOYER, SARAH, 'The Manchester Altus Partbook MS 340 Cr 71', *ML* 72 (1991), 197–213.

—— and WAINWRIGHT, JONATHAN, 'From Barnard to Purcell: The Copying Activities of Stephen Bing (1610–1681)', *Early Music*, 23 (1995), 620–48.

BRIDGEMAN, G. T. O., *The History of the Church and Manor of Wigan* (4 vols.; Manchester, 1888–90).

BRIDGES, ROBERT, 'English Chanting', *Musical Antiquary*, 2 (Apr. 1911), 125–41; 3 (1911–12), 74–86.

BRIGGS, H. (ed.), *The Elements of Plainsong* (London, 1895).

—— and FRERE, W. H., *A Manual of Plainsong for Divine Service* (London, 1902; ed. J. H. Arnold, 1951 [Helmore's original 1849]).

BRIGHTMAN, F. E., *The English Rite* (2 vols.; London, 1921).

Bristol Mirror (1821).

BRITTON, ALLEN P., LOWENS, IRVING, and CRAWFORD, RICHARD, *Sacred Music Imprints 1698–1810: A Bibliography* (Worcester, Mass., 1990).

BROOKS, HENRY M., *Olden-Time Music* (Boston, 1888).

BROUGHTON, THOMAS, *Bibliotheca Historico-Sacra: or, an Historical Library of the Principal Matters relating to Religion, Antient and Modern* (2 vols.; London, 1737–9).

BUCKENHAM, JOHN, *The Psalm-Singer's Devout Exercise* (London, 1741). BuckJPSDE.

BULL, WILLIAM, *Music, Adapted to Language* (Greenfield, Mass., 1819). BullWMAL.

BUMPUS, JOHN, *A History of English Cathedral Music* (2 vols.; New York, 1889).

—— *The Organists and Composers of St. Paul's Cathedral* (London, 1891).

BURNEY, CHARLES, *A General History of Music, from the Earliest Ages to the Present Period* (2 vols.; London, 1789; ed. Frank Mercer, London, 1935; repr. New York, 1957).

BURT, EDWARD, *Letters from a Gentleman in the North of Scotland to his Friend in London* (1754; 5th edn. 1822).

BUTCHER, VERNON, *The Organs and Music of Worcester Cathedral* (Worcester, 1981).

BUTTREY, JOHN, 'William Smith of Durham', *ML* 43 (1962), 248–54.

BYNG, JOHN, *The Torrington Diaries 1781–94*, ed. C. B. Andrews (4 vols.; London, 1934–6, 1938).

BYRD, WILLIAM, *The English Services*, ed. Craig Monson (*The Byrd Edition*, 10a; London, 1980).

CALLCOTT, J. W., *The Anthems, Hymns, Psalms, and Sentences sung at the Asylum Chapel* (London, [c.1799]).

CAMERON, KENNETH W., *Samuel Seabury among his Contemporaries* (Hartford, Conn., 1980).

CARDWELL, E., *The History of Conferences and Other Proceedings Connected with the Revision of the Book of Common Prayer* (Oxford, 1840).

CARR, BENJAMIN, *The Chorister* (Philadelphia, 1820). CarrBC.

—— *Masses, Vespers, Litanies, Hymns, Psalms, Anthems & Motetts* (Philadelphia, [1805]). CarrBMV_a.

A Catalogue of the Extensive and Valuable Music, Printed and in Manuscript, of the Late Granville Sharpe, Esq. (London, 1814).

The Cathedral Magazine (3 vols.; London, 1775–8).

CHETHAM, JOHN, *A Book of Psalmody* (London, 1718; 3rd edn., 1724). ChetJBP.

Church Music and Musical Life in Pennsylvania in the Eighteenth Century (4 vols.; Philadelphia, 1926–47).

CHURCH OF ENGLAND, *The Book of Common Prayer* (London, 1678).

—— *The Book of Common Prayer* (London, 1691), MS additions and commentary, Exeter Cathedral Library.

—— *Facsimile of the Original Manuscript of the Book of Common Prayer Signed by Convocation December 20, 1661, and Attached to the Act of Uniformity 1662* (London, 1891).

CLARK, J. BUNKER, *Transposition in Seventeenth-Century English Organ Accompaniments and the Transposing Organ* (Detroit, 1974).

CLARK, J. C. D., *English Society, 1688–1832* (Cambridge, 1985).

CLARKE-WHITFELD, JOHN, *Cathedral Music* (4 vols.; London, 1800–37).

CLIFFORD, JAMES, *The Divine Services and Anthems usually Sung in his Majesties Chappel, and in all Cathedrals and Collegiate Choires in England and Ireland* (London, 1663; 2nd edn., 1664).

CLIFTON, ROBIN, 'Fear of Popery', in Russell, *Origins of English Civil War*, 144–67.

The Code of Canons of the Episcopal Church in Scotland, Drawn up and Enacted by an Ecclesiastical Synod, Holden for that Purpose at Aberdeen, on the XIXth and XXth Days of June, in the Year MDCCCXI (Aberdeen, 1811).

COLCHESTER, L. S., *Wells Cathedral: A History* (Shepton Mallet, Somerset, 1982).

A Collection of Hymns and Anthems, for the Use of the Episcopal Church of Scotland (Aberdeen, 1779).

COMBER, THOMAS, *A Companion to the Temple and Closet: Or, a Help to Publick and Private Devotion* (2 vols.; London, 1672).

—— *Short Discourses upon the Whole Common-Prayer* (London, 1684).

A Complete Collection of the Psalm and Hymn Tunes, Anthems, and Chants, as used in St. Andrews Chapel (Aberdeen, 1829).

COSIN, JOHN, *A Collection of Private Devotions* (London, 1626).

—— *The Works of the Right Reverend Father in God John Cosin, Lord Bishop of Durham* (5 vols.; Oxford, 1843–55).

COSTELLOW, THOMAS, *A Selection of Psalms and Hymns . . . Bedford Chapel* (London, 1791). CostTSPH.

—— *Sunday's Amusement. A Selection of Sacred Music, as sung at Bedford Chapel* (London, [1801], 1805). CostTSA1_a,b.

COWARD, BARRY, *The Stuart Age* (London, 1980).

CRANMER, THOMAS, *An Exhortation unto Prayer. A Letanie with Suffrages* (London, 1544); facs., ed. J. E. Hunt (London, 1939).

CRAVEN, J. B., *Journals of the Episcopal Visitations of the Right Rev. Robert Forbes, MA of the Dioceses of Ross and Caithness and of the Dioceses of Ross and Argyll, 1762 & 1770* (London, 1886).

—— *Records of the Dioceses of Argyll and the Isles 1560–1860* (Kirkwall, 1907).

CRAWFORD, RICHARD, *Andrew Law, American Psalmodist* (Evanston, Ill., 1968).

CRISP, WILLIAM, *Divine Harmony* (London, 1755). CrisWDH.

CROMPTON, JOHN, *The Psalm-Singer's Assistant* (London, 1778). CromJPSA.

CROSBY, BRIAN, *A Catalogue of Durham Cathedral Music Manuscripts* (Oxford, 1986).

—— *Durham Cathedral Choristers and their Masters* (Durham, 1980).

CROSS, M. C., 'The Church in England 1646–1660', in Aylmer (ed.), *The Interregnum*, 99–120.

CULL, RICHARD, *Garrick's Mode of Reading the Liturgy of the Church of England* (London, 1840).

CUMING, G. J., *The Anglicanism of John Cosin* (Durham, 1975).

—— *The Durham Book* (London, 1961).

—— *A History of the Anglican Liturgy* (2nd edn.; London, 1982).

DAVENPORT, URIAH, *The Psalm-Singer's Pocket Companion* (London, 1755; 1758; 1785). DaveUPPC.

DAVIES, HORTON, *Worship and Theology in England* (5 vols.; Princeton, 1961–75).

DAWE, DONOVAN, *Organists of the City of London 1666–1850* (Padstow, Cornwall, 1983).

DAY, JOHN, *Certaine Notes set forth in Foure and Three Part. Mornyng and Evenyng Prayer and Communion, set forthe in Foure Partes* (London, 1565).

DEARNLEY, CHRISTOPHER, *English Church Music 1650–1750* (New York, 1970).

DICKSON, W., *A Catalogue of Ancient Choral Services and Anthems, Preserved among the Manuscript Scores and Part-books in the Cathedral Church of Ely* (Cambridge, 1861).

DINGLEY, W., *Cathedral Service Decent and Useful* (Oxford, 1713).

DIXON, J., *Canto Recitativo* (London, 1816).

DOANE, JOSEPH, *A Musical Directory for the Year 1794* (London, 1794).

DOE, PAUL, *Tallis* (London, 1968; 2nd edn., 1976).

DON, ALAN C., *The Scottish Book of Common Prayer 1929* (London, 1949).

DONALDSON, GORDON, 'Covenant to Revolution', in Forrester and Murray (eds.), *Studies in the History of Worship in Scotland*, 52–64.

—— *The Making of the Scottish Prayer Book of 1637* (Edinburgh, 1954).

—— 'Reformation to Covenant', in Forrester and Murray (eds.), *Studies in the History of Worship in Scotland*, 33–51.

—— *Scotland—Church and Nation through Sixteen Centuries* (Edinburgh, 1972).

—— *Scotland: James V–James VII* (Edinburgh, 1965; repr. 1994).

DORR, BENJAMIN, *A Historical Account of Christ Church, Philadelphia, from its Foundation, A.D. 1695, to A.D. 1841; and of St. Peter's and St. James', until the Separation of the Churches* (Philadelphia, 1841).

DOUGLAS, CHARLES W., 'Early Hymnody of the American Episcopal Church', *HMPEC* 10 (1941), 202–18.

DOWDEN, JOHN, *The Scottish Communion Office of 1764*, ed. H. Wilson (London, 1922).

Bibliography

DYCE, WILLIAM, *The Order of Daily Service, the Litany, and Order of the Administration of the Holy Communion, with Plain-Tune, according to the Use of the United Church of England and Ireland* (London, 1843).

EBDON, THOMAS, *Sacred Music, Composed for the Use of the Choir of Durham* (2 vols.; London, 1790).

EELES, F. C., *Traditional Ceremonial and Customs Connected with the Scottish Liturgy*, Alcuin Club, 17 (London, 1910).

ELLINWOOD, LEONARD, *The History of American Church Music* (New York, 1953).

EVELYN, JOHN, *The Diary of John Evelyn* (3 vols.; London, 1906).

EVISON, JAMES, *A Compleat Book of Psalmody* (London, 1747; later edns. 1751–69). EvisJCBP_1–3.

FARMER, HENRY, *A History of Music in Scotland* (London, 1947).

FARQUHAR, G. *History of Episcopacy in Perth* (Perth, 1894).

FAWCETT, TREVOR, *Music in Eighteenth-Century Norwich and Norfolk* (Norwich, 1979).

FELLOWES, EDMUND, *English Cathedral Music* (2nd edn.; London, 1945).

—— *The Music of Westminster* (London, 1927).

—— *Organists and Masters of the Choristers of St. George's Chapel in Windsor Castle* (Windsor, 1979).

FERGUSON, WILLIAM, *Scotland: 1689 to the Present* (1968; repr. Edinburgh, 1994).

Fifty Double and Single Chants (London, [c.1770]).

FORRESTER, D. B., and MURRAY, D. M. (eds.), *Studies in the History of Worship in Scotland* (Edinburgh, 1984).

FRERE, WALTER H., *The Use of Sarum* (2 vols.; Cambridge, 1901).

GARDINER, JAMES, *Advice to the Clergy of the Diocese of Lincoln* (2nd edn., London, 1697).

GASQUET, FRANCIS, *Edward VI and the Book of Common Prayer* (London, 1890).

GATENS, WILLIAM, *Victorian Cathedral Music in Theory and Practice* (Cambridge, 1986).

GAUDEN, JOHN, *Considerations Touching the Liturgy of the Church of England* (London, 1661).

GEE, HENRY, *The Elizabethan Prayer-Book* (London, 1902).

—— and HARDY, WILLIAM J., *Documents Illustrative of English Church History* (London, 1896).

GOLDIE, FREDERICK, *A Short Historical of the Episcopal Church in Scotland* (Edinburgh, 1976).

GOULD, GEORGE (ed.), *Documents Relating to the Settlement of the Church of England by the Act of Uniformity of 1662* (London, 1862).

GRAY, JONATHAN, *An Inquiry into Historical Facts relative to Parochial Psalmody* (York, 1821).

GREEN, I. M., *The Re-establishment of the Church of England, 1660–1663* (Oxford, 1978).

GREEN, JAMES, *A Book of Psalmody* (London, 1724, 1730, 1738). GreeJBP.

GRIFFITHS, DAVID, *A Catalogue of the Music Manuscripts in York Minster Library* (York, 1981).

—— *A Catalogue of the Printed Music Published before 1850 in York Minster Library* (York, 1977).

GRUB, GEORGE, *An Ecclesiastical History of Scotland* (4 vols.; Edinburgh, 1861).

HAMILTON, DAVID, and MULLER, J. M., *Harmonia Sancta* (Edinburgh, 1838).

HARRISON, FRANK LL., 'Faburden in Practice', *MD* 16 (1962), 11–34.

—— *Music in Medieval Britain* (London, 1963; repr. 1980).

HARRISON, RALPH, *Sacred Harmony* (London, 1788). HarrRSH_b.

HATCHETT, MARION, *The Making of the First American Book of Common Prayer* (New York, 1982).

HAWKINS, JOHN, *A General History of the Science and Practice of Music* (1776) (3 vols.; London, 1853)

HAYDON, COLIN, *Anti-Catholicism in Eighteenth-Century England, c.1714–80* (Manchester, 1993).

HAYES, WILLIAM, *Remarks on Mr. Avison's Essay on Musical Expression* (London, 1753).

HAYES, WILLIAM, jun., 'Rules Necessary to be observed by all Cathedral Singers in this Kingdom', *Gentleman's Magazine*, 35 (May 1765), 213–14.

HELMORE, THOMAS, *Manual of Plainsong* (London, 1850).

—— *Plainsong* (London, [1877]).

—— *The Psalter Noted* (London, 1849).

HIGGINSON, J. VINCENT, 'Hymn Tunes from the Embassy Chapels', *The Hymn*, 1 (Oct. 1949), 5–12.

HIGHAM, FLORENCE M., *Catholic and Reformed* (London, 1962).

HILL, CHRISTOPHER, *Economic Problems of the Church: From Archbishop Whitgift to the Long Parliament* (London, 1956).

—— *Reformation to Industrial Revolution* (London, 1967).

HOARE, PRINCE, *Memoirs of Granville Sharp, Esq.* (London, 1820).

HOGWOOD, CHRISTOPHER, and LUCKETT, RICHARD (eds.), *Music in Eighteenth-Century England: Essays in Memory of Charles Cudworth* (Cambridge, 1983).

HOLDROYD, ISRAEL, *The Spiritual Man's Companion* (London, [c.1724]; [c.1730–53]). HoldISMC_1–5.

HOLMAN, PETER, 'Bartholomew Isaack and "Mr Isaack" of Eton', *MT* 128 (1987), 381–5.

HOPKINSON, FRANCIS, 'A Letter to the Rev. Doctor White, Rector of Christ Church and St. Peter's on the Conduct of Church Organs', *Miscellaneous Essays and Occasional Writings*, ii. 119–26, quoted in O. G. T. Sonneck, *Francis Hopkinson, the First American Poet-Composer (1737–1791) and James Lyon, Patriot, Preacher, Psalmodist (1735–1794): Two Studies in Early American music* (Washington, DC, 1905; repr. 1967), 59–62.

HOWIE, ROBERT L., Jr., *Architecture and Liturgy in St. Michael's Church* (Marblehead, Mass., 1975).

—— *Organs and Organists of St. Michael's Church* (Marblehead, Mass., 1975).

HUDSON, RICHARD, 'The Folia, Fedele, and Falsobordone', *MQ* 58 (1972), 398–411.

HUNT, J. E. (ed.), *Cranmer's First Litany, 1544 and Merbecke's Book of Common Prayer Noted, 1550* (London, 1939).

HUNTER, DAVID, 'English Country Psalmodists and their Publications, 1700–1760', *JRMA* 115 (1990), 220–39.

HUTTON, RONALD, *The Restoration* (Oxford, 1985).

Hymns, Selected . . . for the Use of Trinity Church, Boston (Boston, [1808]).

IVERY, JOHN, *The Hertfordshire Melody* (London, 1773). IverJHM.

JACOB[S], BENJAMIN, *National Psalmody* (Lambeth, 1817). JacoBNP.

JEBB, JOHN, *The Choral Responses and Litanies of the United Church of England and Ireland* (2 vols.; London, 1847–57).

—— *The Choral Service of the United Church of England and Ireland* (London, 1843).

JOHNSON, DAVID, *Music and Society in Lowland Scotland in the Eighteenth Century* (London, 1972).

JOHNSTONE, H. DIACK, 'The Genesis of Boyce's "Cathedral Music" ', *ML* 56 (1975), 26–40.

—— 'Ornamentation in the Keyboard Music of Henry Purcell and his Contemporaries', in Michael Burden (ed.), *Performing the Music of Henry Purcell* (Oxford, 1995).

—— and FISKE, ROGER (eds.), *The Blackwell History of Music in Britain: The Eighteenth Century* (Oxford, 1990).

JONES, J. R. (ed.), *The Restored Monarchy 1660–1688* (London, 1979).

JONES, JOHN, *Sixty Chants, Single and Double* (London, 1785).

Journals of the Annual Conventions of the Diocese of Connecticut from 1792–1819 (New Haven, 1842).

KIDSON, FRANK, *British Music Publishers, Printers and Engravers* (1900; repr. New York, 1967).

LAURIE, MARGARET, 'The Chapel-Royal Part-Books', in Oliver Neighbour (ed.), *Music and Bibliography* (London, 1980), 28–50.

LAVINGTON, GEORGE, *The Influence of Church-Music* (London, 1725).

LAW, ANDREW, *Rudiments of Music* (Cheshire, Conn., 1783). LawARM_1b.

LAW, WILLIAM, *A Serious Call to a Devout and Holy Life* (London, 1729).

LAWSON, JOHN P., *History of the Scottish Episcopal Church from the Revolution to the Present Time* (Edinburgh, 1843).

LEHMBERG, STANFORD, *The Reformation of Cathedrals* (Princeton, 1988).

L'ESTRANGE, HAMON, *The Alliance of Divine Offices* (London, 1659).

LOUD, THOMAS, *The Organ Study: Being an Introduction to the Practice of the Organ* (Philadelphia, 1845).

LOWE, EDWARD, *A Review of a Short Direction . . .* (Oxford, 1664).

—— *A Short Direction for the Performance of Cathedrall Service* (Oxford, 1661).

LEGG, J. WICKHAM, *English Church Life from the Restoration to the Tractarian Movement* (London, 1914).

LE HURAY, PETER, *Music and the Reformation in England 1549–1660* (Cambridge, 1967, 1978).

LENMAN, BRUCE, *Integration and Enlightenment: Scotland 1746–1832* (Toronto, 1981; repr. Edinburgh, 1992).

MACDERMOTT, K. H., *The Old Church Gallery Minstrels* (London, 1948).

MACE, THOMAS, *Musick's Monument* (London, 1676).

McGARVEY, WILLIAM, *Liturgiae Americanae* (Philadelphia, 1895).

MANGLER, JOYCE, 'Early Music in Rhode Island Churches 1770–1850', *Rhode Island History*, 17 (Jan., July 1958).

MARR, PETER, 'An 18th-Century Collection of Anglican Chants', *Soundings*, 8 (1979–80), 71–80.

MARSH, JOHN, *The Cathedral Chant Book* (London, [1808]).

—— *Eighteen Voluntaries, for the Organ* (London, [1791]).

—— *Twenty four New Chants* (London, [1804]).

MASON, WILLIAM, *A Copious Collection of those Portions of the Psalms of David, Bible, and Liturgy, which have been Set to Music, and Sung as Anthems in the Cathedrals and Collegiate Churches of England* (York, 1782).

—— *Essays, Historical and Critical, on English Church Music* (York, 1795).

MATHER, F. C., 'Georgian Churchmanship Reconsidered: Some Variations in Anglican Public Worship 1714–1830', *JEH* 36 (1985), 255–83.

MATTHEWS, BETTY, *The Royal Society of Musicians of Great Britain List of Members 1738–1984* (London, 1985).

MAXWELL, WILLIAM D., *A History of Worship in the Church of Scotland* (London, 1955).

MERBECKE, JOHN, *The Book of Common Praier Noted* (London, 1550).

MESSITER, ARTHUR H., *A History of the Choir and Music of Trinity Church, New York, from its Organization to the Year 1897* (New York, 1906).

MITCHISON, ROSALIND, *Lordship to Patronage: Scotland 1603–1745* (London, 1983; repr. Edinburgh, 1990).

MONSON, CRAIG, 'The Preces, Psalms and Litanies of Byrd and Tallis: Another "Virtuous Contention in Love" ' *MR* 40 (1979), 257–71.

—— ' "Throughout all generations": Intimations of Influence in the Short Service Styles of Tallis, Byrd and Morley', in Alan Brown and Richard Turbet (eds.), *Byrd Studies* (Cambridge, 1992).

MOORE, THOMAS, *The Psalm Singer's Compleat Tutor and Divine Companion* (London, 1750). MoorTPS2_2.

MORLEY, THOMAS, *A Plaine and Easie Introduction to Practicall Musick* (London, 1597; *A Plain and Easy Introduction to Practical Music*, ed. R. Alec Harman, 1952).

MORRILL, JOHN 'The Church in England, 1642–9', in id. (ed.), *Reactions to the English Civil War*, 89–114.

—— (ed.), *Reactions to the English Civil War 1642–1649* (London, 1982).

MOULD, CLIFFORD, *The Musical Manuscripts of St. George's Chapel Windsor Castle* (Windsor, 1973).

NEALE, J. N., *The Life and Times of Patrick Torry, D.D.* (London, 1856).

NEIGHBOUR, OLIVER (ed.), *Music and Bibliography* (London, 1980).

New Remarks of London (London, 1732).

NUTTALL, G. F., and CHADWICK, O. C., *From Uniformity to Unity 1662–1962* (London, 1962).

OLLESON, EDWARD (ed.), *Modern Musical Scholarship* (Oxford, 1980).

OVERTON, J. H., *Life in the English Church 1660–1714* (London, 1885).

OWEN, DOROTHY (ed.), *A History of Lincoln Minster* (Cambridge, 1994).

PALMER, G. H., *Introduction and Tone-Table to the Sarum Psalter* (2nd edn., London, 1898).

PARKER, JAMES, *An Introduction to the History of the Successive Revisions of the Book of Common Prayer* (Oxford, 1877).

PARKER, JOHN R., *A Musical Biography* (Boston, 1825).

PATRICK, MILLAR, *Four Centuries of Scottish Psalmody* (Oxford, 1949).

PAYNE, BENJAMIN, *The Parish-Clerk's Guide* (London, 1709, repr. 1731).

PEPYS, SAMUEL, *The Diary of Samuel Pepys,* ed. Robert Latham and William Matthews (11 vols.; Berkeley, 1970–83).

PIPER, JOHN [John Alcock], *The Life of Miss Fanny Brown* (Birmingham, 1760).

POCOCKE, RICHARD, *Tours in Scotland*, ed. Daniel W. Kemp (Edinburgh, 1887).

—— *The Travels through England of Dr. Richard Pococke*, ed. J. J. Cartwright (2 vols., London, 1888–9).

PRING, JOSEPH, *Papers, Documents, Law Proceedings, &c. &c. Respecting the Maintenance of the Choir of the Cathedral Church of Bangor* (Bangor, 1819).

PROCTER, FRANCIS, and FRERE, WALTER H., *A New History of the Book of Common Prayer* (London, 1955).

Protestant Episcopal Church in the United States of America, *The Book of Common Prayer, and Administration of the Sacraments, and other Rites and Ceremonies, as Revised and Proposed to the Use of the Protestant Episcopal Church* (Philadelphia, 1786).

—— *The Book of Common Prayer* (1790).

RAINBOW, BERNARR, *The Choral Revival in the Anglican Church 1839–1872* (Oxford, 1970).

RASMUSSEN, JANE, *Musical Taste as a Religious Question in Nineteenth-Century America* (Studies in American Religion, 20; Lewiston/Queenston, 1986).

REESE, GUSTAVE, *Music in the Renaissance* (New York, 1954).

RIDER, GEORGE, *Plain Music for the Book of Common Prayer* (New York, 1854).

RIMBAULT, EDWARD F., *Cathedral Chants of the XVI, XVII and XVIII Centuries* (London, 1844).

The Rubrick of the Church of England, Examin'd and Considered (London, 1737).

RUDDER, S., *The History and Antiquities of Gloucester* (Cirencester, 1781).

RUSSELL, CONRAD (ed.), *The Origins of the English Civil War* (London, 1973).

RYDER, DUDLEY, *The Diary of Dudley Ryder 1715–16*, ed. William Matthews (London, 1939).

SATCHER, HERBERT S., 'Music of the Episcopal Church in Pennsylvania in the Eighteenth Century', *HMPEC* 22 (1953), 372–413.

SAUSSURE, CESAR DE, *A Foreign View of England in the Reigns of George I and George II*, ed. and trans. Madame Van Muyden (London, 1902).

SCOTT, DAVID, *The Music of St. Paul's Cathedral* (London, 1972).

Scottish Guardian (1933).

SEELEY, L. B., *Devotional Harmony*, ii (London, 1806). SeelLDH2.

SEFTON, HENRY, 'Revolution to Disruption', in Forrester and Murray (eds.), *Studies in the History of Worship in Scotland*, 65–78.

SEYMOUR, THOMAS, *Advice to the Readers of the Common Prayer* (London, 1682).

SHARP, GRANVILLE, *A Short Introduction to Vocal Music* (London, 1767; 2nd edn., 1777).

SHARP, THOMAS, *The Rubrick in the Book of Common Prayer* (London, 1753).

SHAW, WATKINS, *The Bing–Gostling Part-Books at York Minster* (Croydon, 1986).

—— *The Succession of Organists* (Oxford, 1991).

SHEILS, W. J., *Restoration Exhibit Books and the Northern Clergy 1662–1664* (York, 1987).

SHERLOCK, WILLIAM, *A Sermon Preach'd at St. Paul's Cathedral, November 22, 1699, Being the Anniversary Meeting of the Lovers of Musick* (London, 1699).

SHORE, S. ROYLE, 'The Early Harmonized Chants of the Church of England', *MT* 53 (1912), 585–8, 650–2, 718–19.

SIMPSON, W. SPARROW, *Registrum Statutorum et Consuetudinum Ecclesiae Cathedralis Sancti Pauli Londinensis* (London, 1873).

Sketch of the History of the Congregation of St. Andrew's Church, Aberdeen (Aberdeen, 1846).

SKINNER, JOHN, *An Ecclesiastical History of Scotland* (2 vols.; London, 1788).

SMITH, A. EMSLIE, *S. Paul's Episcopal Church, Aberdeen* (Aberdeen, 1901).

SMITH, HORACE W., *Life and Correspondence of the Rev. William Smith, D.D.* (2 vols.; Philadelphia, 1880).

SMITH, WILLIAM, *An Assistant to the Evangelical Psalmodist, in Setting Forth the Most Worthy Praise of Almighty God* (New Haven, 1816).

—— *The Churchman's Choral Companion to his Prayer Book* (New York, 1809).

—— *Discourse in Christ's Church at Norwich Landing . . . being the Day of Introducing an Organ into that Church* (Norwich, Conn., 1791).

—— *The Reasonableness of Setting Forth the Most Worthy Praise of Almighty God, According to the Usage of the Primitive Church* (New York, 1814).

SONNECK, OSCAR G., *Francis Hopkinson and James Lyon* (Washington, 1905).

SPARROW, ANTHONY, *A Rationale upon the Book of Common Prayer of the Church of England* (London, 1657).

SPINK, IAN, *Restoration Cathedral Music 1660–1714* (Oxford, 1995).

STEWART, DAVID, and THOMSON, DAVID, A. R., *A Survey of Edinburgh Organs* (Edinburgh, 1975).

STREET, JOSIAH, *A Book Containing a Great Variety of Anthems . . . Sett of Psalm-tunes* (London, [c.1730]). StreJBCA.

SYKES, NORMAN, *Church and State in England in the XVIIIth Century* (Cambridge, 1934; repr. 1962).

TAAS, WILLIAM, *The Elements of Music* (Aberdeen, 1787). TaasWEM.

TALLMADGE, W. H., 'Folk Organum: A Study of Origins', *American Music*, 2 (1984), 47–65.

TANS'UR, WILLIAM, *The Royal Melody Complete* (Book III, London, 1755). TansWRM.

—— *The Royal Psalmodist Complete* (London, 1742–52). TansWRPC_a–g.

TEMPERLEY, NICHOLAS, 'John Playford and the Metrical Psalms', *JAMS* 25 (1972), 331–78.

—— *Jonathan Gray and Church Music in York, 1770–1840*, Borthwick Institute of Historical Research Publications, 51 (York, 1977).

—— 'Music in Church', in Johnstone and Fiske (eds.), *Blackwell History of Music in Britain*, 357–96.

—— *The Music of the English Parish Church* (2 vols.; Cambridge, 1979).

—— 'The Old Way of Singing: Its Origins and Development', *JAMS* 34 (1981), 511–44.

THISTLETHWAITE, NICHOLAS, 'Music and Worship 1660–1980', in Owen (ed.), *History of Lincoln Minster*, 77–111.

THORESBY, RALPH, *The Diary of Ralph Thoresby*, ed. J. Hunter (2 vols.; London, 1830).

TIMBRELL, FRANCIS, *The Divine Music Scholars Guide* (London, *c*.1720). TimbFDM_b.

TREITLER, LEO, 'Homer and Gregory: The Transmission of Epic Poetry and Plainchant', *MQ* 60 (1974), 353–69.

TREVELYAN, G. M., *The English Revolution 1688–89* (Oxford, 1938).

TROWELL, BRIAN, 'Faburden and Fauxbourdon', *MD* 13 (1959), 43–78.

—— 'Faburden—New Sources, New Evidence: A Preliminary Survey', in Olleson (ed.), *Modern Musical Scholarship*, 28–78.

TRUMBLE, ERNEST, *Fauxbourdon, an Historical Survey* (Brooklyn, 1959).

TYACKE, NICHOLAS, 'Puritanism, Arminianism and Counter-Revolution', in Russell (ed.), *The Origins of the English Civil War*, 119–43.

UPDIKE, WILKINS, *A History of the Episcopal Church in Narragansett, Rhode Island*, ed. Daniel Goodwin (3 vols.; Boston, 1907).

VAN DIJK, S. J. P., 'Medieval Terminology and Methods of Psalm Singing', *MD* 6 (1952), 7–26.

VINCENT, WILLIAM, *Considerations on Parochial Music* (London, 1787; 2nd edn., 1790).

WAINRIGHT, JONATHAN, *A Set of Chants Adapted to the Hymns in the Morning and Evening Prayer* (Boston, 1819).

WALCOTT, MACKENZIE, *Traditions and Customs of Cathedrals* (London, 1872).

WALSH, JOHN, HAYDON, COLIN, and TAYLOR, STEPHEN (eds.), *The Church of England c.1689–c.1833: From Toleration to Tractarianism* (Cambridge, 1993).

—— and TAYLOR, STEPHEN, 'Introduction: The Church and Anglicanism in the "Long" Eighteenth Century', in Walsh, Haydon, and Taylor (eds.), *The Church of England*, 1–64.

WARD, W. R., 'The Eighteenth-Century Church: A European View', in Walsh, Haydon, and Taylor (eds.), *The Church of England*, 285–98.

WEBBE, SAMUEL, *A Collection of Masses* (London, [1792]).

—— *A Collection of Motetts or Antiphons* (London, [1792]).

WEBER, WILLIAM, *The Rise of Musical Classics in Eighteenth-Century England: A Study in Canon, Ritual, and Ideology* (Oxford, 1992).

WESLEY, SAMUEL S., *A Morning and Evening Cathedral Service* (London, 1845).

WEST, EDWARD N., 'Music in the American Church', *HMPEC* 14 (1945), 15–40.

—— 'The Music of Old Trinity', *HMPEC* 16 (1947), 100–24.

WHIBLEY, L., and PEARCE, E. (eds.), *The Correspondence of Richard Hurd and William Mason* (Cambridge, 1932).

WHITE, WILLIAM, *Memoirs of the Protestant Episcopal Church in the United States of America* ed. B. F. deCosta (3rd edn., New York, 1880).

WHITEMAN, ANNE, 'The Re-Establishment of the Church of England 1660–1663', *Transactions of the Royal Historical Society*, 5th ser. (London, 1955).

WILLIAMS, GEORGE W., *Jacob Eckhard's Choirmaster's Book of 1809* (facs. edn., Columbia, SC, 1971).

—— *St. Michael's Charleston, 1751–1951* (Columbia, SC, 1951).

WILSON, JOHN (ed.), *Roger North on Music* (London, 1959).

WILSON, RUTH M., 'Episcopal Music in America: The British Legacy', *MT* 124 (1983), 447–50.

—— 'Harmonized Chant', in *The Hymnal 1982 Companion*, i (3 vols.; New York, 1990–4).

—— 'The Old Scottish Chant', *The Hymn*, 31 (1980), 174–82.

WOLFE, RICHARD J., *Early American Music Engraving and Printing* (Urbana, Ill., 1980).

WOOD, ANTHONY, *The Life and Times of Anthony Wood*, ed. Andrew Clark (5 vols.; Oxford, 1891–1900).

WOODFILL, WALTER, *Musicians in English Society* (Princeton, 1953; repr. New York, 1969).

WOODWARD, RICHARD, *Cathedral Music* (London, 1771).

WRIDGWAY, NEVILLE, *The Choristers of St. George's Chapel* (Slough, 1980).

WRIGHTSON, JAMES, *The 'Wanley' Manuscripts: A Critical Commentary* (New York, 1989).

ZIMMERMAN, FRANKLIN B., *Henry Purcell, 1659–1695: His Life and Times* (2nd edn.; Philadelphia, 1983).

INDEX

Abercrombie, Revd James 233
Aberdeen 3, 194, 197, 198, 203, 217
Act of Uniformity 11
Adrian Batten's Tune 46
Advice to the Readers of the Common Prayer 20
Aitken, John 226, 228, 231
Alcock, John 138, 149, 185
    chanting canticles 139
    Divine Harmony 87–8, 90–1
Aldersgate Church, London 303
Aldrich, Henry 162, 228, 243, 257
    Litany-service 46–7, 146–7
    Proper Tunes 75, 80, 83
    Service in A 178
All Hallows Church, London 187
Allison, Richard 120
alternatim canticles 170, 177
    Chetham Te deum 120, 177–82, 246
    repertory 182
alternatim musical practice 8, 43, 103–4, 107, 119,
    167, 177
amen cadence 175–6
Amner, John 116
Andrewes, Bishop Lancelot 8
Anglican Chant 43 n., 44 n., 59, 60, 83, 114, 144
    origin 85–6, 262
    summary history 260–9
    see also chant; chanting; psalm chanting
Anglican Communion 216, 218, 268
Anglican reaction (1660) 5–7
ante-Communion 2, 13, 28, 152, 169, 199
    rubric for 16, 18
anthem 10, 15, 31
antiphons 33, 35
Aplin, John 33, 208 n.
Apostle's Creed 15, 31, 56, 135
Arminianism 2
Arnold, John 166, 167–9, 170, 172
Ash Wednesday 26, 256, 257
Athanasian Creed 15, 26, 27, 32, 37, 122, 140 n.
    and popery 128
Aylmer, Archdeacon John 33

Baltimore 221
Banff 197, 198, 202, 203, 215
Banks, John 201
Banner, Revd Richard 155
Barber, Robert 167, 170, 182, 183, 205
Barnard, John 49
Barry, Jonathan 131
Barthelemon, F. 256

Bath Abbey Church 300
Battell, Revd Ralph 156 n.
Batten, Adrian 40
Battishill, Jonathan 89, 123, 124, 216, 228
Bayly, Anselm 22, 100, 259, 260
    against double chants 121
    on chanting 96, 98, 158, 261
    pointing Lord's Prayer 137–8
Beattie, James 215 n.
Beckwith, John 87, 93–4, 101, 188, 264–5
Bedford, Revd Arthur 92, 162
Beesly, Michael 172
Bellamy, John 171, 183
Benedic anima mea 219, 228, 257
Benedicite 14, 30, 174, 209, 211
Benedictus 15, 30, 104
Bennet, John 140
Bennet organbook 139–44
Bennet, Thomas 140, 141
Bentham, James 92–3, 97, 98, 99
Betts, Edward 172, 185, 205
Bible 2, 8, 12, 187
    see also Scriptures
Billington, Thomas 185
Bing, Stephen 65, 69
Bisse, Revd Thomas 20, 29, 126, 133–4, 137, 156,
    165
Blair, Revd Robert 199
Blake, George 227, 228
Bledlow Church 145
Blow, John 28, 61, 65, 68, 69, 75, 185
    E minor chant tune 141, 175–6, 205, 212, 223,
    224
    Venite chants 76, 138
Book of Common Order, Scottish 2, 4
Book of Common Praier Noted 24, 27, 260
Book of Common Prayer, American:
    Proposed Book, 1786 217, 223, 224
    (1790) 217, 218–20
Book of Common Prayer, English:
    (1549) 2, 3, 10, 13, 17
    (1552) 2, 10, 13, 16, 17
    (1558) 13, 17
    (1604) 2, 3, 5, 17
    (1662) 11, 12, 23, 28, 49, 126, 259
Book of Common Prayer, Scottish:
    (1637) 2–3, 193, 196
    Communion office, 'wee bookies' 192, 194,
    217
Boston, Mass. 221, 238
Bowers, Roger 33

Boyce, William 86, 154
funeral 293–4
see also Cathedral Music
Braehead chapel, Banff 202–3
Brass, Cuthbert 148
Bremner, James 222 n.
Bremner, Robert 184, 203, 205, 208–12, 213, 215, 216
see also Rudiments of Music
Bristol Cathedral 106, 131
Broome, Michael 172, 189
Bryne, Albertus 65
Bull, William 239
Bumpus, John 120 n.
Burney, Charles 96
Butler, Mr 200
Byrd, William 33, 34 n., 49–51, 78, 104, 138

calendar 3, 7, 12, 14
Calvinism 2
Cambridge University 78, 140
Camidge, John 266
Camidge, Matthew 149, 151, 188, 266
Campbell, Alexander 200
Cantate domino 14, 104, 110, 111
Canterbury Cathedral 16, 67, 73, 145, 154, 300–1
Canterbury Tune 38, 40–1, 44, 49, 69–70, 75, 139
for Athanasian Creed 122, 140
for Te deum 94, 140, 141
prelude to 97
canticles 13, 26, 30, 32, 85, 104, 139
see also hymn
Carlisle Cathedral 131, 305
Carr, Benjamin 229, 233, 234, 251, 256, 257, 258
extended chants 252–4
organbooks 239, 243, 245–7
Castleton, Derbyshire 167
Cathedral Music 47, 86, 114, 120, 121, 243, 257, 258
cathedral versus parochial service 4, 20, 126–7, 157–9, 162, 187
Cavalier Parliament 6
Certaine Notes 33
Certayne Psalms Select out of the Psalms of David 34
Champness, Weldon 122, 304
changeable chant 100, 101, 238
chant:
accompaniment 30, 83, 91, 97–8, 141–4, 189
arrangements 177, 209, 234, 252–4
composition of 54, 59, 60
MS repertories 75–9, 84
ornamentation 123–4, 141, 144, 178, 243, 246–50
for parish use 170–6
transmission of 60, 67, 73, 75–9, 205, 213, 216, 223–4
chant books 87, 88, 100–1

American 222, 239, 286–8
for parish churches 170–1, 186, 190, 279–82
Scottish 204, 283–5
chant notation 32, 79–86, 145
scoring 19th c. 233, 241
in Scottish books 205, 209
text coordinated with music 188–9, 229, 231, 239, 241
triple metre 226
chant tunes 28, 44 n., 54, 59, 60–79, 261–2
in chanting services 107, 111–14
for entire service 115, 139–43, 228
chanting 17, 20–1, 33, 40, 54, 91
in America 223, 225
congregational 124, 186–8, 268
in Communion 151–4
improvised 42–4, 264
in the litany 145–7
in parish churches 167, 170
prejudice against 127–8
in Scottish chapels 215, 216
whole service; 115–16, 139, 299
see also choral service; psalm chanting
chanting service 103, 104, 105, 113–15, 124
by James Hawkins 107–12
MS repertory 106–7
chanting–tunes 166
chapel movement 127, 130, 262
Chapel Royal 23, 26, 27 n., 30, 105, 131, 132, 299, 304
giving up chanting 155
and royal chapels repertory 60–1, 68, 69
initiating Sanctus as introit 154
charity children singers 163, 187, 295, 303
Charles I 3, 7, 10, 16
Charles II 5, 6, 11, 127
Charleston, SC 221, 242
Chetham, John 164, 165
Chichester Cathedral 67, 72, 107, 131, 301–3, 304
Child, Simon 117, 119
Child, William 40, 47, 61, 65, 68
Child's of Windsor Tune:
on tone 8 47, 69
on tone 1.4 78
choirs in parish churches 4, 165, 166, 177, 188
American 234, 247, 254
Scottish chapels 201–2, 215
surpliced 202, 242, 267
choral service 8, 17, 20, 23–4, 29–32, 134–8, 160–2, 267
chanting given up 154–9
clerical arguments for and against 8–10, 132–4
economic factors 105–6, 130–1
restoration 55–8
rubrics 28
the tradition 125–6, 260–1, 262–4
Christ Church, Oxford 23, 67, 75, 161

Christ Church Tune 38, 46
Christmas 4, 26, 45, 116, 301
Church of England 1–5, 125–6, 127, 129–30, 262–3
Church, John 77, 80–2, 146
Civil War 2, 3, 4
Clapham sect 89 n.
Clarke, Stephen 200
Clarke, William 200, 216
Clarke–Whitfeld, John 87, 160, 161
Clifford, James 24, 46, 47, 54, 69, 99
  'Brief directions . . . Divine Service' 26–32, 35–40
Cock, Robert 201
Cole, John 226, 228, 231
  aligning text and music 239, 266
  Episcopalian Harmony 239
A Collection of Private Devotions 7
Commandments responses 18, 31, 32, 152, 167–9, 201–3
Commonwealth 3, 4, 5, 7, 11, 22, 24, 47
  see also Interregnum
Communion 3, 4, 13, 16, 31–2, 149, 151–4
  1662 rubrics 18–9
Compton, Bishop Henry 145, 154
Convention Parliament 5
Convocation 6, 9, 11, 128, 130
Cooke, Benjamin 91, 94, 100
Cooper, James 83–4, 119, 147, 148
Cordiner, Revd Charles 202
Corfe, Joseph 300
Cosin, Bishop John 7–8, 9, 24, 26, 29, 34
Cotton, Humphrey 85
Cowan, William 120 n., 208 n.
Cowgate Chapel, Edinburgh 200
Cranmer, Archbishop Thomas 26, 31
Creighton, Robert 25, 107
Croft, William 114
Cromwell, Oliver 3
Crotch, William 123, 124, 260, 303–4
Crowley, Robert 34
Culloden 195

Dallas, James 204–8, 209
Dallas/Bremner canon 209–12
  text–tune pairings 213, 214
  transmission 213, 216, 243
Darley, W. H. W. 245
Davenport, Uriah 183, 222
Davies, Horton 255
Davis, Mr 121, 228, 256, 258
Daye, John 33
Deane, Thomas 107
Dearnley, Christopher 85
Declaration of Breda 5
Deus misereatur 15, 27, 104, 110, 111, 219
Dibb, J. E. 267

Ding, Laurence 213, 214, 215
Directory for the Public Worship of God 4, 9
dissenters, *see* nonconformists
Divine Service 13–16, 26, 28
  see also choral service
Dixon, J. 186, 265, 266
Doe, Paul 46, 85
Dorian Service 47, 104
double tune 89, 103, 116–24, 178
Dundee 197
Dupuis, Thomas S. 87, 228, 243, 257, 258, 299
Durham Book 8
Durham Cathedral 8, 61, 67, 74, 145, 147

Easter 4, 16, 26, 151
Ebdon, Thomas 90 n., 152 n.
Eckhard, Jacob 233, 239
  organbook 242–4
Edinburgh 184, 197, 204, 208
  Episcopal chapels in 193, 198, 199, 200
Edward VI 12, 27
elevated voice 21, 22, 135, 137
Elgin 197, 204
Ely Cathedral 60, 67, 75, 106
  chanting practice 93, 97, 134–7, 145, 151
  organ in 113
  saying service 155, 156
Ely Tune 38, 75
embassy chapels 191
Episcopal Academy, Cheshire, Conn. 226
Episcopal Church in Scotland 192–3, 196, 216
Erben, Peter 233
Eton College 131
Evangelical Lutheran Synod, New York 243
Evangelicals 89, 130, 188
  ideal of church music 186, 187, 232, 268
Evening Prayer 13, 26, 28–32, 104, 141, 142–3
  1662 rubrics 14–15
Exeter Cathedral 24, 25, 106, 289, 300

faburden 34, 40–4, 103, 260
falsobordone 43, 44
Farrant, Richard 47, 48, 85
feast and fast days 12, 17, 26, 32, 44
  see also holy days
Fellowes, Edward 85
Fergus, John, jun. 201
festival psalms 44–8
Finch, Edward 73 n., 76, 189
fine reading 261, 302
Five Articles 3
Flintoft, Luke 89, 120, 121
Forbes, Revd Robert 161, 195–6
Ford, Robert 49 n., 65 n.
Forgue 204
Founder's Day 47
Foundling Hospital, London 245

Free and Candid Disquisitions 128
Fuller, Robert 140
Fuller, Wendy 140, 141

Garrick, David 261
Gauden, Bishop John 10, 11
Geddes, John 202
George III 123, 196
Gilbird, Mr 141
Glasgow 197, 198, 200, 201, 202
Gloria in excelsis 17, 19, 20, 151, 154, 235–8
Gloria tibi 28, 31
    see also Gospel acclamation
Gloucester Cathedral 116, 139, 157–9
Good Friday 26, 258
Goodson, Richard 75
Gospel acclamation 28, 29, 50, 58, 221
Goss, John 304
Gostling, John 67
Gow, William 200
Grand Chant 139, 141, 299
Gray, Jonathan 188, 266
Great Warley, Essex 167
Green, James 171, 172, 182, 183, 184, 205, 216
Greenshields, Revd James 193
Gunning, Revd Henry 93 n.
Gunpowder Treason 32, 128

Halifax 182
Hall, Henry 119, 185
Hallifax, Bishop Samuel 158
Hampton Court Conference 1
Harley, Robert 138
Harrison, Ralph 120, 122, 184, 186, 205
Hawkins, James 106–14, 178
Hawkins, John 154
Haydn, Franz Joseph 123–4
Haydon, Colin 128
Hayes, William 94 n., 130, 131
Henry VIII 12
Hereford Cathedral 67, 116, 139, 305
Heywood, Thomas 61
high church 2, 3, 130
Hodges, Edward 188, 264
Holdroyd, Israel 182, 183
holy days 3, 10, 12, 26, 32, 218, 257–8, 261
    see also feast and fast days
Holyrood 3
Hooker, Revd Richard 155
Hopkinson, Francis 221, 223, 225
Humfrey, Pelham 65, 68, 69, 141
    see also Grand Chant
Hurd, Bishop Richard 155 n., 158
Husbands, Charles 61
hymn 13
    see also canticles

Imperial Tune 47–9, 68, 69, 70, 75, 85
    in canticles 184, 185, 206
    in Turner dbl tune 119
Innes, Bishop George 203
Interregnum 4, 10
    see also Commonwealth
Introduction to the Skill of Musick 28, 167 (Playford), 172 (Betts)
Inverness 197, 204
Invitatory 14, 29, 33, 85
    see also Venite exultemus
Isaack, Barnabas 117
Isaack, B. 75, 117
Isaack, Bartholomew 116–17, 119
Ivery, John 165

Jackson, George K. 231, 238, 243, 254, 256
    A Choice Collection of Chants 239–41
Jackson, John 75
Jackson, Thomas 166, 174, 228
Jacob[s], Benjamin 189
Jacobite uprisings 194 (1715), 194–5 (1745)
Jaffray, Revd Andrew 198
James I 1, 2, 12
James II 127, 128
Jebb, John 146 n., 147 n.
Jenks, Stephen 226
Jennings, Kenneth 85
Jolly, Bishop Alexander 161 n.
Jones, John 87, 100, 123, 124, 187, 189 n., 243, 258
Jones, Revd Walter 27
Jones, William 186
Jubilate deo 13, 15, 30, 104, 115

Kelway, Thomas 223–4, 243, 257
Kemp, Joseph 87
Kempton, Thomas 97, 106, 113
Kent, James 256, 298
Key to Chanting 267
Kilgour, Bishop Robert 203, 204
King, Charles 107
King's College, Cambridge 140, 161
Knapton, Philip 186
Knight, William 73, 76
Knights of the Garter 61
Kyrie, English, *see* Commandments responses

Lamb, Benjamin 78, 141
Langdon, Richard 106, 114–15, 169, 227, 258
Lasher, Revd Joshua 75
Latitudinarian 129, 130
Laud, Archbishop William 1, 2, 3
Laurencekirk 193
Law, Andrew 222, 223
Law, William 186
Leeds Parish Church 170, 190

le Huray, Peter 40, 85
Leith 195
Lent 155
Lichfield Cathedral 87, 88, 161, 305
Lincoln Minster 33, 24 n., 106, 111, 145, 155, 162, 262
Lincoln Tune 38, 49, 75
Litany 13, 26, 31, 50–3, 145–51
litany desk 145
liturgy:
    Ordinary 12, 23, 25–6, 32, 55–8, 125–6
    Extraordinary 12, 25–6, 32, 50, 55–8
    see also Book of Common Prayer; holy days; rubrics
liturgical anthems 222, 229, 232, 234
London 6, 26, 27, 28, 60, 61, 65, 223, 260
Loosemore, John 25
Lord's prayer 14, 15, 18, 19, 137–8
Loud, Thomas 249, 251, 252
Lowe, Edward 23, 69, 75, 80, 99, 105, 139
    A Short Direction 25–6, 29–32, 55–8
    Tallis and Byrd arranged 49–53
Ludlow Parish Church 33
Lumley partbooks 33, 44, 45
Luther, Martin 44
Lutheran 222, 243

Mace, Thomas 105
Magdalen College, Oxford 26, 129, 146, 160, 161
Magnifcat 14, 104, 107, 108, 141, 144
Manchester Collegiate Church (now Cathedral) 129, 305
Mann, A. H. 120 n., 140
Marsh, John 131, 160, 161, 265
    on chant accompaniment 83
    Cathedral Chant Book 87, 91, 101
    journal 298–305
    pointing system 98–9, 188–9, 266
    service playing 294–7
    on triple metre chants 226
Mary II 127, 129
Mason, Lowell 238
Mason, William 99, 100, 131, 154, 158
    Commandment responses 152, 169, 227, 228, 257
Mather, F. C. 160
Merbecke, John 24, 27, 32, 40, 185
    see also Book of Common Praier Noted
Merton College, Oxford 146
Methodism 130, 262
metrical psalms 4, 9, 10, 34–5, 120, 132, 144, 170
    in cathedral nave 156
    improvised 176
    tune naming 38
    versus chanting 232
Millenary Petition 1
'mixed service' 267, 268

Montrose 197
Morley, Thomas 40, 42, 43, 44 n., 116
    Eight Tunes 34, 35, 38, 41, 60, 70, 85
Morley, William 120
Morning Prayer 13, 26, 28–32, 104, 135–6, 138–43
    1662 rubrics 14–15
Mornington, Garret Wesley, Earl of 223
Morrill, John 4, 5
Murgetroyd, Charles 76
music MSS:
    Bennet organbook 139–43
    chant tunes 271–8
    chanting services 106
    Episcopal organbooks 242–6, 247–51
    relation to printed music 24, 59, 101, 254, 264, 268
    royal chapels repertory 68, 70
    Wanless litany 148
musical orders of service:
    Clifford 26–7, 55–8
    Lowe 25–6, 55–8
    Merbecke 24, 27
    Playford 28, 29, 32, 55–8
    parish 167–70
musical service 13, 104
    chanting 103–15, 124
    verse 178
Musical Society, Aberdeen 198
Musical Society, Edinburgh 204

Nalson, Valentine 75, 76
Nares, James 107, 238, 299, 300
Newark on Trent 166
New Chapel, Edinburgh 199, 200
New College, Oxford 117, 160, 161
A New Version of Psalms 219
New York 221, 232
Nicene Creed 18, 26, 31, 58, 159
Nicolson, Bishop William 154
nonconformists 1, 6, 10, 127–30
    see also nonjurors; Puritans; Presbyterians
nonjurors 129, 161, 186
    in Scotland 192, 194, 195, 198, 199, 200, 202
Norris, William 106, 111
North, Roger 17, 29, 83, 134, 151
    'plainsong practice' 152
    on psalm chanting 92, 96–7, 264
Norwich Cathedral 25, 30, 67, 83–4, 106, 147, 159–60
Nunc dimittis 15, 104, 107, 108, 174, 175

Obiit Sunday 47
Octagon Chapel, Bath 187
octave chant 123, 124
Old St. Paul's, Edinburgh 200

Old Scottish Chant 235–8, 243
  see also Dallas Te deum
Old Way of Singing 177, 190
Ordinal 3, 12
organ:
  accompaniment techniques 246–52
  chant accompaniment 26, 30, 83, 96–8, 141,
    189, 191, 296
  chant interludes 178, 238, 240, 245–50
  chant preludes 97, 178
  barrel 166, 212
  in parish churches 4, 163
  responses 303
  in Scottish chapels 193, 198, 199, 200, 201, 204
organ voluntary 32, 55, 57, 140, 141, 154, 191
organist's role 96–8, 189, 221, 294–7
Oxford Movement 89, 263, 267, 268
Oxford University 23, 27, 78, 146, 160, 303–4

parish clerk 4, 54, 156
Parish–Clerk's Guide 54
parochial service 126–7, 152
  imitation of cathedrals, 162, 163, 164, 165, 170,
    177, 189
  reform movement 163, 166
Parr, Henry 120 n.
Patronage Act 1712 199
Payne, Benjamin 54
Pembroke College, Cambridge 47, 48
Penal Laws 192, 194–6
Perth 197
Pescatori, Mr 200
Peterborough Cathedral 24, 106
Peterhead 204
Peterhouse College, Cambridge 8, 34
Peterhouse tunes 34, 35–8, 40–2, 85
Philadelphia 217, 221, 224, 242
plainchant [plainsong] 17, 20, 24, 26, 32–3, 44, 54,
    125
  in Communion or ante–Communion 151–2
  extempore harmonization 43, 59
  in Ely service 135–7
  rationale for 133–4, 158
  revival 27
  transmission 24, 35, 43, 59
Playford, John 24, 54, 99, 120, 167, 172
  Order of performing Divine Service 28, 29, 32,
    55–8, 60, 69
Pococke, Bishop Richard 167, 198, 200
pointing 137, 189, 190, 219, 266–7
popery 1, 3, 127, 128, 129, 133, 191
Portland Chapel, London 187
Portsoy 198, 203
Preces and Responses 14, 29, 31, 45, 55
  Byrd 49–51, 78, 138
  Tallis 50, 52–3
Presbyterians 5, 6, 8, 10

in Scotland 129, 193, 195, 197
Protestant Episcopal Church in the United States
    217, 218, 239
psalm chanting 29–30, 54, 92–7, 125, 138, 154,
    161, 261, 264
  matching tune with text sentiment 99–101
  parish directions for 171, 189, 223, 225, 241, 265
  pre–Restoration practice 32–5, 40, 43, 104
  see also *rule of 3 & 5*
Psalmes of David in Metre 120
psalmodist 163–4, 19
psalm tone 26, 27, 32–49, 60, 118, 171
  harmonized 30, 34, 40, 59, 69–71, 75, 174,
    261–2
  psalm settings on 44–8, 104
psalm tune 60
psalter 12, 13, 34, 35, 126, 219, 267
Psalter of David 34
Purcell, Edward 69, 70, 75, 205
Purcell, Henry 65, 69, 70, 185
Purcell, Revd Henry 242
Purcell, Thomas 68, 69, 243, 293
Puritans 1, 2, 4, 7, 27 n., 151, 262

qualified chapels 129, 192, 193, 194, 197, 199,
    200, 203
Queen Anne 197, 200
Quicunque vult 27, *see* Athanasian Creed

Rattray, Bishop Thomas 197
Ravenscroft, Thomas 54
Rea, James 201
Reading, John 76
reading–pew 2
reading psalms 27, 92, 171, 186, 189
  see also psalm chanting
Reformation 4, 24, 33, 103, 105
Reinagle, Alexander 201
Repeal Act 1792 196
Restoration 4–6, 22, 23–5, 196
Revolution of 1689 127
Rimbault, Edward 89 n.
Robinson, John 86 n., 216, 243, 257, 258
Rochester Cathedral 131
Rogation 4, 174
Rogers, Benjamin 65, 139, 185
Roman Catholics 1, 127–8, 134, 157, 191, 195
  and Episcopalians 231, 234
Romanticism 264
Ross, John 198
royal chapels repertory 28, 60–70, 72, 75, 138, 140
  musical style 69–71
  transmission 67, 73, 205, 223
royal peculiar 11, 28, 61
Rudiments of Music:
  Bremner, R. 203, 208, 209, 215, 222
  Law, A. 222, 223

rubrics 12, 22, 26, 35, 140
  American BCP 218–19
  1662 BCP 14–15, 18–19
  interpretation of 13, 17, 20, 55–8, 259
  and music 126
  in Sarum rite 16, 17
rule of 3 & 5 93, 94, 101, 189, 227, 239
Ryder, Dudley 54 n.

sacraments 2, 3, 16, 151
St Alban Wood Street, London 238
St Andrew Holborn, London 65
St Andrew's Chapel, Edinburgh 200
St Andrew's Church, Aberdeen (now Cathedral)
  198, 204 n.
St Andrew's Episcopal Church, Banff 202
St Andrew's Episcopal Chapel, Glasgow 190,
  200–2, 242
St Andrew's University 238
St Asaph Cathedral 131
St Bartholomew's Day 11
St George's Chapel, Windsor 47, 61, 67, 78, 116,
  131
St John's College, Cambridge 161
St John's College, Oxford 67, 117
St John's Lutheran Church, Charleston, SC 242
St Mary's Church, Chelmsford (now Cathedral)
  229
St Mary's Church, Oxford 146
St Michael's Church, Cambridge 140
St Michael's Church, Charleston, SC 221, 242
St Michael's Church, Marblehead, Mass. 225
St Paul's Cathedral 26, 30, 31, 35, 105, 131, 154,
  304
  Boyce funeral in 293–4
  chanting in 54 n., 124, 139
  charity children chant 187
  litany desk 145
  Psalter 61, 65–7
  responses with organ on Whitsunday 303
St Paul's Church, Aberdeen 194, 198
St Paul's Church, Narragansett, RI 225
St Peter's and Christ Church, Philadelphia 222,
  223, 243, 245, 248
St Philip's Church, Charleston, SC 242
St Saviour, Southwark (now Cathedral) 116
St Sepulchre, London 65
Salisbury Cathedral 27, 35, 298–9. 300
Salisbury Tune 120
Sanctus 19
  as introit 154, 169–70, 241
Sanderson, Bishop Robert 11
Sarum rite 12, 16–17, 24, 25, 32–3, 59, 103–4
Sarum Tonal 33
Saussure, Cesar de 134, 155
Savoy Conference 6–10
Scripture 8, 9, 13, 132

Seabury, Bishop Samuel 199, 217
Seager, Francis 34
Second Service 26, 31, 32, 149, 151–4
  see also Communion; ante-Communion
Seeley, L. B. 188
Selby Abbey, Yorkshire 167
service 13, *see* musical service
set–tunes 185
Seymour, Thomas 20, 21
Shand, James 202
Sharp, Granville 74, 88–90, 148, 149
  Durham responses 152–3
  Fifty Double and Single Chants 87, 223
  music MSS 89, 90
  on psalm chanting 96, 187, 292–3
Sharp, Archbishop John 74
Sharp, Archdeacon Thomas 74, 89
Shield, William 90 n.
Shoneman, Mr 202
Short, Benjamin 65, 66
sing versus say 8–11, 17, 126, 132–3, 154–6,
  158–9, 164–5
  see also cathedral versus parish service
singing gallery 156, 177
Skilton, Edward 81 n.
Skinner, Bishop John 199, 203
Skinner, Revd John Jr 203, 209, 212
Skipton, Yorkshire 164
Smith, John 199
Smith, John Stafford 87
Smith, Mr 75
Smith, Revd William 185, 203, 226, 251
  aligning text and tune 239, 266
  on chanting 225, 268
  Churchman's Choral Companion 231–8, 256–8
Soaper, John 90 n., 152 n.
Society for Cultivating Church Music, New York
  233 n.
Solemn League and Covenant 6, 11
Southwell Collegiate Church 262–3, 304, 305
Speymouth 203
Sreeve, John 172
Standbridge, J. C. 245
Stephens, John 298, 299
Sterling Tune 120, 184
Street, Josiah 183
Suffrages 21, 31, 56, 78, 135, 136
Sykes, Norman 129

Taas, William 215–16
Tait, Andrew 198, 202
Tallis, Thomas 26, 31, 45–6, 50–3, 104, 146, 147,
  175, 259, 260
  Mr Thomas Tallis's Tune 46–7
Tans'ur, William 169, 172, 189, 216
Taylor, Rayner 231, 234, 243, 252, 257
  Te deum 246–50

Taylor, Rayner (*cont.*):
  Venite dbl chant 229–31
  see also Old Scottish Chant
Taylor, Stephen 130
Taws, Joseph 245
Te deum 13, 14, 30, 94, 104, 114
  Chetham 177–83, 208, 222
  Dallas 184, 185
  with tone 8 40, 49
Temperley, Nicholas 34, 268
Temple Church, London 28, 35
Terril, Israel 226, 227
Test Act of 1673 127
Thomson, James 214, 215
Thoresby, Ralph 170
Timbrell, Francis 171, 172
Toleration Act:
  (1689) 127
  (1712) 193, 194, 197
Torrington, John Byng, 5th Viscount 159, 262–3
Torry, Bishop Patrick 204, 209
Travers, John 80
Trinity Church, New York 218, 233
  St George's Chapel 233, 238
  St John's Chapel 233
Trinity College, Cambridge 161
Trisagion 154, 241, 249, 250
Trowell, Brian 42 n., 43
Tucker, William 65
Tuckey, William 218
Tudway, Thomas 126, 138, 140, 141, 146, 162
  cathedral versus parochial service 126
  'Chappel Tunes' 77–9
  state of choral service 105–6, 132
Turner, William 28, 61, 67, 68, 69, 70
  autograph chant tunes 71–3
  double tune 116, 118–19
  sgl chant in A 94, 177, 205, 223, 228, 243, 257, 258

United Brethren 233, 257, 258

Vanderman, Thomas 87, 114, 120, 121
Veni Creator 51
Venite exultemus 29–30, 33, 34, 93, 99, 119, 138
  chant for musical service 138

and origin of Anglican Chant 85–6, 79–80, 262
Versicles and Responses 15, 20, 27, 31, 50
Victorian era 267
Vincent, Revd William 187–8

Wainwright, Revd Jonathan 238
Wainwright, Richard 169
Walker, Bishop James 161 n.
Walond, William 301, 303
Walsh, John 130
Waltham Holy Cross 42
Wanless, Thomas 75, 90 n.
  Litany 147–51
Wanley, Humphrey 77, 78, 79, 140
Wanley partbooks 33, 44, 45
Watkins, Thomas 136
Watton, Robert 80, 81
Webbe, Samuel 257
Wells Cathedral 25, 60, 75, 107
Wesley, Revd Charles 138
Wesley, Samuel S. 103, 107
Westminster Abbey 23, 30, 68, 105, 131, 139, 154, 301
Westminster Tune 120–1, 122
White, Bishop William 219, 221, 223, 231, 232
Whole Book of Psalms in Three Parts 120
William III 127, 129
Wimborne Minster 61, 67
Wimpole 138, 140
Winchester Cathedral 5, 24, 139, 159, 304
Winchester College 151
Windsor 60, 61, 74, 138, 140
Winton, George Seton, Earl of 194
Wise, Michael 61, 257
Withye, Francis 75
Wood Anthony 23
Woodward, Richard 228
Worcester Cathedral 16, 67, 155, 158
Worcester House Declaration 6
Wren, Charles 81
Wren, Bishop Matthew 7, 8
Wylde, John 42

York Minster 67, 73, 75, 76, 154, 161, 263
  instructions for choral service 96, 137, 289–92
  York (Wanless) Litany 148, 149